Kingdoms Beyond the Clouds

Also by Jonathan Gregson

Bullet up the Grand Trunk Road

Jonathan Gregson

KINGDOMS BEYOND THE CLOUDS

Journeys in Search of the Himalayan Kings

MACMILLAN

First published 2000 by Macmillan
an imprint of Macmillan Publishers Ltd
25 Eccleston Place, London SW1W 9NF
Basingstoke and Oxford
Associated companies throughout the world
www.macmillan.com

ISBN 0 333 76550 8

1 3 5 7 9 8 6 4 2

A CIP catalogue record for this book is available from
the British Library.

Typeset by SetSystems Ltd, Saffron Walden, Essex
Printed and bound in Great Britain by
Mackays of Chatham plc, Chatham, Kent

To

Sarah

CONTENTS

List of Illustrations   ix

Maps   xi

Acknowledgements   xxi

INTRODUCTION   1

1. AN ENTRY TO BHUTAN   7

2. FIRST TIBET   47

3. AN AUDIENCE WITH THE DALAI LAMA   78

4. BEYOND DHARAMSALA – WHAT FUTURE?   124

5. NEPAL I – THE RULING DYNASTY   157

6. MUSTANG – KINGDOMS WITHIN KINGDOMS   202

7. NEPAL II – MONARCHY AND DEMOCRACY   280

CONTENTS

8. SIKKIM – THE KINGDOM THAT DISAPPEARED   320

9. BHUTAN II – THE KING AT LAST   361

10. BHUTAN III – A RETIRING MONARCH   409

  EPILOGUE   468

  Glossary   479

  Bibliography   482

  Index   495

List of Illustrations

All photographs are the copyright of Sarah Woodward unless otherwise stated.

1a The fortress-monastery of Tashichodzong, Thimphu
(*Jonathan Gregson*)

1b Tongsa Dzong, birthplace of Bhutan's monarchy

2a Tibetan nuns during the Full Moon Festival, near
Drigung, Central Tibet

2b Monks announce the beginning of the day's teachings

3a A discipline monk controls the crush of pilgrims at the
Drigung Festival

3b His Holiness the Dalai Lama with the author,
Dharamsala

4a HM King Birendra of Nepal and Queen Aishwarya,
Kathmandu, 1975 (*by kind permission of HM King
Birendra Bikram Shah Dev of Nepal*)

4b Entrance to Hanuman Dhoka, the old royal palace,
Kathmandu (*Jonathan Gregson*)

4c Durbar Square, Patan (*Jonathan Gregson*)

5a The road to Lo Manthang

5b The Gateway to Upper Mustang, Kagbeni

5c Lo Manthang, the capital of Mustang

6a Tsarang Monastery, Upper Mustang

6b King Jigme Dorje Palbar and Queen Ridol of Mustang

7a A chorten and prayer flags mark the spot where the first Buddhist King of Sikkim was enthroned in 1642

7b Tea pickers on the Temi Estate in West Sikkim

7c Captain Yongda, warrior-monk

8a The King of Bhutan, HM Jigme Singye Wangchuck *(by kind permission of HM King Jigme Singye Wangchuck of Bhutan)*

8b Novice monks, Tashigang, East Bhutan

MAPS

1. General Map of the Himalayan Region

2. Bhutan

3. The Kingdom of Lo, known as Mustang

4. Kathmandu Valley

5. Sikkim

MAP I

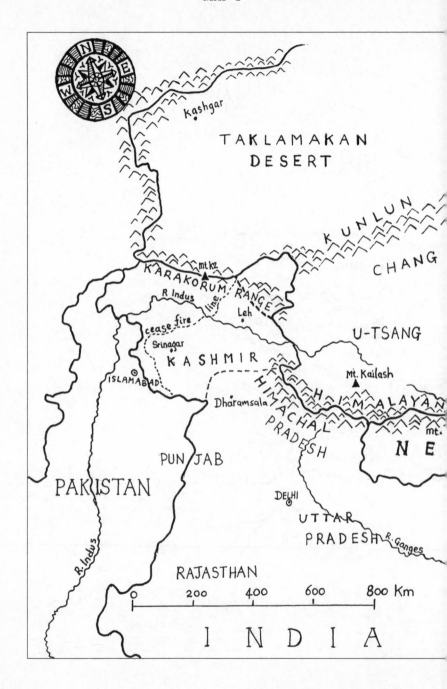

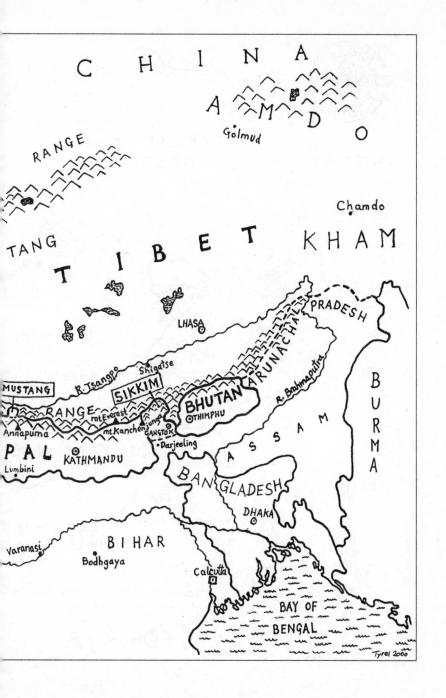

MAP 2

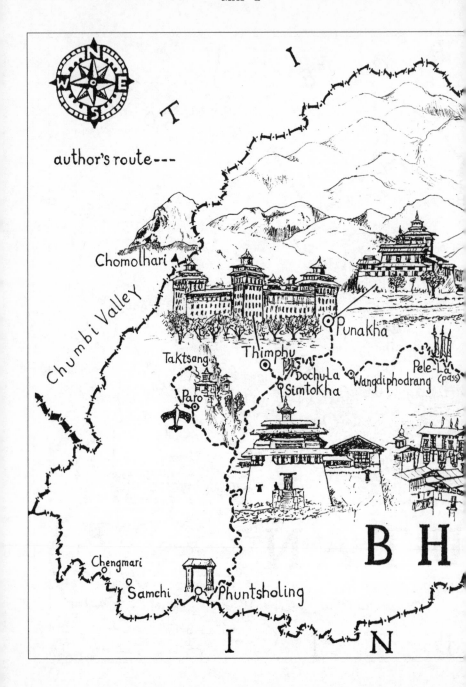

author's route---

N E W S

T I

Chomolhari

Chumbi Valley

Taktsang
Thimphu
Paro
Dochu-La
Simtokha
Punakha
Wangdiphodrang
Pele-La (pass)

B H

Chengmari
Samchi
Phuntsholing

I N

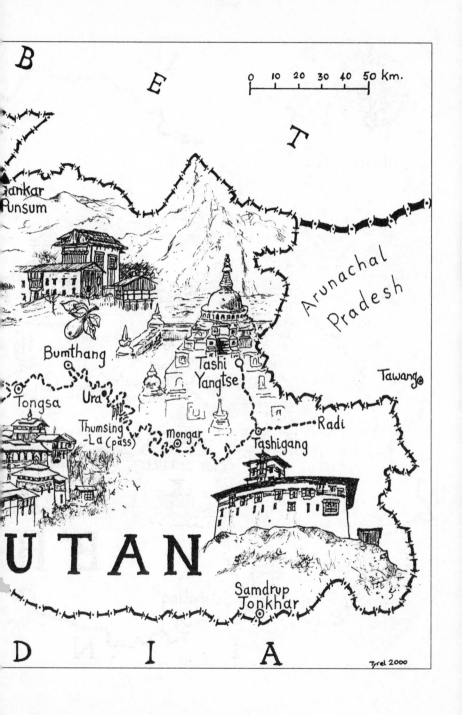

B E T

0 10 20 30 40 50 km.

ankar
Punsum

Arunachal
Pradesh

Bumthang

Tashi
Yangtse

Tawang

Tongsa

Ura

Thumsing
-La (pass)

Mongar

Radi

Tashigang

UTAN

Samdrup
Jonkhar

D   I   A

Tyrel 2000

MAP 3

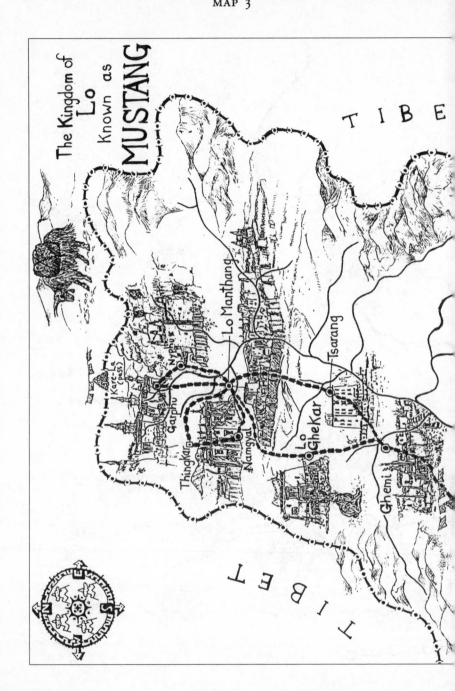

The Kingdom of Lo known as MUSTANG

TIBE

TIBET

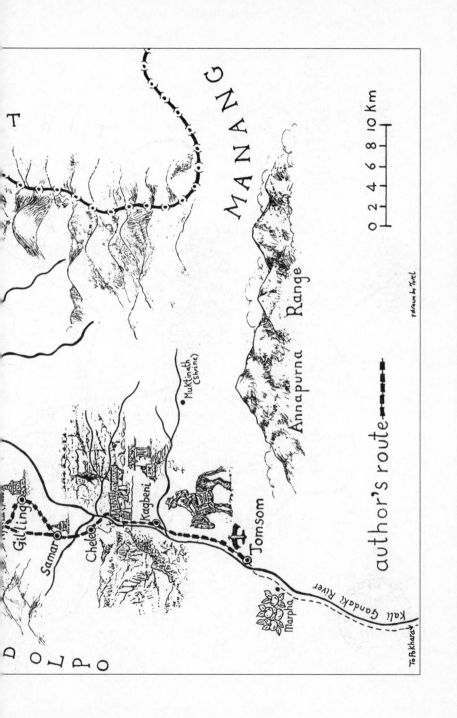

T

MANANG

DOLPO

Gilling
Samar
Chele
Kagbeni
Muktinath (Shrine)
Jomsom
Marpha

Annapurna Range

Kali Gandaki River

To Pokhara

author's route

redrawn by Turtl

0 2 4 6 8 10 km

MAP 4

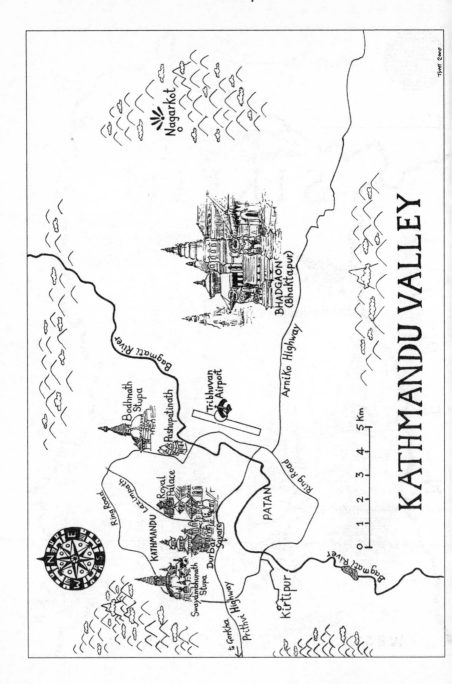

KATHMANDU VALLEY

MAP 5

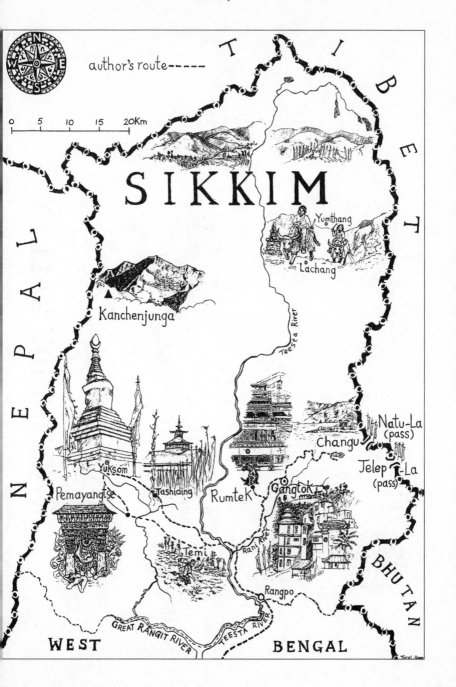

author's route - - - - -

0 5 10 15 20Km

TIBET

SIKKIM

NEPAL

Yumthang

Lachang

Kanchenjunga

Teesta River

Natu-La
(pass)

Changu

Jelep-La
(pass)

Yuksom

Pemayangtse

Tashiding

Rumtek

Gangtok

Temi

Rani River

BHUTAN

Rangpo

GREAT RANGIT RIVER

TEESTA RIVER

WEST

BENGAL

ACKNOWLEDGEMENTS

My thanks must go first to those Himalayan monarchs who agreed to be interviewed and showed me much kindness: H.H. the Dalai Lama; H.M. King Jigme Singye Wangchuck of Bhutan; H.M. King Birendra Bir Bikram Shah Dev of Nepal; and the Lo Gyalpo, King Jigme Palbar Bista of Mustang.

Of the many individuals who offered advice or helped me on my travels, I can mention only a few. I do not include members of the royal families concerned, nor the many government officials and royal secretaries who helped me out, nor those who are already named in the text. But without their assistance this book could not have been written.

Others I wish to thank are: in New Delhi, Mark Tully and John Lall, for their wisdom and experience, and Madan Kumar Bhattarai and Yadav Khanal of the Royal Nepalese Embassy.

In Dharamsala, Professor Samdong Rinpoche, Tsewang Yeshi of the Tibetan Children's Village, Dolma Choephel of the Tibetan Youth Congress, and Pema Yangchen for acting as translator during interviews with recent political refugees, whose names, and those of the many Tibetans who helped me inside Tibet, are perhaps best not revealed.

In Bhutan, Ugyen Wangchuck, Kinley Dorji (editor of *Kuensel*), Sangay Wangchuck of the Special Commission for Cultural Affairs, Pema Dorji of the Institute of Traditional Medicine, Karma Ura, Michael and Bina Vinding, headmaster Lhundup Dukpa, and Lili Wangchuck and Ngawang Pem for looking after us so well.

In Kathmandu, the late Manmohan Adhikari, 'Comrade Rohit' (Narayan Man Bijukacche), Professor Dilli Raman Regmi, Rishikesh Shaha, Chiran Thapa, Professor Tri Ratna Manandhar, Kanak Mani Dixit (editor of *Himal*), Mana Ranjan Josse, Pasuram Kharel, Erkki Heinonen of UNHCR, R.B. Basnet of the Bhutan National Democratic Party, Samdup Lhatse (the Representative of H.H. the Dalai Lama) and Lobsang Tsultrim for his help in meeting former Khampa fighters, and Dr Ramesh Dhungel for his guidance on the early history of Mustang.

In Mustang, Maya Bista, Gyanendra and Yanji Maya Bista, Lama Nagwang Kunga Bista, the royal priest Gyatso Bista, and Pema Tsering.

In Jhapa (E. Nepal), Ratan Gazmere, Quazi Ghiasuddin of Save the Children, the Lutheran World Service for their hospitality, headmaster B.P. Acharya, Tendzin Pasang of the Druk National Congress, and Thinley Penjore of the Druk-Yul Peoples Democratic Party.

In Sikkim, Pema Namgyal and family, the late Ganju Lama VC, 'Kailash', Diki Wangchuk, and the Lachungpa family.

In London, Tsering Shakya and Michael Hutt at the School of Oriental and African Studies, for their help and learned advice; P.K. Pradhan of the Royal Nepalese Embassy; Rory Mungoven and Ingrid Massagé of Amnesty International.

Above all I wish to thank my agent Derek Johns at A.P. Watt, who gave me invaluable guidance and support throughout, and my editor Catherine Whitaker, who stayed with the project despite physically moving to New York, deftly editing and commenting on chapters about incarnate lamas that had been transferred electronically back and forth across the Atlantic. Also the 'home team' at Macmillan, Becky Lindsay, Nicky Hursell and Ann Cooke, for putting the book together, and my publicist Katie James for her infectious enthusiasm. And a true twenty-first century hero, Jonathan Ladd, musical and computer virtuoso, who spent an entire night talking me through how to retrieve a section of the book that had disappeared into the void.

Also Tyrel Broadbent, a great travelling companion and artist, for having drawn and embellished the maps, and Graeme Grant for his comments on the early drafts. Among others who have shared my Himalayan journeys, Pat Mellor (the long-serving secretary of the Britain-Nepal Society), Alan and Stella Woodward, and of course my wife, Sarah, whose forbearance extended to the home front.

And not least, my parents and my godfather, the late Charles Ingram, for having introduced me to the Himalayas and India's north-east frontier.

Therefore, though it may be good sometimes to think particularly of God's kindness and worth, and though it may be enlightening too, and a part of contemplation, yet in the work now before us it must be put down and covered with a cloud of forgetting. And you are to step over it resolutely and eagerly, with a devout and kindling love, and try to penetrate the darkness above you. Strike that thick cloud of unknowing with the sharp dart of longing love, and on no account whatever think of giving up.

The Cloud of Unknowing,
Anon, English, fourteenth century.
Translated by Clifton Walters (1961)

INTRODUCTION

I cannot recall the first time I set eyes on the Himalayas, since I was then just sixteen months old. Whatever subliminal images are lodged in my memory have merged into the impressions gathered from half a dozen other visits before I reached the age of twelve.

My family were living in Calcutta, and most years we took our holidays up in the hills, in Darjeeling or Kalimpong. After the sweltering humidity of the Bengal plains, to breathe in the cool, crisp air around these hill stations was like taking some energy-enhancing drug. The air was scented with wood smoke, and in the evenings it was cold enough for us all to huddle around a blazing fire.

By the age of five I was running up and down mountains, usually accompanied by a stray pi-dog which had attached itself to me. These solo expeditions were a source of some anxiety for my parents, since I was forever getting lost among the labyrinth of raised grounds that ran between the steeply terraced paddy fields and the bamboo thickets. I was warned particularly not to go in amongst the bamboo because snakes made their homes there. So of course I did.

The hill people were very different from the plains people, both in physique and demeanour. Most of the hill farmers were of Nepalese origin: short, stocky, easily given to laughter. I had picked up some phrases of Nepali by sitting around the kitchen at our home in Calcutta and listening to our Nepali head bearer, Dil Bahadur, talk with his many friends. So on my hillside explorations I could exchange greetings at each hamlet and, when I got lost, I was able to ask the way home. Sometimes, when the path was difficult, they would send one of their younger sons to accompany me part of the way. The sight of the two of us clambering up ridges made villagers laugh and shout out, 'Sair Hilaree! Tenzing!' – the ascent of Everest by Sir Edmund Hillary and Sherpa Tenzing Norgay then being fairly recent news.

But there were even stranger people to be found in town. Tibetan refugees came flooding over the border after the Chinese army's suppression of the Lhasa Uprising in 1959, but even before then there were many Tibetans living in Darjeeling. The women with long plaited hair and weather-worn faces who hired out riding ponies were Tibetans, as were the strange medicine men down by the bazaar whose 'remedies' included various bits of wild animals – claws and horns and ground-up bones. Then there were the beaming, shaven-headed monks. The 'moon-men' I called them, for they seemed to inhabit a sphere so very different from the rest of us that I imagined they lived on the moon. Of course I knew nothing then about Buddhism; but they were much gentler, much kinder, than any of the many varieties of godmen I had encountered in India.

Yet more Tibetans lived around Kalimpong, since this had long been the main entrepôt on the trade route between Lhasa and Calcutta. I remember once being dragged to safety out of the path of a caravan bringing raw wool down from Tibet. The lead mules had bells on their harnesses and the muleteers, with their great boots and long earrings, were the wildest looking men I had ever seen.

Walking through the bazaar I would run into all manner of different peoples: Bengali clerks and Marwari traders come up from the Plains; Bhotias and Lepchas down from Sikkim or the surrounding hills; the occasional Bhutanese wearing their distinctive, brightly striped robes. For, despite their 'Anglo-Himalayan' architecture and other reminders of the British raj, these hill stations perched on the first range of the Himalayas also served as a meeting place between native highlanders and plainsmen. The Tibetans and other highland peoples preferred not to go down any further into India, for they could not abide the heat and often fell ill; while the Indian administrators and merchants found the Himalayan winters too cold. They went about wrapped in woollen blankets and balaclavas or squatted around their inadequate stoves.

I remember, when I was seven years old, my father waking me well before dawn so that we could go up from Darjeeling to Tiger Hill. There had been a sharp frost overnight, and the stars shone high above us. With luck we would have a clear view of the Himalayas. A jeep dropped us beyond Ghoom, but because it was so icy we made the final ascent on foot. There was nobody else at the top, and we stood in silence as the sun came up to reveal range upon range of mountains, their snowy peaks glowing first a dull red, then golden, before finally assuming their habitual daytime brilliance.

Perhaps to help take my mind off how cold it was my father decided to give me an impromptu geography lesson. It was a lesson I would never forget.

He began by turning to face west, where the snows of Kanchenjunga glistened in the morning light. Tracing an imaginary arc to the south, he led my eye to a small white triangle, which barely poked above an intervening ridge. 'That', he announced, 'is Everest, the tallest mountain in the world.'

'Then why does it seem so much smaller than the others?' I queried.

'Because it's much further away. And all those hills in between are part of another country, the Kingdom of Nepal, where nobody from outside has been allowed to go.'

I did not really understand why outsiders couldn't go there – especially since I knew this was where our bearer, Dil Bahadur, came from. Whenever he took leave to visit his family, he always came to say goodbye and tell me he was off to Nepal.

My father was not going to be distracted from his lesson. Pointing up the cloud-filled Teesta Valley, he told me that that way lay the Kingdom of Sikkim. 'And beyond the Sikkim mountains', he added, 'is another country called Tibet.'

Of this he had personal experience. He explained how in 1939, long before I was born, he had walked into Tibet over 14,000-foot passes, and then across a high desert plateau until he had reached a town called Phari Dzong, where the people left dead dogs lying in the streets. But they did not go rotten – as they would have done very quickly in my hometown of Calcutta – because the air was so cold and so dry up there. He also told me that until the previous year this country had been ruled over by a god-king called the 'Dally Lama'; but now he had fled to India and his people were being oppressed by the Chinese. Again, it seemed impossible to visit this country.

Finally, my father turned me eastward and pointed to a range of snow-dusted hills. 'And over there', he said, 'is the Kingdom of Bhutan, also known as the Land of the Thunder Dragon. Nobody can go in there.' Which naturally made me want to go there very much indeed.

From that vantage point on Tiger Hill I had peeked into four separate Himalayan kingdoms, all of which were very difficult – if not impossible – to enter. And from that moment I was fascinated by these hidden kingdoms and determined that, sooner or later, I should go to each and every one of them.

Chapter One

An Entry to Bhutan

Up until the 1960s, Bhutan remained the most isolated country in the Himalayas. It was far easier to enter Tibet than Bhutan, which to all intents and purposes remained a 'forbidden kingdom'. Only a handful of foreigners had managed to penetrate its mountain ramparts since the eighteenth century, when an agent of the East India Company called George Bogle passed though Bhutan on his way to Tibet, where he visited the Panchen Lama. Most of these outsiders were political officers stationed in Gangtok. Some, like John Claude White, have left vivid descriptions of a feudal and warlike country, and of the enormous difficulties of travelling through such mountainous terrain. Even when the Indian prime minister, Jawaharlal Nehru, visited Bhutan in 1959, the expedition travelled from Sikkim through Tibetan territory to reach Paro Dzong, any direct approach from the Indian plains being considered too hazardous a journey.

In the winter of 1964, the Bhutanese royal family visited Calcutta. I was eleven years old, back in India for the Christmas holidays, when one day my mother came looking for me. 'You must go and get scrubbed and change your clothes,' she announced. 'We've been asked to go to Raj

Bhavan to meet the Queen of Bhutan. They're thinking of sending their son to your school and want to ask you about it.'

I knew nothing of the complicated chain of events which persuaded the Bhutanese royal family to send their son to a boarding school in England. They had arrived in Calcutta and were installed as state guests in one wing of Raj Bhavan – the vast Palladian mansion modelled on Chatsworth House which had in British times served as the official residence of viceroys and governor-generals of Bengal. Discreet enquiries were being made about anyone in Calcutta whose son was attending a suitable English school.

But when I discovered I was going to meet the future king and that, if all went well, we might become friends, I entered a state of extreme excitement. As we drove past the sentries outside Raj Bhavan, my mother told me not to speak unless directly asked a question. 'And for God's sake,' she added, 'do try to be on your best behaviour.'

I tried, mother . . . oh, did I try. But by the time we had been ushered into the royal apartments past the big man with the shaven head and massive biceps (the royal bodyguard) and I had messed up my bow before Her Majesty, I was not feeling very calm. The crown prince helped out by advancing and shaking hands. But when the smooth private secretary leaned over and asked me: 'And do they practise corporal punishment at your school?' all I could do was blurt out, 'What's that?'

'Have you ever been beaten?' he whispered.

'Oh, yes,' I replied, happy to be on firm ground again. 'Ten stripes last term.'

This was a matter of some pride to me. But my mother looked daggers and started explaining that I had been a particularly ungovernable child just lately and that such punishment was highly unusual.

At this point the secretary suggested the crown prince and I go outside to play. He escorted us out onto the immense lawns surrounding Raj Bhavan where he proposed a game of tag. Jigme was nine years old at the time. I was two years his senior, but none the less deeply perplexed about the protocol involved in chasing a boy who was heir to the throne. Should I play for real or let him catch me?

I looked for guidance to the royal secretary, but his face was impassive. 'Why don't you begin?' he suggested. So I did, and played for real. We dodged around the flowerbeds and potted dahlias for twenty minutes, at which point the score was two-all.

'Now for the decider,' announced the secretary. I took off after Jigme like there was no tomorrow, as by now I'd forgotten all about protocol. He made me run like hell, and when I eventually got him he started laughing. Only then did I realize that he had allowed me to catch him all along.

As we re-entered the royal apartments I saw the muscular bodyguard trying to stretch the heavy silver and gold bracelets which the queen had chosen as gifts for my mother and sister (the Bhutanese have slimmer hands than most Europeans). Though he flexed his muscles mightily, still the bracelets refused to slide on. This caused acute embarrassment all round, at which point the queen decided to end the interview.

On the way home from Raj Bhavan my mother upbraided me for admitting to being caned. 'Now he'll never come to your school,' she declared. And I had to admit that, all in all, things didn't look good.

The beginning of next term, however, I discovered Jigme

had joined the school. There he was, with his shock of blue-black hair, looking uncomfortable in new grey flannels. There also was his Bhutanese companion, a wiry boy called Dodo with a knowledge of the martial arts. I took on the role of being their 'minder', explaining all the arcane school rules and steering them away from the worst bullies.

I think I only really helped on one occasion, when the future king was rounded up with the usual suspects during a clampdown on inter-dormitory warfare. I was called down to the headmaster's study, stood by my story, and in doing so averted the hand of calamity. But Jigme and Dodo paid back the favour in spades. Dodo's martial arts skills mesmerized the school; there was serious betting in contraband sweets on how many wooden rulers he could break with his little finger; and I ran a book on it while being privy to insider information. I made a killing in sweets that term.

Jigme commanded respect in subtler ways. We realized that anyone who could learn Latin from English when English was only his second language must be putting the rest of us to shame. I remember him fighting like a tiger against a much bigger boy in the boxing ring; and coming off the rugby pitch muddied, smiling, and still wearing his skull-cap. It must have been strange for him, leaving the enclosed, hierocratic, almost medieval society that was Bhutan, and then travelling halfway across the world only to find himself in a British boarding school – another enclosed hierocracy, though this time built around Victorian values. He kept to himself for the most part, and rarely talked about his homeland. Despite my curiosity I didn't push him; for when he did mention Bhutan he seemed to be overcome by a deep sadness.

Only later did I learn about some of the pressures he

had been under. His parents had been living apart for some time since his father, King Jigme Dorje Wangchuck, had taken a Tibetan mistress by the name of Yanki. Provided the affair remained discreet, the queen might have borne out this indignity quietly. But Yanki began making the most of her status as 'royal favourite'. Moreover, she had a son by the king who was the same age as the crown prince. The possibility arose of an alternative succession to the throne.

Then, on 5 April 1964, the prime minister and queen's elder brother, Jigme Palden Dorji, was assassinated by traditionalists who may have thought they were acting in the king's best interests. The king returned immediately from Switzerland, where he had been receiving medical treatment, and reasserted his authority. The prime mover behind the assassination, Brigadier Chapda Bahadur, was condemned to death, and something resembling the old balance was restored when the younger of the queen's brothers, Lhendup Dorji, was appointed acting prime minister. But things could never be the same.

The Dorji family were well known for their open-minded, progressive values, and their influence within Bhutan was second only to the king's. Opposed to them were the traditionalists – including senior members of the monastic body and the Wangchuck family – who resented the Dorjis' Western education, their arrogance, and their pushing for modernization too rapidly. As two hostile camps emerged, the direction of national policy and dynastic politics became inextricably linked. The king suspected the Dorjis of trying to set up a parallel government, reducing his own role to that of a constitutional monarch. All of which left Queen Ashi Kesang Choden in an invidious position. She was estranged from her husband, had lost a brother to an assassin's bullet, and now probably feared for the life of her son.

The king returned to Switzerland to resume his treatment. Back in Bhutan, it didn't take long for another crisis to emerge. The pistol used to assassinate Jigme Dorji was traced to none other than the king's mistress, Yanki. Worse still, it had been a gift to her from the king. Fearing for her life, Yanki fled with her entourage but was detained before making it across the border into India. For a moment it seemed that the Dorjis might have their revenge. But when news of this reached the king in Switzerland, he let it be known that he considered Yanki's arrest a serious insult both to himself and to his country. 'I am not going to take this insult lying down,' he declared. 'Anyone who insults me in my own kingdom must pay for it and pay for it many times over.'

Lhendup Dorji and his sister Tashi sought political asylum in Nepal, leaving the queen in an extremely isolated position. All this had happened during the two months immediately preceding my first meeting with the crown prince in Raj Bhavan. Moreover, there was disagreement between the king and queen as to whether their children should have a Western education or remain in Bhutan. For the time being the queen's opinion prevailed. It was decided to send the royal children to England – if only to have them removed from the tensions and intrigues that had gripped Bhutan since their uncle's murder.

This was the background to my mother and I being asked to an audience with Queen Ashi Kesang Choden. It may well explain why the king was absent. It also goes a long way towards explaining why Jigme was so solemn a schoolboy. And the trouble did not stop there. Later that year an attempt was made on the king's life. A grenade was lobbed at him outside the Kyichu Temple in western Bhutan, but he ducked just in time and was unharmed. The assailant was discovered to be a former cook of the Dorji family. Under interrogation he confessed to having been paid a large sum by Tashi Dorji, the queen's elder sister, to assassinate the king (though subsequently, when re-examined in the queen's presence, he retracted this).

Whatever the truth, the impact of these events on the ten-year-old crown prince must have been traumatic. While the letters I was sent from home dwelt on how my father was doing in the latest golf tournament, the letters Jigme received must have contained more worrying news – no matter how gently it was put. I was at least partly aware of the difficulties he faced. My parents had told me about the assassination attempt on his father, but warned me not to spread it about the school.

Though we later went on to different schools, I kept in touch with Jigme and very much wanted to meet up with him again out in Bhutan. But just 'dropping in' was not an option in those days. Quite apart from questions of protocol, Bhutan had no air link with the outside world and had only just completed its first road passable by motor vehicle. Then my family left India, and it was not until I was at university that I was able to go out to the subcontinent during the long vacation to see my school friend.

I had got as far as Delhi, after travelling overland through Iran and Afghanistan, when the news reached me that Jigme's father had died of a heart attack. There followed a handwritten letter from the new seventeen-year-old king of Bhutan. 'Dear Gregson,' it began, keeping to schoolboy usage. He dwelt on the sadness caused by his father's death, adding that he would remain in official mourning, surrounded by hundreds of monks, for many weeks to come. Obviously, my plans to visit Bhutan had to be cancelled.

More than a decade passed before the next opportunity arose. It was the winter of 1986. I was recently married, and had returned with Sarah to Calcutta so that she could discover for herself where 'I had come from'. Once there, I decided to try for permission to enter Bhutan, which by then allowed in a strictly limited number of foreign tourists. To my surprise, authorization came straight back from the capital, Thimphu. It looked likely that I would very soon see my old friend again.

Nowadays, most foreigners arrive on the regular Druk Air service, the airport at Paro being less than two hours' flying time from Delhi or Calcutta. And that was how Sarah and I arrived for the first time, cruising high above the Bengal plains until the snowy masses of Kangchenjunga and Chomolhari filled the northern horizon.

Even from an airborne perspective, which has a tendency to diminish and flatten out any landscape, it was obvious we were passing over extremely rugged country. Thrust into the foreground were occasional hill-top hamlets, close enough for me to notice how they clung to the slightly flatter, more manageable land around the summit of a ridge. Steeply terraced fields coiled about these homesteads and, with the harvest in and the land newly ploughed, they resembled a dormant snake sloughing off its skin. They seemed terribly isolated, these islands of cultivation in a deep green sea. For everywhere else you looked, a carpet of unbroken forest softened the sharp contours of the hills. After India's teeming plains – or even Nepal, with its bare and all too often eroded hills – this land of Bhutan looked remarkably empty.

The aircraft had been gradually losing altitude when the pilot put it into a tight enough turn for the G-force to send the blood rushing to my feet. Then the nose went down and we were dropping fast into Bhutan's broadest valley. Not that Paro's valley seemed that spacious from where I was sitting. I peered out of the window and saw a farmer ploughing his field. What was slightly unsettling was that he was standing a good hundred feet above me. Seconds later the pilot touched down and feathered the props. It was the first time I had landed at an international airport where you look upwards to see peasants going about their daily rounds.

Arriving at Paro for the first time is a surreal experience. There is a windsock – that you expect at an airfield. But the Lilliputian airport building was fronted with multi-coloured prayer flags. There were more of them – faded white ones this time – fluttering in the breeze beside a row of half-timbered houses beyond the airport's perimeter fence. Just up the valley stood a massive and apparently still functioning castle, which I took to be Paro Dzong. The air was crisp and clear; the mountains to the north dusted with recent snowfall; the valley floor lined with graceful willows. Except for the airport there was not a modern building to be seen. Stepping straight off an aircraft into this, the first-time visitor might well imagine they have landed in some Shangri-La.

Inside the airport building, Sarah and I presented our passports to a smartly uniformed official. He studied the gratis visas issued by the Bhutanese trade delegation in Calcutta.

'What is the purpose of your visit to Bhutan?' he queried.

'Just visiting,' I replied.

He seemed perplexed. 'But you both have gratis visas. Are you not a diplomat? Or working for an aid organization?'

'Neither. I think we've been issued that visa because I'm an old friend of the king.'

'But there is nobody to greet you,' he said in disbelief, and busied himself checking through his records.

This being our first time in Bhutan, I did not know that all foreign visitors are met on arrival and chaperoned throughout their stay: tourists by their authorized tour guide; official visitors by the protocol officer assigned to them. Entry to Bhutan was limited to around 3,000 well-off tourists, preferably in pre-organized groups, each year. The fees, paid up front, are set at $200 a day – for which sum one could survive for a month in India or Nepal. But it is precisely to discourage mass-tourism or low-spending backpackers that the royal Bhutanese government has adopted this policy of controlled tourism. They want to maximize foreign exchange earnings, while keeping the possibility of 'disruptive' contact between outsiders and their own traditional society to a minimum. Hence the importance attached to their always being an official guide or chaperon.

The rationale of this highly controlled approach was explained to me later in the capital, Thimphu. 'Look at what's happened in Nepal. We don't want to sell out to tourism and ruin the country, as they have, without drawing any benefits.'

A fair enough point; but this control syndrome did not ease our unexpected arrival at Paro Airport. Unexpected, because we had managed to get on a flight a day earlier than originally planned.

'I will telephone for instructions to Thimphu,' announced the immigration officer.

But what was he to do about us in the meanwhile? According to his records we simply did not exist.

'You should stay at the tourist hotel here in Paro,' he decided.

Fine, but how were we to get there? By this time all the vehicles that had been waiting for 'expected' arrivals had driven off, and there seemed to be no taxis in this country. Eventually we hitched a ride with an airport employee who refused any payment.

There were more scenes of confusion at the hotel over our status. Were we not attached to a group? People didn't just walk in and ask for a room. The manager was called and, once again, I tried to explain this was a private visit, that I had known the king when he was at school in England and expected to meet him in the capital.

'So you are officially guests of His Majesty?'

'Not that I'm aware of.'

'Then I will have to contact Thimphu for further instructions.'

Clearly, we had entered a country where all decisions – even over what to do with a stray visitor – came from the top down.

For the time being, we were shown to a cottage in the grounds. Like the main hotel building, it was newly constructed but decorated with traditional Bhutanese motifs (I later learned these cottages were built for guests attending Jigme's coronation in 1974). There we were left to contemplate our predicament. Officially speaking, we did not exist. Since nobody knew how to categorize us, we had become 'non-persons'. It was an odd and not altogether unpleasant sensation.

As it was a fine afternoon we decided to walk into Paro town. The way led past wood-framed farmhouses, whose overhanging roofs of shingles weighted down by stones reminded me of Alpine chalets. Some were quite substantial buildings, large enough to house several generations, with two or three rows of small windows rising above a blank-eyed ground floor used for storing hay or keeping livestock. The window frames were intricately carved of softwood and painted in primary colours; access to the upper floors was often by an external ladder. Most of these dwellings stood four-square within a generous plot planted with willows and fruit trees and vegetables. The land was watered by diverting mountain streams through a maze of stone-lined channels. It seemed to me that Paro was a prosperous valley, its houses larger and more solidly built than any I had seen in other parts of the Himalayas.

Arriving in the main street, we found the town completely deserted. Not that Paro really qualified as a town in any strict sense of the word. There was just one street along which stood two uniform rows of shops – most of them general and hardware stores, though some doubled up as bars or simple hotels. At one end was a petrol pump; at the other a cluster of very large chortens surrounded by willow trees. Sarah entered one of the shops in the hope of finding some tea. It was empty apart from the young daughter of the house. She spoke good English, free of the odd sentence constructions and cadences typical of English-medium schools in India. Nowadays, she told me, all pupils learn English at school.

'So where has everybody gone?' I asked.

'Paro is new-built, in these last two years only,' she answered. 'The people will come later.' Whether this meant later that afternoon, or that the new-built houses and shops still awaited tenants, was not clear. I tried another tack.

'Can I visit the dzong?'

'The dzong is closed now. They have official guests staying. You see, Her Majesty the Queen Mother is now in residence at Ugyen Pelri Palace.'

Again, her answer seemed to stray off at a tangent. It was an upside-down world I had entered, where the twelve-year-old daughter of a shopkeeper knew all about the movements of the royal family, and could mention this in the most matter-of-fact way.

'If you want to see something,' she ventured, 'you can go walking only five minutes. Today there is an archery competition.'

An archery competition? I should not have been too surprised by this, archery being Bhutan's national sport. In fact, the subject had been raised the very first time I met the crown prince in Calcutta. During that audience the queen, Ashi Kesang, had asked me whether archery was among the sports practised at my school in England. Jigme was apparently rather good at it. The answer, sadly, was 'no'; although after Jigme had joined the school an arrangement was made with the local archery club whereby they could use the sports fields for practise if the Bhutanese students were allowed to join in. My schoolboy memories of summer's evenings and gentlemen in flannels shooting at regulation-sized targets did not, however, prepare me for a Bhutanese archery contest.

For one thing, all the contestants were wearing the *kho* – the loose, knee-length robe that is Bhutanese national dress. Normally it is made up of either brightly coloured striped silk or large-checked woollen stuff and it reminded me of a dressing-gown, though with stiff white cuffs attached. Even the spectators were all wearing traditional dress: the women in long wrap-around kiras of striped material, their hair cropped short in the pudding-bowl style of Bhutanese highlanders; the young boys in diminutive versions of the kho. It was like dropping in on a medieval pageant. Except this was not dressing up in historical costume; it was simply the equivalent of putting on their 'Sunday Best'.

The rules of the contest were equally extraordinary. There were two teams of eleven archers, and they were shooting over a distance of some 150 yards with bows and arrows made of a special variety of bamboo which grows mainly in the province of Khyeng. But the target was tiny and members of both teams crowded round it, ducking and weaving to avoid the incoming arrows. Whenever an archer scored a hit, his own team members joined in a victory dance, waving their bows in the air. When he missed the target the opposing team did much the same.

Meanwhile the spectators were constantly shouting and jeering at the contestants, doing their best either to encourage them or put them off their shot. And while the archers are supposed to refrain from alcohol and stay away from their wives before an important match, the crowd had been imbibing serious quantities of home-brewed *arra* and were in high spirits. But whenever a bowman stepped forward to take his two allocated shots, they looked deadly serious – a reminder that not so long ago such archery matches were used to train ordinary tenant farmers in the arts of war.

Proper respect – for one's elders, one's teacher, for office-holders and, of course, for the royal family – is deeply ingrained in Bhutanese society. An archery contest, however, is not the best occasion to observe such qualities. All the shouting and jeering, the uproarious laughter among the women when one of them hurled a particularly risqué taunt at some hapless bowman, gave quite the opposite impression. And while some of the contestants wore khos of finer stuff than others, it was hard to single out who were the local big shots and who were just ordinary farmers. I guessed that some royal officers would be present; but, if so, they bore no discernible badge of office. Nor were they accompanied everywhere by an obsequious entourage – as can usually be found surrounding any Indian politician who graces such sporting events with his presence.

Suddenly the match was over, one team was proclaimed victors, and the spectators either trooped off home or made for one of the bars along the main street where they ordered tea and locally produced spirits to ward off the cold. I soon discovered that Bhutan is home to a thriving distillery, and from a bewildering array of bottles selected one labelled Bhutan Mist. This turned out to be halfway between rum and whisky; but it warmed me up for the climb back to the hotel. By now it was dark, and since there were no street-lights we lost our way a couple of times. Then, alone in our room, the sensation of being a 'non-person' returned. What should we do next? If I hoped to see the king, then I supposed we should make our way to the capital.

The next morning I was offered a lift to Thimphu in an old Hindustan Ambassador. It got us as far as the main road before the engine gave up completely, so we simply hopped on the first public bus. The interior was already packed with families and vendors who were taking vegetables and live poultry in wicker baskets to market, but somehow two extra places were found. It soon became apparent that foreigners were not expected to travel in this fashion. My fellow travellers asked where we came from and what we were doing in Bhutan, showing astonishment when told that neither of us were aid workers. Only foreign aid workers, it seems, ever travelled on the buses.

We were offered sweet tea from a Thermos and betel nut (the Bhutanese are addicted to chewing this carcinogenic substance whose use, I was told, is sanctioned by no less an authority than Padmasambhava, the legendary Indian Buddhist mystic). As the bus swooped around the road's endless curves I began to enjoy the experience of travelling incognito through this country, hopefully to meet it's ruling monarch. Then the absurdity of our situation struck home, and as we approached Thimphu I began worrying about what to do next.

I need not have bothered. The moment Sarah stepped off the bus, a dignified gentleman rushed up. He was wearing a dark blue kho whose arms ended in extravagantly crisp white cuffs, one of which was extended in tentative greeting.

'You are Mrs Gregson?' he enquired, as fellow passengers jostled past with their baskets of squawking poultry. Then, turning to me, he added, 'Mr Gregson, I presume.' I wondered if he knew the same line is supposed to have been uttered when Stanley met up with Dr Livingstone in darkest Africa.

'Thank goodness we have met up,' he continued. 'We were expecting you to arrive on today's flight, and have just driven to Paro in order to greet you.'

I apologized for putting him to any inconvenience. 'It is a small misunderstanding,' he smiled, 'but now all is well. I am the protocol officer assigned to you; and this is your car and driver.'

I stared in disbelief at a brand new Toyota saloon. 'The vehicle is provided by the Foreign Ministry,' he explained. 'But now you will want to refresh yourself at the hotel.'

And so we were whisked off to the Mothitang Hotel, a modern building decorated in traditional Bhutanese style. It was set high up on a hill with fine views over the Thimphu valley, just far enough out of town to discourage visitors from walking down on their own.

'Why don't you take some luncheon?' suggested the protocol officer. 'Meanwhile, I must return to the office in order to confirm your schedule.'

What was this schedule? I wondered. And, more to the point, was I going to meet up with the king? Obviously we were no longer non-persons. Instead, we had entered a new, and from my own point of view, less comfortable state of limbo.

Over the next two days a succession of government officials came to see us. They regretted our visit had been arranged at too short notice. His Majesty was unable to see any visitors at present. In between these meetings Sarah and I were shown around Thimphu's ancient monasteries and temples, the great white chorten that Jigme had built as a memorial to his father, even the fortress-monastery of Tashi-chodzong which houses the royal secretariat. But the king was not there.

I wondered whether I had done anything to cause this change of heart. Or might there be some kind of palace revolution going on, an 'evil uncle' holding the king in his thrall? For a foolish moment I even imagined myself in some sort of Scarlet Pimpernel role, arguing my way past serried ranks of officials into the royal presence and then carrying away, secreted about my person, a desperate message to the outside world. Fortunately I did not act on these fantasies since, as usual, it turned out to be a case of 'cock up' rather than 'conspiracy theory'. We had arrived earlier than expected, and the king was out on tour in the provinces. All the same, I was saddened at having got so near and still not met up with my old school friend.

Sarah and I decided to cut short our visit to Bhutan. Apart from anything else, we were running up bills so fast at the official tourist rate that very soon we would be broke. This, I was told, was not a problem; we could always settle the account later (which I duly did by bankers' draft from London). Besides, it would be such a shame if we left without seeing something else of the country. To refuse would be an affront to Bhutanese hospitality. Why not a visit to Punakha, and then more time to explore the Paro Valley? A face-saving formula was worked out. But I was left with the distinct impression that I had played by the rules and that, in doing so, I had lost out.

Clouds hung over Thimphu on the morning we were meant to set off for Punakha. Not even the ever-optimistic protocol officer thought we would have a clear view of the Himalayas from the top of the Dochu-La pass. So instead of hurrying on, we agreed to stop first at Simtokha Dzong – the dour fortress which stands guard over both the approaches to Thimphu and the main road linking western and eastern Bhutan. It was begun in 1629, the first of many such fortress-monasteries ordained by the Great Shabdrung as part of his masterplan to impose unity and internal peace on the Bhutanese clans.

The Shabdrung Ngawang Namgyel is a seminal figure in Bhutan's history. Born into the Tibetan princely family of Gya in 1594, he was enthroned at an early age as eighteenth abbot of the main Drukpa monastery at Ralung. And so he might have ended his days undisturbed, were it not for disputes which arose over the possession of a sacred bone relic and his claim to be the reincarnation of an earlier Drukpa scholar, Pema Karpo. Chased out of Tibet by the powerful ruler of Tsang province, he sought refuge among the Drukpa community in Bhutan. But although he came as a political refugee, the Shabdrung was a charismatic leader of men. Within the space of thirty years this warrior-monk had united the Bhutanese clans behind him, subdued any rival monastic orders, established a code of laws throughout the country, and repulsed no less than four invasions from Tibet.

He is still revered as the 'founder of the nation'. The most tangible expression of his authority is the chain of dzongs he had constructed right across Bhutan. Most of these are still standing and continue to function, as he intended, both as monasteries and centres of regional government. Simtokha Dzong is an exception to the rule. In its layout it is more a fortified palace, intended for the Shabdrung's personal use, than a military-monastic complex. While the temples and sanctuaries inside the main tower are still attended by monks, nowadays the out-buildings house a school where lay-students from all over Bhutan can learn the Dzongkha language and traditional culture.

A group of young scholars were rehearsing a masked dance in the first courtyard. They wore a uniform of simple khos rather than the heavy masks and costumes of a full-dress performance; but they followed the traditional steps with precison, rolling their bodies and kicking their legs high as they leapt. Then we entered the main temple, whose gloomy interior contains some very fine wall-paintings and statues of bodhisattvas. A curiosity, which I had not seen elsewhere, was the presence of two life-size figures in antique armour which guard the door to the Gongkhang, the secret, black-walled room wherein the temple's fearsome deities reside.

The armoured figures are a reminder that Simtokha was also a fortress, that within three years of its completion it was captured by an army sent by the 'Five Groups of Lamas'. Their success was short-lived, however; for as the chronicles known as 'The Blue Annals of Bhutan' relate, 'Due to the spiritual power of the Shabdrung Rinpoche, the dzong caught fire and most of the enemies were burnt, while the rest fled to Tibet.'

The Shabdrung's successes in battle and in unifying Bhutan were ascribed to his superior spiritual powers rather than mere statecraft. And, until quite recently, the exercise of supernatural powers was central to waging war – and not just the provision of holy charms and amulets for one's troops to ward off the arrows and sword blows of the enemy, but the use of magical rituals effective over a long range to disrupt the enemy's plans or induce the death of their leader. It was to protect his country against another invasion from Tibet that the Shabdrung went into indefinite retreat in 1651, so that he could devote himself single-mindedly to such magic practices. Meanwhile his principal enemy at the time, the Fifth Dalai Lama, claimed to have won this spiritual duel by inducing the Shabdrung's death through his own secret rites.

The drive from the Shabdrung's first dzong, Simtokha, to his last resting place in Punakha, takes less than three hours along a twisting but well-paved road. Until this was built in the 1960s, the journey took two or three days – depending on how light you travelled. For much of the way the modern road shadows the old mule-track. It was a much-used route, for each year the Wang people migrated between their summer farmsteads around Thimphu and their winter homes in the much warmer Punakha Valley. From this habit arose the practise of having twin capitals, with Tashichodzong in Thimphu being the seat of government during the summer months and Punakha Dzong serving as the winter capital. This remained the rule until the late King Jigme Dorje began building a fixed capital in Thimphu during the 1950s. But that status applies only to secular government; the central monastic body continues to move twice a year between the traditional capitals. As this was December, the monks would be in Punakha now with their chief abbot, the Je Khenpo.

To begin with the road climbed steeply through orchards and blue pine forest. Then we entered thick cloud, and I began to wonder whether we would ever see Bhutan's snow-peaks. But just as we reached the top of the pass the clouds parted and there, crowding the northern horizon, were at least six Himalayan giants I had never seen before, all of them rising 23,000 feet or more. The driver steered around the left of the white chorten that marks the top of the Dochu-La. Devout Buddhists always go past a holy place in a clockwise direction, and in Bhutan this rule applies equally to motor traffic. All around the chorten were clusters of prayer flags, some very old and faded. There was no doubting that Bhutan remains a profoundly Buddhist country.

The 5,500-foot descent to Punakha combined the sensations of a roller-coaster ride and watching a nature video on fast-forward. The road was one succession of hairpin bends, and we were dropping so fast that the type of forest cover changed every ten minutes. Eventually we emerged into more open country, and I was surprised to find that the same sturdy, wood-framed farmhouses as in the higher valleys were now surrounded by tropical vegetation and banana trees. We stopped for lunch in a field lined with prayer flags. A warm wind was gusting up the valley, and the flags whipped noisily to and fro against their bamboo poles.

Rising above the confluence of two fast-flowing rivers, and with the distant snow mountains as a backdrop, Punakha Dzong is blessed with a spectacular setting as well as a pleasant climate. The monk body were out in force, the older ones enjoying the afternoon sun as they strolled beneath the red-and-white walls of the dzong, all the while turning their rosaries or commenting on the progress of a file of young novices which just then issued forth from the main gate.

Even the novices conducted themselves with a certain hauteur, and I was reminded that this was an elite monastic body to which the leading families of Bhutan would seek to enter their sons. For the Drukpa church is hierarchical in its organization: and for a promising young monk to shine here, beneath the eyes of the Je Khenpo or one of the Lopen – the high masters in charge of the different scholastic disciplines – is as sure a path as any to rapid advancement. Previously the monk body had owned large feudal estates; but from 1982 onwards these were surrendered so that landless farmers could be resettled on them. Nowadays the needs of the monkhood are provided for by the state.

As supreme head of religious affairs in Bhutan, the Je

Khenpo still commands enormous respect. Photographs of him arm-in-arm with the king are to be seen everywhere, in public places and private homes alike. The monk body also retains its own representatives in the National Assembly and on the Royal Advisory Council. They remain a powerful influence in the land, a bastion of monarchy (provided the king does nothing that upsets them too much), their natural instinct being to favour a conservative approach and to be suspicious of novelties.

Within Punakha Dzong we found more than twenty temples, each of them containing a wealth of statuary and wall-paintings. For, despite having been damaged many times by fire and floods, Punakha is a storehouse of religious treasures. Some of the murals are designed as aids to meditation, and for a while I lost myself staring at the cosmic mandalas outside the main assembly hall. But there is one temple, at the top of the central tower, forbidden to anyone save the king, the Je Khenpo, and the temple guardian. This is the Macchen Lhakang, and the body of the Great Shabdrung is preserved within its sanctuary.

The Shabdrung died at Punakha in 1651, shortly after going into indefinite retreat so as to concentrate his spiritual powers against the invading armies of the Fifth Dalai Lama. But to most Bhutanese, their Shabdrung remained a living presence for many years after. It may seem remarkable, but his death was successfully concealed for another fifty-four years. Only a handful of his closest advisers knew the truth. To keep up appearances they arranged for food to be passed through the opening to his meditation cell. It helped that most Buddhists believe that holy lamas can live to a great age, and that even after their physical death the conscious principle remains present until such time as it is willingly expelled. And there were pressing reasons to keep the Shabdrung's death a secret – not least the continuing threat of invasion from Tibet.

The ferocity of the Tibetan assault on the fledgling state of Bhutan runs hard up against the prevailing orthodoxy that once Tibet converted to Buddhism it ceased to be a militaristic power. The first three invasions, led by the princely rulers of Tsang, carried an internal dispute over monkish office and religious relics across the Himalayan divide. Such esoteric concerns still motivated later expeditions, as when a Tibetan army laid siege to Punakha Dzong in 1659 because the Shabdrung had placed a disputed bone relic there. (The attack was repulsed, and the relic remains within Bhutan's state treasure to this day.) But the cumulative effect of five invasions, particularly the later ones despatched by the Fifth Dalai Lama, was to kindle an enduring hostility between Tibet and Bhutan.

As leader of the dominant Gelugpa sect, the Dalai Lama had stamped out resistance from other Buddhist sects and their princely patrons within Tibet. Now that process was being taken to the periphery, with the assistance of Mongol troops furnished by the Dalai Lama's chief patron, Gushri Khan. But the Bhutanese, inspired by a charismatic leader, fought on with grim determination to defend their political independence and the established rights of the Drukpa church. This was, I believe, a formative experience. At some point in history, all the other Buddhist satellites among the Himalayas have fallen under Tibetan suzerainty. Bhutan alone can claim never to have been conquered. This spirit of resistance continues to inform Bhutanese nationalism – as does the close identification of the Drukpa church with what is considered to be most typically 'Bhutanese'.

Of course, links with Tibet did not dry up completely. Traders continued to cross the Himalayan passes, exchanging Bhutanese rice and chillies and dyes for Tibetan wool and salt and livestock. Revered lamas from Tibet continued to be welcomed into Bhutan (the first two chief abbots following the Shabdrung's death were Tibetans, and later on the post was filled by lamas from Ladakh), while some Bhutanese monks crossed over the Himalayas to study at the great monasteries of their order. There were matrimonial alliances between leading Bhutanese families and the Tibetan aristocracy, though less so than in neighbouring Sikkim.

There also existed large monastic estates in Ladakh and around Mount Kailash in western Tibet that had been originally granted to the Great Shabdrung. These remained under Bhutanese administration until 1960, when China's crackdown inside Tibet and the Dalai Lama's flight prompted the withdrawal of Bhutan's representative in Lhasa. At the same time, the border with Tibet was closed.

But by then a new and not always comfortable source of contact had arisen in the form of some 4,000 Tibetan refugees who crossed into Bhutan to escape the Chinese. Initially they were housed in large camps; but jealousies and resentments grew up between this exiled Tibetan community, who mostly refused to take up Bhutanese citizenship and paid voluntary contributions to the Dalai Lama in Dharamsala, and their Bhutanese hosts.

Things came to a head during the preparations for Jigme's coronation in 1974. The Bhutanese authorities claimed to have uncovered a plot to usurp the throne, replacing King Jigme Singye Wangchuck with one of the children of the late king's Tibetan mistress. The Dalai Lama's representative in Bhutan and – worse still – his Darjeeling-based elder brother, Gyalo Thondup, were implicated. A number of Tibetan refugees inside Bhutan were arrested for carrying arms. There followed an acrimonious correspondence between Dharamsala and Thimphu. But what is most remarkable about this episode is that when the world press arrived in Bhutan to cover the coronation, they were informed of this attempted coup but then asked not to report on it until after Jigme had been crowned – so as not to upset such an 'auspicious occasion'.

The affair did not bode well for the exiled Tibetan community in Bhutan. First the larger Tibetan refugee camps were disbanded and their occupants sent in small groups to remote and inhospitable corners of the land. Eventually they were given the blunt choice between accepting Bhutanese citizenship or being expelled. Most left in 1979, for another life of exile in India. With hindsight, Bhutan's treatment of its fellow Buddhist refugees has been less generous than either India's or Nepal's.

In view of this episode, it is hardly surprising the Dalai Lama has never been invited to Bhutan. Nor, for that matter, have King Jigme and the Dalai Lama ever met. Bhutanese reluctance to have any formal relations with the exiled Tibetan leader may well have been influenced by other considerations, such as not wanting to upset its 'big neighbour' China unnecessarily. All the same, it is odd that the king of the last Mahayana Buddhist state should never meet the spiritual leader of all Mahayana Buddhists.

Unless, that is, you look back to the old antagonism between the Druk people and the Dalai Lamas in their role as head of the Gelugpa order. That this antagonism still endures was brought home to me when, years later, I visited a Drukpa temple in eastern Bhutan. It contained a large 'tree of life' sculpture, upon which were carved figures embodying all the main sects of Tibetan Buddhism. 'But not the Gelugpa,' announced the incarnate lama who presided over the monastery. 'In Bhutan, we never have the Gelugpa.'

The threat of invasion from Tibet had receded by the time that the first Shabdrung's death was finally acknowledged. There was no natural heir, so the senior monks and nobility who had ruled in his name for more than half a century had to decide on how to find a duly sanctioned ruler of Bhutan.

The method chosen was the discovery of the Shabdrung's reincarnation. Or rather, reincarnations: for when the Shabdrung's consciousness was finally deemed to have departed, the three vital principles of body, speech and mind were found to have taken up separate embodiments – one in the boy-child of the Chogyal of Sikkim, one in southern Bhutan, and one in central Tibet. The Sikkimese line of 'body principle' incarnations was never fully recognized; but there have been reincarnations of both the Shabdrung's verbal and mental principles through to the twentieth century. Precedence has normally been given to the mind incarnations, and it was they who became – in theory at least – supreme rulers within Bhutan for the next two hundred years.

While the discovery of reincarnations may be theologically a sound enough instrument for transferring spiritual and secular authority from one generation to the next, it does not make for efficient government. None of the founding Shabdrung's successors demonstrated anything like his charisma or leadership, and for most of the next two centuries they had little to do with actually ruling the country. Like so many of the Dalai Lamas, they were mere figureheads.

Temporal authority was exercized on their behalf by a succession of regents whom the Bhutanese call Druk Desi. (When the British came into contact with Bhutan they applied Hindu terminology, referring to the Shabdrung as the Dharma Raja or 'religious ruler' and his regent as the Deb Raja.) But whereas some of the earlier Druk Desi provided firm government, by the nineteenth century it was unusual for any regent to last more than a year or two. An alarming number were either assassinated or forced to leave office. Arguments over who should hold the regency often boiled over into civil war. Real power fell away from the centre into the hands of the Penlops or regional governors, the commanders of dzongs and other feudal lords. If the Shabdrung's legacy was to ensure Bhutan retained its independence, it also installed a system of government that can at best be described as a dysfunctional theocracy.

Standing at the foot of the steep wooden staircase that led up to the forbidden chamber in which the Shabdrung's embalmed body is guarded day and night, I wondered how the 'founder of the nation' might have judged the system of government – and the two centuries of more or less continuous anarchy – carried out in his name.

I also wondered how he would have reacted to the

historic assembly of abbots and high lamas, ministers of state, regional governors, lesser officials 'entitled to riding mounts' and village headmen from each region of Bhutan, which gathered here within Punakha Dzong on 17 December 1907, to undo that system of theocratic rule and accept in its place a new hereditary monarchy. The imposing figure who ascended the Golden Throne to become the first king of Bhutan was Sir Ugyen Wangchuck, Tongsa Penlop and de facto ruler of the entire country for more than two decades. The present king is his great-grandson.

The novel institution of monarchy was accepted unanimously by the assembled notables and representatives of the people, who duly attached their seals to the contract. At the top of this parchment the Shabdrung's Great Seal, then in the keeping of the chief lama or Tatsang Khenpo, was applied. The contract makes plain that the king was taking on all the secular powers previously exercized by the regent. But it did not touch upon the spiritual authority of the Shabdrung, the most recent 'mental incarnation' having been born four years previously just across Bhutan's eastern border in a Tibetan-controlled region around Tawang monastery. For the next twenty-three years, monarchy and the remnants of theocracy would co-exist in Bhutan side by side.

The Sixth Shabdrung, Jigme Dorje, was brought to the monastery of Talo in central Bhutan where his predecessors had normally resided. And it was there that he died, under mysterious circumstances, when still only twenty-six years old. What happened on that night of 12 November 1931 has been whispered – but never openly stated – in Bhutan for more than two generations.

It was well known there had been a quarrel between the Shabdrung and the second king, Jigme Wangchuck. Its origins probably go back to the Shabdrung's granting disputed grazing rights within Bhutanese territory to his relatives from across the border, who were technically either Tibetan or British subjects. The king viewed this as an infringement of his authority over all secular matters.

Then it became known that the young Shabdrung had abandoned his celibacy by sleeping with a woman of Talo, a devotee who believed that in doing so she would become a dakini or spiritual consort of so holy a lama. Worse still, the Shabdrung's court sent a mission to seek out Mahatma Gandhi in India, where they asked the independence movement leader to help in restoring the Shabdrung to his rightful authority. Such a move could easily be construed as treason. Moreover, it was certain to alarm the British authorities in India who were paying an annual subsidy to Bhutan and generally supported the monarchy. Finally, King Jigme was informed that the Shabdrung was invoking maledictions and performing black magic ceremonies intended to do him deadly harm. Royalist troops were despatched to surround Talo Monastery.

While it has long been suspected that the Shabdrung was assassinated, this was only admitted publicly in 1998. And the source of this confirmation is even more remarkable. It appears in a book, *Of Rainbows and Clouds*, authored by one of the present queens of Bhutan, Ashi Dorji Wangmo Wangchuck. For the most part it is a family history, as told by her father, Yab Ugyen Dorji. However, Yab Ugyen is well placed to know what really happened at Talo since the Shabdrung was his maternal uncle.

According to this account, when news reached Talo that royalist forces were approaching, some of the Shabdrung's advisers urged him to flee to Tibet. Others offered to defend the monastery with what weapons they had. He refused to be moved, believing that nobody would dare to harm the Shabdrung. Later, on retiring to his bedchamber, he told the monk-servant who stayed beside him: 'If my death is of any benefit, it is all right by me. I am not afraid to die. For me, it is like changing clothes.' That same night, ten or eleven men carrying torches entered the chamber. Some refused to advance any further, but three of them encircled the sleeping Shabdrung and, having pinned him down and kicked him in the scrotum, stuffed a silken scarf down his throat until he suffocated.

Such detailed confirmation that Shabdrung Jigme Dorji died not of a heart attack or by committing suicide – as some earlier versions claimed – but was assassinated by high-ranking and loyal officers of the king – would appear to lay the mystery to rest. The fact that it was made public by the queen of Bhutan may seem bizarre, although in a way this is also an act of reconciliation. As close relatives of the dead Shabdrung, her family was chased out of Bhutan. Both her parents and grandparents suffered because of this affiliation. On the other hand, the family can claim descent not only from the sixth mind incarnation but also from the fifth speech incarnation of the Shabdrung. So when the present king of Bhutan married Ashi Dorji Wangmo and her three sisters in 1988, it was in a very real sense a union of the Royal House of Wangchuck and the heirs of the Shabdrung.

Fittingly enough, the wedding took place within Punakha Dzong, for it was here that Yab Ugyen's daughters had first met Crown Prince Jigme in 1969. Now the four queens ascended the steps leading to the Founding Shabdrung's antechamber, where they made obeisance to his embalmed body before each of them was draped with royal scarves by the chief abbot. They then went down to the main temple, where they received long-life blessings and enthronement offerings. The long-standing relationship between the king and the four sisters (Jigme later told me they had been 'unofficially married' in 1981) was now solemnized, and the succession of the seven-year-old Crown Prince Jigme Khesar Namgyal confirmed.

There was also the expectation amongst ordinary Bhutanese that 'the Shabdrung's Curse' might now be lifted. I was told that this curse – which is closely linked to the Sixth Shabdrung's untimely death – was the reason why both the previous two kings of Bhutan had died before reaching the age of fifty.

But the long shadow cast by the Shabdrung does not stop there. The very manner by which incarnations are discovered means that after one embodiment has died new claimants are likely to appear. At least two children born in eastern Bhutan were claimed to be true embodiments – before, that is, they mysteriously 'disappeared'. Another claimant born outside Bhutanese territory, in Tawang, caused a security scare when the Chinese invaded that area in 1962. The Indian authorities feared the Chinese might use him in the same way as they had the Panchen Lama in Tibet, as a mouthpiece for their own propaganda, and made sure this claimant was escorted down to safety.

Within Bhutan, no incarnation of the Shabdrung is recognized. Yet another so-called Shabdrung is very much alive and well (he is the same age as the king) and living a life of exile at Manali in northern India. I have never seen a photograph of him inside Bhutan. Indeed, it was only much later that I first saw his image – enlarged and framed and respectfully draped with white scarves – hanging on the office walls of exiled Bhutanese politicians in Nepal. He was up there on the wall of the Druk National Congress, whose party manifesto states it 'is committed to restoring his glorious place as the Spiritual Head of Bhutan'. And he was present at the breakaway Druk-Yul Democratic Party's HQ in Birtamod, which likewise promises 'to ensure the reinstatement of the ninth Shabdrung, Ngawang Namgyel, and the Mind incarnate of the first Shabdrung, to his legitimate position'.

It occurred to me that he is being promoted as a Dalai Lama-like figure, a religious figurehead who might appeal to pious Buddhists of whatever political persuasion. And in this they are probably correct, for the Shabdrung's memory is still venerated in Bhutan. I was told that when a rumour went around Thimphu that the exiled Shabdrung was in town, a crowd assembled outside the hotel where he was supposed to be staying. Likewise, some Drukpa pilgrims continue to go up to his retreat in Manali. But for the dissident leaders in Nepal, pushing the claims of the exiled Shabdrung gives them an additional excuse for cutting Bhutan's monarchy down to size. And having listened to some of these angry dissidents, I was left in no doubt that should they ever 'return in victory' to Bhutan, they would reduce the monarchy to a cypher. As for their Shabdrung, it is unlikely that he would be reinstated in anything more than a purely honorific position.

Punakha, the resting place of the First Shabdrung, was as far as we got on that first visit to Bhutan. But before flying out there were two glorious sunlit days exploring the Paro Valley. The mid-winter light was crystal clear, and up towards the Tibetan border the snows of Chomolhari gleamed against the pale blue sky.

We climbed up to Taktsang Lhakhang, one of the holiest sites in Bhutan. It is known as 'the tiger's lair' because, back in the eighth century, the miracle-working Padmasambhava is believed to have reached this inaccessible spot by flying on the back of a tigress. He then spent three months meditating in a cave there, subdued the evil spirits then presiding over the Paro Valley, and converted its inhabitants to Buddhism.

It is easy enough to understand the story of the flying tigress, for the diminutive temples at Takstsang cling to a vertical rock face. How else could the Buddhist saint have reached such an inaccessible spot? Even now a path has been built, the final approach had me worried about Sarah's vertigo taking hold. The main temple hangs slightly out-wards from the cliff and its narrow windows look straight out into the void. A single guardian-monk sat cross-legged on the polished wooden boards, reciting his prayers. The temple was both a haven of peace and an artistic treasure house, its walls covered with ancient paintings of Padmasam-bhava and his disciples.

Padmasambhava is still deeply venerated throughout Bhutan. His role in bringing Buddhism to its upland valleys, his subjugation of demons and conversion of the 'One Valley Kings' who then held sway, his concealing of sacred texts and other religious objects to be unearthed centuries later by treasure-discoverers or tertons – all qualify him as a founding figure in the emergence of Bhutan as a Buddhist state. His doings are celebrated in school texts that portray him as a 'cultural hero'. Clearly this Guru Rinpoche or 'precious teacher', as he is commonly known, is central to the Bhutanese sense of identity. Yet, one only has to look across the valley from Taktsang to know that he was not the first Buddhist missionary in Bhutan.

For there, surrounded by prayer flags, stand the twin temples of Kyichu Lakhang. By tradition, the first temple here was built by the great Tibetan king, Songtsen Gampo, as part of his endeavour to pin down a giant demoness whose body stretched across Tibet and the Himalayas. The Jokhang Temple in Lhasa was built over her heart in AD 638, while the temple at Paro was precisely positioned to pin down her left foot. There is another of these architectonic temples founded by King Songtsen Gampo in what is now Bhutan – Jampa Lhakhang, in the valley of Bumthang. This temple was designed to hold down the demoness's left knee and, on a more practical note, 'to subjugate the frontiers' of Tibet. Both temples were already there when Padmasambhava visited them in the eighth century.

Sceptical minds might dismiss all of this as fanciful. And yet, hidden behind this rich overlay of religion and legend lie the few clues we have to the early history of Bhutan. Two of the key elements, the coming of Buddhism and the migration of Tibetan peoples across the Himalayas, are closely intertwined. They had already begun by the seventh century, when the Tibetan Empire extended its sway over Bhutan and all the southern slopes of the Himalayas. Tibetan control of these regions may only have been indirect – witness the declared purpose of Kyichu Lhakhang and other outlying temples being to 'subjugate regions beyond the frontiers'.

None the less, it seems that Buddhism first entered from

Tibet, and under royal patronage. Thirteen hundred years later the links between religion and kingship are still there. The kings of Bhutan are considered to be, first and foremost, protectors of the Buddhist dharma. Members of the royal family remain great patrons of religion, and it was the Queen Mother who had a second temple built at Kyichu in exactly the same style as the old. And turning the wheel full circle, there is a statue of King Songtsen Gampo hidden within the older sanctuary.

For all the supernatural powers of Padmasambhava and his like, the country that is now Bhutan was not converted to Buddhism overnight. It was a gradual process, the work of countless lamas and ordinary monks over more than a thousand years. Along the way they had to come to an accommodation with earlier animist beliefs, incorporating local mountain deities and spirits within the Buddhist pantheon.

The forests and valleys on the southern slopes of the Himalayas were already inhabited by various Mongoloid peoples who practised a form of animist religion, worshipping the spirits in certain rocks, the forests and mountains. Some were ruled by 'One Valley Kings' (Padmasambhava is said to have reconciled two warring kings of Indian origin and then converted them to Buddhism); others stuck to tribal ways. The incoming Tibetans lumped them all together and called them 'Mon'.

Precisely who these 'Mon' peoples were, and where they originally came from, remains a matter of informed guesswork. Most probably they belonged to hill tribes similar to those still found in Arunachal Pradesh who migrated westwards through the Himalayan foothills. Among the main ethnic groups now living in Bhutan, the Sarchops or 'Easterners' fall into this category, while in the west there are small pockets of Lepchas – a timid, forest-dwelling people also found in the neighbouring Kingdom of Sikkim. But throughout Bhutan, there are still many isolated villages where pre-Buddhist rites are observed alongside the 'official' religion.

The early Buddhist missionaries did not find a united or even a homogenous country. Some lamas came as refugees from sectarian struggles within Tibet; others were invited by existing Buddhist communities or accompanied Tibetan clans as they migrated south of the Himalayan divide. But both priests and laymen knew they were heading for the periphery of the world of Mahayana Buddhism. Either as refugees or conquerors, they were going into exile. This, I believe, has had a lasting impression on how the Bhutanese see themselves. So, too, has the determination of those early missionaries and settlers that they would conduct their religion and run their new-found country their own way. In this respect, they resemble the Pilgrim Fathers, who founded their colonies in New England around the same time that the Shabdrung unified Bhutan.

Many of these Tibetan settlers entered Bhutan through the Paro Valley, travelling down the trade route from central Tibet by way of Phari Dzong and then crossing over one of the easier Himalayan passes. They brought with them their Buddhist religion and the rivalries which already existed between the different monastic orders and schools within Tibet. Most of those who came to Bhutan belonged either to the 'old' Nyingmapa school or to one of the sub-sects of the Kagyupa order. The other two main orders of Tibetan Buddhism – the Sakyas and the Dalai Lama's Gelugpas – are scarcely represented. Many of the later migrants who arrived in Bhutan were fleeing from persecution at the hands of the Gelugpas.

Around Paro and the western valleys, the Lhapa sub-sect of the Kagyupa order held sway from the late twelfth century until challenged by the Drukpas, another offshoot of the Kagyupa school ruled by hereditary prince-abbots of the Ralung Monastery in Tibet. Their name derives from the rolling of thunder (*druk* in Tibetan) when their first monastery was consecrated, this being deemed an auspicious sign. Over time their influence spread from Ladakh to the eastern Himalayas. But only in Bhutan did they achieve such dominance over other sects that their branch of Buddhism became the official state religion. The very name by which Bhutanese refer to their country, Drukyul, means 'Land of the Drukpas' or 'Land of the Thunder Dragon' – a direct reference to their first foundation.

As in Tibet, charismatic lamas exercised both spiritual and secular authority, which in due course was passed on through their 'lineage' – either by direct descent if they married, through nephews or other family members, or by recognizing their subsequent reincarnations. Very often these different means of transmission were combined, so it was not unusual for family heirs also to be recognized as reincarnations. Thus in western Bhutan, there developed a system of theocratic rule where all authority derived from a supreme spiritual ruler – rather like the Dalai Lama, though on a much smaller scale.

Monastic rule was not nearly so entrenched in central and eastern Bhutan. This was partly because the less centralized Nyingmapa school of Buddhism was more active there. Also, there was a long tradition of rule by clan chieftains or 'One Valley Kings'. By the eleventh century, most eastern parts of the country were ruled by a nobility of Tibetan stock who claimed descent from Prince Tsangma, elder son of the last Buddhist king of Tibet. This devout prince was expelled by his younger brother, the violently anti-Buddhist Langdarma, before eventually finding refuge in Bhutan.

It is through the offspring of this royal refugee that the old religious nobility of Bhutan – including the royal house of Wangchuck – trace their origins back to the Yarlung dynasty, and ultimately to the first divine kings of Tibet who descended from the sky along a cord. Kingship, then, has very deep roots in Bhutan; and while the Wangchucks do not claim divine ancestry in the same way as either the Japanese emperors or the kings of Nepal, 'that divinity which doth hedge about a king' is still very much a reality.

The present king, as I discovered, is also hedged about with bureaucrats and protocol officers whose business it is to screen anyone seeking a royal audience. They apologized profusely that 'His Majesty was out-of-station', that it was most unfortunate he was 'unable to receive any private guests at this time'. Perhaps I had been naïve in thinking I could just drop in on my old school friend now that he was absolute ruler of this bizarre country. Or could it be that my letter never got through this protective cordon; that Jigme wasn't even aware of my being in his kingdom?

Whatever the truth (and I shall never know), my first visit to Bhutan had not been an unqualified success. To have come all this way and not met up with King Jigme was a serious disappointment. At least I had fulfilled my child-hood ambition of entering Bhutan. And yes, on that first trip, I thought I had entered some enchanted kingdom where so much that was good from the past – the buildings, monastic learning, a sense of dignity and independence that expressed itself even in the way ordinary people wore their traditional clothes – had been preserved. These people, I sensed, were proud to be Bhutanese. They lived in peace and there was an abiding sense of tranquillity. But then that was in 1986, before the troubles erupted in the south.

I was also aware that I had not ventured beyond the cultural heartland of the Ngalong or 'western Bhutanese': that further to the east, or down in the southern foothills, there existed peoples of different ethnic backgrounds who spoke half a dozen other languages or dialects. In other words, I had seen only one aspect of the country; and that (as I later realized) was the part most likely to confirm the visitor's view of Bhutan as a sort of modern-day Shangri-La. For all these reasons, I was determined to return to this Himalayan kingdom and finally meet up with Jigme again.

Chapter Two

FIRST TIBET

The People's Liberation Army invaded Tibet in 1950 and rapidly overran the poorly equipped Tibetan forces. While the Chinese were still advancing, the fifteen-year-old Dalai Lama was made head of state and invested with powers that, under more normal circumstances, he would not have exercised until he had reached his majority at eighteen. But it was too late to save the Tibetans' independence. Since then Tibet has been a captive land.

I suspected this Chinese-controlled Tibet would be very different from the country my father had walked into in 1939. He had taken the old trade route through Sikkim and over the Himalayan passes, continuing through the Chumbi Valley and up onto the Tibetan plateau, where he stopped at Phari Dzong. He never reached Gyantse, let alone the 'forbidden city' of Lhasa. But the Tibet he saw was unchanged from medieval times. The monasteries and high officials were supported by armies of serfs, and at the head of this feudal hierarchy a god-king, the Dalai Lama, ruled over a vast country much as the medieval popes and prince-bishops had once done in Europe.

The Fourteenth Dalai Lama, latest reincarnation of this living Buddha, had recently been recognized to be a young boy called Lhamo Dhondup from Taktser, a village in the north-eastern province of Amdo. That same summer, in 1939, a huge caravan assembled to escort him across the Tibetan plateau – a journey of more than three months – to Lhasa, where he was installed in the fortress-like palace of the Potala. News of these events was sent to the British Government of India from the small British Mission in Lhasa, which had its own radio transmitter. As my father walked into Tibet, he was overtaken by a mule-train carrying batteries made by his own company that were destined to power this transmitter. He also brought with him a case of beer that had been packaged in cans – this being a very recent invention. He has always claimed that these were the first canned beers ever seen in Tibet. By such means did the trappings of modernity (or, as the Chinese saw it, 'Western imperialism') enter this ancient and previously undisturbed land.

One reason I wanted to visit Tibet was to retrace part of his original route. To travel the old trade route is impossible these days, for both the Indians and Chinese have created restricted military areas on either side of the Himalayan divide. But I hoped to get as far as Phari Dzong, or possibly even the Chumbi Valley (which he recalled as being the loveliest of places, all flowering meadows and crystal-clear mountain streams). But he also saw the darker side of Old Tibet – the wooden stocks outside the governor's palace in Phari Dzong where criminals were flogged or were disfigured by having their noses slashed or an ear cut off. Not everything under the feudal regime that then ruled over Tibet was admirable.

I did not expect to find many traces of kingly rule. If the Dalai Lamas are considered as priest-kings (and 'The

Great Thirteenth' certainly ruled over Tibet like an absolute monarch), then all that is left is their palaces – the Potala and the Norbulingka or summer palace, both of which have been turned into museums. More than thirty years had passed since the Dalai Lama fled from Lhasa in 1959. A new generation had grown up which had known nothing but Communist rule. The vast country that had once been Tibet had been carved up between different Chinese provinces. Most of the north and east, the ancient provinces of Amdo and Kham, had become parts of neighbouring Qinghai, Ganzu, Yunnan or Szechuan – a deliberate act of dismemberment which left only around half of the six million Tibetan-speaking peoples within the so-called Tibetan Autonomous Region or TAR.

Sarah and I succeeded in entering Tibet in the summer of 1992. Just five years earlier there had been more anti-Chinese demonstrations in Lhasa. The authorities' response was to fire into the crowds and re-impose martial law. And because these events were witnessed by foreign tourists who smuggled out reports and photographs of the security forces' response, the authorities had tightened up on who was allowed into Tibet. Only organized tour groups who could be chaperoned by their Chinese-authorized guides were permitted.

But by 1992 there was supposedly another period of political thaw. Monasteries were being rebuilt and religion practised more openly – though I was also aware that millions of Han Chinese were being encouraged to settle in Tibet. Already they formed the majority in the larger towns. Indigenous Tibetans were becoming increasingly marginalized in their own land. This massive population transfer of Han Chinese ranks alongside Indonesia's 'transmigration' programme as one of the worst examples of neo-colonialism from the late twentieth century.

The Chinese authorities still preferred that all visitors be part of guided tour groups and generally restricted access to a few 'open' cities including Lhasa, Shigatse and Gyantse. This did not fit with our plans, so Sarah and I applied to the Chinese Embassy in London for visas permitting us to travel independently. Visas were issued for most of China, but not for Tibet. Rather than sign up with a tour group run by one of China's state-owned travel agencies, we took a flight to Kathmandu; but the Chinese Embassy there was equally unwilling to grant independent entry to Tibet. There were Nepalese-run tours going overland into Tibet, however, and after considerable wrangling we attached ourselves to one of these. Usually you have to buy a return flight from Lhasa; but, as we pointed out, both of us had valid visas to continue our journey through China proper. Which is how we managed to obtain a one-way ticket into Tibet.

I had met Tibetans in exile many times before – in Delhi and Kathmandu, on pilgrimage to the Buddhist shrines at Sarnath and Bodh Gaya, in England and in Canada. In fact, one of my earliest memories is of a Tibetan couple in Calcutta who used to take their early morning walk around the same public gardens as I did. He wore a heavy woollen robe called a *chuba*; she a long striped apron. For them, even the relatively cool hours just after dawn were oppressive, and they wiped away little beads of sweat on their foreheads with a handkerchief. All of which struck me as wrong-headed but refined.

My first encounter with 'real' Tibetans – that is to say,

part of the supposed six million who remain under Chinese rule, as opposed to the 100,000 who live in exile – occurred at the border crossing with Nepal. And, to tell the truth, they frightened me.

There were maybe twenty of them, mostly teenagers, though all were of much larger build and physically more intimidating than anyone I had run into in Nepal. What's more, they were eyeing up us foreigners – or rather our baggage – with the concentration of a bird of prey about to swoop down on its quarry. Their dress was an ill-fitting mixture of traditional and modern: weather-stained chubas over drab Chinese work clothes; but they all wore their long hair bound in tresses, and some had pendants of coral or turquoise dangling from one ear. None of them had known anything but rule by Communist China.

'These men are seeking to be porters,' explained a Nepalese businessman who had come up on the same bus from Kathmandu. 'But do not trust them. So many times at this border, valuables have disappeared.'

His remarks reminded me of accounts written by nine-teenth-century travellers to Tibet, who reported back that most Tibetans were either thieves or ruffians and generally not to be trusted. Nowadays such sweeping condemnations are no longer acceptable – particularly since the Tibetan cause has been taken up by so many opinion-formers in the West – and it is only fellow Asians who air them without embarrassment.

I took a closer look at these would-be porters. Their broad faces might have shone with the 'rosy complexion' so typical of highland-dwelling Tibetans, were it not for the fact that they were covered in many layers of ingrained dirt – a characteristic also noted by earlier generations of travellers, my own father among them. The Tibetans' reluctance to wash frequently may be explained by the severe climate up on the plateau, where, for most of the year, water would freeze on the body before it could dry. Also, as protection against the biting winds, yak butter or grease is sometimes smeared on the skin to form an insulating layer. Naturally, this film of grease traps any wind-blown dirt and in time gives off a slightly rancid odour.

Some Westerners, and more recently the Chinese, have interpreted Tibetans' disregard of personal hygiene as a sign of their being a 'backward' people. Others explain such customs as a sensible enough response to living in a near sterile environment, where the air is so cold and dry that most of the diseases spread by poor hygiene simply cannot take hold. I remembered my father telling me how, when he trekked into Phari Dzong, he 'found the inhabitants healthy enough, though they didn't seem to wash much'; and that 'despite all the dead dogs lying around the streets there was no stench or putrefaction'.

But then Phari Dzong lies in the rain shadow of the Himalayas at an altitude of nearly 16,000 feet. Where I was now, the border town of Zhangmu, stands less than 7,000 feet above sea level, and the road was still waterlogged from that afternoon's monsoon downpour. So while Tibetan sanitary customs might have evolved differently up on the world's highest plateau, they are not well adapted to living at lower altitudes. The plight of newly arrived Tibetan refugees in India, so many of whom died of tuberculosis, dysentery, cholera, and other tropical diseases against which they had no resistance, bears this out. All of which made me wonder about the health of those fierce-looking and grimy young men waiting to carry my rucksack. Half of them had streaming noses which they occasionally wiped on their sleeves. As for the tall Khampa with red silk tassles woven into his hair, the cold sores around his upper lip had split open and were weeping badly.

For the time being, he and his colleagues were kept at bay by a Chinese policeman wielding his baton. They were playing at a game of cat-and-mouse which I suspected was enacted every time a fresh batch of travellers came through the border. The ground rules were simple. The policeman had to keep the Tibetans on the far side of the pagoda-embellished gateway which formally welcomes all those travelling from Nepal across the Friendship Bridge into the People's Republic of China. The Tibetans' game was to taunt him, either by shouting abuse or by making a fake run at the invisible border. He then had to chase them back, baton waving in the air, only to be greeted by more jeering and insults.

The duration of the game was set by the amount of time the Chinese immigration and customs officers needed to process a group. Since individual travel was prohibited, travellers were not allowed to pass through the Welcome Gateway individually. Which meant that even those who had been processed had to wait around in no-man's land until the last had been dealt with. The best part of an hour passed before I was called in. Although I knew my visas were valid, the immigration officer made me feel like some sub-species very far down the evolutionary ladder.

The only hitch occurred when the customs men started pulling out my books to check whether I was carrying any subversive literature. They found a volume entitled *Foreign*

Devils on the Silk Road and I knew I was in for trouble. A woman officer who spoke better English was called in to question me.

'What is the meaning of this book?' she asked.

'It is about the archaeological treasures in western China, and how the Westerners came to take them away,' I answered quite truthfully.

'So why are you bringing this book into China?' Her tone made it clear that she suspected me of smuggling in some sort of DIY manual for grave-robbers.

'It is a serious historical work,' I said in desperation. 'The author condemns the imperialists who stole the treasures from Dunhuang and other places I will be visiting. He also says these treasures should now be returned to the people of China.'

My explanation seemed to satisfy her and she handed back the book. But, by the time Sarah and I had re-packed, all the other foreigners were ready to go. Some were already starting to pick up their bags when there was a huge commotion up by the gateway. This, apparently, was the agreed signal for the Tibetans to come rushing over the border.

They ran in great leaps and bounds, whooping and hallooing as they came. One made a beeline for Sarah's rucksack.

'I can manage perfectly well, ' Sarah declared. She tried to wrest it back and there ensued a brief tug-of-war, but it was hopeless to resist. He had a tight grip on it and the only possible outcome was a ripped strap or two. So off he went, to yet more exuberant whooping, through the Gateway to China. I ran behind, trying to keep an eye on our bags among all the luggage bobbing up and down. Amidst this confusion, I did not even register that I had finally entered Tibet.

We caught up with my self-appointed porter outside the Zhangmu Hotel, where he had tipped my bag onto a communal pile of luggage. I was carrying no Chinese currency, but payment in Nepalese rupees was acceptable. They might have looked poor, dirty and dishevelled, yet these kids knew the current exchange rates. But then Zhangmu lives off the cross-border traffic, the trade in Chinese, Tibetan and Nepalese goods, not to mention a little smuggling on the side – including, I suspected, assisting Tibetan refugees to cross the border.

We were told to wait in the hotel lobby for information about onward travel arrangements. This was to be provided by Mr Zhou of the CYTS (China Youth Travel Service), who introduced himself as our Group Leader. But first he had to go through his 'welcome speeches'. He began with a general address on how our visit to China would undoubtedly contribute to mutual understanding and peace between our respective peoples. To mark the end of this speech he began clapping and encouraged others to join in – not, it should be understood, in praise of his oratory, but out of respect for the high principles of international solidarity he had just enunciated. My reluctance to participate was overcome by the desire to be back on the road, so I clapped along with the others.

But Mr Zhou was not finished yet. Far from it. He now called on individuals of each and every nationality on the bus – Spanish, French, British – to stand up in turn so that he could deliver a personalized welcome speech during which the 'special friendship' between the People's Republic and Britain, France, Spain, etc, could be praised, ending with another round of mutual applause. Even the bus driver had to stand up while Mr Zhou listed his comradely virtues, culminating with his technical proficiency in having driven the Lhasa–Zhangmu route for two and a half years without being involved in a single accident. For this he received the loudest applause yet from our newly constituted group.

I had not counted on having Mr Zhou along when I bought my ticket back in Kathmandu. Not that there was anything intrinsically objectionable about him. He was from Shanghai, a reliable Han Chinese who had been drafted into this distant and inhospitable province mainly because of his language skills. There was a shortage of English-speakers because a number of Tibetans previously employed as official guides had been dismissed. Some were former refugees who had learned their English while in India, and were therefore suspected of giving foreigners 'unreliable' information. So Mr Zhou and his colleagues had been sent in to fill the gap.

Unfortunately he knew very little about Tibet. This became apparent the next morning. After driving up a precipitous gorge where waterfalls came tumbling over the road we finally reached the high plateau. We stopped to visit Pengyeling Monastery and the icy cave where the eleventh-century Buddhist saint, Milarepa, meditated while wearing only a thin cotton shawl. Mr Zhou had mugged up on how 'Milarepa' means 'cotton-clad'; but when he tried to explain the significance of the temple's recently restored murals he found himself being constantly corrected by one of the passengers, a Frenchwoman on her second visit to Tibet.

This caused serious 'loss of face' which may well have persuaded Mr Zhou that there should be no further visits to cultural monuments until we reached Shigatse two days later. And so the bus trundled east across the Tibetan plateau with a minimum of wayside halts, its occupants as effectively cut off from the world outside as aboard the 'sealed train' that carried Lenin to St Petersburg in 1917. It was as though we carried some deadly bacillus that might infect the native population. Even the most fleeting contact with local people was discouraged; though whenever we stopped peasant women would advance shyly and ask if we had any Dalai Lama photos.

Sealed within this artificial world, we looked out on landscapes so vast and empty that it seemed impossible that anyone could live there at all. We crossed passes still covered in snow at the end of July. We saw nomads with their herds of yaks – massive beasts that appeared to be only half-domesticated – moving on to new pastures. For most of the time the High Himalaya was buried in cloud and, although we passed close by, not once did we see the northern slopes of Mount Everest. The monsoon had been particularly heavy that year and moisture was spilling over the Himalayan divide.

Some of the passengers asked Mr Zhou if we could visit Sakya Monastery. It used to be the seat of the Sakya Lamas, heads of one of the four main orders of Tibetan Buddhism. Indeed, it was one of the Sakya Lamas who in the thirteenth century went to the court of Kubilai Khan and so impressed the Mongol leader that he was made head of the Buddhist religion throughout his domains, including China. The Sakya Lama was also granted the right to rule over the whole of Tibet. While incarnate lamas and the abbots of larger monasteries had previously exercised temporal powers, ruling like princes over different regions of Tibet, this was the first time the entire country was subjected to a single monkish ruler. This experiment in theocracy was to be taken up in the sixteenth century by the heads of the reformist Gelugpa order of monks, to whom their Mongol patrons accorded the title of Dalai Lama or 'Ocean of Wisdom'. The relationship between these high lamas and their powerful supporters, the Mongol Khans and Chinese emperors, was essentially that of priest and patron. More recently, the Chinese have interpreted this historic relationship to support their claims to exercising 'sovereignty' over Tibet. For them, Tibet has always been part of the 'Great Motherland'.

Mr Zhou flatly refused to undertake any side trip to Sakya, declaring that it was not on the agreed schedule. It may also have been that he did not want us to see the immense damage wrought by the Chinese after they discovered the Sakya Lama and practically the entire monk body had fled across the Himalayas to India, where he eventually set up the order's headquarters in Dehra Dun. Whatever his reasons, the bus kept ploughing on towards Shigatse. In an attempt to cheer us up, Mr Zhou tried to get us to sing along to a Bob Marley tune he had picked up somewhere. 'Don't worry, be happy,' he chortled, 'be-cause every little ting's going to be all right.' Nobody else joined in, but he kept on singing and smiling none the less.

It was in Shigatse that Sarah and I decided to bail out. If we were ever going to follow a portion of my father's route into Tibet, we needed to obtain a piece of paper authorizing us to travel independently around the country and not just as part of a tour group. The document we required was called an Alien's Travel Permit or ATP, and these were only issued in larger towns like Shigatse by the Public Security Bureau, otherwise known as the Gong An Ju. The very name of this secret police force inspires dread amongst most Tibetans. But both Sarah and I had valid Chinese visas, and we could argue that all we needed was an extension to our visit within the Tibetan Autonomous Region. At least it was worth a try.

To our immense surprise, we were issued with ATPs authorizing a further month inside Tibet. It was only valid for travel between the larger cities, however, and my attempts to add Phari Dzong and the Chumbi Valley to the list were firmly crossed out. Still, it was better than nothing, and we left the PSB headquarters with a sense of liberation. 'No more Mr Zhou,' Sarah shouted to no one in particular as we made our way down the broad and empty boulevards of Shigatse's new town. This had all gone up since the Chinese occupation and the drab office blocks and apartments, the high-walled compounds concealing government offices and state-owned enterprises, were identical to those of any provincial town in central China.

I decided it was best not to reveal our hand until after we had left Shigatse. Otherwise Mr Zhou might arrange to have our travel permits cancelled; so we tagged along on the visit to Tashilhunpo. This great monastery is the seat of the Panchen Lama, the second highest reincarnation after the Dalai Lama. The previous Panchen Lama had been kept under close house-arrest in Beijing and made numerous pro-Chinese statements. For most of his life he was considered by Tibetans as a stooge; but after he returned to Tibet he was critical of China's imposition of socialist programmes and even came out in favour of the Dalai Lama. Shortly afterwards he died of a 'heart attack', as did several members of his family and closest followers. That, at least, was the official version.

Three years later, when I visited Tashilhunpo, the Chinese authorities were well advanced in the search for 'their' Panchen Lama. As we entered the monastic precincts an official motorcade swept out of the main gates, the faces of the dignitaries inside the black limousines concealed behind darkened glass. As for the monastery itself, with its colleges and dormitories and innumerable shrines linked by narrow lanes that wind up the hill towards the main prayer hall, it resembled an enclosed city rather than what one normally thinks of as a monastery. But it was a deserted city, with only a handful of visibly disgruntled monks in residence. One of them asked me for a Dalai Lama photo. Otherwise, they stared in silence at these foreign intruders in their midst.

It was only a half-day's drive to Gyantse, which is where we planned to strike off on our own. The old town lies at the foot of a medieval fortress which was thought to be impregnable until Colonel Younghusband's expeditionary force brought modern mountain guns to bear on it in 1904. For all that, it is still an imposing sight, its walls rising above vertical cliffs up towards the citadel.

As in Shigatse, the authorities were in the process of building a new town. To encourage the population, a public address system had been rigged up which broadcast a mixture of uplifting speeches and patriotic songs. But the day we arrived was a holiday, and the largest crowds gathered in the old town, where they joined in tug-of-war competitions – the women as well as men straining at the ropes while their group leader waved a big red flag and yelled at them through a megaphone. They put their all into it; but when one team eventually won both sides sat down in the dust and laughed uncontrollably. It was just a game, after all.

The next morning I told Mr Zhou that, regretfully, Sarah and I would be leaving his party. He protested vociferously, but when I showed him our ATPs he knew there was nothing he could do. So the tour coach left for Lhasa without us, and revelling in our new-found freedom we hurried down to the public bus depot to see if we could buy a ticket to Phari Dzong. Although a bus was headed that way, its driver refused to let us aboard. It was, we understood, 'not permitted'.

We tried hitching a ride with a team of American and French geologists; but they also declined, saying that our presence might 'jeopardize' their expedition. There was nothing left for it but to walk down to the junction where the road to Phari Dzong branched off and try hitch-hiking. Our first lift was with a Communist cadre driving a Chinese version of a Jeep. He wore a black Mao jacket and had a portrait of the 'Great Helmsman' encased in plastic dangling from the rear-view mirror; but he drove us right out of the valley and up to a mountain village. Beyond that he said he could not take us, since there was a police checkpoint. But he did suggest we walk through the fields of ripening barley, thereby avoiding the checkpoint, and try our luck on the other side. I later learned that this is fairly standard practice in Tibet, where 'dodging the system' has become almost second nature.

Our next lift was on a truck carrying timber. There was no room in the already overcrowded cab so the driver suggested we climb up top. It felt rather precarious perched on top of a load of untrimmed tree trunks – especially once we started climbing in earnest and the logs started shifting every time we went round a sharp bend. We kept climbing for more than an hour, the fertile valleys around Shigatse giving way to open grasslands where yaks and hardy Tibetan ponies had been let out to graze. Then the truck came to an abrupt halt. I peered over the top of the cab and saw we had arrived at another checkpoint. And this time there was no way of walking around it. The valley rose on either side right up to the snow line without so much as a bush to hide behind. Our only hope of continuing towards Phari Dzong was to talk to the officer-in-charge and hope that he was so bewildered by the appearance of two foreigners that he would let us proceed on our way.

The Chinese officer on duty was indeed surprised to find us at his checkpoint, but there was no way that he would permit us to continue any further. I tried to persuade him to let us go on to Yala, the next township up the road, where the authorities could decide what to do with us. He would not give an inch. I pointed out there was no traffic going in the other direction. So what did he want us to do about the situation? His response was to order some tea.

We spent six hours under detention at that checkpoint, during which time I bought soft drinks for half the garrison and watched them line up the empty bottles and throw stones at them. There was nothing else to do apart from wait and watch the ponies graze in the water meadows or look up towards the snow line.

For me, the desolate beauty of this high pass was some consolation for having blown any chances of making it as far as Phari Dzong, where half a century earlier my father had been stopped coming in the opposite direction. It was only a personal quest, after all. But for the Chinese soldiers who had to man this outpost of empire, the immensity of the sky and the green meadows rising to snow-capped peaks held no consolation at all. For them, this was the back-end of hell – except it was freezing cold at night even in mid-summer. They didn't want to be here. And they expressed their boredom and resentment by throwing stones at empty bottles all afternoon. There was nothing else to do.

Towards evening, a truck heading towards Shigatse drew up. We were told to jump in the back. The goods platform was empty apart from a few sacks of rice and two dozen incontinent sheep. We clung to the rice sacks as the truck sped downhill through endless hairpin bends all the way to Shigatse, since that was the only way to avoid being rolled in among all the sheep's droppings. I cannot say I felt entirely covered in glory when we finally staggered back to our hotel room.

The bus from Gyantse to Lhasa was full of Taiwanese tourists on a Buddhist cultural pilgrimage. Throughout the journey they all wore anti-pollution face-masks against the dust – except when they passed round little plastic bags of dried seaweed or sweet-cured octopus tentacle to help relieve the boredom. Sarah and I mastered the art of polite refusal pretty quickly. Moreover, the route we took – over three high passes and along the shores of an unnaturally blue lake – was far from boring. I also noted that the Taiwanese showed no interest in Tibetan people or culture unless there was an overtly Buddhist connection. They seemed to share the same condescension towards 'barbaric' peoples as their ideological rivals on mainland China.

The Taiwanese were staying at the Lhasa Holiday Inn, a concrete fortress in which you could munch on 'yakburgers' and enjoy the specially laid on 'cultural programmes' of

Tibetan music and dance. Sarah and I hot-footed it out of there, though not before running into a still outraged Mr Zhou. We moved into the Yak Hotel, a Tibetan-run establishment popular with independent travellers who had made it overland from China. It was only a few minutes' walk from the centre of the Barkhor, the old Tibetan quarter with its once crowded markets and narrow streets.

We found many of the older houses had been emptied prior to demolition, the authorities having grandiose plans to 'improve' the Barkhor and, in the process, uproot its distinctly Tibetan character. But there were thousands of pilgrims down by the Jokhang Temple, where they performed the *kora*, walking in a clockwise direction around its walls before entering this holiest of shrines. They had journeyed from all over Tibet, some of them covering the entire distance by making full-length prostrations every yard of the way. The temple entrance was crowded with these devout pilgrims prostrating themselves countless times before they judged themselves worthy to enter the inner sanctum.

There were armed police everywhere and plain-clothesmen in among the crowds. Throughout our stay in Lhasa I was aware that a watching game was going on: the Public Security Bureau and their informers keeping up constant surveillance of the Tibetan population while a few young men, usually Khampas, kept an eye on the police. It didn't take long before we too became aware of the unmarked cars belonging to the dreaded Gong An Ju. The atmosphere was tense, I was told, because a Buddhist nun had recently been arrested and the authorities were determined to prevent any further protests. The advice to foreigners was not to be seen talking to local people and certainly not to go around handing out Dalai Lama pictures. Simply contacting a foreigner could result in a Tibetan being arrested and interrogated. Lhasa – or at least the Tibetan quarter around the Barkhor – was a city under invisible siege.

The atmosphere in the new town was quite different. There, most of the shops and restaurants were run by Chinese settlers. The broad, tree-lined avenues adhered to a grid pattern, and the town-planners had obviously left plenty of open space for further expansion. For the time being, however, business was slack. The only customers at the street stalls were other Chinese stallholders. When we stopped at a restaurant there were no other customers – nor, to judge from the bored nonchalance of the teenage girl left in charge, had there been any for some time. She just sat there, leaning against the counter, listening to Chinese pop songs, passing the time of day.

I got the impression that she didn't want to be in Lhasa in the first place. For her it was a backward, deeply provincial township where it was difficult to find even the simplest of modern amenities. The locals were hostile and spoke a barbaric and incomprehensible language. It was something to be endured. That, I am convinced, is how many Han settlers feel about living in Tibet.

Soaring high above this new town is the former palace of the Dalai Lama, the Potala. Seen from below it looks more like a fortress than either a palace or a monastery, though before 1959 it combined these roles with that of being the seat of the Tibetan government. Most of this imposing, eleven-storey structure was built by 'The Great Fifth' Dalai Lama in the seventeenth century, and for the next three hundred years it was the nerve centre of a highly unusual form of theocracy that ruled over the whole of Tibet.

Not that many of the 'Great Fifth's' successors exercised the absolute powers attached to their office. The method of succession, whereby a boy child was found to be the reincarnation of the previous Dalai Lama, ensured that there would be long periods when the young god-king was still a minor and a regent governed in his name. Through most of the eighteenth and nineteenth centuries, real power fell into the hands of these regents; and to forestall the possibility that their young charges might assume their rightful authority, the regents ensured that they never reached the age of majority. No less than four consecutive Dalai Lamas died at a suspiciously young age during the nineteenth century – possibly with the connivance of the *ambans*, the powerful ambassadors sent by the Manchu emperors of China who claimed an ill-defined suzerainty over Tibet, and whose interests were best served by there being a weak government in Lhasa.

All that changed with the Thirteenth Dalai Lama, who not only survived to his majority but then proved himself to be a firm and forward-looking ruler, asserting Tibet's full independence of China and creating the nucleus of a modern army which might defend it in future. But the 'Great Thirteenth's' move towards modernization was too much for the more conservative monks, who viewed any change as tending towards the dissolution of the Buddhist dharma. This was especially true of the three great monasteries around Lhasa – Drepung, Sera and Ganden – whose private armies of warrior-monks openly threatened the Dalai Lama's ministers. The previous policy of modernizing the army and building diplomatic relations with foreign powers was put on hold. After the Thirteenth Dalai Lama died in 1933, this proudly independent but inward-looking country was woefully ill-prepared to meet any external challenge.

That challenge came in 1950 when the Chinese invaded. The Fourteenth Dalai Lama, who was still a teenager, was invested with full powers. But there was little that he could do. Despite desperate pleas to India, Britain and the United States that they raise the issue before the United Nations, no major power came to Tibet's assistance.

The Dalai Lama fled towards the Indian border while a Tibetan delegation tried to come to an accommodation with the Chinese. They were given the choice of continued destruction or signing the Seventeen Point Agreement, which outlined how Tibet should be peacefully integrated into the 'Great Motherland'. The young god-king returned to Lhasa, where he remained for most of the next eight years. Then, in March 1959, rumours that the Chinese planned to kidnap the Dalai Lama sparked a spontaneous uprising. The people of Lhasa formed a human wall around his palace and were mown down as they tried to protect their god-king.

But the Dalai Lama had already fled in disguise and was making his way once more to the Indian border. This time he crossed over and into a life of exile – which is what he and 100,000 Tibetan refugees have known ever since. The Lhasa Uprising was brutally suppressed, and over the next twenty years the Chinese did their best to destroy Tibet's ancient civilization, its Buddhist faith, and any sense of separate identity that ordinary Tibetans might feel. More than a million Tibetans were killed and 6,000 monasteries destroyed as the Chinese carried though their programme of cultural genocide. The suppression of the Khampa revolt in eastern Tibet (1956–8) and the Cultural Revolution marked the high tides of this destructive frenzy; but even after Deng Xiaoping ushered in a more 'pragmatic' approach and allowed some freedom of religion, Tibet remained a captive land.

These days the Potala has been turned into a museum, mainly for the benefit of foreign tourists. But it was also open to Tibetan visitors to Lhasa who treated the museum tour as a kind of pilgrimage. As we all filed through dark internal corridors the Tibetans kept trying to stop and prostrate themselves before a particular chapel or one of the gilded images of a previous Dalai Lama, only to be prodded onwards by irate museum guards. The private apartments in which the present Dalai Lama spent so much of his youth had been left much as they were found. But without the presence of their rightful occupant, they felt unnaturally empty. Some of the Tibetans were weeping as they filed out of the Potala's back gate.

It was at the Yak Hotel that we first caught wind of the Drigung Festival. Two visiting tibetologists wanted to attend since 'something special' was expected. One tibetologist was a bearded Frenchman who reminded me of Rasputin; the other an American called Robert Thurman (he was teaching at Columbia University in New York; only later did I discover he was the actress Uma Thurman's father and a close friend of the Dalai Lama). Their contacts had helped find some local transport, but they needed some extra people along to share the costs. Would we like to come?

Sarah and I leapt at the opportunity. The next morning

we hit the road, passing beneath the dynamited ruins of Ganden Monastery. Given our 'unofficial' status we were lucky there were no checkpoints on the way. Even as we climbed the final section on foot, past natural hot springs where weary pilgrims eased their aches and pains, there was an unspoken fear that we might still be turned back. But, probably because our presence was unexpected, we slipped through the net.

The final ascent to the monastery is possible only by foot or pack animal. It takes three hours, and my rucksack full of provisions seemed to grow heavier and heavier the higher we went. At nearly 16,000 feet the thin air made my lungs ache and my legs feel like lead. It was time for a rest. A patch of soft turf beneath a wayside shrine covered in prayer flags was irresistible. Below us a swift-running stream threaded its way past boulders and clumps of juniper. Above, the mountainside rose sheer and naked towards ornamental clouds that seemed so close you could stretch out your hand and touch them.

No sooner had we halted than a circle of inquisitive faces surrounded us. There were nomads from the high plateau and majestic, big-boned Khampas – until quite recently the most feared warriors in Central Asia, their long tresses bound with scarlet tassles. Both men and women wore earrings of turquoise and coral. Some had portable shrines of finely worked silver around their necks; others were clicking their prayer beads as they looked on in fascination. Few had ever set eyes on a 'long nose' before. So strange did we seem that an inquisitive ten-year-old approached and stroked my forearm – to confirm stories he had heard that Western 'monkeys' are indeed covered all over in hair. But otherwise they did not press forward intrusively, as a similar crowd would have done anywhere in the Indian subcontinent.

Most Tibetans are quite shy by nature. They are also remarkably hospitable. An old woman, her deeply lined face testament to many winters passed on the windblown plateau, insisted we each accept a small round loaf of bread. Then a young mother, baby slung across her shoulders, drew a small parcel from the folds of her shawl. It contained tiny dried yak cheeses which resemble the French *crottin*; but try to bite into them and you are likely to crack a tooth. My mistake caused much giggling – the Tibetans have a mischievous sense of humour – before I was shown the right way to tackle this delicacy. You shove the cheese between gum and cheek and suck on it like a wad of tobacco.

I rejoined the procession as it wound up the mountain. There was a special excitement about this festival because it had not been held properly for almost forty years. The previous occasion, I was told, had coincided with a clampdown by the Chinese authorities, and before that Tibet was going through the worst excesses of the Cultural Revolution. So the last time that the pilgrims had attended in anything like these numbers was when the Dalai Lama still ruled over Tibet from the Potala.

After climbing for three hours I had ceased to care about being stopped by officials. The track narrowed in places so that whenever a train of shaggy Tibetan pack ponies clattered past there was a danger of being jostled over the brink.

'Not far now,' said a youth who was studying English at

school. And sure enough, the gorge opened up into a sunlit valley carpeted with blue and white tents.

If Genghis Khan had ever decided to lay on a rock concert, it might have looked like this. For it seemed that all the tribes of Central Asia had descended on this remote valley in eastern Tibet to celebrate the Full Moon Festival. Thousands of pilgrims had journeyed for days, or weeks even, from Amdo in the far north, from Lhasa, from Kham in the east, to this spot. And here they had created a tent-city around which their yaks and ponies were grazing peacefully, storing up strength for the return journey.

In the centre of this encampment, at the confluence of two streams, stood a great blue and white canopy beneath which perhaps four hundred monks were chanting. The air was thick with the smoke of dried yak dung mingled with the sweeter smell of sacred juniper burning in braziers. High above the throng, a thousand prayer flags had been strung between neighbouring crags so that they spanned the entire valley. A devotional hum rose from the pilgrims as they processed around a large white chorten, always in a clockwise direction.

This festival was organized around a smallish monastery, daughter house of the Drigungpa, an important sub-sect of the Kagyu order. Their principal lamasery clings to a hillside above Drigung, which lies about six hours' drive north-east of Lhasa. The site of this daughter house, hemmed in on three sides by mountains, had been deliberately chosen by the monks for its isolation. But now it had become the focus of a great pilgrimage.

That night we slept in the prayer hall of the monastery. It was cold and the floor was hard, but we were none the less privileged guests. As bedtime approached, the resident monks calmly stretched out on their low bunks, casting only the occasional glance in our direction as we struggled into sleeping bags. On my right the tibetologists – both practising Buddhists – murmured their mantras and twiddled their rosaries, while on my left Sarah (probably the most irreligious member of our party) was already fast asleep, leaving myself as a vaguely agnostic buffer zone. When I woke up in the night I saw a solitary monk tending the butter lamps beneath the golden figures of buddhas and incarnations.

The monks woke us well before dawn with bowls of yak butter tea – a thick, slightly rancid brew which, once the initial nausea has been conquered, is remarkably sustaining. Outside, the vast encampment was beginning to stir. Two young monks blowing on conch shells announced the beginning of the day's ceremonies. Laymen and women bared their heads in reverence as the abbot and other dignitaries processed behind an orchestra of trumpets and gongs to the blue and white pavilion where the assembled monkhood sat intoning. Their day was divided loosely into 'wet ceremonies', when the monks took refreshments of *tsampa* (a sort of barley porridge) and butter tea, and 'dry ceremonies' of initiation and teaching.

But pilgrims came and went as they pleased, slipping off to take food in their tents or to do some shopping at the market stalls around the main enclosure. There appeared to be no rigid order in the round of prayer and rest. I was surprised, however, to discover Sarah hunkered down with a group of discipline monks – fierce-looking giants with long staves and shoulder pads like American footballers who, by tradition, are entitled to police religious events.

They had been brewing up some tea and had asked her 'to be mother'. But her attempt at the tea ceremony – Tibetan style – only produced roars of laughter. She had forgotten the yak butter. One of the monks intervened: seizing the Thermos of tea he gathered a fistful of blue-veined butter and forced it down the neck. After adding salt to taste and handling the Thermos like a cocktail shaker, the tea was poured into bowls and consumed with much smacking of lips. It had perhaps twice as much butter as normal Tibetan tea. 'To keep up their strength,' I suggested, little suspecting that just two hours later I would witness their physical prowess in action.

The incident occurred as the incarnate lama, a bespectacled youth dressed in an embroidered robe of red and yellow silk, began dispensing blessings to the crowd. Eager to get close, some pilgrims rushed forward, their heads bared to receive the blessing. But in doing so they were crushing those already in the front rows. Our erstwhile friends the discipline monks swung into action, laying into the crowd with their long staves. They were joined by uniformed police wielding sticks – the first time the Chinese authorities had made their presence felt. For a moment it seemed that things were turning nasty.

From where I stood it looked as though the discipline monks were handing out the heaviest blows, singling out troublemakers and forming a protective ring about the incarnation. Then, as swiftly as it had begun, the trouble blew over. The discipline monks continued to look threatening and prodded the occasional interloper. Some of the pilgrims appeared to accept the monks' blows almost as an honour. But I had seen the darker, feudal side of Tibetan religiosity.

I also saw the more spiritual, mysterious aspect of Buddhism as practised by this unreformed branch of the Kagyu sect. The Full Moon Festival culminated in a ceremony reserved for spiritual adepts who through intense concentration attain a higher state of consciousness. The French tibetologist explained that there was a strong vein of tantrism in these practices and that they were dangerous for the unprepared. Figuratively speaking, the spirit escapes through a hole in the top of the head; and after the ceremony the adepts fall into a state of exhaustion and have to be carried off to meditate in isolation. Certainly, this ceremony drew a powerful response from the crowd. To my untutored mind, the monks appeared to become the human equivalent of lightning conductors.

Despite forty-two years of Communist rule, it was obvious that Buddhism remained a living force in Tibet. But it was not the arcane practices of the monkhood which conveyed this most forcibly. It was the simple faith of ordinary laymen, the way in which religion is not something distinct but part of the fabric of everyday life. There was a calm dignity in the faces of pilgrims. Many of them were completing the kora – the prescribed route around a monastery or sacred spot which pilgrims tread in order to gain merit. In this case, the sacred site was a cave high up the mountain face where Guru Rinpoche – as Tibetans normally refer to the eighth-century saint Padmasambhava – is believed to have meditated.

Some of the pilgrims completing the kora were old enough to be great-grandparents, yet they had climbed 2,000 feet over the shoulder of a mountain to visit the cave. As they passed by, the clack of rosaries measuring each step of the way, they murmured *tashi delek, tashi delek* – the traditional Tibetan greeting which means 'good fortune'. Then another group – nomads from the northern province of Amdo to judge from their dress – passed by. Again we were met with a chorus of greetings. I smiled back. But when I tried to reply a thin, rasping noise came out of my mouth: '*Tah-shah-dah-lah*'.

The altitude and lack of oxygen had me gasping. Yet it did not seem to matter that my accent was atrocious or that I probably sounded like an asphyxiated android: the magic formula brought forth smiles or polite giggles. So, as another group of pilgrims approached, I wished them *tashi delek*, probably for the hundredth time that day. It was rather like reciting a mantra; only the effect was tangible and immediate.

Back in Lhasa, the atmosphere felt oppressive – especially after seeing what Tibetans are like when they are not under constant surveillance. Sarah and I could have stayed on in central Tibet and taken a flight back to Kathmandu, but, armed with our Chinese visas, there was an alternative option.

We could head north across the Chang Tang, the vast high-altitude desert that occupies more than half of historic Tibet, to the newly founded city of Golmud. Then, after crossing a salt desert and two more mountain ranges, we would reach Dunhuang – an oasis that had once been the main entrepôt on the Silk Road, its enormous wealth and Buddhist piety hidden for centuries in the 'Thousand Buddha Caves' out in the adjacent desert. From there we would join the railway linking Xinjiang (as Chinese Turkestan is now called) with the rest of China, moving north-west to

Urumchi before turning south again to Kashgar and down the Karakorum Highway into Pakistan.

It would require many days' hard travelling to complete this immense loop through Inner Asia. We did not even know for certain whether we would be allowed to leave Tibet this way. But it was worth a try.

And I was aware that when some of the earlier Buddha caves at Dunhuang were founded, practically all of this enormous territory had been ruled over by Tibetan kings of the Yarlung dynasty. Their seat of government had been at Lhasa, and nearly a thousand years before the existing Potala was built there had been another royal palace on the same site. Nothing remains of that palace, but between the seventh and ninth centuries AD the Yarlung kings were one of the great military powers of Asia. Their armies fought off the Umayyad Arabs in what is now northern Pakistan and swarmed over the Chinese border like ants, taking the fight right to the gates of the Imperial capital at Xian.

Now the tables have been turned, and much of historic Tibet has been 'reallocated' to neighbouring Chinese provinces. But that overland journey gave me a sense of the immensity of the Tibetan plateau, even though a Chinese bus can now reach its limits in three days, whereas before the Lhasa–Golmud Highway was opened it took as many months to cross it by pony or yak.

As we rumbled across the Chang Tang we saw great herds of *chiru* or Tibetan antelope – a species once commonplace, but which is now being slaughtered indiscriminately to provide the fine wool known as *shahtoosh*, used in weaving the most expensive (and illegal) Kashmiri shawls. We saw encampments of black tents in which the nomadic yak herders still live in preference to the pre-fabricated housing provided by the Chinese.

Sometimes, when we were in the middle of nowhere, one of the passengers would ask the bus driver to stop and let him off – our last sight of him being a speck-like figure marching purposefully off into the surrounding emptiness. For much of this route, the plateau is more than 15,000 feet above sea level and the air is so thin, the light so intense, that you can see for miles. It also has the properties that create mirages, and we got used to seeing lakes surrounded by green meadows vanish into thin air as we approached, only to be replaced by another empty stretch of desert.

All along the Lhasa–Golmud Highway there were road gangs at work, trying to use the brief summer months to repair the damage caused by the underlying permafrost expanding and shrinking. Some of these labourers were civilians, but mostly they were inmates of China's hidden Gulag. Political prisoners were mixed up with common criminals, and when the bus slowed down to pass them some of the Tibetan passengers threw parcels of food and cigarettes out of the window. It was a sad reflection on what has happened to Tibet these last fifty years. For having journeyed across Greater Tibet from south to north, it seemed to me that the whole country was run like one vast open prison.

Chapter Three

AN AUDIENCE WITH THE
DALAI LAMA

Tibet is one thing; Dharamsala, the hill station in northern India where the Dalai Lama usually resides, quite another. It has become known as 'Little Lhasa' because it is the seat of the Tibetan government-in-exile; and since everything is crammed onto a narrow ridge, the town is built on a diminutive scale. After the empty expanses of the Tibetan plateau it might well feel claustrophobic – especially during the monsoon, when it is dank and humid and the mountains are obscured by cloud for weeks on end.

But the most striking contrast to Communist-run Tibet is the sense of freedom. The narrow streets are full of refugee monks and nuns who can practise their religion in India without fear of state intervention. The Dalai Lama and his exiled government are free to voice their criticism of what is going on inside Tibet – from human rights abuses through to China's policies of dumping both nuclear waste and surplus population. Ordinary Tibetans are free to disagree with their leadership on crucial issues.

Even the chaotic manner in which the town has grown up reflects the workings of the free market, albeit in a distinctively Indian style. It is a far cry from the authoritarian planning that goes into every new town the Chinese have built in Tibet. And there is none of the fear of being caught out that lingers over Lhasa and other large towns. While I deliberately refrained from ever discussing politics inside Tibet – not on account of my own safety, but because anyone I talked to might well be arrested – in Dharamsala I felt no such constraints.

I went up to Dharamsala in early 1999 with one object in mind: to interview His Holiness the Fourteenth Dalai Lama. I had arranged to go there shortly after Losar, the Tibetan New Year, and was fairly confident an audience would be granted. For, unlike most other Himalayan monarchs, the Dalai Lama is only too happy to talk to film stars and celebrities, journalists, writers, and anyone else who might promote his cause. As an exiled ruler, he needs all the help he can get.

I flew into Delhi and immediately booked a sleeping berth on the Frontier Mail. It runs overnight to Pathankot, the nearest mainline station to Dharamsala. This, I knew, was the way the Dalai Lama prefers to travel, in a private coach, to and from his mountain retreat.

I boarded the train at Old Delhi Station, having struggled first through the evening rush hour and then through all the hawkers and vendors who crowded the station, trying my best to avoid the little islands of bodies lying asleep on the platform. I found that I was sharing a four-berth sleeper with a Buddhist nun from Canada. Her maroon robes were so formless, her grey hair cropped so short, that initially I took her for a monk. In fact she was an abbess, or at least 'director', of the Enjoy the Sky Nunnery near Vancouver. There was another nun from England, a more recent convert to Buddhism, on the train. They were going up to Dharamsala to hear the series of teachings given by the Dalai Lama every year after the Losar Festival has ended.

The train pulled into Pathankot early next morning, and we mustered enough passengers to hire a minibus to take us on to Dharamsala. I left the task of haggling over the fare to the nuns, who were past masters at it.

We crossed the bridge over the Sutlej and were soon climbing through wooded foothills towards the Kangra Valley. The valley was once itself an independent Hindu kingdom which produced a distinctive school of miniature painting before it was swallowed up first by the Sikhs and then by the British Empire. There was a brief halt beside a river gorge to breakfast on puris and tea. A troop of monkeys clambered over a temple built out from the trunk of a peepul tree, but were too shy to approach us.

We drove on, past thatched farmsteads set among emerald fields of winter wheat. In places these were interspersed with the brilliant yellow of flowering mustard. The snow-peaks of the Dhauladhar Range came into view, and we knew Dharamsala could not be far off.

The English nun was excited at the prospect, and rattled on about how she had got stuck at certain stages of meditation before advising me on what were the best Buddhist retreats back in Britain. The Canadian, who was older and a great deal shrewder, kept her silence.

'And you mustn't believe all Tibetans are nice,' continued the red-robed Englishwoman. 'Why, last time I was here for His Holiness's teachings they forcibly removed me and a lot of other nuns from where we were sitting. They don't seem to have even heard about gender-equality . . .'

The older nun clucked in disapproval, but her colleague was so caught up in her own world that she bashed on regardless. Turning to me, she asked whether I would be attending a meditation course.

'No. I'm here to interview the Dalai Lama.'

'But if you're going to see His Holiness, then surely you'll want to stay on for his teachings?'

'Perhaps I want to ask him about other matters.'

'Oh, I see,' she replied, looking distinctly puzzled. I supposed she could not imagine anyone seeing the Dalai Lama without seeking some spiritual benefit.

By now we were entering Lower Dharamsala, and she requested the driver stop in the bazaar where she wanted to buy a hot-water bottle. The dormitories in the nunnery where she would be staying could get rather chilly at night. 'I nearly froze to death last time,' she explained, clutching her newly acquired, bright pink rubber bladder to her chest.

The driver changed into low gear to tackle the old cart road which climbs more than a thousand feet through many twists and turns before reaching the upper town. I got out about halfway, opposite the offices of the government-in-exile, and began walking to a Tibetan-run lodging house I had been told about. The two nuns waved goodbye as the minibus lurched onwards, the younger one calling out, 'See you around town.' Which was almost certain to happen, since Dharamsala is so small that you are bound to run into everybody and anybody sooner or later.

Even by the standards of higgledy-piggledy Himalayan hill-top towns, Dharamsala is an oddity. For a start, it is not really a single town at all. At the base of the hill stands the market town, with its crowded bazaars and transport depots, that is properly known as Dharamsala. It is here that the offices of local government, the GPO and police station are to be found. And although there are many Tibetans, both monks and laymen, to be seen shopping for vegetables or cooking pots in the bazaar, here one is still palpably in India.

The other Dharamsala sits high on a ridge overlooking the Kangra Valley. It started life as a minor hill station, where British officers and their families could find relief from the Punjab's torrid summers. It never acquired the fashionable status – or notoriety – of the larger hill stations like Simla or Darjeeling, though one of the few British viceroys who died in harness, Lord Elgin, chose to be buried here in the Church of St John-in-the-Wilderness because the surrounding forests of fir and pine reminded him of his native Scotland. Properly speaking, this upper town should be called McLeod Ganj; and while ribbon development is steadily narrowing the gap between the two Dharamsalas, there remains a stretch of fir and rhododendron forest separating them.

When the Dalai Lama first arrived in 1960, McLeod Ganj was a sorry sight. It had been devastated by earthquakes and abandoned by its colonial clientele. Most of the genteel villas stood deserted, the gingerbread woodwork around their porches rotting after being left untended through a dozen monsoons, their corrugated iron roofs falling in.

The Dalai Lama was originally housed, at Prime Minister Nehru's insistence, in one of the larger colonial villas. In the Dalai Lama's autobiography, he remembers those early years in Dharamsala as one of the happier periods of his life, when he was able to cultivate his flower garden and wander in the forests. The silver ramparts of the Himalayas were there to remind him of 'The Land of Snows' that he had lost – and of his lifelong duty somehow to repair that loss.

Then began the task of rebuilding Tibet in exile. Monasteries and temples, schools and orphanages, libraries and institutes for the propagation of Tibetan culture, were established and gradually added to. They were built using such untraditional materials as concrete and brick; but upon the whole they faithfully replicate Tibetan designs and motifs.

Within twenty years this derelict hill station in Himachal Pradesh was transformed into 'Little Lhasa', a bustling township that was predominantly Tibetan in character. And, as the Dalai Lama became better known internationally, more and more foreigners started turning up in Dharamsala. There were backpackers and celebrities, ordained monks and nuns, spiritual seekers and ordinary tourists, all drawn by tales of a little corner of Tibet that had been miraculously reborn in the hills of northern India. To cater for their needs, a rash of new hotels and restaurants and meditation centres sprang up, with the result that today Dharamsala is a peculiar hybrid of Tibetan, Indian and Western cultures.

That much was apparent as soon as I stepped down from a shared taxi at the bus stand, which in the absence of any grander monument serves as the focal point of McLeod Ganj. The sound of taped music floated over to me on the light breeze, but not the Hindi pop songs which must usually be endured all over the rest of India. From the open picture-windows of McLlo's, a multi-storey eatery across the way, came trance music; from the dark portals of the Tibet Hotel a rock anthem with lots of drums and bass, though the vocalists appeared to be singing in Tibetan. As I wandered around the central market area, I picked out the strains of Bob Marley and Pink Floyd and just about every variety of world-fusion music you could think of. Then I heard the sound of Buddhist monks chanting. It came from a shop selling guides to meditation and devotional cassettes.

Along the road running down to the Dalai Lama's palace, the line of street-stalls were crammed with mass-produced tangkas and reliquaries and Buddha statues, most of them turned out in Kathmandu. Some of the newer shops were run by Kashmiri merchants who have become economic refugees since the fighting in their homeland killed off the tourist trade. There were shops offering colour film development and Internet access, restaurants specializing in spaghetti and pancakes, placards that sought to entice the passer-by into a 'real Tibetan artist studio' or wished them 'Well Come' to the world of traditional medicine. If anywhere deserves to be labelled Karma-Cola City, it is uptown Dharamsala.

And this being Losar, there were plenty of foreigners in town. They sported suntans from South India, hennaed hands from Rajasthan, nose jewellery, tattoos, ankle bracelets ... They enthused about meeting 'this really cool reincarnation who just meditates all the time' and obsessively compared how much they were paying for their rooms. Women travellers outnumbered the men, and many of them were accompanied by 'Yeti Boys' – local school drop-outs who have discovered that a few words of English, a mane of blue-black hair, and, above all, the mystique attached to all things Tibetan, can get them a very long way indeed. Alcohol and drug abuse is becoming a problem, and above the central bus stand is a sign that warns 'Aids Can Happen to You'.

But it is not just the influx of foreigners seeking a whiff of Shangri-La that brings a sense of lost innocence. Relations between the Tibetan exiles and the local Himachali people used to be easygoing and, for the most part, mutually beneficial.

All that changed in April 1994, when a Tibetan youth was accused of stabbing an Indian student. The atmosphere at his cremation was already highly charged when local politicians began whipping up the crowd into shouting slogans like 'Death to Dalai Lama', 'Tibetans Quit Dharamsala', and 'Long Live Deng Xiaoping'. The enraged crowd then went on the rampage, smashing up Tibetan government offices and looting Tibetan shops, while the Indian police turned a blind eye.

True, many of the ringleaders had been bused in specifically to cause trouble. But the 'April Incident', as it came to be known, destroyed much of the goodwill that had been built up over thirty years. The Dalai Lama even suggested moving away to Delhi or some other city where the presence of 7,000 Tibetans was less likely to be a problem. At which local representatives pleaded with him to stay in Dharamsala, for they knew only too well that their shops and construction businesses depended almost entirely on his remaining in their midst.

Not long afterwards, an eight-year-old Tibetan girl was raped and strangled by a recently arrived 'refugee'. It was discovered that he had already been convicted of murder in Lhasa, but had been spared the death penalty so that he could go on a 'surveillance mission' to Dharamsala. Then, in 1996, the bodies of a venerable lama and two young monks were discovered in a room not far from the Dalai Lama's residence. They had been ritually stabbed to death by monks linked to an unorthodox Buddhist sect who had escaped – most probably to Tibet. Such horrible crimes shattered whatever sense of peace and security had previously existed among the Tibetan community in Dharamsala.

A long-distance bus pulled up in front of Nowrojee & Son (General Merchants, Estd 1860, now one of the few surviving remnants of old McLeod Ganj) and passengers started spilling out over the pavement. While foreigners might be more conspicuous, I soon realized most of the people arriving by bus were Tibetans.

They had come from all over India to be in Dharamsala for the Losar Festival. Ancient matrons in their brightly striped aprons and heavy silver jewellery, proud to arrive wearing their best Tibetan dress, struggled with baskets of cheap vegetables from the plains and other presents. One had even brought a new mattress, still wrapped in its plastic, and stood wondering how to remove it from the roadside as a traffic policeman yelled at her.

Another bus pulled in carrying a group from Bylakuppe, one of the Tibetan rural settlements in South India founded in the 1960s to provide a home for the poorer class of refugee. They had travelled five days by bus and train to reach Dharamsala and looked exhausted. They had not bothered to put on any finery and, as a rule, carried less luggage than the passengers from Delhi.

The question of what to do with the tens of thousands of refugees who followed the Dalai Lama into exile after the Lhasa Uprising of 1959 posed a major problem for the Government of India. To begin with, they were kept in refugee camps. But the Tibetans were unused to the heat of the Plains and had no in-built resistance to the multitude of virulent bacteria that thrive there. Whereas the high Tibetan plateau provided a virtually sterile atmosphere, once down in India the refugees' living habits, their warm clothing and carefree sanitary arrangements, spelt disease or death. Crowded together in camps like Misarami, thousands succumbed to typhoid, cholera and, above all, to tuberculosis. The Indian government responded by sending off the able-bodied to join labour gangs building roads into the Himalayas. At higher altitudes the refugees stood a much better chance of surviving. Besides, India desperately needed military roads to counter the new threat to its northern frontier from Chinese forces in Tibet.

But these were only temporary measures. More permanent refugee settlements were gradually established along the Himalayas, from Ladakh to Arunachal Pradesh, at altitudes where Tibetans were less prone to disease. However, New Delhi had misgivings about allowing too many of these refugees to settle close to its sensitive border with China. They were not Indian citizens, and most were firmly committed to restoring Tibet's independence. So it was arranged for land to be made available to settle more refugees in the South Indian state of Karnataka, far away from any potential conflict. The land grants were generous, but they were mostly in bush country, which had to be cleared before housing could be built and the first maize crops sown. The spirit of those pioneers, struggling to build a new life in a scorching and inhospitable land, must be admired – especially since they still dreamed of returning to their own homeland, now more than two thousand miles away.

New monasteries were built to re-create Tibet's greatest monastic houses – Sera and Tashilhunpo at the Bylakuppe settlement, Drepung and Ganden at Mundgod. The Tibetan language was taught in schools, and, because they live in isolated rural settlements, these 'southern' Tibetans have preserved more of their culture than those who have moved to big cities and entered the all-inclusive embrace of what Indians call 'the mainstream'.

But after two generations, the kibbutz-style idealism of the pioneers is fading. Many settlers used to leave for the cities during winter to sell 'Tibetan' sweaters (in fact they are turned out by factories in Punjab) and return for the harvest. Now they are staying away, the young especially. This is partly due to the widening gulf between what you can earn in cities as opposed to rural India. But there are also doubts about the point of being a perpetual refugee, of denying your family opportunities in order to retain a separate Tibetan identity when the likelihood of ever returning to Tibet is as remote as ever.

I reckoned none of those people off the Bylakuppe bus could afford to live in Dharamsala. For one thing, the Tibetan government-in-exile discourages the settlement of long-term refugees, priority going to government servants, the monkhood, and refugees newly arrived from Tibet who are put into temporary lodgings or schools while their case is being processed. But the wealthy can always find a way round, and they keep up residences in Dharamsala. It is expensive because the town straddles a narrow ridge. There is a scarcity of good building land, and most of that has been given over to creating yet more hotels and shops. The end result is spiralling land values and high living costs. It is this, more than anything else, which prevents many exiled Tibetans from living near their god-king.

Like me, they had arrived too late to witness the prayer festival that marks the first day of the Tibetan New Year. I had seen it all two years before. After a thorough security vetting I had been admitted to the upper floor of the Tsuglakhang, the central cathedral which serves as a sort of replacement for the Jokhang Temple in Lhasa. There, under a canopy, the claret-robed monks of Namgyal Monastery were already sitting cross-legged in neat rows, chanting prayers or letting off spiralling crescendos on Tibetan trumpets known as *jalings*. They wore the distinctive arched yellow headgear that has given the Gelugpa sect of Buddhism the nickname of 'yellow hats'. Namgyal is the Dalai Lama's private monastery.

He was seated on a slightly raised throne, a yellow hat perched above his familiar bespectacled features, leading the prayers and occasionally reaching forward to grasp a ritual dorje dagger or tinkle a hand-held bell. To his left were assembled important lamas and foreign dignitaries. After the prayers were finished, we all filed down to the main hall. The Dalai Lama sat upon a throne beneath a huge gilt statue of the Buddha, from where he closely observed a series of scholar monks conducting dialectical debates with much stylized gesturing and stamping of feet. At all times, armed security guards lurked behind pillars, machine pistols at the ready.

The monks' debate was followed by a performance of Tibetan dance – the girls in bright, colourful silken gowns, the boys waving silver daggers, while the musicians wore vividly embroidered caps and jackets. They were mostly students at the Institute of Tibetan Performing Arts, one of many cultural foundations set up by the Dalai Lama to preserve traditional culture. Their repertoire owed much to Tibetan opera. But it was also intended as a celebration of youth, symbolizing the future of Tibet, and there was a regimented quality about it all that reminded me strangely of mass spectacles laid on by the Communist authorities in China. Perhaps it is a matter of 'anything they can do, we can do better'.

The performance over, the Dalai Lama strode out onto a balcony to address the crowds gathered outside. Most of them were Tibetans and as soon as their spiritual leader appeared they dived forward in full prostration. The handful of Westerners who remained standing looked around nervously, bowing their heads slightly and clutching their hands together as though in church. The Dalai Lama's personal standard hung limply from a flagpole, but there were plenty of Tibetan national flags being waved among his audience. He spoke briefly, Losar being a time for uplifting sentiments. The more heavyweight political speeches are held over for 10 March, the anniversary of the Lhasa Uprising.

Losar marks the beginning of an extended holiday that is accompanied by much drinking and feasting. It is very much a family affair. As I stood by the bus stand watching the late arrivals, I wondered whether, like me, some of them hoped to have an audience with the Dalai Lama. The busload from Bylakuppe settlement soon dispersed, seeking out distant relatives and friends fortunate enough to live in 'Little Lhasa'. I decided to walk down the hill to my guest house.

I took the old mule-track, which runs above a yellow-roofed monastery. For the first half-mile or so the path skirts the edge of town, and here all the unwanted by-products of Dharamsala's rapid expansion are plainly on view. Where the buildings stop, the rubbish tips begin. I had to make my way through open sewers and mountains of refuse that were left for the crows to pick over. Sadly, they weren't the only ones. A pair of indigent Tibetans were sifting through the tips' rubbish in the hope of finding something that might buy them their dinner.

I was happy to leave the town's limits and enter the pine forests beyond. Although this footpath is the most direct link between Upper and Lower Dharamsala, it is little used these days. I passed a gaggle of maroon-robed monks and a few local farmers; that was all, apart from a troop of monkeys which shadowed my progress down though pine and flowering rhododendron into the sparser broad-leaf forest of the lower slopes.

Then, right in the middle of nowhere, I heard women shrieking. I ran ahead, only to find the sounds emanated from a nunnery belonging to the Nyingmapa sect. Some of the younger nuns were playing volleyball, while others were cheering them on.

Perhaps I should not have been so surprised. It was a lovely spring day, after all, and even nuns need to let off steam sometimes. And while this was a very isolated spot, I knew that more than a dozen monasteries and nunneries have been established around Dharamsala as part of a concerted effort to re-create Tibetan monastic life in exile. The nunnery's buildings were modest and roofed over with corrugated iron; but the setting certainly lent itself to the contemplative life.

The foundation of monastic houses – not only in Dharamsala or India, but throughout the Free World – has been one of the Dalai Lama's priorities. Like this nunnery, many belong to Buddhist orders other than the Dalai Lama's own Gelugpa sect, and came into being without any direct input on his part. But all the orders of Tibetan Buddhism revere the Dalai Lama as their supreme head, just as the different Catholic orders all owe obedience to the Pope. If you added up all the Tibetan Buddhist foundations around the world made during his lifetime, I expect he would emerge as the most prolific monastic founder of all time.

But this was only part of the task of rebuilding Tibet in exile. The Communist occupation ushered in the wholesale destruction of manuscripts and books which had for centuries preserved the unique traditions of Tibetan Buddhism. As the destructive frenzy built up during the Cultural Revolution, it was left to a handful of brave individuals to carry out what they could over the Himalayan passes.

'They brought with them some very important manuscripts,' said Amchok Rinpoche, an incarnate lama from Amdo who is now director of the Library and Archives of Tibetan Works in Dharamsala. 'We think maybe seventy-five per cent of manuscripts inside Tibet have been destroyed, though we have copies of some of these works.' None the less, he estimated that roughly half of Tibet's enormously rich literature has disappeared for ever. 'Almost every monastery would have had its own unique traditions and writings, and many of these have been totally destroyed.'

He had been recognized as a young child as the reincarnation of a high lama of Amchok Monastery, which he described as being 'three to four months' journey from Lhasa – though if you do the pilgrimage making prostrations all the way, it will take three years. And yes, I have heard some still do it.'

The Rinpoche had been fifteen years old when he escaped from Tibet in 1959. He spent two months in the notorious Misamiri transit camp in Assam where, like so many Tibetan refugees, he contracted tuberculosis. 'I kept it secret because otherwise the doctors would have sent me to hospital, and so many monks spent years and years in such places. Miraculously, the TB held up by itself, and was only diagnosed twenty years later when I visited Vienna University and was obliged to have a health check.' The memory caused him to laugh; but I now knew why his skin had the pale, almost transparent quality of fine parchment.

'Before coming here I was abbot of Ganden Monastery in South India. His Holiness recommended me as the new director. You know,' he added, his eyes twinkling, 'usually we Rinpoches are not very efficient in the field of administration.'

I visited the library most days, since it was just across the road from my guest house. The exterior was brightly painted in the manner of a Tibetan temple, though inside all was bare and functional. Apart from its collections of priceless manuscripts and wood-blocks traditionally used for printing, there was a good range of secondary sources in several languages.

The Amchok Rinpoche explained that microfiche readers had been installed to make some of the collection's rare manuscripts more accessible to the public. 'We also run classes in the woodcarving skills necessary to make wood-blocks, and in tangka painting. The painting techniques are taught by senior monks, who follow precise rules in order to preserve this unique Tibetan art form. So many distorted tangkas with Hindu elements mixed up in them were being mass-produced in Kathmandu and elsewhere, that His

Holiness insisted it be done properly. And over the past twenty years we have had many good students from both the monastic and lay communities.'

Instruction is also given in Tibetan language and philosophy for visitors from Japan, Taiwan and Western countries. Conversely, one of the tasks entrusted to the Amchok Rinpoche by the Dalai Lama was to explore means of having Western textbooks on science translated into Tibetan. 'Up to now, Tibetans' knowledge of science has come through China, not from the West. I'm going to the United States soon, to Dallas, where I will discuss this and also do some fundraising.' He smiled at the prospect, and I was made aware that I was in the presence of a very worldly-wise high lama.

In those first years of exile, many Tibetan refugees had to struggle simply to survive, let alone think about preserving their sense of identity or culture. Thousands were less fortunate than Amchok Rinpoche and died in the transit camps, leaving behind many orphans and destitute children. Others were sent as labourers to build military roads through the mountains.

It was the arrival in Dharamsala of a truck full of very sick and malnourished children from the road construction camps in Jammu that prompted the Dalai Lama's elder sister, Tsering Dolma Takla, to take charge of their care. At first the children were assigned to members of the Dalai Lama's entourage. Then, with Indian government assistance, a building was rented so that all the children could be housed together. This was the beginning of the Nursery for Tibetan Refugee Children.

Then more children arrived from road-workers' camps all along the Himalayas, and the dilapidated Egerton Hall was pressed into service as a combined orphanage and school. When the elder sister died unexpectedly in 1964, the Dalai Lama placed his younger sister, Jetsun Pema, in charge of the project. Thirty-five years later she is still there. But, in the meantime, it has changed its name to the Tibetan Children's Village (usually abbreviated to TCV) and has expanded to the point where it runs more than a dozen boarding schools and educational centres, from Ladakh and Kullu in the north to Bylakuppe in southern India.

Its headquarters remain near Dharamsala, in a purpose-built 'village' above the military cantonment. These days it has become something of a tourist attraction, and many well-meaning foreigners go out to see its impressive facilities besides those who have a direct interest in it because they are sponsoring a Tibetan child there. I had run into one of these benefactors in McLlo's restaurant, where he had invited the two children he was sponsoring though TCV for a special treat. They were brother and sister, and they sat there dutifully pretending to draw pictures with the coloured crayons he had just given them while he made encouraging noises.

Both sides were trying their best to bridge the gap, but there was no real communication. The children recognized that this strange man was their patron, but they could not think how to please him apart from being quiet and well-behaved. And the sponsor, whose regular remittances were paying for these children's education, looked awkward and embarrassed. It was all rather sad, and it made me wonder whether such individual sponsorship is the right approach to helping children in need.

Having been up to the TCV, I also had my doubts about its aims and how it is run. Its original purpose was to look after and educate the children of poor Tibetan refugees in India. Now that the exiled community is more firmly established, the TCV's focus has shifted to providing an education for children who are sent by families inside Tibet. The number of such young 'refugees' has risen dramatically in recent years. This is partly due to the limited educational opportunities within Tibet, and partly because of the TCV's stress on Tibetan language and culture, its relatively high academic standards, and the possibility of learning some English and Hindi. These are all strong attractions for parents who want their children to get on in the world.

In other words, the TCV increasingly resembles an offshore academy. It is understood that once the children have completed their education they should return to Tibet. They are, in fact, not so much 'refugee children' as 'educational migrants'. The schooling they receive may help preserve certain aspects of Tibetan culture inside Tibet and enhance the Dalai Lama's standing among those who stayed behind. All of this is funded by mainly foreign sponsorship through what is the largest non-religious charitable organization run by Tibetans in exile.

Jetsun Pema was 'out-of-station' while I was in Dharamsala but the TCV's executive director, Tsewang Yeshi, made it abundantly clear that she is still very much in charge. It was 'Madam Pema' this and 'Madam Pema' that. The lobby to the main administrative building was full of promotional literature, all very persuasive and user-friendly. I have visited other TCV schools in the Himalayas, and they seem to be doing a good job. But the question still arises as to why this charitable empire should be so dominated by the Dalai Lama's family, as though it were a personal fiefdom. And it was not me who raised such questions, but disgruntled Tibetans in exile.

The same goes for the very high-profile roles assumed by the Dalai Lama's brothers. Of these, Gyalo Thondup has played the most decisive role in Tibetan affairs. Cosmopolitan, multilingual, and with his own network of contacts around the world, for more than forty years he has been the Dalai Lama's personal emissary and fixer.

Even before the Communist invasion of Tibet, Gyalo Thondup was active in seeking support from the Chinese Nationalists, India's intelligence services, and the Americans. From his base in the former British hill station of Kalimpong, he received promises of modern armaments for the Tibetan army (though none arrived until it was too late). After the mass exodus of 1959, he was instrumental in recruiting former Khampa guerillas now working on road gangs to form a new armed resistance. Some five hundred were smuggled out of India and flown by the CIA to Camp Hale in Colorado, where they received parachute training and instruction in covert operations. The plan was to have them set up an underground movement inside Tibet. Despite individual feats of endurance and bravery, Chinese intelligence soon had the upper hand and these covert operations were discontinued.

Meanwhile, thousands of Khampa refugees had heard the call to arms and secretly made their way to Mustang, a remote region of Nepal bordering on Tibet. This, it had been decided, would serve as a forward operating base. The CIA provided arms and training on the understanding that this would be 'a secret war'.

Gyalo Thondhup used the Darjeeling-based Tibetan Welfare Committee as a front for these operations. It was his CIA contacts who brought in the armaments and military instructors. From the outset, it was very much 'his show'. Some of the older, more conservative members of the government-in-exile had serious misgivings about this. They saw it as an exclusively Khampa movement, which was liable to run beyond their control and threaten the fragile unity of the exiled community. They also wanted to question Gyalo Thondhup about how he had managed to lose most of the Dalai Lama's personal fortune – all the pack-loads of gold dust and silver ingots that had been carried over the Himalayas in 1956 and secreted in Sikkim – through rash investments on the stock exchange. But the Dalai Lama's elder brother went to Dharamsala and brazened it out, accusing government ministers of being feudal relics left over from the old Kashag in Lhasa.

To begin with, the Khampa guerillas operating out of Mustang achieved some morale-boosting successes. During the early sixties they shot up Chinese convoys and disrupted traffic along the Xinjiang–Lhasa Highway. But their base in Mustang was too remote, their field of operations too peripheral, to cause the Chinese anything more than mild irritation. If the outside world had known about this armed struggle for Tibetan independence it might have had a greater impact; but that was not part of the deal, and for fourteen years the Khampas fought on without any external recognition, silent warriors in one of the most bizarre epsidodes of the Cold War.

*

India's reluctance to play host to any form of armed Tibetan resistance changed overnight when open warfare between Chinese and Indian forces broke out along the Himalayan frontier in October 1962. The Indian army was in desperate need of troops capable of operating at high altitudes and began recruiting Tibetans into units of its Special Frontier Force – otherwise known as Establishment 22. Thus began an arrangement whereby young Tibetans were inducted into specialized army units that continues to this day. I was told that Tibetans had fought in the 'Kargil Conflict' between India and Pakistan during the summer of 1999. It is like a tax that the exiled community must pay to the host country.

The Khampas in Mustang were abandoned by their American backers after 1971. Their successes had been very limited, and once US policy shifted to a rapprochement with China this band of Tibetan freedom-fighters became dispensable. Then the Nepalese government, anxious to strengthen its own relationship with China, began moving army units up to Jomsom in preparation for an attack on the guerilla bases. By then the Khampas had split into two rival factions and the flow of CIA supplies had stopped. But the coup de grâce was the delivery of a taped message from the Dalai Lama himself ordering them to lay down their arms.

Some committed suicide rather than abandon the cause they had fought for. Others followed their commander, General Gyatso Wangdu, in a desperate attempt to escape to Indian territory. The Chinese attacked them in Tibet, the Nepalese in Nepal, and the remnants were killed in an ambush just short of the Indian border. The dead General Wangdu's personal effects were triumphantly displayed back in Kathmandu. But most of the Khampas obeyed the Dalai Lama's orders and surrendered to the Nepalese army. Those who are still alive mostly eke out a living in Pokhara or Kathmandu. I talked to some of them, and although they feel betrayed, there is no rancour against their supreme leader. They simply said they had done their duty as best they could. But with their surrender in 1974, all armed resistance against the Chinese occupation of Tibet collapsed.

Meanwhile Gyalo Thondup, the man who had set up this long and ultimately futile struggle, had moved to Hong Kong, where he looked after his business interests and observed the changing political scene in China. With Mao dead and the more pragmatic Deng Xiaoping in the ascendant, feelers were put out for a renewal of direct talks about the 'Tibetan question'. And who should the Chinese contact first, with a view to his being an intermediary? Not a representative of the Tibetan government-in-exile or the Dalai Lama himself, but his elder brother.

Gyalo Thondup had always liked being at the centre of things. Having been the chief organizer of the armed resistance against China, he now became the 'bridge builder'. As the Dalai Lama's personal emissary he visited Beijing no less than twelve times. Again, the end result was stalemate – possibly because Gyalo Thondup was distrusted by both sides, but also because the Chinese did not want to discuss Tibet's status, only the conditions on which the Dalai Lama might be persuaded to return. It is remarkable, all the same, that a 'private businessman' should be entrusted with negotiating the future of a country. He had neither formal authority nor any representative capacity. But on the strength of the messages he conveyed as go-between, Dharamsala's hopes were raised and a completely different policy towards China adopted.

And the Chinese made sure that their 'old friend' Gyalo Thondup would continue to string along by refusing to talk to anyone else. In desperation, Dharamsala turned to him again in 1986, hoping that a resumption of talks might somehow break the deadlock. So the Dalai Lama's brother resumed shuffling between Beijing and Dharamsala, again without any tangible result. More than a decade had passed since the first overtures. Silent diplomacy had not worked. Finally, in September 1987, the Dalai Lama went public. In Washington DC, on Capitol Hill, he announced his Five-Point Peace Plan. From here on Dharamsala's strategy was to 'internationalize' the issue. Some Tibetans now feel that this should have been done much earlier.

After two very different approaches had failed so dismally, one might imagine that their chief proponent would be quietly shelved. But no, Gyalo Thondup was still trying to advance talks with the Chinese and being stone-walled. In the strange world of exiled Tibetan politics, kinship with the Dalai Lama is enough to cancel out any number of failures. In 1992 Gyalo Thondup was chosen by the elected representatives of the Tibetan community-in-exile to become a government minister, a member of the Kashag.

The Dalai Lama claims to have favoured the democratization of Tibetan institutions even before he fled from Lhasa. After arriving in India, he set about drawing up a democratic constitution for a free Tibet, the results of which were made public in 1963. For the interim years, while the refugee community remained in exile, a representative body was to be elected. It was not a fully fledged democracy in the Western sense, since political parties were banned and the Dalai Lama continued to appoint all ministers. Moreover, the people voted according to what region they originally came from in Tibet – for Amdo or Kham or U-Tsang – rather than where they lived in exile. The four main orders of Buddhist monks elected two members each, as did members of the ancient Bon religion.

Initially these elected members of the National Assembly tended to be quiet, if not subservient. But gradually their political competence grew and there were some stormy debates – especially after the Dalai Lama's renunciation of the claim to Tibet's independence through the Strasbourg Proposal of 1988. In the next session, members were granted much fuller powers, including that of voting in candidates for ministerial office who would then be confirmed by the Dalai Lama. And yet this very process of democratization has brought the Dalai Lama's family back into the political limelight.

For amongst the first elected to the cabinet was Jetsun Pema, who somewhat unwillingly took office as minister of education. The following year the Assembly voted in Gyalo Thondup, who was also prevailed upon to accept. But he had made many enemies in Dharamsala, and even though most Tibetans thought that to oppose him was tantamount to being 'anti-Dalai Lama', there were knife-fights and rioting between his supporters and other factions. Some of his party went so far as to issue death threats and a commission of enquiry had to be called (Gyalo Thondup was personally exonerated).

Brother and sister both resigned in 1993, but the Ministry of Education now went to Rinchen Khando, wife of the Dalai Lama's younger brother. Again, she was elected by the people's representatives. There are worrying parallels to be drawn between what might be called the dynastic tendency in South Asian democracies – the Gandhi dynasty is best known, but very similar political dynasties have emerged in Bangladesh, Pakistan and Sri Lanka. The informal, family-based 'kitchen cabinet' that has always supported the Dalai Lama is being replaced by a situation where family members get voted into ministerial office. Perversely, democratization serves to reinforce this dynastic tendency; and the Dalai Lama, who never appointed a family member to the Kashag before the rules were changed, does not appear to object.

These days, the Dalai Lama spends almost as much time visiting foreign countries as he does in Dharamsala. Sometimes he gives teachings to Buddhist converts; but mostly he is busy winning new friends to the Tibetan cause. He is the key spokesman, the headline-grabber, the central cog around which the whole strategy of 'internationalizing' the question of Tibet's status revolves. It certainly helped that in December 1989 he was awarded the Nobel Peace Prize. This raised his personal profile enormously and won much broader support among the liberal democracies. At roughly the same time, Dharamsala shifted the focus from Tibetan claims for independence to human rights abuses committed by the Communist authorities inside Tibet. Through this potent combination of popular adulation and outrage, the Dalai Lama and his advisers hoped to persuade Western governments to apply diplomatic and economic pressure on China.

But at this stage the whole stratagem of 'internationalizing' the Tibet issue broke down. The Chinese government took umbrage, and the already feeble channels of communication with Dharamsala were shut down. As for the world's democracies – or at least their elected governments – while expressing great sympathy for the Tibetan leader they stuck firmly to their 'business as usual' policies. Which means, when it comes to the crunch, good relations with China always come first. And the Chinese made sure that any country which raised the Tibet issue or human rights in an international forum paid for it severely. Denmark did, and Danish companies suddenly found their business prospects in China had gone up in smoke.

So we are faced with a paradox. The Dalai Lama's international standing has never been higher. He regularly scores highly in polls asking who are the most influential leaders of our time. But in terms of bringing any meaningful pressure on China, 'internationalizing' the issue has produced few results so far. Indeed, it may well have backfired. For the dialogue with China appears to have dried up. Perhaps I was ill-informed, but to me it seemed the trail had gone cold.

To catch up on events, I went across the road from my lodgings to see Tsewang C. Tethong in the offices of the Tibetan government-in-exile. He is Kalon or minister in charge of international relations and information. He is also the only member of the old Tibetan aristocracy still holding ministerial office. In the early days of exile things were different. Appointments to the Kashag went mainly to aristocrats who had served the Dalai Lama, either as ministers or high officials, in Lhasa before the exodus of 1959.

Kalon T.C. Tethong's office enjoys a panoramic view of the Dhauladhar Range. Provided you prefer snow peaks to skyscrapers, this may well be the finest view from any office in the world. It had been snowing recently and even the forested slopes lower down were well covered. This had the effect of making the mountains seem nearer and larger than they really are. They appeared to me as an impenetrable curtain of ice, blocking all access to the Tibetan plateau beyond. And so they might seem to the courteous aristocrat who is responsible for the government-in-exile's international relations.

There was a kindly, if somewhat world-weary, quality to his greeting – as though he had seen it all before. He wore a tweed jacket over a cardigan, for the air was still sharp. Unlike most other Tibetan officials I met, he smoked continuously.

'We have made it clear to the Chinese', he said, 'that we are willing to meet them anytime, anywhere – if not for a formal dialogue, then for informal discussions. But that has not happened for many years now.

'So we were puzzled when they said they had several channels still open. They do have one or two individuals to convey messages, though these are not officials. What channels exist were created by His Holiness's personal friends or have come via the US president. After President Clinton's meeting in Beijing, we heard from the Chinese side that, yes, talks will come. But then there was a sudden change after President Clinton mentioned the Tibet issue and it was broadcast on Chinese television. The hard-liners denied that any talks were being considered.

'Since then, any moves towards talks or dialogue are at a standstill. The Chinese have introduced a linkage with Taiwan, making it a pre-condition of any talks about Tibet that His Holiness endorse their position that Taiwan is a province of China. We believe that is something for the

Chinese people in Taiwan to decide. My personal suspicion is that they introduced this linkage because they were angry that His Holiness had visited Taiwan. They wanted to keep Tibetans away from the Taiwanese. And I know another reason why they did this. It creates a total road-block.

'And it is the same with His Holiness's wish to go on pilgrimage to Wutaishan, a place in China which is sacred to Buddhists and was previously visited by the Fifth and Thirteenth Dalai Lamas. This was first expressed publicly at Yale University in 1991, but his request has repeatedly been refused. Perhaps the Chinese leadership are worried about the overwhelming response he would receive in China – and even more so if he went to Tibet.'

I asked the Kalon about the Dalai Lama's response to recent nuclear tests conducted by India and Pakistan. As a committed pacifist, whose declared goal was to transform the Tibetan plateau into a nuclear-free 'Zone of Peace', his views on nuclear proliferation in South Asia appeared, at best, lukewarm.

'Ah, but that was China's reaction to His Holiness's statement.' The Kalon bristled. 'If you look at the whole statement it becomes clear he is in favour of a total test-ban worldwide.'

That may be true, though the section dealing with India's nuclear programme is distinctly restrained in tone. It is difficult for a refugee leader to be too critical of the host country. By the same measure, both Bhutan and Nepal took an equivocal line on India's nuclear tests. For people living on the southern side of the Himalayas, the dangers of criticizing 'Big Brother' normally outweigh any moral imperatives.

*

I felt slightly sorry for T.C. Tethong. As a government minister, he is responsible for explaining Dharamsala's position to the outside world and handling any criticism from Tibetan delegates in the National Assembly. But very often it is the Dalai Lama's Office that takes the initiative in foreign affairs, and he himself is by far the most effective mouthpiece through which these decisions are made known. Which leaves the ministers toiling down in Gangchen Kyi-shang – 'The Abode of the Snow-Happy Valley', as the government offices are known – in a position of responsi-bility without being in full charge of events.

If misunderstandings sometimes arise, the dual system of government in Dharamsala is at least partly to blame. Not only is the Office of the Dalai Lama housed apart from the rest of the administration, it operates quite separately and, in some respects, covers the same remit as the individual government departments do from further down the hill. It is a curious hybrid, combining as it does certain character-istics of presidential palace, royal household and papal secretariat. And for all the Dalai Lama's championing of democratization and open government, the workings of his private office are singularly opaque. Some even see it as a sort of parallel government to the Kashag or Cabinet, which is formally vested with executive powers. Most of the key decisions over the future of Tibet have been taken in Thekchen Choeling, 'The Island of Mahayana Buddhism', where the Fourteenth Dalai Lama resides.

The entrance to the Dalai Lama's residence is directly across the square from the Tsuglakhang Temple. Most Tibetans refer to it as 'His Holiness's Palace'. In fact it is a large, low-built structure which has few palatial pretensions. Security at the front gate is tight – far more so than with other Himalayan monarchs who still rule over a country. But then, although the Dalai Lama is merely an exiled leader who is not recognized internationally as a Head of State, he has a far higher profile than the kings or presidents of most developing countries. I guessed there would be many potential threats – anything from religious nutters through to Chinese-sponsored assassins. So I submitted meekly to a thorough body search and watched the contents of my camera bag being taken to pieces.

I was escorted up the drive by a junior member of His Holiness's Office. Security guards armed with machine pistols patrolled the grounds. Mostly they were Tibetans, though I noticed a bearded Sikh lurking beneath a flowering cherry tree. Even at this early season there were flowers everywhere, and I was reminded of how the Dalai Lama has written lovingly of his garden. The official left me in a waiting room with an old-fashioned wood-burning stove at its centre. Three Tibetans, two monks and a layman, were huddled round it.

I had arrived early and had plenty of time to look around this ante-room. A portrait of Mahatma Gandhi in meditative pose hung in pride of place. Above the entrance stretched a fairly recent panorama of Lhasa, with the Potala at its centre. On either side of the door were glass-fronted cabinets filled with medals that had been presented to the Dalai Lama on his travels, certificates conferring honorary degrees from American and European universities and keys granting him the freedom of cities he had visited around the world. I was informed that my audience would be a little later than scheduled. His Holiness had many visitors to meet at this time of year.

The principal press secretary arrived and guided me along the veranda, past flowering pot plants and yet more security guards, to a small audience room. Its walls were painted turquoise and left for the most part bare. There was a marble-ended cabinet containing a thousand miniature Buddhas, and from the end wall hung a large tangka depicting Avalokiteshvara, the Bodhisattva of Compassion, whose emanation the Dalai Lama is supposed to be. There was a modern oil painting of the Buddha attaining enlightenment under the bodhi tree. But, for me, the most curious item was a picture of a king receiving a princess. I recognized the king as Songtsen Gampo, who ruled over a huge Tibetan Empire in the seventh century; but whether the princess was Wengcheng, his Chinese bride, or Bhrikuti of Nepal, I could not tell. Both are credited with spreading Buddhism throughout Tibet. But, given the present Dalai Lama's policy of seeking rapprochement with China, I reckoned the symbolism worked best if it was the Chinese princess.

The Dalai Lama entered the room, shuffling hurriedly and rearranging his robes as he advanced. He pressed his palms together briefly in the Namaste greeting, but before I could respond likewise he had grasped my hand and was pumping it up and down. From behind his gold-rimmed glasses he peered at me with such intense curiosity that I might have been the first Englishman he had ever met.

My own first impression was that he looked exactly like every picture of the Dalai Lama I had ever seen. This might be taking things the wrong way around; but it is often the case with public figures like the Dalai Lama, who have been photographed so many times, that they end up resembling their images rather than vice versa. Only when he settled in a chair beneath the representation of Avalokiteshvara did I notice that, despite his abundant energy, he had aged somewhat since I had watched him conduct the Losar ceremonies two years before. As he raised his bare right arm to rearrange his monkish robes, the flesh sagged. I calculated he must be nearly sixty-four years old. In a waiting game, time is not on his side.

Nor did it seem to be on mine. After a brief discussion in Tibetan with his secretary, the Dalai Lama consulted his wristwatch. It looked expensive, and I was reminded that tinkering with watches and other pieces of machinery had been one of his hobbies since he was just a boy. I was also reminded that His Holiness has to keep to a tight schedule, that there were other audiences after mine.

'So, let us begin,' he boomed, rather like a schoolteacher taking on a recalcitrant pupil.

I asked him about his own role in preserving Tibetan culture outside Tibet. He was self-deprecating about his own part in this. 'There are other scholars . . .' he began, before expressing how deeply concerned he was about the preservation of Tibetan culture. Not so much the outward manifestations as the passing on of knowledge that, for him, contained the essence of Buddhist civilization. 'Inside Tibet it is a problem, because the last generation of learned scholars is almost gone. Many were eliminated early on, between 1956 and 1958, and more during the Cultural Revolution. Those who survived are very old. So we are left with very few genuinely qualified teachers.'

The situation among the exiled community was, he said, much better. 'The Tibetan identity and spirit has been preserved very well.' But he perceived some slippage – a recent instance being the formal debate between two monks that had just been held in his presence during the Losar celebrations. 'This time the debate was not very rich,' he said. It did not compare to similar debates he could still remember from when he was in Lhasa.

'They were similar types of scholars. But then it was so forceful. There was so much to debate about. Maybe now they do not have the same confidence. In debating, they were so very humble and meek. Before, they fired off arguments like a machine gun!' – at which the Dalai Lama started laughing at so incongruous a comparison. 'Now, it sounds more like a toy rifle!'

He slapped his knee with his right hand, his whole body rocking as laughter filled the room. But there was no doubting that he was displeased with the scholar monks' performance.

The degeneration of the Tibetan language was also a cause for concern. 'Inside Tibet they are deliberately discouraging Buddhist practices and culture – including the use of Tibetan language. Here, it is taught in schools from first to fifth class; and the language itself is very rich, adequate to explain even electricity and other scientific subjects. For philosophy, Tibetan is one of the richest languages, almost equal to Sanskrit. Here in India also, the younger generation still makes mistakes – even when they have some school education. They mispronounce words. They are using Hindi words in debates. When there is no equivalent word in Tibetan, that is excusable. Otherwise not. They will have to do better!'

This was clearly no laughing matter. The Dalai Lama took on the appearance of an irate schoolmaster. At which his private secretary decided to intervene. 'His Holiness is very concerned with Buddhist studies,' he explained.

'Traditional custom does not matter so much', declared the Dalai Lama. 'Custom is only the reflection of a social system. This changes.' He paused, as if to contemplate the transience of such external phenomena. 'There are other types of values, respecting the elderly, being humble, which I feel it is very important to preserve. Inside Tibet, they are deliberately reducing these customs. But also here in India, there is some degeneration there.

'It is important to keep the essence of Tibetan tradition and custom,' he continued. 'Why? Because it is useful to becoming a good human being – sensible, disciplined, compassionate ... All these are associated with Buddhist knowledge. But there is this misconception among Tibetans that the study of Buddhist philosophy is only for monk-scholars. I think that each family should have a greater knowledge about Buddhism, so parents can explain to their children what is the real meaning of lighting a butter lamp. Or what is the Buddha.'

I had the impression that the Dalai Lama could have talked for hours along these lines. But my own time with him was limited, and I wanted to move on to more political matters. I knew him to be a great admirer of Mahatma Gandhi, so I asked him about his own espousal of non-violent resistance and how this differed from the Mahatma's. Could such methods work when you are dealing with Communist China rather than the British?

'The situations are different,' he said. 'The British were imperialists. Their ruling India was bad enough; but they still had an independent judiciary. For us Tibetans, even a small sign of resistance and we are immediately arrested and tortured, and then forced to make a false statement. I doubt this would happen if we were under British rule rather than the Chinese.'

'But has non-violence worked?'

'At Chinese government level?' He rubbed his chin and made a humming noise. 'But among the Chinese public, especially intellectuals among the democracy movement, they very much appreciate our non-violent struggle. Also our Middle Way approach (not demanding full independence for Tibet). So I think our non-violent struggle does have a good result. We have genuine support for this worldwide.'

I asked whether international support was enough. He explained that this was only part of a two-pronged strategy, the other being to seek direct negotiations with the Chinese.

'Let us start from the beginning,' he smiled. 'Around 1973, when the Cultural Revolution was still going on, we set up a plan here in Dharamsala. We decided that sooner or later we would have to talk with the Chinese government.

'On some things we would have to compromise. But to have talks in a spirit of reconciliation was the only possible way forward. Therefore we adopted the Middle Way approach – not independence, but a genuine settlement. And this was to be through direct talks with the Chinese government, not through the UN. If our main goal was to push through the UN, then we would have demanded independence or the right to self-determination.

'Then, at the end of 1978, we received some signal from Peking. In 1979 my elder brother, Gyalo Thondup, went to Peking for talks. In the years which followed we sent many delegations . . .'

I knew about these fact-finding missions, which the

Chinese allowed to visit Tibet. Despite China's attempt to orchestrate these tours, limiting the delegates' contact with Tibetan people and showing them only the new factories and schools and other symbols of the material progress brought by Communism, the immense destruction carried out during the Cultural Revolution could not be hidden. Nor could the authorities always prevent ordinary Tibetans from telling the delegates of their plight. Notes were some-how smuggled to them, and wherever a delegation stopped there was a crowd of people desperate to make some contact with, or even to touch, these representatives of the Dalai Lama.

Meanwhile, Dharamsala persevered in its discussions with Beijing. 'But the Chinese government's position remained that there was no 'Tibetan issue' to be discussed. The only issue was whether the Dalai Lama would return to Tibet or not.'

The ridiculousness of this attempt to separate his personal status from the whole question of Tibet's future, to concentrate on arrangements for his own comfort, had the Dalai Lama laughing again – though this time it was tinged with regret. 'Some Chinese officials admit privately that this approach caused a problem,' he confided, 'but not officially, of course.'

'And so', he continued, 'in 1987 we were compelled to make public our stand in Washington, with the Five-Point Peace Plan.' These five goals were carefully chosen to appeal to a broader audience. Tibet, he declared, should become a demilitarized 'Zone of Peace' and the flood of Chinese migrants halted; human rights and democratic freedoms should be respected; Tibet's wildlife and the environment protected. Naturally, all of this was music to the ears of

Western liberals. The final clause, that sincere negotiations take place with the Chinese, was the only one directly linked to reality. Moves towards such negotiations had already been going on secretly for eight years.

Bringing them out into the open was a desperate attempt to get the Chinese around a conference table. In the event, this strategy backfired. The Chinese were furious, and the Dalai Lama was edged towards making the most crucial concession of all – abandoning Tibetan claims for full independence. 'Then in 1988, we offered a compromise in the Strasbourg Proposal,' he said simply. In return for a degree of internal autonomy, Tibet would still be part of the 'Great Motherland', its defence and foreign relations remaining under Chinese control. It unleashed a storm of protest among the Tibetan community-in-exile.

But from there on, Dharamsala was committed to this 'Middle Way' and concentrated on getting its message across to a broader audience, winning influential friends in America and Europe who might be able to persuade their governments to bring some pressure on the Chinese. Naturally, the Chinese did not take kindly to this 'internationalization' of what they considered an internal matter. Protests by exiled Tibetans and their sympathizers around the world were likely to cause embarrassment.

The Chinese responded by stalling on direct talks with the Dalai Lama's representatives. Inside Tibet, they launched a series of crack-downs, the latest being the 'Strike Hard' campaign, which specifically targeted the Dalai Lama's adherents. Partly this has to do with consolidating Communist control in Tibet. But it is also a means of putting pressure on Dharamsala to call off its bid for international support.

The monks and nuns who willingly go to prison rather than give in to demands that they publicly denounce their spiritual leader are, in a sense, the 'Poor Bloody Infantry' in this war of attrition. But the Dalai Lama is adamant that his Middle Way policy, this combination of seeking renewed talks with the Chinese and building up international pressure over human rights abuses, is 'the only way forward'.

He expressed his concern over 'the worsening situation in Tibet'. The stories he heard from newly arrived refugees were deeply distressing. But even as he contemplated such terrible events, he could not help giggling at how the Chinese portray his own role. 'They accuse me of being a splittist!' he chuckled. And there is a deep irony here – that the man who jettisoned the campaign for an independent Tibet, accepting that it should be part of China, ends up being branded a splittist.

Meanwhile, in the West he is commonly referred to as a 'god-king'. I knew that he dislikes the term, preferring to describe himself as 'a simple monk'. But the Dalai Lama still embodies supreme spiritual and temporal power. He is venerated by most Tibetans as the reincarnation of the God of Compassion. Moreover, he commands the kind of unconditional allegiance that any king would envy. And the more I saw of his situation in Dharamsala, the more I was reminded of a royal court in exile. 'Did it help the cause of Tibetan freedom', I asked, 'that you are both a spiritual and political leader? Or does this dual role sometimes prove a hindrance?'

'In the past', he said, 'it had been beneficial most of the

time – though not always. Today, when we are facing an extremely difficult situation, this combination is helpful in promoting popular unity.'

And it is true that Tibetans in exile have maintained a remarkably united front, given the tendency of most refugee movements to split into rival factions. The Dalai Lama's dual role, and his unquestioned authority, has certainly played a major part in this. Yet he does not come over as a politician. Nor does he appear to relish that side of the job. 'I have already made clear that in future our religious and political institutions should be separate,' he declared. 'Myself, I prefer that monks and nuns should not be involved in political activities.' And he was laughing again.

The Dalai Lama is very much aware that the Tibetan community-in-exile is becoming increasingly politicized. Even the monastic orders, he said, found it hard to stay out of politics. 'From Ladakh to Arunachal Pradesh, when elections come round there are disturbances among the monasteries. Politics also causes disagreements and discord among relations or family members, and this is not good. Of course, politicians argue at elections; then afterwards they are all friends again. I think democracy is good, but our democratic practices are not yet mature. More experience is needed, and much also depends on education.

'Up to now, we Tibetans have been carrying on a struggle for freedom, for our national survival. This is very much to do with the survival of the Buddhist Dharma. Therefore, my involvement in this political struggle is part of my spiritual practice.' In this scheme of things, the crossover between religion and politics occurs at many different levels. It also provides the rationale for delaying further moves towards multi-party democracy.

The Dalai Lama explained that 'while Tibetans are a refugee community, we don't have political parties based on ideology or policies. Eventually, when we return to Tibet, it will come. Back in 1992, I made clear that on the day of our return – with a certain degree of freedom – I will hand over all my legitimate authority to the Tibetan government, and then there should be an elected, democratic government. Together with other Tibetans, we will work hard to create a multi-party democracy and ... [already his eyes were twinkling, his whole body shaking in anticipation of the punch-line] and a little corruption, also.'

This time his laugh rose from somewhere deep inside him and ended in a high-pitched squeak of delight. He had to remove his glasses and wipe a tear from his eye. The very thought of it – all those years of struggle in exile, and for what? Hopefully to see things through to the election of a mildly corrupt Tibetan administration. The Dalai Lama had been in South Asia too long, had met with too many seriously corrupt politicians, to know that it could not be otherwise. But the absurdity of it all had him in stitches.

Once he had composed himself, the Dalai Lama began discussing what this imagined Tibet of the future should be like. 'It is no use to think that we can return to our old lifestyle. That's finished. Much better for us to join with modern society. In Tibet, therefore, I think there will be a kind of socialism – but with complete freedom of speech, a free press, full guarantees of human rights.'

I knew that since his youth the Dalai Lama had admired socialism, and had even been drawn to the Communism of Chairman Mao, because there is a moral basis to such systems of thought. What kind of socialism did he have in mind?

'Socialism usually means an economy. My wish is to adapt the dynamism of the capitalist system to increase the economy; but there should also be an effective method to reduce or check the gap between rich and poor . . .'

Now this seemed a serious moment for it to happen, but I sensed laughter bubbling up again. Another absurdity must have occurred to him. 'Many years ago,' he began, 'I was discussing with an Indian friend the disparity of wealth between two persons. What is acceptable, and what is not? He thought about it and offered this difference – one had five rupees, the other five lakhs (500,000 rupees). To him, this was an acceptable gap!

'Another time, a party of wealthy industrialists came and asked me for a blessing. I told them I have nothing to offer but the outward form of blessing. Real blessing must come from within the self. Their profits should not be spent on luxuries, but more on education and health in the slums and rural areas. It is not wrong to make profits, but you should then distribute them in a socialistic way.'

Since we had entered the realms of idealism, I asked him about his vision of Tibet becoming a 'Zone of Peace'. His proposal was that the Tibetan plateau become a demilitarized zone. All nuclear installations and nuclear waste should be removed, and the region's fragile environment protected by stringent regulations. Of course, all this depended on Tibetans first gaining real autonomy. The Dalai Lama had unveiled this blueprint twelve years before in Washington. Was it still part of the plan?

'The Zone of Peace? Yes, it is still possible. Look at Gorbachev's idea for the Sino–Russian border to be demilitarized.

Tibet is not so different. And once we are inside Tibet and there is genuine stability, then there will be no need to station large numbers of Chinese soldiers there.'

'And the border with India?'

'On the Indian border also. When there is no threat, most of the Indian forces can leave. Only a few border police will be needed. But first there must be mutual trust between India and China. Then both can reduce their military forces in the region.'

'And Pakistan?'

The Dalai Lama frowned severely at this, and any sense of benevolence evaporated. Possibly I was pushing things too far from the topics he liked to discuss.

'The India–Pakistan relationship', he said resignedly, 'is very important for regional stability. I think relations should improve if they can find a more meaningful way to solve the Kashmir issue. Meanwhile, we shouldn't put responsibility at the government level only. Cultural exchanges of ordinary people, artists and sports players, these can be more important.'

'Do you think that the Zone of Peace concept can be extended to the whole Himalayan region, to create a buffer zone similar to the one that British India established?'

'I think it will be difficult. The reason is that Tibet would not be independent. Also, there would be no development, and in Tibet we have to develop a modern society. We need machines, factories, roads, hydro-power, trains. These are necessary for development. We also need experts and capital from other countries. For this we have to work with the Chinese, though we would like some experts from India also.

'It is better we join with a big nation,' he said enthusiastically. 'In the long run, I see Tibet becoming a genuine friend of China. Independence is no longer realistic. But first many things must change. The Chinese still look down on Tibetans, and the Tibetan people suffer.'

I was surprised how suddenly he switched from optimism to heartfelt sorrow. He had left the Tibet of his dreams, a sort of Never-Never Land where freedom and human rights were assured and everybody worked together, both Tibetans and Chinese, towards creating an ideal Buddhist-Socialist future. Now he returned to his current predicament.

As tactfully as possible, I asked the Dalai Lama about what would happen when he died. He seemed completely unphased by this, admitting that 'it is a difficult situation. Obviously, if I pass away among the exiled community, my reincarnation would be discovered outside Tibet. The purpose of a reincarnation is to carry on the work started in the previous life but not yet accomplished. If a reincarnation is a hindrance, then it is not a true reincarnation.'

'What if the Chinese recognize another boy in Tibet, as they did with the Panchen Lama?'

'In a family', replied the Dalai Lama, 'if the son does everything absolutely against his father's wish, naturally he is not considered a good son.' Then he suddenly switched moods again, and started joking about how it would be much easier if, instead of searching for another reincarnation, the Dalai Lama's lineage could be passed on like the Sakya Lamas from father to son. 'The Sakyas,' he giggled, 'they have no problem.' I must confess that I had not expected him to be joking about his own death.

The audience had already overrun and there was time for only one more question. Now one of the criticisms I had heard among Tibetans émigrés was that the Dalai Lama's family, his brothers and sisters, were too closely involved in decision-making. The entire Tibetan movement was run like a family firm. If Dharamsala was a court-in-exile, then the Dalai Lama's siblings behaved as though they were royalty. And this is not always appreciated by fellow exiles who are not so well connected. A Khampa trader even suggested that when the Dalai Lama dies, the knives will be out for those around him who have misappropriated funds or otherwise abused the authority they held.

I knew that this was only hearsay, and that in asking such a question I would be treading on dangerous ground (which was why I had deliberately left it until last).

So I went ahead anyway; and the Dalai Lama riposted most adroitly.

'In earlier times,' he said, 'when my younger sister and brother were in school, my three elder brothers sometimes came to see me. Otherwise there was no involvement in government.

'Then, since the Middle Way was opened some twenty years ago, my eldest brother (Thubten Jigme Norbu) has been very anti this policy. On this we disagree. But here we have a very good democracy. As a brother, he is very close.

'My second brother (Gyalo Thondup) is quite active – in some ways controversial. He was very much involved in the Tibetan Revolt. Sometimes he has great enthusiasm for good relations with China; sometimes with Taiwan. If he was not involved in all these complicated issues, he would be a very good brother. But he is a very good person. I appreciate his good heart.'

On this warming note, the audience drew to a close. Unfortunately, there had been no time to discuss the way that his brothers had been allowed to organize a guerilla war while the Dalai Lama preached non-violence, or how much involved they were in conducting secret talks with the Chinese government before that approach also broke down. Neither had he touched upon his two sisters' uninterrupted reign at the Tibetan Children's Village; nor upon Jetsun Pema's being a minister in the Kashag and several of his nieces and nephews being politically active as deputies in the National Assembly.

Instead the Dalai Lama blessed and presented me with a *kadda*, the ceremonial white silk scarf that is customarily exchanged on such occasions. He left swiftly, barrelling along the veranda before veering left towards an open door. Inside, a group of maybe twenty Westerners stood respectfully, awaiting his presence.

Chapter Four

Beyond Dharamsala –
What Future?

I handed in my security badge and walked out of the monastic-palace complex that is generally known as the 'Little Potala'. I needed to find somewhere quiet, where I could think through what I had heard. The area just outside the gates was crowded with pilgrims and beggars and hawkers of religious offerings, so I took a steep path through the woods towards Lower Dharamsala.

About halfway down I climbed up to a flat rock and rested there, my back against the trunk of a fir tree, the snowy Dhauladhar range spread out before me. What was I to make of this remarkable man? At one level, he appears to be a bundle of contradictions. He proclaims himself to be 'a simple monk' and yet accepts that he is revered by most of his people as a god-king. He is a freedom-fighter who professes non-violence; an enormously popular spiritual leader who is also, in his own way, an adept politician.

One thing I now knew for certain. The Dalai Lama possesses what is known in acting circles as 'tremendous presence'. I could see how this could become overpowering, especially if you happen to be a Buddhist; though precisely how far it all comes down to his having 'inherited' the office of Dalai Lama – as opposed to having any charismatic qualities of his own – is hard to tell. Such matters are not easily disentangled when applied to an individual who is held to be the reincarnation of Chenrezig, the protective deity of Tibet, as well as all thirteen Dalai Lamas who preceded him. As with royalty, much of what is perceived as 'star quality' may really be a question of lineage rather than the individual's attributes.

That said, the Fourteenth Dalai Lama has made a deliberate break with the past. In his youth he was a distant and unapproachable figure, sealed off from his people by the Potala's stout walls and by an equally impenetrable code of court etiquette. He himself has described how much he resented this situation. And, like other monarchs who have for reasons of custom or political expediency been kept as prisoners in their own palaces, he has gone to the opposite extreme. Now he holds opens house, and virtually every new refugee from Tibet is vouchsafed a brief audience – not to mention all the Westerners who either make it to Dharamsala or meet him during one of his many international tours. He has deliberately dispensed with ceremony (although Tibetans still prostrate themselves three times when first entering His Holiness's presence) and makes light of formalities, punctuating even the most serious conversations with his reverberating belly laughs.

This shift towards informality is in keeping with the times. Most of the world's reigning monarchs and heads of state have gone down the same route, though few appear to relish their new role quite as much as the Dalai Lama. And while Rupert Murdoch and other 'friends of China' can make cheap jibes about this 'old monk shuffling around in Gucci shoes', the informal style adopted by the present Dalai Lama does seem to fit his character as naturally as his monkish robes. He deliberately plays down the mystical (or mysterious) aspects of his office, saying that he has no recollection of his previous lives. But he is still the Dalai Lama.

What can be said of him is that he is warm, compassionate, and deeply committed to non-violence. Of course the same could be said of any Buddhist monk who is true to his vocation. He is also reputed to have a sharp temper, and I caught a glimpse of him consciously exercising self-control when some of my questions touched on matters he might rather have avoided. Very often he seems to be regarding the subject being discussed from a perspective completely different to that of anyone else in the room. This habit of looking at things familiar as though for the first time, of examining a concept as though from a great distance, may be the fruit of his spiritual exercises and initiations. It certainly makes for unpredictability in his conversation. And I suspect it feeds into his already lively sense of the absurd – which so often ignites into uproarious laughter.

Then there is his curiosity, his willingness to learn, to gather information from whatever source is available. This might stem from his youthful experience in Lhasa when, although technically the head of government, his own ministers kept him so ill-informed that he became a radio ham, tuning the Potala's wireless set into foreign stations to discover what was happening in the outside world or even within his own country. In my own case, he quizzed me about Tony Blair's 'Third Way' and how New Labour sought to combine capitalism and socialism. Given his own leanings towards socialism, and his desire that an autonomous Tibet should have some form of mixed economy, I could understand why this interested him.

Whether I was the right person to explain the ambiguities of New Labour's approach to socialism is another matter entirely. And herein lies one of the Dalai Lama's weaknesses as a political leader. He is too ready to listen to unqualified 'well-wishers', too indiscriminate in his choice of advisers. At certain crucial junctures, as when he publicly renounced Tibet's claim to full independence, he may have allowed himself to be influenced by outsiders rather than listening to his own people.

And while Tibetans are generally unwilling to criticize the Dalai Lama himself, they are not so restrained when it comes to his coterie of advisers. I found the same to be true of other Himalayan monarchies where the king's ministers and advisers — even other members of the royal family — may be criticized publicly, but the monarch himself stands above the fray, totally immune. The age-old principle that 'the king can do no wrong' still holds good; and, in the Dalai Lama's case, this is overlaid with an additional coating of spiritual authority not far removed from Papal Infallibility.

The Dalai Lama's reliance on well-meaning 'volunteers' may be explained by the very limited resources at his disposal. As an exiled ruler, he depends largely on voluntary contributions of both money and expertise. Members of his own family have been entrusted with the most sensitive missions. But beyond that, he needed experts in constitutional and international law, political lobbyists and spin doctors, development planners, IT technicians, communicators, technocrats ... The 100,000-strong Tibetan community in exile could not furnish all these skills; so the Dalai Lama and his government called upon outsiders whose advice, though well meaning, may not always have been in the best interests of the Tibetan cause.

Foreign advisers are suspected of being behind the Dalai Lama's decision to change his declared goal of full independence for Tibet to that of adopting some form of autonomy within China. Those Tibetans who opposed this change in policy (and there were many) complain that everything was done in great secrecy. Their elected representatives in the Tibetan National Assembly were not consulted beforehand. Certain ministers of the government-in-exile were involved in the discussions. But back in the 1980s all appointments to the Kashag were made directly by the Dalai Lama himself.

For most exiled Tibetans, the Strasbourg Proposal came as a great shock. 'People were weeping openly,' I was told. 'They felt betrayed. Everything they had struggled for had been abandoned. They just couldn't believe it.' But being Tibetans, they found it hard to blame the Dalai Lama. It was the foreign advisers who had steered him down that road.

The timing of the Strasbourg Proposal, the way it was announced – that had certainly been influenced by foreigners. But from what the Dalai Lama had just told me, he had determined on this 'Middle Way' policy of compromise with China at least five years earlier. Moreover, given his deep commitment to non-violence, it was for him the only way forward.

As a pragmatist, he declared that any attempt by Tibetans to mount violent resistance to Chinese rule was tantamount to 'suicide'. As an idealist and spiritual leader, his adherence to the Buddhist principle of ahimsa or non-violent struggle ensured that he occupied the moral high ground. His pacifism, his teachings on showing compassion to your enemies, his renewed emphasis on human rights – all these won him glowing accolades from Western liberals.

But by trying to build on this and make Tibet an international issue, the Dalai Lama alienated the Chinese. Proposals for further talks never got off the ground. Twelve years on, and the prospect of a negotiated settlement is as distant as ever. The Dalai Lama sticks to his Middle Way even though it has brought no tangible results, while his unswerving commitment to non-violence prevents Tibetan nationalists from doing anything to put pressure on the Chinese other than mounting peaceful protests. As a political stratagem, as a means of securing freedom for Tibet, it can scarcely be seen as an unqualified success.

All of which made me wonder about the Dalai Lama's pacifism. Was it purely a matter of his consistently following Buddhist teachings on compassion and non-violence? Or was there something else, deep within him, that made him shy away from any course of action that might result in bloodshed? For whenever he has been confronted with such harsh realities, he has always given in. He accepted China's Seventeen-Point Agreement in 1951. Two years later, he went to Beijing and virtually kow-towed to Chairman Mao. He disassociated himself from the armed revolt in eastern Tibet and then, during the Lhasa Uprising of March 1959, he abandoned his people, leaving thousands of Tibetans protecting an empty palace while he fled south towards the Indian border.

Nor was this tendency to acquiesce always directly linked with his pacifism. He tacitly accepted CIA support for the continuation of armed struggle against the Chinese, both within Tibet and from guerilla bases in Mustang, but preferred that this war be kept a secret. From the 1960s up to the present day he has allowed Tibetans to join India's special forces. When the United States sought a rapprochement with China and wanted Tibetans to cease their guerilla war, the Dalai Lama ordered the Khampas in Mustang to lay down their arms. Only since then has he been consistently wedded to non-violence and seeking an understanding with China.

Pacificism alone does not explain why the Dalai Lama has so often chosen the path of least resistance. Moreover, while claiming to be in the tradition of Mahatma Gandhi's non-violent resistance, the Dalai Lama's version is quite different. Gandhi confronted the British head on, deliberately courting arrest by leading illegal demonstrations and marches. For which he was imprisoned many times; though each time he was jailed he became more popular, his stature as an independence fighter growing until he was widely regarded as a sort of secular saint.

The Dalai Lama has adopted a less confrontational approach. He has repeatedly called for a free Tibet; but he practices what might be termed a 'remote-control' variant of non-violent struggle, leaving it to ordinary Tibetans to mount peaceful protests that will almost certainly land them in jail for many years. Western supporters of Tibet have also courted arrest when protesting against Chinese delegations to their countries, though their brief detention is in no way comparable to the punishments endured within Tibet.

The Dalai Lama cannot apply the same confrontational tactics because, as he had explained to me, dealing with the Chinese is a completely different matter to the British in India. There is no independent judiciary, no freedom of the press. But what if the Dalai Lama were to follow Gandhi's example and lead a peaceful march into Tibet? That would certainly demonstrate his personal commitment to a free Tibet, his willingness to share in the sufferings of his people, in a far more convincing manner than any speeches he may give from the safety of Washington or New Delhi.

Comfortably perched on my rock, looking northwards towards the Himalayan barrier, I tried to imagine the scene at the Tibetan border. The Dalai Lama surrounded by a human wall of Tibetans as Chinese troops tried to hold them back, for once not daring to fire into the crowd. It would be a magnificent gesture, and I wondered whether the Dalai Lama did not sometimes dream of playing out such a heroic Gandhian role. For a brief moment it would focus the world's attention on the Tibetan issue. But then what?

Then the Chinese would send in a snatch squad or find some other means of gaining custody of the Dalai Lama's person. Even the presence of the world's media would not guarantee his safety. The Chinese have learned much since Tiananmen Square, and understand well how to limit hostile coverage. The Dalai Lama would 'disappear' for a while, just as the Panchen Lama did. And when he finally did reappear in public, it would be as some brainwashed puppet leader swearing undying friendship with the People's Republic of China. Worse still, when he died the Chinese would be able to control the search for his successor. There exist many sound reasons why the Dalai Lama should not risk either his life or his liberty, as Gandhi once did.

The same goes for Gandhi's other 'weapon' – his repeated threats of fasting to death unless certain demands were met. The Dalai Lama has never sought to emulate him in this respect, and with good reason. If Gandhi had died during a hunger strike he would have become a martyr to the cause of Indian nationalism. There would have been massive civil unrest. A wave of strikes would have paralysed the country. And there were plenty of other nationalist leaders like Nehru to take on the great man's mantle.

None of this applies to the Dalai Lama. He does not need to seek the sanctity bestowed by martyrdom. He is already the reincarnation of the Bodhisattva of Compassion, and as such fulfils his role best simply by continuing to live in this world of suffering to assist all sentient beings. If he were to declare a hunger strike, his example would be followed by countless monks and nuns and lay Tibetans. It might even precipitate another uprising inside Tibet, causing yet more suffering. And even if Tibet erupted in turmoil, this would have little impact on China's economy.

Moreover, Tibetan Buddhism is profoundly anti-suicide, teaching that it wipes out the merits earned in countless previous existences (which, in the Dalai Lama's case, would pose some serious theological problems). That said, hunger strikes do form part of the Tibetans' meagre arsenal. Political prisoners in Drapchi and other such places in Tibet have undertaken hunger strikes, though usually they are force-fed sooner or later. And when a group of Tibetan exiles were determined to fast to death in New Delhi, the Dalai Lama went to them and counselled against their continuing to the bitter end. The hunger strike was finally abandoned, though one of its supporters poured petrol over himself and was so badly burned that he died in hospital. Again, the Dalai Lama went to comfort him. He also pointed out the error of carrying protest to such extremes, even if the motivation was of the purest kind.

As for himself, the Dalai Lama probably does serve his people best simply by being there. He gives them a sense of unity, and is by far the most effective spokesman for the Tibetan cause around the world. While he is alive the thorny question of who is to succeed him is postponed. For the very nature of his office means that unlike hereditary monarchies – or, indeed, the entrenched political dynasties which rule in most of the developing world – there can be no heir-apparent.

Although he is able to joke about his own death, the Dalai Lama knows that this is likely to be followed by a fiercely disputed search for his new incarnation. The Chinese could easily arrange for their own candidate to be discovered, using compliant lamas to draw up a shortlist while the final choice would be left to the Golden Urn – a straight lottery which has been the method preferred by the Chinese since it was first introduced by the Ming emperors. The authorities could also apprehend any candidate from inside Tibet chosen by other means, and ensure that this boy and his family 'disappear'. That was what happened after the last Panchen Lama died.

Measures have been taken to prevent a re-run of those unfortunate events when the Fourteenth Dalai Lama dies. The last thing that Tibetans in exile (and nationalists inside Tibet) want is to have a puppet Dalai Lama, selected, groomed and carefully indoctrinated by the Chinese, enthroned in Lhasa. Which is why the present Dalai Lama has dropped heavy hints – to many others besides myself – that if he dies in exile then his next reincarnation would live in a free country where he can 'continue his predecessor's work'. But the selection of a 'free' Dalai Lama would not prevent the Chinese from installing their own candidate in the Potala. In fact, it would become all the more essential. So there would be two Dalai Lamas: one recognized by the Chinese; the other living in exile.

Such a situation is unlikely to enhance the respect in

which the institution of the Dalai Lama is held. The Chinese would be able to use the full range of options – from re-education campaigns through to imprisonment and torture – to 'persuade' people inside Tibet to acknowledge their candidate. Presumably they will also be able to rely on Gyaltsen Norbu, the boy they had installed as Panchen Lama in 1996, to fulfil his 'patriotic duty' and recognize their chosen candidate as Dalai Lama. And in this they have tradition on their side: for in the past the Panchen Lama has always recognized the Dalai Lama and vice versa.

Meanwhile, adherents of the 'free' Dalai Lama would be pressing for his recognition throughout the world. Within Tibet itself, their options are more limited. Some courageous individuals – high lamas, monks, devout laymen and women – might speak out in his support before they can be silenced; though the most effective form of passive resistance would be for Tibetans to boycott the 'Chinese' Dalai Lama's enthronement and any other ceremonies at which he is present.

But the authorities are skilled in stage-managing such events and one can be sure that Lhasa would be filled with crowds of 'faithful adherents' prostrating themselves before the official claimant for the benefit of the cameras. The Potala and the Jokhang Temple could serve as backdrops. While it may seem fantastical that the organs of a Communist and officially atheist state would use such overtly religious imagery, the authorities have overseen the enthronement of 'their' Panchen Lama and a new Reting Lama (whose predecessor was regent on behalf of the present Dalai Lama). All the signposts are there. The Chinese are great pragmatists. They have a saying that it matters not if a cat is black or white, so long as it is good at catching mice.

Only a very determined group of Tibetan protesters could break up such carefully orchestrated proceedings. The authorities would have plenty of time to prepare against such an eventuality by infiltrating dissident groups, rounding up all the usual suspects, and mounting security operations on an intimidating scale. To demonstrate against the 'Chinese' Dalai Lama would be tantamount to suicide.

Even more damaging to the office of the Dalai Lama, a war of words would almost certainly break out between the two camps long before either of the young boys chosen as Dalai Lama was able to read (or memorize) their carefully scripted messages to the world at large. And this time the arguments would focus not on the status of Tibet but on the position of the Dalai Lama himself. The legitimacy of each candidate would be called into question. So too would the theology and spiritual beliefs that validate the choosing of a Dalai Lama, and the reverence which is accorded to that office. The Chinese can play their cards any number of ways, confident that the existence of two rival Dalai Lamas will undermine the institution itself in the long run.

The very nature of the office means that, whatever happens, there will be a space of roughly fifteen years when both claimants are still minors. Traditionally, a regent or regency council has governed on behalf of the Dalai Lama until he comes of age. In Dharamsala, at least, arrangements are in place for a regency council comprising 'high lamas and government ministers' to run the Tibetan government-in-exile during the future Dalai Lama's minority. But these long regencies have always been the greatest weakness of passing on temporal and spiritual authority through reincarnations. Already many Tibetan exiles fear that without the living presence of the Dalai Lama to provide a sense of unity and purpose, internal divisions will come to the surface, and that any unseemly infighting would permanently damage the cause of a free Tibet.

On their side, the Chinese would ensure that 'their' Dalai Lama is carefully educated – most probably in Beijing, where he can be kept in close custody, completely isolated from his people and anyone who can inform him of his historic role. There, he can be indoctrinated so as to ensure he causes the Chinese leadership no embarrassments. Meanwhile the Tibetan Autonomous Region will be run by loyal Party members, just as before – until such time as it is expedient to elevate their puppet Dalai Lama to a symbolic leadership role.

Of course, that is just one option. The Dalai Lama might just as easily be left in obscurity, completely sidelined. But as long as Beijing thinks he has a useful role in countering the protestations of the Dharamsala 'splittists' or keeping pious Tibetans more or less on side, then there will be a future Dalai Lama in the Potala.

For most Tibetans, this is a nightmare scenario. The idea of there being a puppet Dalai Lama in Lhasa, a man who was supposedly their spiritual leader though, in all likelihood, his early indoctrination would mean that he was anti-religious and secretly working against the Buddhist faith. Just imagine how the Catholic Church would react if the Pope was discovered to be an atheist, deliberately seeking to destroy Christian doctrines and values. It is easy to see why such a figure might be compared to the Anti-Christ. For Tibetan Buddhists, something very like that is not just a bad dream.

That is the emotive impact of there being a false Dalai

Lama. As for the effect of such a split on the institution itself, one can see what happened to medieval Christendom when there were two Popes – the one in Rome, the other in Avignon. Each party accused the other of being the Anti-Pope, the Whore of Babylon, and much else besides. In the long run, such partisan propaganda seriously undermined the Papacy; and it is likely that any war of words between Dharamsala and Beijing would have a similar effect on how the institution of the Dalai Lama is perceived.

There are, as far as I could see, only two ways out of this impasse. Either the present Dalai Lama lives long enough to reach an accommodation with China that allows him to return to Tibet with some credibility intact. In that case, the Dalai Lama would hand over his temporal authority, and the whole question of his succession would be far less politically charged. But for this to be possible, certain changes must first occur in China; and most China-watchers do not expect sufficient movement towards democracy – or the acceptance of self-rule by 'national minorities' like Tibetans – for at least ten, maybe twenty years.

Of course, the Dalai Lama may live even longer than that. He works out on an exercise bicycle in his private gym. And if one looks at Pope John Paul II, there is no reason why the Dalai Lama should not see in the Losar celebrations in the year 2020.

The other option is that there may be no more Dalai Lamas. He himself raised this possibility by declaring that it was for the Tibetan people to decide whether the office of the Dalai Lama should continue in future. Theologically there is no problem, for any incarnate lama can choose not to be reborn. But most Tibetans find it impossible to imagine living without their Dalai Lama.

While I was in Dharamsala I heard many prayers for His Holiness's long life. And yet, as I picked myself up from the rock where I had been sitting, I was pretty certain that I had just met the last undisputed Dalai Lama.

During this long and not especially joyous contemplation, I had been only vaguely aware of external events. Various people had moved up and down the track below me. A group of schoolchildren had gone skipping over the steps. An old Tibetan monk and a much younger Westerner passed by. For maybe half an hour my eyes followed a pair of Himalayan vultures as they circled in the void.

I was aware that time had passed because the snows had taken on a buttery hue as the sun moved round to the west, and the air felt much sharper. Looking around, I found this side of the hill was now cast in shadow. So I started walking down the trail towards my lodgings. As the sun dipped behind the western foothills, its last rays suffused the evening mist with an unearthly luminescence. Down in Lower Dharamsala the electric lighting was being switched on. Beyond, in the Kangra Valley and the foothills stretching down towards the Punjab, there was hardly a light to be seen. It was as though the surrounding country had been consumed in an ocean of blackness.

Losar festivities continued in and around Dharamsala long after the official public holidays were over. Special Losar offerings of fried biscuits and brightly coloured cakes were laid out in the dining room at my lodgings and in the

entrances of various government offices I visited. A large
blue-and-white Tibetan tent went up in the back yard of a
house just down the road from where I was living. 'They
will be having a big party,' my landlord's daughter
explained. But these are mostly family affairs to which
outsiders are rarely invited.

There is not much to do in the evenings in Dharamsala,
apart from joining in an impromptu party thrown by
travellers in the spaghetti house or other eateries around
town. I even found myself wandering down to the small
cinema on the bazaar which runs behind a Buddhist temple
surrounded by prayer wheels. Most of the films were Hollywood blockbusters and action movies which appealed to the
local youth as well as Western visitors. But they also had
showings of *Kundun*, Martin Scorsese's film about the Dalai
Lama's life up to his journey into exile in 1959. Unlike
other Hollywood renditions, most of the cast were Tibetans
(including several of the Dalai Lama's family relations). The
audience for such a film in Dharamsala is almost exclusively
Westerners, the locals having either already seen it or being
all too familiar with the story it tells.

Kundun means 'the presence' in Tibetan, and is one of
several respectful terms used when referring to the Dalai
Lama. It is not a bad film, but I must confess to a sense of
absurdity watching this reconstruction of events in Lhasa
forty years back while sitting in a dank theatre just up the
hill from the Dalai Lama's residence. The normal boundaries
between what happens on screen and the outside world
became blurred. After leaving the cinema I found myself not
on a neon-bright urban pavement but following a Tibetan
matron up a dark alley lined with prayer wheels.

The film's portrayal of the young Dalai Lama is upon the whole sympathetic. He comes over as an isolated and helpless figure. The underlying message is that once the Chinese invaded Tibet, there was not a lot that he could do about the situation. It was a tragedy – both for himself and the Tibetan nation. This is also how the Dalai Lama describes that crucial phase of his life in his autobiography. It is the orthodox version.

But having first seen the Dalai Lama, and then the Hollywood rendering of his early life, made me want to draw up a checklist of what he had in fact achieved. So I stopped off at an eatery for a plate of *momos* – plump Tibetan raviolis stuffed with meat and vegetables. A young monk, still in his teens, sat at the next table. Once he had finished his bowl of soup and noodles, he leaned back on his chair and started swaying to the rock music coming out of the speakers.

While waiting for the food to arrive, I got out my notebook and wrote down a few key events. He was recognized as the Dalai Lama. He lost his country to a foreign invader. He accepted the situation and even cosied up to the occupying power. When his own people rose in his support, he abandoned them. He led 100,000 of his people into exile with the assurance that they would be returning 'soon'. More than forty years later, he is no nearer to achieving that goal.

When assessed as a political rather than a spiritual leader, the record did not look good. And there were so many themes from his early life (his fear of confrontation, for instance) that seemed to repeat themselves up to this day. Even the arcane process of choosing him as the true reincarnation of the Thirteenth Dalai Lama – the visions that appeared in a holy lake in Tibet, the way in which the young boy unerringly chose the personal effects of his predecessor rather than identical copies — these moving scenes have more recent echoes that have rocked the stability of Tibetan Buddhism. For no matter how many supernatural signs are made evident in the finding of a high incarnate lama, his recognition is and always has been a political act.

And viewed in this light, the Dalai Lama's recognition of other high lamas has been one long series of political fiascos.

He went public on recognizing the Panchen Lama before that boy could be smuggled out of Tibet. Neither the boy nor his family have ever been seen since, and the Chinese candidate has been enthroned. As for the furore surrounding the rival claimants to be the Karmapa, the head of the five million-strong Kagyu sect who is normally ranked third in the Tibetan hierachy of living gods, that has rumbled on for more than eight years and shows no sign of a peaceful outcome.

In fact, the dramatic escape from Tibet of the fourteen-year-old Urgyen Thinley in December 1999 and his sudden arrival at Dharamsala have brought matters to a head. This is the boy whom the Dalai Lama had recognized as the Seventeenth Karmapa seven years earlier — even though he had never met the candidate and communicated his approval by fax from Brazil, where he happened to be travelling at the time. Urgyen Thinley was also recognized by the Chinese authorities as part of their new policy of manipulating Tibet's religious hierarchy rather than trying to suppress it.

He made appropriate 'patriotic statements' and was locked up in Tsurphu Monastery, the traditional seat of the Karmapas high in the mountains above Lhasa. It was from there that he escaped with suspicious ease in the winter of 1999 and crossed the Himalayas, claiming he wanted to meet his spiritual teacher.

The Tibetan government-in-exile hailed this as a great triumph. It proved that the Dalai Lama's choice had been right all along, that the Tibetan Karmapa was not a Chinese stooge. Despite fifty years of Chinese occupation and religious persecution, the spirit of Tibetan Buddhism remained unvanquished. The ruddy-cheeked teenager who posed for the cameras in Dharamsala was the living proof.

But that is only half the story. There is another claimant, a boy who was successfully smuggled out of Tibet, and who is recognized by around half of the Kagyupas living in the free world as the true Karmapa. These days Thaye Dorje lives under close guard in the hill station of Kalimpong, preparing for his role as head of the Kagyu sect. Security guards are necessary because already the conflicting claims of the two would-be Karmapas have resulted in bloodshed. Monks have been murdered and thrown out of their monasteries. There is also a pile of court actions waiting to be heard by the Indian judiciary as the two parties try to gain control of the Kagyu order's multi-millon-dollar assets worldwide.

Many adherents of the 'Delhi Karmapa', as Thaye Dorje is commonly known, resent the Dalai Lama's intervention in the choosing of their spiritual leader. He, after all, is head of the Gelugpa sect of Buddhism. They are Kagyupas, heirs to far older spiritual traditions. Besides which, they have been more active than the other Tibetan orders in founding monasteries and meditation centres in the West. Hence their enormously enviable wealth.

So why did the Dalai Lama intervene? Some say that it

was part of his attempt to build bridges with the Chinese government. For the first time, a very senior incarnation would be recognized both in Dharamsala and Beijing. Others, that he was personally convinced by reports of the search party (which included members from Samye Ling Monastery in Scotland) that the boy-child Urgyen Thinley was indeed the true Karmapa. A less charitable interpretation is that he simply sided with one of the two parties and used the divisions within the Kagyu order to impose his own authority. Ever since the reformist Gelugpas rose to prominence in the fifteenth century they have played off the leaders of rival sects against each other – a very Tibetan version of 'divide and rule'.

And as the Dalai Lama has demonstrated by banning certain teachings of other nonconformist sects, he is determined to retain control of the Tibetan church. The dislike he expressed during my audience of 'politics' infecting the monastic life is largely because such political or sectarian arguments undermine his central control. Though exceptionally pliant in his dealings with the Chinese or Indian governments, when it comes to ecclesiastical politics he can be as authoritarian as Pope John Paul II.

That said, the Dalai Lama is an extremely charismatic figure. In due course the historians will probably list him up there with 'The Great Fifth' and 'The Great Thirteenth'. If nothing else, his capacity to transform a fairly obscure Himalayan variant of Buddhism into a non-doctrinal code for 'living a good life', a stripped-down version of ethics that has appealed to a truly global audience – for that alone the Fourteenth Dalai Lama might well qualify as one of the 'Greats'.

He has maintained hope and unity among the Tibetan

exiled community while building a huge following around the world. But what about the vast majority of Tibetans, the six million who have never left their homeland? What has he done for them?

To most Tibetans the Dalai Lama is a beacon of hope, a natural focus for their aspirations to be a free nation once more. That much I knew from my encounters with ordinary Tibetans in Lhasa and Shigatse who pleaded for a Dalai Lama photo. And yet, as their remembered images floated before my eyes, I realized their veneration and loyalty were to the Dalai Lama as an institution, the most potent symbol imaginable of their own identity as Tibetan Buddhists, and not to the individual who lived in a distant land, whom they had never once seen and, most likely, never would see in this life.

Simply by existing, the Dalai Lama inspires hope. But there is a price to pay: and it is his adherents inside Tibet – political dissidents, human rights activists, the hundreds of monks and nuns who suffer humiliation, imprisonment and torture rather than denounce the Dalai Lama – who have done so. While I was in Dharamsala I went to the refugee rehabilitation centre, a dank and severely overcrowded concrete building, and talked with three of the more recent arrivals. Two had been monks, and their stories of being locked in freezing cells and prodded with electric batons are unfortunately only too typical of what is still happening inside Tibet. They were still waiting for political asylum and worried that they might not be allowed to join a monastery in India. The layman, who had been arrested for possessing pro-Dalai Lama pamphlets, was concerned he might be sent back to Tibet.

Both Dharamsala and international human rights organizations monitor individual cases and protest against such abuses. The Chinese authorities take little notice. Rather, any initiative by the Dalai Lama to raise the issue of Tibet in the international arena usually prompts another clamp-down inside the country. Other factors – the internal struggles between hard-liners and liberals within the Communist Party hierarchy in Beijing or, indeed, in Lhasa – may determine the timing or severity of 'patriotic re-education' campaigns and other forms of political repression. But, by inspiring his people to continue their passive resistance to China's occupation of Tibet, the Dalai Lama is caught up in a dreadful game of consequences.

By insisting that this struggle is carried on through non-violent means only, the Dalai Lama demands of his people an exceptional degree of self-restraint. Although their religion tends towards pacifism, most Tibetans are not naturally inclined to take things lying down. Sometimes their anger boils over. During the protests in Lhasa of 1987–8, furious crowds attacked a police station where monks and other pro-independence demonstrators were being held. And when three EU ambassadors visited the notorious Drapchi Prison in May 1998, political prisoners staged an uprising which resulted in ten deaths.

That incidents like these are so rare is testimony to the moral hold the Dalai Lama still has over his people. But how much longer can they be expected to exercise such self-restraint? There is a world of difference between the well-looked-after, quasi-monastic community in Dharamsala and the desperate condition of those inside Tibet. More than twenty years have passed since the Dalai Lama promulgated his doctrine of passive resistance, without any tangible progress. Instead, millions of Han Chinese settlers have moved in and Tibetans now find themselves increasingly marginalized in their own country.

Among the younger generation, both inside Tibet and among the exiled community, there is a mounting sense of frustration. Indeed, the wisdom of the Dalai Lama's 'Middle Way' is openly questioned by youth leaders who are variously described by the officials I met as 'radicals' or 'hot-headed'. I decided my next move should be to find one of these 'hot-headed' radicals. Maybe the Tibetan Youth Congress, which acts as a sort of unofficial opposition, would be a good starting point. In the event, I didn't have to look too far.

'The Dalai Lama is a saint. I'm not a saint. So why should I love my enemy?'

I looked into the eyes of Lhasang Tsering, former President of the Tibetan Youth Congress, and they glowed with fervor and conviction. These days he runs a book shop in McLeod Ganj; but he has lost none of his youthful radicalism.

Once he had found out why I wanted to see him, he locked up his shop and led me to a newly opened restaurant where we were the only customers. 'Here we can talk openly,' he declared.

Lhasang Tsering had been TYC President through the turbulent years from 1986 to 1989. He has been outspoken in his opposition to the Dalai Lama's policies of pacificism, seeking reconciliation with China, and abandoning the call for a fully independent Tibet. Since then, both he and his family had been subject to intimidation. Local heavies had been around to his apartment in Dharamsala. He has a wife and two children to consider. When the tea came he scanned the restaurant again. Two others had arrived, but they were sitting out of earshot.

'My single appeal to His Holiness was not that he should support violence,' Lhasang Tsering continued, 'but that in a situation like the Lhasa protests in 1987, it was not right to condemn people for throwing stones at armed police. Some had watched their best friends killed beside them. They were desperate people using any means to defend everything that was dear to them. All that I was advocating is the right of people to defend themselves, to rise up against repression. So I asked of His Holiness: "Please give us the freedom to be human, to seek ordinary aims through ordinary human means." But His Holiness only repeated his threat to resign if the violence continued.'

Self-defence was not the only kind of violent resistance proposed by Lhasang Tsering. He believed that armed struggle, even against overwhelming odds, was better than doing nothing. This he summarized in what he calls his 'Four Humble Truths'.

Freedom is a basic necessity.
Freedom will not come just by waiting.
Therefore freedom must be fought for and won.
Freedom doesn't come for free. There's a price to pay.

'And that's not in dollars and cents,' he added. 'It must be paid for with life and blood.

'We Tibetans have had enough "autonomy with Chinese characteristics",' he said scornfully. 'To live with integrity — that is as basic a necessity as air and water. Unless this generation finds the courage and is willing to pay the price, the next generation will not be free.'

This militancy goes back to when, as a teenager, he gave up his studies to join the Khampa guerilla army in Mustang. He only reached there in 1974, shortly before the final surrender, and according to Khampa commanders I met elsewhere this young volunteer played only a marginal role. None the less, he still argues that the Khampas could have held out.

'The Khampas' fighting abilities were legendary,' he declared, excitement now in his voice. 'We didn't want to fight the Nepalese army, only to defend our capacity to continue the struggle against China. Orders had already been given, ammunition distributed, our troops had moved down to surround the valley at Jomsom where the Nepalese had gathered. We were ordered to begin the attack at 3 a.m. The taped message from His Holiness arrived just before midnight. It was that message which brought about the ignominious and sad surrender of these courageous people.'

Lhasang Tsering still blames the Dalai Lama for having 'let down' the Khampa movement. As for the CIA's involvement, he did not think they had used the Tibetans and then dumped them. That decision came from a higher level within the US government. And if the Tibetans had been duped into fighting a secret war for fourteen years, they had only themselves to blame. 'As far as I am concerned the CIA provided us with the means to fight, and even now I would welcome another such opportunity.'

I asked him whether he thought armed struggle was a feasible option. 'I believe conditions since 1990 have been much more favourable to Tibetans and other occupied peoples in China. Before, there was an acceptance of a fixed post-World War order. But since 1990 there is an acceptance that maps can and will continue to be redrawn. What gives me courage to continue the armed struggle is the example of Chechnya,' he declared. Unfortunately, he made that statement only a few months before the Chechen capital of Grosny was flattened by the armed might of Russia. But he also mentioned East Timor, which, after enormous suffering, has at least gained its independence.

'But, surely,' I said, 'you can't expect to take on China? Everything depends on internal changes coming from within China first.'

'We should not just wait for trouble to happen in China,' he replied. 'We should set about creating instability. Not that I have anything against the Chinese people. This I feel in my heart. But they have no right to rob my land and my people and then not accept the consequences.'

One of the unmentionable consequences, should Tibet ever regain its freedom, is what would happen to the Han Chinese settlers already there. 'Morally', he declared, 'we must not have ethnic cleansing. But politically we must not find ourselves a minority in our own country. The Chinese government has always denied there has been any population transfer. If that's the truth, then we don't expect to find any Chinese settlers in Tibet.

'But in reality we know there has been settlement, so with international involvement a safe haven must be found for these people. However, if we achieve freedom through our own struggle, the very nature of that struggle will reduce both the number of Chinese in Tibet and the willingness of the remainder to stay on.'

I noticed how Lhasang Tsering worked through to his conclusions with a cold, almost Maoist, logic. At the same time he spoke of Tibet with a romantic fervour that reminded me of Polish émigrés I had met years before, when their country was still dominated by the Soviet Union. But there was something refreshing in the way he was willing to face up to unpalatable truths.

One thing he could not abide was hypocrisy. 'Our leaders keep talking about peace,' he said, 'but they allow the cream of our young men to be recruited by the Indian army. That may be because as an exiled community we are too dependent on India. But let's have some honesty here. Our own Tibetan government has no moral right to push school leavers into the Indian army.'

He was equally brutal about 'moral support' for the Tibetan cause. 'It would be much kinder of the West to tell us the truth – that they will not really help us because no government in the world is in a position to put pressure on China. It would help us Tibetans to face the truth. But instead, we Tibetans have this mental habit of always transferring hope to the future. We love to say to ourselves: "The whole world is behind the Dalai Lama and the Tibetan cause." But what has this nebulous entity – the freedom-loving peoples of the world – ever done for us? Nothing. When His Holiness goes to Washington, it should not be just for a pat on the back from Bill Clinton.

'We are partly to blame for this because we are perpetuating this Shangri-La image of Tibetans. When His Holiness travels abroad, everyone finds him so sweet, so compassionate. They love his message of ahimsa, of having compassion for the enemy. I say that the application of such absolute concepts is for saints, and we don't have many of them. It is a misleading image of what Tibetans are really like. I think that in perpetuating this image, His Holiness is just trying to pander to his New Age supporters. I also believe that in extolling non-violence we destroy the memory of all those Tibetans who laid down their lives, who made the ultimate sacrifice, for their country.'

Many young Tibetans — and not just members of the 15,000 strong Tibetan Youth Congress — share these views. They have grown weary of Dharamsala's fixation with winning moral support internationally when this does not translate into any real economic or diplomatic pressure on the Chinese. They continue to demand full independence for Tibet, not the watered-down version of autonomy within China that has been the target set by the Dalai Lama and his government for the last two decades. The question of whether or not to stick to the original goal of independence has created bitter divisions within the Tibetan community-in-exile ever since the Strasbourg Proposal of 1988.

Lhasang Tsering blames certain of the Dalai Lama's foreign advisers — the Dutch lawyer Michael van Walt van Praag and 'friendly' US Congressmen — for pushing a more conciliatory line towards China. 'Was this in support of Tibetans' interests?' he asked. 'Or was it because they thought they could make a quick deal with Beijing? His Holiness subsequently defended this decision by saying what was on offer in the Strasbourg Proposal was the "bottom line". But from the tactical point of view, it is an error to place your rock-bottom price on the table before the Chinese had even agreed to having talks about talks.'

He was honest enough to admit that Tibetans are always looking for scapegoats, someone other than themselves to blame for their misfortunes. The fault, he said, lay closer to home. 'After we were invaded in 1950, His Holiness went to Beijing and pleaded with Mao. Later he said the Chinese had gone back on their promises. Then, for twenty years we transferred our hope to India, the United States, the United Nations. What good have all three noble-sounding UN Resolutions done us? Finally, we transfer our hopes back to China – assisted, maybe, by moral pressure from the West, though basically everything depends on China. We have pursued this Middle Way for twenty years, and still the Chinese will not negotiate. Why should they? The Chinese are playing a waiting game, and we Tibetans are playing into their hands.'

Nor is he impressed by the current orthodoxy, that one must wait for democratic changes to come about in China and, in the meantime, try to forge links with Chinese dissident leaders abroad. He rejects this waiting passively for something to happen, just as he rejects non-violence, as being contrary to Buddhism. 'The Buddha's message was that we must take positive action to help ourselves', he declared, 'and not just wait for things to happen. The Law of Karma is that we are ultimately responsible for everything – for our will, our actions, and the results thereof. So I say it is better to do something rather than just wait.'

I left Lhasang Tsering at the front door of his bookshop, an angry and embittered man. Of his nationalist fervour, his idealism, his commitment to a free Tibet, I was left in no doubt. But whether his confrontational stance would do any more good than the Dalai Lama's more conciliatory Middle Way, I cannot say. Both approaches have been tried for roughly the same amount of time since 1959, and with equally dismal results.

What I do know is that pinning one's hopes on the Chinese – even pro-democracy Chinese dissidents – suddenly changing their minds about Tibet is not realistic. This was brought home to me when I met Xiao Qiang, executive director of a dissident group called Human Rights in China, whose head office is on Fifth Avenue in New York. He had been brought over on an all-expenses-paid trip to meet the Dalai Lama, and I encountered him in one of the smarter hotels in McLeod Ganj where he was staying. While he found his meeting with the Dalai Lama 'extremely useful', and was sure that 'further cooperation on human rights issues will be of mutual benefit', he would not be drawn on whether Chinese dissident movements would actually support the Tibetan cause.

Such reticence is hardly surprising. Anyone who has spent any time in China knows that the vast majority of Han Chinese — and not just the Party leadership — are fully convinced that Tibet has always been part of the 'Great Motherland'. For a dissident leader like Xiao Qiang, furthering the cause of democracy and human rights in China proper is the first priority, not Tibet. In fact, he told me his immediate concern was in forging some kind of unity among all the different Chinese dissident groups. Tibet was a long way down the agenda. And even if China does turn to democratic institutions, it would be a brave politician who offered concessions on Tibet's status. Electorally it would be courting disaster; for Han nationalism remains a potent force.

In this respect, I think Lhasang Tsering was right when he said there must be some quid pro quo. But he and the other 'hot-headed nationalists' are probably wrong about how to engineer this. For Tibet to be free again, there must be some internationally brokered deal whereby the Chinese can be seen to benefit — in terms of enhanced security, more favorable trade agreements, greater acceptance within the

international community. India would have to make concessions by demilitarizing its Himalayan frontier; the great
trading blocs by allowing China a far larger say than at
present. That, I believe, is the way forward; not another
doomed insurrection within Tibet, which would only encourage the Chinese to take another 'Great Leap Backwards.'

So perhaps the Dalai Lama's waiting strategy is correct
after all. Since I was last in Dharamsala he has moved yet
closer to China, asking the international community not just
to condemn human rights abuses but to do more to welcome
the Chinese into WTO and other such bodies. The declared
aim is to thaw relations and open up the way to reforms
within China. But to ardent nationalists like Lhasang Tsering, that is throwing in the towel. Just waiting passively for
something to turn up is no comfort to them. Nor does it
alleviate the desperation of those inside Tibet.

The last night before I left Dharamsala, I joined some
Westerners doing voluntary work on human rights for a
Losar supper. It was held at a little restaurant near my
lodgings run by a couple from Amdo. He had been a lawyer
in Qinghai province, a well-qualified and respected member
of provincial society in China. He told me how he had
walked through snowfields with a baby strapped to his back
to reach 'freedom in exile'.

I looked around the busy dining room. Most of the
other tables were occupied by novice monks. They were
watching a televised football match involving Manchester
United and some other European team.

After dinner I hitched a ride up to McLeod Ganj, but

there was no way we could make it to the central bus stand. A large crowd had formed and they were watching a group of Tibetans perform a traditional dance. The men wore trousers, shirts, even baseball caps; but the women were resplendent in their best striped aprons and had ornaments of silver and coral attached to their long tresses. They all locked arms and formed a circle. An old lady began the singing, and then the responses ran to and fro, the men answering the women and then the women taking up the refrain. Some of the younger men were obviously unfamiliar with the rapid dance steps, but the elders showed the way.

'Hey, what's this going on?' shouted an American woman just behind me.

'They are from Amdo', replied a soft-spoken Tibetan, 'from near where the Dalai Lama was born. This is the dance of their village.'

'But why go dancing right here?' she queried. And it is true, dancing around Dharamsala's central bus stand does have certain drawbacks – including frustrated taxi drivers honking their horns at you.

'They do not live in Dharamsala,' he explained. 'The Losar Festival is now finishing. They are waiting for the bus to take them back to their settlement.'

The bus must have been very late in arriving, for the dance and the sad refrains continued for more than an hour. I never discovered what settlement in India they came from. But that was not the point. Their dance was to mark the ending of the Losar celebrations and to reaffirm their identity as Amdowas and Tibetans. It was a dignified and haunting performance; but the reaction from other Tibetans in the crowd was subdued. Perhaps they recognized in that dance an expression of their own yearning to return in freedom to their homeland. And perhaps they too knew, in their heart of hearts, that it would not happen during their lifetimes.

Chapter Five

NEPAL I – THE RULING DYNASTY

I arrived in Kathmandu with a sense of foreboding. There was no rational explanation for this. The weather was clear and we had enjoyed spectacular views of the Himalayas during the flight up from Delhi. Looking down, I could follow our progress across the Terai, the low-lying belt of country that borders on India. Once it had been covered in dense, malarial jungle; but since eradication programmes were introduced in the 1950s much of the forest has been cleared, making this the richest agricultural land in Nepal.

This fertile landscape was frequently scarred by pale slash-marks which broadened out as they entered the plains. These I recognized as the flood-courses of rivers; but during this season they carried little water and sandbanks glittered in the spring sunshine. Then we crossed the first range of foothills, gradually losing height, so that when we met the much higher Mahabharat Lekh the confusion of hill-top hamlets and bare paddy were in plain view, only a few hundred feet below.

The country was so broken up by mountain ridges and gorges that it was easy to see why, for much of its history, Nepal had remained divided between fifty or more princi-palities, each of them based around a river valley. Also, why it had not attracted many invaders. That series of natural barriers, the Terai's jungles, the successive ranges of hills, the physical difficulties of moving an army from place to place, posed a serious deterrent to all but the most determined conqueror.

The plane banked and dropped into the Kathmandu Valley. Now there was less to see, for above the capital there rose a dense pall of half-combusted diesel fumes, the noxious exhalations of thousands of clapped-out trucks and buses and motor-rickshaws. I knew from previous visits that Kathmandu had a pollution problem, but now it has grown so bad that it makes your eyes sting. It was impossible to see the mountains even on a clear day like this one.

Maybe that was what had brought on my depression. Or maybe it started during the ride in from the airport, when I caught a glimpse of the sacred Bagmati River and saw how it has been reduced to a pitiful trickle, clogged with refuse and untreated sewage and the outpourings of all the carpet factories that have sprung up around Kathmandu.

Or was it the taxi-driver's attempt at conversation, his explaining how he was a Sudra – a member of the lowest of Hindu castes except the Dalits or 'untouchables' – in the hope that this would make me give him a bigger tip? Or allowing him to take me first to 'his best friend's' hotel in Thamel? It was, predictably, a dump; though I was less upset by this than seeing how the entire district of Thamel has become a rats' nest of budget hotels, souvenir shops, trekking agencies, Internet cafes, and eateries selling every kind of food apart from Nepali. It now claims to be the 'Ibiza of the Himalayas', whatever that means apart from being able to purchase just about anything that money can buy – drugs, child prostitutes, you name it. Anyway, it looked to me as if Thamel had sold its soul, and a lot more besides, to earn just a few more tourist dollars.

'Poor old Kathmandu . . .' I have heard that refrain too many times – from Nepalese, long-term expats, anyone who can remember how things were before. But before what? The late arrival of democracy in Nepal in 1990? Or does it go further back, to the decades when the Shah Kings were still in charge and prodded their subjects down the road to modernization and 'development'?

These were some of the questions I wanted to ask the present monarch, His Majesty King Birendra Bikram Shah Dev. But first I had to get to see him. And here, on top of all the other reasons for feeling down, was the real source of my anxiety. For despite countless communications with His Majesty's Press Secretary, I had no inkling of whether I would be granted a royal audience or not.

I had arrived in Kathmandu not exactly unannounced, but uninvited. I had no previous connexion with Nepal's royals, so this would be a very different scenario from my seeking to renew my old acquaintance with the King of Bhutan. It would also be different from my visit to the Dalai Lama, who seems to be happy to talk to anyone who might support his cause. I knew that King Birendra liked to keep a low profile. What I did not yet know was that he had not spoken to any foreign writer or journalist for more than eight years. If I had been aware of the odds I wouldn't have caught the flight that morning.

On the other hand, I very much wanted to meet King Birendra. Not only is he is the only ruling Hindu monarch in the world, he is still revered by many Nepalese as an incarnation of Lord Vishnu. In other words, he is a god–king – though I was aware that this very modern-minded monarch, who was educated at Eton before going on to the universities of Harvard and Tokyo, prefers not to be referred to in such terms.

And I wanted to learn more about how monarchy functions in Nepal these days. For the Kingdom of Nepal is by far the largest Himalayan country to have retained its independence. It covers 90,000 square miles of extremely varied terrain, and its 24 million people speak as many different languages and dialects as survive in the whole of Western Europe. That they should have been welded together into a single nation state, and then remained free of colonization, is nothing short of miraculous. For as the founder of the Nepalese state, King Prithvi Narayan Shah (1743–75), famously asserted, Nepal is 'like a yam between two boulders', having as its immediate neighbours two of the most expansionist powers in Asia – Imperial China and British India. Of course China is now a 'People's Republic', while India prides itself on being 'the world's largest democracy'. But the geo-politics are much the same.

Everything would seem to have conspired against Nepal's emerging as an independent sovereign state – its geography, the diversity of its peoples, the proximity of colonial powers. Until the eighteenth century it was just a collection of squabbling principalities ruled over by 'hill rajas', no different from any of the minor princely states that were being absorbed into British India. Then along came the Shah dynasty. Rarely has the creation of a unified country, its survival as an independent entity, and its final emergence into the modern world, been so closely linked with a single royal house. It was the heir to this remarkable legacy that I wanted to meet. To be honest, that was the only reason I had come back to Kathmandu.

I moved into the Manaslu, a quiet place in Lazimpath that seemed a world away from all the hawkers and hustlers of Thamel. The hotel is surrounded by gardens that had once formed part of the grounds of an old Rana Palace, and there is a large aviary stocked with Himalayan pheasant and other rare birds. It was within easy walking distance of Narayan-hitti Palace, should I be required to go there. I had a beer and some vegetable pakoras out on the lawns before putting through a call to Mr Panday, the king's press secretary.

'Mr M.B. Panday is not here. Are you also wishing to speak to Mr N.R. Pandey?'

This left me somewhat confused, as the two surnames are pronounced exactly the same. So there were two Mr Pandeys in the same office? I was aware that this was a fairly common name among Nepalis of the Brahmin or priestly caste. I also knew that Brahmins enjoyed a near monopoly of all the higher positions in government service. Even so . . .

While I was still hesitating, the voice down the line chipped in: 'Mr M.B. Panday is only secretary. Mr N.R. Pandey is principal press secretary. Therefore he is Mr Panday's boss.'

'Then please could you put me through to Mr N.R. Pandey.'

'Please wait.'

I did so, wondering all the while whether I was doing the right thing by changing horses – or Pandeys – in midstream. The Palace switchboard took an unconscionably long time finding the right extension.

Then I heard someone clearing their throat.

'Pandey speaking,' he announced. No Mr. No identifying initials. This must be the head man.

I told him about my long-standing request for an audience, all the correspondence with his colleague, Mr M.B. Panday.

'Yes, yes. I have seen the file.'

'And do you think it is possible?'

'Perhaps . . . But I must inform you that His Majesty is actually out-of-station. He is taking some rest, together with Her Majesty, in Pokhara. For the sake of his health. You know that only recently His Majesty was in London on account of his heart condition? Their Majesties will not be returning to Kathmandu for some days now.'

Not the best news in the world. And his tone was that of a deliberately busy man who found himself being irritated by a fly.

'Well, perhaps after they return,' I suggested hopefully.

'We shall see. This matter has yet to be put before His Majesty.'

'In the meantime,' I persisted, 'I would like to meet up with you.'

'Both tomorrow and the day after are public holidays,' he said, scarcely concealing his glee. 'The earliest I can see you is after three days. Come to the West Gate of the palace at, say, 2 p.m. Goodbye, Mr Gregson.'

I had the distinct impression of having been given the brush-off. Also, that Mr Pandey might have been economical with the truth about the king's whereabouts. That same afternoon I watched a large helicopter swoop down and land in the palace grounds. The next morning I learned that the king and queen had made a visit by helicopter to Lumbini, the birthplace of Lord Buddha in southern Nepal, though where they flew on to was unclear. Still, I had no choice but to hope that Mr Pandey would be more positive next time, for I was told that access to the king is strictly controlled by the Palace Secretariat.

I now found myself with time on my hands, but I was not in the mood for sightseeing. Instead I looked through my notes on Nepal's history and more recent political developments, to prepare myself for an interview which now seemed unlikely to happen.

It was scant consolation to reflect that at one time the odds against there being a member of the Gorkha branch of the Shah family on the throne of Nepal were even more unlikely. If such a proposition had been raised before Robert Clive in Calcutta or the Mughal Emperor in Delhi, it would have been laughed out of court.

For the distant ancestors of King Birendra were very minor hill rajas indeed. Like most other princely rulers in the central Himalayan region, they were Hindus of the Kshatrya or warrior caste. They claimed to be the descendants of Rajput princes of the Khan family who left their homelands in Rajasthan after the invading Muslims sacked the great citadel of Chittor. Like many other Rajput clans, they sought refuge in the hills, entering what is now western Nepal at some point between the fourteenth and late fifteenth century (the chronicles offer varying accounts). In other words, they arrived as refugees.

Different branches of the same Khan family set themselves up as rajas of eight Chaubisi principalities, including Gorkha, calling themselves Shaha or Shahi. They brought with them traditions of Hindu kingship going back to Vedic times, including the belief that they were ultimately descended from the gods. While it may seem remarkable that the kings of Nepal are still regarded as incarnations of Vishnu, similar genealogies claiming divine descent were commonplace among the hill rajas – and, indeed, among the Hindu rajas and maharajas down in the plains of India who continued to rule over far more extensive princely states until after the British left in 1947.

The Shahs of Gorkha controlled a small territory immediately to the west of the Kathmandu Valley. Until the mid-eighteenth century, the Kingdom of Gorkha was just one of twenty-four Chaubisi principalities – some larger, some even smaller – which divided up the central hill country between them. Further west were the twenty-two Baisi principalities, each ruled by one of the Baisi rajas. Such was the political fragmentation that no dominant power could emerge in the hills; for as soon as one hill raja looked threatening, the others joined together in a defensive alliance.

The only region with sufficient manpower and economic resources to become a dominant power was the Kathmandu Valley. It was then known as Nepal (originally the term applied only to this fertile and populous valley), and during the Middle Ages its Malla kings had extended their rule over large areas beyond the surrounding mountains. But in 1482 the Malla dynasty had split into three rival branches, each of them ruling from one of the valley's historic capitals – Kathmandu, Patan and Bhadgaon. From then on, these three kingdoms vied with each other for supremacy; though usually the most powerful was held in check by the other two combining against it.

The wealth and refinement of these courts can still be seen in the palaces and temples around the Durbar Squares where religious festivals and mass audiences were held. True, the mainly Buddhist Newari population of the Kathmandu Valley was more given to trade and artisanal crafts than to soldiering. But their kings could command enough members of the martial castes – principally Magars and Chhetris – to defend themselves against even a confederation of hill rajas.

In terms of resources, then, any one of these valley kingdoms was more than a match for the tiny hill state of Gorkha. It had no significant industries of its own and was not even situated on a major trade route. By the mid-eighteenth century its population was around 12,000 households – hardly a sound base from which to set forth and conquer the greatest empire ever seen in the Himalayas. Yet that is precisely what the rajas of Gorkha did within just two generations, beginning with King Prithvi Narayan Shah the Great.

From the outset he realized that the Kathmandu Valley was the key. In the collection of his sayings known as the *Dibya Upadesh*, Prithvi Narayan recalled how he once climbed a ridge overlooking the valley and was inspired by a vision of glorious conquest:

'From Chandragiri's top I asked, "Which is Nepal?" They showed me, saying "That is Bhadgaon, that is Patan, and there lies Kathmandu." The thought came to my heart that if I might be king of these three cities, why, let it be so.'

It took more than twenty-five years of hard campaigning to achieve his aim.

Initially he tried a direct assault and was repulsed before the hill-top town of Kirtipur. He then switched to a strategy of encirclement, occupying the high ridges and laying siege to forts which guarded the main routes into the valley. One of his aims was to cut the twin trade routes to Tibet, for one of the valley kings' most lucrative businesses was minting coins – the Tibetans having plentiful supplies of gold dust and silver bullion, but no coinage of their own. The Malla kings made a handsome profit by turning out an increasingly debased coinage for use in Tibet. By cutting the trade routes, Prithvi Narayan Shah denied his enemies these revenues and mounted what was effectively an economic blockade on the whole Kathmandu Valley. The beleaguered Malla kings called on the East India Company for assistance, but the British expeditionary force was ambushed and cut to pieces in this, their first ever encounter with the Gurkhas.

The Gorkhali armies then moved down into the valley and laid siege to Kathmandu. The attack was timed to coincide with the Hindu festival of Indra Jatra. While King Jaya Prakash and his subjects were busy with their religious celebrations, the Gorkhalis appear to have just marched into the city. Prithvi Narayan Shah ascended the throne already set up in Durbar Square for the festival. The date was 26 September 1769.

The neighbouring city of Patan fell two weeks later without a fight. Bhadgaon, where King Jaya Prakash had taken refuge, put up much stiffer resistance. But after two days of street-to-street fighting, the last of the Malla strongholds surrendered. Prithvi Narayan Shah had, against all the odds, conquered the entire Kathmandu Valley. It is for this determined feat of arms that he is still acclaimed as the founder of the modern state of Nepal.

It would be more accurate to say that he placed the Shah dynasty of Gorkha firmly on the throne of Nepal (in its original sense) and made it possible for a unified country roughly corresponding to modern Nepal to emerge. Although he has left many useful precepts on good governance, from the need to maintain a sound currency through to making generous allowances to war widows, Prithvi Narayan Shah did not attempt to build a unified state. When he conquered a kingdom he generally left the machinery of government unchanged.

What he did build up was a very effective and disciplined army. Recruits were drawn to his service by the promise of grants of land for their families in newly conquered territories. The rank and file were usually given *jagirs*, temporary land grants that reverted to the crown. Generals and highly valued officers were rewarded with *birta*, lands held in perpetuity.

Members of the warrior castes and tribes were enticed into Prithvi Narayan Shah's service because there was already a shortage of fertile land in their native hills. It was land-hunger that provided the manpower needed to make fresh conquests, which in turn could be distributed among the soldiery. This system of recruitment and reward had a built-in impulse to further territorial expansion. Everything turned on the king's success in battle.

The Gorkhali armies were among the first to make effective use of muskets in hill warfare and, once he had the riches of the Kathmandu Valley at his disposal, Prithvi Narayan Shah was able to purchase more of these weapons. He now turned his armies west against the Chaubisi rajas who had so often tried to invade Gorkha while his main army was deployed elsewhere. But so fearful were these hill rajas of the new power in the land that for once they forgot their internal disputes and formed a grand alliance which succeeded in holding back the Gorkhali advance. So Prithvi Narayan Shah turned east, conquering all the hill states as far as the Kingdom of Sikkim and acquiring a valuable strip of the eastern Terai.

This was the extent of his conquests when he died of a fever at Nuwakot in 1775. He was fifty-two years old. Queen Narendra Laxmi followed her husband's corpse to the funeral pyre where, in keeping with Hindu traditions, she performed sati and perished in the flames.

Prithvi Narayan Shah was first and foremost a great military leader. Given the slender resources at his command, military adventurer might be more accurate. He committed the forces of tiny Gorkha against the powerful kingdoms of the Kathmandu Valley and won out. For this, he might be compared with King Gustavus Adolphus of Sweden or Frederick the Great of Prussia. By the end of his life, the House of Gorkha held all of what is now central and eastern Nepal. He had also created a military machine capable of further conquests, so that within forty years the Shah dynasty ruled over a vast Himalayan empire that is usually referred to as 'Greater Nepal'.

It is hardly surprising that Prithvi Naryan Shah was held up as a model for later kings and crown princes of Nepal. His deeds were recorded in many chronicles; his dictums in the *Dibya Upadesh*, the collection of discourses he gave shortly before his death. But perhaps his greatest quality was the ability to inspire his people to follow him through so long and hazardous an undertaking.

He made his dreams of conquest something akin to a joint enterprise from which the ordinary peasant-soldier – and not just the royal family and nobility – stood to gain. He is portrayed as having been close to his people, always ready to listen to their problems and to provide some remedy. 'If you seek justice, then go to Gorkha' remains a popular expression to this day.

This image of an understanding and caring ruler has come down to inspire – or haunt – later generations of the Shah dynasty. Did the present monarch, King Birendra, ever try to measure up to his celebrated ancestor? And how far do any of these traditions survive in the way a modern monarchy sees itself and operates? These were some of the questions I wanted to put to the king – if, that is, I was ever allowed to see him.

The evening before I was to meet His Majesty's principal press secretary I felt a fresh wind blowing out of the north-west. This usually clears the smog and haze which had made the Himalayan peaks invisible for three days, so I decided to rise well before dawn and go out to Nagarkot, an old hill fort perched high above the Kathmandu Valley's rim which has become a popular spot for viewing the mountains.

The drive out was in the dark and we were delayed by all the other buses carrying hopeful dawn-watchers, arriving just too late to see the sunrise. But the air was crisp and clear, and the mountains in full view. I scurried up to a railing just as they turned from gold to palest yellow. For a moment the Great Himalaya, the mightiest mountain range on earth, appeared to be composed not of rock and ice but of some soft, malleable substance like yak butter – the dark, snowless ridges resembling the veins of mould which impart such a distinctive flavour to Tibetan-style tea. Then the sun climbed above a ridge to the east and the eternal snows assumed their daytime brilliance.

'The finest natural boundary in the world.' That is how Sir Henry McMahon viewed the Himalayas. Given his concerns over the security of the Indian Empire, he was only too happy to propose that their highest ridges should form the dividing line between British India and Central Asia. This principle was officially adopted in 1912, and the 'McMahon Line' is still the basis for much of the Sino-Indian border. Certainly, looking out from Nagarkot at that line of majestic giants, from the Annapurna Massif in the west to Everest and Kanchenjunga far to the east, they seemed an impenetrable barrier.

But to the people of the high country – who venerated their mountains as the abode of the gods and would never have dreamt of climbing them before the 'mad foreigners' arrived – there has always been a way through. Many of the rivers that flow south to meet the Ganges have their head-waters beyond the main Himalayan range, on the very rim of the Tibetan plateau.

Not far from where I now stood was the gorge carved out by the Bhote Khosi. I had travelled that way into Tibet along the new highway, crossing the 'Friendship Bridge' into Chinese-controlled territory. But for more than two thousand years beforehand it had been an established trade route between Tibet and the Kathmandu Valley.

To the west was another of the main arteries of trans-

Himalayan trade, which passed through Kyrung. The basic necessities of life passed through this mountain barrier: salt and wool coming down from Tibet, rice and worked metals going up. The high passes had their dangers; but so too did the malarial jungles of the lower hills and the Terai that lead down to the Gangetic Plain.

The Himalayas may present a formidable obstacle, but they are not impenetrable. Armies have crossed them many times and fought successful campaigns, despite extended lines of communication. The Tibetan King Songsten Gampo extended his rule south of the Himalayas. More recently, Gorkha armies invaded Tibet and a Chinese-led army advanced to just short of the Kathmandu Valley. In 1904 Colonel Younghusband led the British expeditionary force to Lhasa. In 1962 the People's Liberation Army fought its way across the McMahon Line and pushed the Indian army down to the plains. Impressive they might be — awe-inspiring, even — but the Himalayas have never been the impenetrable barrier that armchair strategists imagine them to be.

Apart from the panoramic views and a rash of recently built hotels with names like Space Mountain and At the End of the Universe, there is not much to Nagarkot. It used to be a fort and look-out post, not a hill village. I had breakfast in a teashop before returning to Kathmandu. As we descended towards the valley we passed a line of elephants being led down to a river. Bare trees were about to come into bud; the terraced paddy was ploughed and ready for planting. But there had been no rain for weeks, and the farmers were complaining.

Soon we rejoined the strip development that spreads like tentacles along the main roads out of Kathmandu. New-built houses, each sitting in the centre of a generous plot, were eating up what is left of the valley's arable land. Many were left unfinished, with steel struts sticking up above the roof like prayer flags, awaiting such time as when the owner's finances might permit adding another storey. A property boom had come and passed, leaving many half-finished buildings (which are also exempted from taxes). There was no evidence of planning controls and land use was extremely wasteful. Still, the situation in this eastern part of the valley was better than in the west, where scattered building projects have crept up into the surrounding hills.

It is only when seen from above, in its entirety, that the sheer size of the Kathmandu Valley can be appreciated. It resembles a huge bowl, and legend has it that this was once a lake which was drained by either Manjushri or Krishna carving out a gorge. Geologists have confirmed that the central valley was indeed once the bottom of a lake, which accounts for both its rich soil and unusual breadth compared with the steep river valleys normally found in the Himalayan region. Only the Vale of Kashmir, centred around its lakes, is of greater extent.

The availability of so much fertile land made it possible for cities to develop earlier around Kathmandu than else-where in the hills, and its position astride two trans-Himalayan trade routes encouraged a rich and diverse culture. The valley was home to both Hindus and Buddhists, as is attested by such ancient temples as Pashupathinath and the great Buddhist stupa at Boudhanath.

It was from here that one of the main impulses that

spread Mahayana Buddhism throughout the Tibetan world originated. The Nepalese princess Brikhuti, who married the Tibetan King Songsten Gampo, is credited with bringing with her to Lhasa some Newari craftsmen who built the original Jokhang Temple. The pagoda style of architecture first developed in the Kathmandu Valley, from where it spread to Inner Asia, China and Japan. As a cultural crossroads, the cities of the valley had an importance far beyond their size and population.

And from the earliest times there had been kings in this land. The historical Buddha was himself a prince of the Sakya line who, even if they were little more than clan chieftains, ruled over an area of what is now the Nepalese Terai in the sixth century BC. Since then many dynasties – the Kiratas, the Licchavis, the Mallas – have come and gone.

Last in this line are the Shah dynasty, still reigning after more than 200 years. Would I be allowed to meet King Birendra? As we drove through the grimy outskirts of Kathmandu, I began worrying about what kind of reception I would get from the present king's press secretary, Mr N.R. Pandey.

It was only a short walk to the royal palace from where I was staying in Lazimpath. I had put on a jacket and tie for the interview and felt conspicuous out on the street. Westerners who wear this kind of rig usually move around Kathmandu in chauffeur-driven cars, not on foot. So it was only to be expected that one richshaw-wallah after another pedalled slowly alongside, touting for business. 'You go to Thamel?' they shouted. 'Durbar Margh?' If I had told them where I was walking to they would have thought I was either lying or utterly mad. Visitors to Narayanhitti Palace don't walk the streets.

And perhaps they are right. During that short stroll I very nearly fell into an uncovered manhole while trying to avoid stepping on a pile of refuse that overflowed the gutter. A stray dog cocked its leg and came close to pissing on my foot. Even as I walked beside the palace's high, blank walls I tripped over a broken paving stone. My legs seemed unable to cope with all the uneven surfaces. Maybe it was because I was nervous. I knew a lot depended on this interview.

At the West Gate were half a dozen smartly turned-out soldiers, small men in khaki green uniforms with red sashes which signified they belonged to the Royal Guard. They wore the broad-brimmed hats made famous by Gurkha regiments all over the world and each had a *kukri* – the deadly curved blade concealed within a plain leather scabbard – tucked into his belt. I gave them Mr Pandey's name and was told to wait.

After five minutes a civil servant wearing a black coat and similarly sober version of the traditional Nepali cap known as a *topi* appeared at the gate. It was not Mr Pandey, but a junior official who was to escort me to the Palace Secretariat. I was told to wear a visitor's badge with the royal emblem – a six-sided star encompassing a raised sword – embossed upon the plastic, and given a paper chit which I was to hand in on leaving the palace precincts. The official accompanied me up the drive towards the palace's west wing before steering me towards an undistinguished range of secretariat buildings on our left. I was shown into a barely furnished waiting room.

'Mr Pandey will not be long now,' I was told.

I had plenty of time to observe the spring sunlight filtering in through the barred windows, the unmoving fans overhead, the room's drably functional desks and plastic-covered chairs. All the fittings seemed to date from the 1970s, which was when the present Narayanhitti Palace was rebuilt. I tried to think up reasons I should be granted an audience with the king. None of them were that convincing. In fact, I was in much the same position as any other humble petitioner, totally dependent on the king's favour. If, that is, he was even aware of my existence. The Palace Secretariat filters out most such requests in advance. Which was why I needed to persuade Mr N.R. Pandey to present my case favourably to the king.

The door opened, and the same junior official announced the arrival of His Majesty's principal press secretary. He was older than I had expected, and from behind his gold-rimmed glasses he eyed me up with a world-weary tolerance that is rarely attained except by members of the priestly caste, the Brahmins. He wore a dark jacket over the tight trousers and loose shirting that is Nepalese national dress, and perched on his head was the obligatory topi. Under his arm was a documents folder which I guessed contained their dossier on me. He didn't bother to open it.

Instead, he examined me as if I were some strange creature from another world. It made me feel like an importunate schoolboy who had been put forward for a top scholarship. He spoke slowly and deliberately, spelling out for me what he called 'the reality of the situation'.

His Majesty had been unwell, and it was unlikely that he would be seeing any additional visitors. As yet, my request had not been put before the king. Of course this could still be done, though Mr Pandey 'doubted very much' that a decision could be taken on it within the next fortnight. His Majesty had many public engagements and needed to attend to his constitutional duties. Also, it was 'most unfortunate' that I had arrived in Kathmandu while there was a general election pending. In such circumstances it was impossible for His Majesty to talk to any journalists or even for it to become known that he had met them. Otherwise it might be construed that he had in some way influenced the outcome of the election.

'Since the reinstatement of the multi-party system', Mr Pandey informed me, 'the role of our king has been fixed by the constitution. And all matters pertaining to this constitution have been most scrupulously observed by His Majesty. Indeed,' he continued with a wintry smile, 'there are those who say that His Majesty is the only one to have done so.'

I tried to protest that I was not writing for a newspaper and that whatever I learned would not become public until long after the elections were over. He could have full confidence in me. After all, I had always gone through the correct channels, the embassy in London and his own office, rather than trying to get to the king through other members of the royal family. Mr Pandey's eyes showed a flicker of interest at this possibility of an outflanking manoeuvre.

This was pure bluff on my part. I had no such royal connexions; but Mr Pandey wasn't to know that. It was like playing a game of poker. Unfortunately, I had the feeling that my adversary had dealt with this particular gambit many times before.

Mr Pandey held up his hand. 'We shall see what can be done,' he announced, keeping alive a glimmer of hope and at the same time minimizing the attractions of my seeking help outside the proper channels. He made it clear that he was the official gatekeeper and I, for all intents and purposes, potentially an intruder. If I tried to gain access through any other means he would get to know about it. And his report would be very negative indeed.

Most of this was intimated rather than spoken out loud. The palace is home to an old-fashioned court culture where disagreeable consequences are merely hinted at. Throughout the interview, Mr Pandey remained courteous in the extreme. Yet I was very much aware that I had stumbled into a world of palace politics, of internal rivalries and unseen pecking orders, and that I had no idea whatsoever how to deal with it. I would have preferred a straight answer – even if it was negative – to the prospect of having to remain in orbit around so nebulous a world.

I thought of the frustration of the British Residents despatched to Kathmandu in the early nineteenth century, who were shown every courtesy but rigorously excluded from the Durbar. Their reports to the governor-general in Calcutta complained of the obsessive secrecy of the Nepalese court, its intrigues and deliberate misinformation, the unwillingness of any public official to take a decision or even utter an unqualified statement.

They at least had their spies. I was left second-guessing every word and gesture. As when Mr Pandey suggested I contact certain court officials to learn more about the traditional aspects of Nepal's monarchy – the royal preceptor on religious rituals; the astrologer royal on the choice of auspicious dates. Taken at face value, it was extremely helpful of him. But by now I was sufficiently suspicious of his motives to wonder whether this was just another ploy, a means of putting me off the scent. I was also pretty certain that these same officials would report straight back to him about the kind of questions I had been asking. Did I really want to let myself in for this type of positive vetting? Already I felt infected by the climate of doubt and suspicion.

What Mr Pandey did not tell me was that he was about to retire as His Majesty's principal press secretary, or that during his term of office he had consistently kept writers and journalists at bay. Why should he risk a different approach at this stage in his career? When I asked him what the Press Secretariat actually did, he replied that they provided His Majesty with speeches and messages for the Nepalese New Year's Day, for Constitution Day, for Democracy Day, and for the festival of Durga Puja, when Nepalis come in their thousands from all over the country and line up in front of the palace to receive the *tika* – a Hindu blessing which involves smearing the forehead with a coloured paste – from the king's own hand. His Majesty had also given a major speech on World Food Day. Obviously the press secretaries had enough on their hands without actually having to deal with the press.

At the close of this interview, Mr Pandey and I shook hands most cordially. I already knew he wasn't prepared to help me. And I was convinced that King Birendra hadn't even been told of my request. My only chance was to play along with the press secretary while trying to find some other avenue into the palace – and not just the officials whose names he had given out.

But what really worried me was the constitutional position of the king. If he was really so constrained in what he could do and say, then I was doomed to failure. And with gatekeepers like Mr Pandey, how could the king ever get his message across? *If* he had a message, that is. For while I was aware that King Birendra graced the openings of international conferences and the like with his presence, in his speeches he was steered away from saying anything that could be construed as politically charged. As for the formal messages to the Nepalese people delivered on national holidays, their content was so bland they made Queen Elizabeth II's Christmas broadcasts seem positively riveting by comparision.

It occurred to me that since the coming of multi-party democracy to Nepal eight years previously, the king had maintained such a low profile as to be almost invisible. And while he could come and go as he pleased, he could not let the outside world know what he thought.

Such self-restraint may have become habitual among longer-established constitutional monarchies in Europe. But Nepal is a very different case. King Birendra was effectively in charge of the government until the 'Spring Uprising' of 1990, and the democratic parties still worry about the possibility of a royalist coup – however remote that may be. The leaders of political parties are very sensitive to anything that might promote the king's power-base or popularity among his people. His movements may be free; but in terms of what he can say or do, the king is surrounded by invisible constraints. In that sense, at least, he is like a prisoner in his own palace. Those were my thoughts as I handed in my security badge and was escorted through the steel gates out into Kathmandu's rush-hour.

It would not be the first time Nepal's kings have been kept as virtual prisoners within their palaces. For most of the nineteenth and early twentieth centuries they had been deliberately secluded and kept away from the real levers of power until they were little more than figureheads. That was certainly the case throughout the 104 years of Rana Oligarchy, though the decline set in much earlier.

Prithvi Narayan Shah recognized some of the potential dangers. Before he died, the founding monarch foresaw problems arising over the succession. He therefore forbade his brothers to carve up the lands he had united – as was common practice among hill rajas – and ordained that the principle of primogeniture always be observed.

His eldest son, Pratrap Singh, inherited the nascent Kingdom of Nepal more or less intact. But his premature death in 1780 meant there would be a long minority, for his son Rana Bahadur was still an infant. Before long the court in Kathmandu was riddled with intrigue and the unity of purpose that had previously distinguished the House of Gorkha from other hill rajas was dissolved. The Queen's Mother's party remained in control until her death, whereupon the boy-king's uncle, Bahadur Shah, assumed the regency and promptly purged the court of hostile factions.

Such infighting might well have spelt doom for the Shah dynasty. But, although they failed to produce another king of Prithvi Narayan's stature, they were great survivors. The Kingdom of Nepal did not disintegrate into rival principalities. Rather, the military machine they had created required fresh conquests. The war effort itself imposed a semblance of unity among the rival factions. And in mountain warfare the Gorkhalis achieved one stunning success after another.

Within forty years of Prithvi Narayan Shah's death they had conquered all the territories that make up modern Nepal and much else besides. To the east, their armies conquered a large part of the Kingdom of Sikkim, plundering the wealthy Buddhist monasteries there and extending

Gorkha control as far as the River Teesta. But their westward expansion was even more spectacular. In a series of swift campaigns, Gorkha armies overwhelmed the hill rajas of Garwhal and Kumaon (now part of India) and pushed on towards Kangra, the hill region around Dharamsala. At its height this Himalayan empire, commonly known as 'Greater Nepal', covered an area almost twice as large as the present kingdom.

Gorkha expansion was only checked when they ran into even stronger military powers – the Sikhs in the west and the British down in the plains. The Gorkhas laid claim to extensive tracts down in the Terai, but some villages were contested by local Indian rulers who called on the British to support them. The East India Company was only too happy to do so, for it had long sought an excuse to intervene in Nepal with an eye to opening up its markets and installing a British Resident in Kathmandu.

Since their previous expedition into Nepal had ended in disaster, the British mustered a huge force and advanced in five separate columns along a seven hundred-mile front. Initially the Gorkhalis' knowledge of mountain warfare gave them the upper hand, and four columns had to withdraw with heavy casualties. But eventually weight of numbers and the effective use of mountain artillery told. With British forces poised to march on Kathmandu, the Nepalese government was forced to sue for peace.

By the terms of the Treaty of Sugauli (1816), roughly a third of the Kingdom of Nepal was lost for ever. The western provinces of Kumaon and Garwhal were annexed outright by the British. In the east, all the lands between the Teesta and Mechi rivers were restored to the Kingdom of Sikkim (the British immediately 'leased' Darjeeling District from the Chogyal and started employing Nepali labour to clear the land for planting tea). A broad strip of valuable Terai lowlands was either annexed by the Company or restored to an Indian princely ruler. Apart from these territorial concessions, Nepal was in future to be 'guided' by Britain in its foreign relations. The British Resident was to be the only foreign representative in Kathmandu. It was an 'unequal treaty' which left Nepal seriously weakened, its status reduced to that of a client state.

The British promised not to intervene in Nepal's internal affairs. They knew only too well the difficulties of campaigning in the hills. The costs of maintaining direct rule would almost certainly outweigh any commercial benefits. Besides, the British were more interested in recruiting members of Nepal's fighting tribes, whose valour had left a deep impression, into their own Indian army. Arrangements for the recruitment of Nepalese subjects were built into the peace treaty and, although the authorities in Kathmandu initially resisted this outflow of skilled mercenaries, the Gurkha Regiments usually trace their origins back to 1816. They soon won the respect of their British officers, and it was this, as much as anything, that persuaded the Imperial Power to stay out of Nepalese affairs and eventually to recognize that the kingdom's status should be on a different footing to that of other Indian princely states. Besides, as a nominally independent country, Nepal served as a useful buffer zone against any incursions by the Chinese or Russian empires.

Now that the kingdom was hemmed in on three sides by British India there was little scope for military expansion (henceforth the dream of a Greater Nepal would be pursued by emigration, not annexation). For a society in which honours and rewards depended so heavily on new conquests, this was a disaster. Forced to turn inwards, the court in Kathmandu engaged in increasingly bitter infighting where poisoning and a swift thrust of the kukri were the preferred means of achieving one's objectives. In 1806 King Bahadur Shah was stabbed to death by his illegitimate brother in front of the assembled court. Over the next forty years, numerous prime ministers were murdered and entire noble families massacred. The Borgias could scarcely have done worse.

The Shah dynasty survived this turmoil, though its kings were no longer fully in control. The rules of primogeniture were generally observed, the succession going to the senior queen's eldest son. While the custom of the crown prince taking several brides at a very young age ensured that the royal line continued, it also produced a host of royal siblings – half-brothers and uncles and royal bastards – whose position at court was assured, but who had no fiefdoms of their own. They had little to do apart from conspiring with one or other of the leading Gorkha families – the Pandes, the Thapas, the Basniats – in the hope of furthering their personal position.

The junior queens and royal mistresses had a more immediate interest in promoting the chances of their own offspring ascending to the throne. Attempts at poisoning or deliberately infecting other royal claimants with deadly diseases were just a part of their repertoire. Behind the veneer of ceremony and exquisite manners, the court was riddled with intrigue; and for this the royal family itself was as much to blame as anyone else. So long as the powerful Prime

Minister Bhim Sen Thapa remained in control, nobody dared make a move. But when King Rajendra attempted to rule by himself all the conspirators came out of the woodwork.

The fifteen years of Rajendra's direct rule (1832–47) were an unmitigated disaster for the Shah dynasty. Unable to control his capriciously cruel son, Crown Prince Surendra, the king chose to co-opt him as joint ruler. Then, at the request of the Council of Nobles, his junior queen was also brought into the government – at which the British Resident quipped that the country was now ruled by 'Mr Nepal, Mrs Nepal and Master Nepal'. But the inclusion of the Junior Queen Laxmi Devi brought new dangers. She was a determined woman, and her real aim was to replace Surendra as crown prince with her own son.

Convinced that her former ally, Prime Minister Mathbar Singh Thapa, had betrayed her and was now pushing for the crown prince to take over the throne, she decided he must be assassinated. The man chosen for the job was a daring young officer called Jang Bahadur Konwar, the eldest son of the kazi who had throttled King Rana Bahadur's killer back in 1806. He also happened to be the proposed victim's nephew.

It is related that the Prime Minister once told Jang Bahadur: 'If the queen orders it, I will kill you and you will kill me.' And that is exactly what happened. Mathbar Singh Thapa was summoned to the queen's chamber and coolly despatched with a bullet to the head by his own nephew.

The royal troika of King Rajendra, Queen Laxmi Devi and Prince Surendra continued much as before. But now the queen's favourite, the low-born Gagan Singh Bhandari, looked after civil affairs, while military matters were dealt with by Jang Bahadur. Both were included in the next coalition ministry, which was equally divided between those whose loyalties lay with the king and crown prince, and the queen's men. Hostility between the two camps prevented any effective government. Then King Rajendra ordered the two sons of the late senior queen to restore the family's honour by assassinating Gagan Singh Bhandari, the junior queen's lover. Not knowing how to go about it, the two princes consulted the Prime Minister and other loyal members of government, who advised they hire a professional assassin to do it for them.

When Queen Laxmi Devi heard that her lover and chief political ally had been murdered, she was determined to wreak revenge. All senior officers of state were summoned to an army depot, known simply as the Kot, which stood just to the north of the royal palace. Jang Bahadur, ostensibly the queen's supporter, arrived early with three full regiments in support. When the king arrived with members of government who, like him, were part of the conspiracy, some sort of showdown seemed inevitable.

The queen demanded to know who had ordered the assassination. There was no response from the assembled notables. She then accused the wrong man and, with exquisite irony, ordered one of the real conspirators to execute him on the spot. The king, fearing that his own part in the plot might be revealed, quietly made his escape. The prime minister arrived and tried to buy time for his fellow conspirators, arguing there should be no executions without a trial. All around the Kot's central courtyard different groups of retainers were preparing for a fight. But the queen, furious that her orders were not being carried out, ran down brandishing a sword at the accused, whom she intended to despatch in person.

It was only then that Jang Bahadur moved forward to escort the queen back to the safety of her balcony. Seconds later firing broke out around the Kot. Jang Bahadur's troops were already in position and massacred everyone inside the courtyard. Among the dead were some thirty nobles, including three out of the four remaining ministers of state. Before the slaughter was over Queen Laxmi Devi had conferred the dual posts of prime minister and commander-in-chief upon Jang Bahadur.

The Kot Massacre of 1846 marked the end of an era. Jang Bahadur swiftly assumed control, deposing both king and queen and installing the feeble-minded Crown Prince Surendra on the throne of Nepal. To consolidate his power-base, he made the prime ministership and all other important positions hereditary, setting up a new Rana dynasty that would rule Nepal for more than a hundred years.

Now the Shah kings really were prisoners in their own palaces. They were revered, even respected. But throughout the Rana oligarchy they had no real power at all.

I went down to the old royal palace, which stands to the east of Durbar Square, with several objects in mind. I wanted to visit the museum inside devoted to more recent kings of Nepal; but this turned out to be shut. I also wanted to seek out the ghosts of royal conspirators, and for this I threaded my way through an archipelago of pagoda-roofed temples to the far side of Upper Durbar Square. It was here that the Kot Massacre took place.

Of the old arsenal, the balcony from which Queen Laxmi Devi demanded revenge for her lover's murder, nothing remains. But there is a certain irony that the site of an infamous massacre should now be occupied by a police station, and I learned that sacrificial buffaloes are still decapitated with a single stroke of the kukri in Kot Square during the festival of Dasain. Whether this is in any way linked to the old nobility who perished here, or is in celebration of Jang Bahadur's triumph, I could not ascertain.

It was late afternoon and worshippers were preparing for their evening *puja*. The soft light glinted off the golden finials projecting skywards from the pagodas around me. Stalls selling incense and other puja materials, garland-vendors with their strings of marigolds, were all doing a brisk trade. The sound of chanting and tinkling bells came from the inner sanctum of one of the larger temples in the square. Now that the daytime tourists had departed, the people of Kathmandu were reclaiming the Old City for themselves.

I walked back towards the old palace, dodging the bicycle-rickshaws and souvenir salesmen who are allowed to ply their trade in Durbar Square, and rested on a stone plinth opposite the vermilion-stained statue of the monkey god, Hanuman, which stands just to the left of the palace gates underneath a gold umbrella. It is from the presence of this deity that the entire royal palace took its name, Hanu-man Dhoka. I noticed that people were still being allowed to enter its precincts and went over to see if I could join them.

'Museum is closed,' announced the ticket-vendor, 'but you may view the chowk and old wing.' So I paid for a full ticket anyway, and scurried past the palace guard. Their uniform was off-white and of an antique design, and on their shoulders rested rifles with bayonets fixed which seemed to be of equal antiquity.

I entered a spacious courtyard known as the Nasal Chowk which is still used for coronations and other royal ceremonies. Most of the buildings to the north and east were originally built in the seventeenth or eighteenth centuries when the Malla kings ruled over Kathmandu. They were refined patrons of the arts, and the delicacy of the carvings around the doorways or along the wooden struts supporting the pagoda-style roofs showed that they used only the best Newari craftsmen.

The Shah dynasty also resided here, for more than a hundred years. It was in this square that Prithvi Narayan Shah was made king during the Indra Jatra Festival, and the image of Indra is still brought from a nearby temple and placed on the coronation platform at that time. Beneath a line of royal portraits stands the ceremonial throne, a sword of state symbolizing the monarch's presence. It is here that the kings of Nepal are still crowned.

Across the courtyard stood an ancient brick building surmounted by pagoda-roofed towers, its upper floor adorned with intricately carved windows that were screened so that the ladies of the court could see what happened below while themselves remaining invisible. I climbed a steep wooden staircase up to the gallery, from which I could look into half a dozen other courtyards.

The old palace appeared to have grown organically rather than according to any clear architectural plan, but I could see how its many separate wings and chowks melded together to create an enclosed world, completely cut off from the crowded city outside. It was well fitted to act as a

royal prison. Which is what it effectively became after Jang
Bahadur and the Ranas took charge.

The people knew that their monarch was in their midst,
even though he was rarely seen and then only on ceremonial
occasions. But before the Shah kings were reduced to mere
figureheads, when they and their ambitious queens held the
power of life and death over even the most exalted of their
subjects . . . then all these different courtyards, this whisper-
ing gallery where I now stood with its screened alcoves and
hidden stairwells, would have been well suited for plotting
treachery. As I walked the empty boards, descending towards
the main courtyard, I could almost hear the ghosts of long-
dead conspirators.

Jang Bahadur was only the first in a long line of all-powerful
Rana prime ministers. He raised up a parallel dynasty by
making himself and his heir maharajas of Kaski and
Lamjung. Appointment to the prime ministership and every
other office of any importance, both civil and military, was
reserved for members of the extended Rana family and made
subject to strict rules of hereditary succession. Jang
Bahadur's niece was married to King Surendra and two of
his daughters to Crown Prince Trailoyka, beginning a tradition of intermarriage between the royal family and Ranas
that continues to this day.

There was a coup d'état in 1885, when the Shumsher
branch of the Ranas replaced the Jang Bahadur line. Otherwise, the Rana oligarchy ran Nepal like a private estate.
They jealously guarded their independence through a combination of currying favour with Imperial Britain and ensuring that, apart from the British Resident, it remained

completely isolated from the outside world. In the first half of the twentieth century it was easier to enter Tibet than Nepal, which under the Ranas really was a 'forbidden kingdom'. That is why all attempts to climb Everest were made from the Tibetan side until after the Rana regime collapsed in 1951.

For all the new building developments, there are still many reminders of the Rana era around Kathmandu. Many of their palaces are still standing, though most of these have now been turned into government offices or luxury hotels. They rear up from behind their high walls like ocean liners of a bygone age, massively impractical.

While the Ranas did not want Europeans entering Nepal, they soon developed European tastes. They wore European-style military uniforms (the officer corps was and still is stuffed with Ranas) with lashings of gold braid, though their headgear – usually a bejewelled helmet with a curving plume of bird-of-paradise feathers – gave them an exotic appearance. Their taste in domestic furnishings was eclectic – chinoiserie, Venetian glass, enormous chandeliers and gilt-framed mirrors. Although their food was cooked according to the strict prescriptions of Hindu caste laws, their dinner service was either of European manufacture or copies made of solid silver and gold.

The Ranas had their palaces built along neoclassical lines, with pediments and colonnades and sweeping drives leading up to pillared carriage-houses. But their preference lay with a heavy, sub-Palladian strain of classicism which they borrowed from the palaces of Indian maharajas rather than the more austere colonial buildings of the British. Whenever there was a choice between a simple or ornate pattern, they plumped for the latter. So the impressive façades of Rana palaces are broken up by overblown Corinthian capitals and cornices from which the carved figures of fishes or auspicious animals peer out. Sometimes this luxuriant detail is further emphasized by being painted in ochre or aquamarine, in striking contrast to the crumbling white stucco of the rest of the building.

While doing the rounds of government officials I visited several of these Rana palaces. The Foreign Ministry occupies a neoclassical pile up in Lazimpath that has been repainted in red, while the most extravagant palace of them all — the thousand-room Singha Durba that was home to the Rana prime ministers — now houses half a dozen departments of government. Perhaps the most evocative of all is the Keshar Mahal, just across the way from the royal palace. Most of it is taken up by the Ministry of Education; but the library wing, complete with the remarkably eclectic collection of books assembled by its former owner, Keshar Shumsher Rana, has been turned into a museum. Here, the spirit of this erudite aristocrat (he was married to King Tribuvhan's sister) still presides.

However, the vast majority of these Rana palaces have been left to rot. For most contemporary Nepalese they represent the values of an era that they feel is best forgotten. True, they are monuments to ostentation and ill-gotten wealth; but they do still form part of the national heritage, and this desire to ignore anything that recalls the 104 years of Rana domination betrays a sense of insecurity about Nepal's recent history.

I put in another call to the royal palace to see if my request to meet King Birendra had progressed in any way. Mr

N.R. Pandey himself took the call. What he told me was not encouraging, though he still would not 'rule it out completely'. I sensed he did this only to keep me dangling, to forestall any moves I might make to open up other lines of communication to the Palace. Which is precisely what I planned to do next.

'Oh, and I almost forgot,' he added, 'I have thought of some people you should see concerning the religious aspects of our monarchy. Their telephone numbers are as follows . . .'

While noting these down I had the distinct impression that, even though we were not in the same room, Mr Pandey was capable of reading my mind. Did he know I had already contacted people with Palace connections? As for the list of names he gave me, I doubted any of them would assist my suit. They might, however, be able to clarify some of the more arcane aspects of Nepal's monarchy, such as the belief that Birendra is a god-king.

For this I went directly to the royal preceptor, who is responsible for instructing the king on religious matters. Like the king's press secretary, his name was Pandey – Nayan Raj Pandey – though there are so many Brahmin families called Pandey that I had no idea whether the two were related or not. He lived in Dilli Bazaar, a busy area south-east of the royal palace. As usual in Kathmandu, there was no proper address. 'Just go to the bus stand', he said confidently down the phone, 'and ask the people there. They will know of my residence.'

Unfortunately, the people I asked by the bus stand had never heard of this Mr Pandey – even though he is the royal preceptor – and I was directed to various other residences, down narrow lanes hemmed in by moss-encrusted walls, before finding the right house. It was an undistinguished modern building in which the Pandey family occupied the first two floors. Removing my shoes by the door (this was a Brahmin household) I was shown into a room full of overstuffed furniture. A little girl rushed in, stared at me in amazement, and rushed out again. Obviously she had the run of the house.

She returned clutching an elderly, bare-headed priest by the hand. 'My grand-daughter,' he explained, smiling benevolently, before detaching his hand and performing a rapid Namaste in my general direction. Shaking hands was obviously out of the question, so I pressed my palms together and returned his salutation. Some tea was ordered for me; he himself would take nothing.

Nayan Raj Pandey sat very upright, his eyes drinking me in as if searching for some invisible aura. 'What do you seek from me?' he asked with disarming simplicity.

I explained that I was interested in the religious aspects of the monarchy. But still he seemed to be under the impression that I had come, like most other visitors to his household, for some advice of a more personal nature. He was relieved to discover that I did not belong to any of the cults that profess some form of Hinduism, for his was an old-fashioned, conservative approach.

'Those who are not born Hindus cannot in this life become Hindus,' he smiled. 'It is not possible. Even when Sonia Gandhi [the Italian-born widow of India's former Prime Minister, Rajiv Gandhi, who now heads the Congress Party] came to Kathmandu, she was not permitted to go into Pashupathinath, our holiest temple. You see, she was born a Catholic, and only became a Hindu later.'

Such conservatism is perhaps only to be expected of a

Brahmin whose family have been royal preceptors since the beginnings of the Shah dynasty. The post, he explained, used to be hereditary, but is now open to all eligible Brahmins who have graduated in Sanskrit. Although belonging to a long line of royal priests, he himself had undertaken lengthy studies of Sanskrit and the Hindu scriptures.

In former times the royal preceptor had also played an important part in meting out justice, for it was he who interpreted the shastras and from his reading of these holy scriptures advised on what was the appropriate punishment. This applied particularly when issues of caste were involved. But since the laws of Nepal were codified in the nineteenth century, the royal preceptors have been more or less excluded from the judicial system. Nowadays their responsibilities are of a more personal or ceremonial nature.

'The royal preceptor must arrange for all religious works. Most especially, he officiates at the coronation, the anointing and placing of the crown on the king's head. My own father anointed our late King Mahendra; my grandfather his father, King Tribhuvan.' He pointed to black-and-white photographs of solemn, priestly figures around the walls, his ancestors and predecessors in the job he now held.

'The ceremonies continue for two days, with many religious works in preparation. The rites go back to prehistory, to the beginning of Vedic times, and the same ceremonies have been in use since before the ancestors of our kings ruled in Rajputana. Some Western scholars say this corresponds to around 500BC, but I do not know.'

I learned something of these coronation rituals – the series of purifying baths the sovereign must undergo before being crowned, the application of a compound of holy herbs, of seed grains identified with different gods and goddesses, the bringing of holy fruits and flowers as prescribed in the scriptures. This is followed by a ritual bath for which water is brought in an earthernware jar by low-caste Sudras, milk in a copper vessel by the Vaishyas, the trading class, curd on silver by Kshatriyas of the warrior caste, before butter is brought by Brahmins in a golden vessel, thereby symbolizing how the monarchy embodies the unity of all the people of Nepal. Representatives of the four main castes are also involved in the Abhiskehha, the ritual sprinkling of waters drawn from holy rivers.

The king is ceremonially enrobed and puts on his regalia. Then, at the auspicious moment, as determined by the royal astrologer, he is crowned by the royal preceptor and his forehead is anointed with a mixture of sandal paste, rice and curd — a variant of the *tilak* ceremony that all Nepalese can readily identify with. The king then announces an amnesty to prisoners in jail and commends the freeing of caged birds and animals destined for the slaughter house. He ascends the serpent-headed Golden Throne, the national anthem is played, and his enthronement is announced to the crowds outside by cannons firing a royal salute.

The royal horse in its trappings of silver and gold is then led to its master, who takes it for a short ride. Next, a mighty tusker, richly caparisoned and with a golden howdah on its back, is brought forward for the king and queen to ride in grand procession, accompanied by Hindu priests and high lamas, military bands and yet more elephants carrying Nepalese and visiting dignitaries, to the open space at the heart of Kathmandu known as Tundikhel Maidan, where the king repeats his coronation pledge and the crowds cheer wildly.

As sheer spectacle, not much can equal the coronation of a Nepalese monarch. But it was the importance of the ancient Vedic rites that the royal preceptor wished to dwell upon.

'You see, Nepal is the last Hindu monarchy on earth, the last place where these rites, which have been practised for many thousands of years, are still carried out correctly. And so it must continue, because in our constitution it is stated that the king must be Hindu, just as in your country the queen must be a Protestant.'

'But we don't believe our queen is descended from the gods.'

'That is true,' he conceded. 'But here in Nepal we believe our king is the reincarnation of the supreme God, Lord Vishnu. It is similar, I think, to the reverence in which the emperors of Japan are held.'

'Aren't such attitudes changing nowadays?'

'Of course, with modernization this is so. Everything must run according to its cycle. And we are now in the Age of Kali, when all these things, even religion and morality, must change. But still we believe most firmly that our king is the reincarnation of Narayan, one of the manifestations of Vishnu.'

By now Nayan Raj Pandey's eyes were glowing, as if he had rediscovered some hidden metaphysical truth. I knew better than to argue with him over this matter. For him to deny the divinity of his monarch implied the negation not only of his own life's work, but that of countless generations of his ancestors.

*

Another court adviser on the principal press secretary's list was Mangal Raj Joshi, the astrologer royal. He lived over in Patan, which although visible from downtown Kathmandu was formerly the capital of a separate kingdom.

I arrived with enough time in hand to take a look around Patan's Durbar Square, which is at once smaller and more harmonious than its counterpart in Kathmandu. Pagoda-roofed temples rise from this open space like those mushroom-shaped islands often found in tropical seas, while one side of the square is lined with the palaces built for the former kings of Patan. The oldest parts go back to the fourteenth century, and practically everything here was first built long before the Gorkhas conquered Patan in 1768. Sitting on top of a 20-foot pillar in the middle of the square is a bronze statue of King Yoganarendra Malla, a sacred cobra rising behind his head to form an umbrella.

He reminded me of Simeon the Stylite, the early Christian saint who spent forty years on top of a pillar in Syria. This regal stylite, however, was fixed in the lotus position for all time to come.

Much restoration work had gone on since I last visited Patan, and parts of the old palace had been turned into a museum. In fact, the whole of Patan's Durbar Square felt like an open museum, there being none of the urgent activity that enlivens its ancient rival just across the Bagmati River.

I had some trouble finding the astrologer's residence. It is not on one of the main thoroughfares, and I had to duck down narrow alleyways before entering a hidden courtyard. A small boy was playing with a hoop which turned out to have been fashioned from a disused bicycle wheel. Apart from a couple of stray dogs, there was no one else about.

Most of the old town-houses had been left with their faded brickwork showing. The astrologer's was the exception; for it had been painted a lively shade of green. One of his assistants led me upstairs and asked whether I wanted some tea. Apparently his master had been summoned to the royal palace and would be late for our appointment.

The room was a hive of astrological industry. Three other assistants were seated cross-legged against a wall where they were engaged in drawing up horoscopes. This involved peering through ledgers of loosely bound astrological tables before punching the data into an electronic calculator.

It was growing dark by the time that the astrologer royal arrived. Still pinned to the lapel of his jacket was a palace security pass, identical to the one I had to wear when I saw Mr Pandey. Mangal Raj Joshi looked pleased with himself, and I guessed he had just been through a satisfactory consultation. His unusually thick spectacles suggested his eyesight was fading.

Just like the royal preceptor, he initially thought I had come to see him in his professional capacity. Was I seeking my horoscope to be drawn up or some other kind of consultation? When I explained that I wanted to learn about his role as astrologer to the royal family he began looking increasingly dubious. 'These are most delicate matters,' he explained.

He was certainly not going to tell me what had been the subject of his latest consultation in Narayanhitti Palace. Instead, he gave me a very broad-brush description of the types of decisions he was involved in.

'For the king', he said, 'I advise on when he should be

going out of the country, the dates for the celebration of a marriage and so on. Sometimes there are bad planetary influences present. Therefore, they must have some religious rites performed to prevent any upset. And naturally the king is very closely connected to the country — its future, its prosperity. On these matters also I must make predictions.'

Then he switched to talking about his qualifications for the job. 'I started at seven years old,' he declared, 'like my father and grandfather before me. For thirty-six generations of my family, we have practised astrological predictions.

'Also, many years of study is necessary. You must learn Sanskrit — which is the basic language for oriental astrology — geology, meteorology, mathematics, modern astronomy. I myself studied at the Queen's College in Banaras, the same which is now the Sanskrit University. The full course requires sixteen years; twenty-one if you do the PhD. I am seventy-nine years old and always I have been increasing my knowledge.'

He claimed to have predicted the Gulf War six months in advance, right down to the day and time when it would begin. Similarly, he had given advance warnings of earthquakes. These global predictions were, he said, extremely complex. 'Without a computer, the calculations take two months or more. But now they can be made much more quickly.'

He said his approach to astrology combined oriental tradition with the precision of modern astronomy and mathematics. He had used these techniques to predict when certain Nepalese politicians would become prime minister. And he hinted that serious political decisions were taken on the basis of his advice. The same was true of politicians in Delhi and other capitals throughout Asia, where astrological predictions are taken very seriously indeed – even in the highest circles.

I tried to steer the conversation back to his role as astrologer to the king. He preferred to keep to generalities. 'For most important occasions,' he said, 'such as the king's coronation, one must make lengthy calculations. The positions of the Moon, the Sun and Jupiter – these corresponding to the day, the month, and the year – are central to all religious functions. If they are not good for that year, then the coronation should be postponed. This is what happened before choosing the day and hour of His Majesty's coronation.'

By the time I left Mangal Raj Joshi's house I was about halfway converted to his brand of 'scientific astrology'. What I was convinced of is that his predictions still carry weight when important decisions are discussed within the palace. I was also pretty certain that a report of our conversation would go back to the Press Secretariat. As for my own hopes of seeing the king, I felt the stars must be against me. At least for the time being.

The sun shone every day and the Kathmandu Valley was growing perceptibly warmer. Spring was giving way to summer. I decided to phone Mr Pandey one last time to see whether it was worth prolonging my stay.

The news was not good.

'Up to now', he said, 'the opportunity has not arisen to bring this matter to the attention of His Majesty.'

'How long do you think I'll have to wait?'

'I do not think it will be possible before these elections are over. Even then, His Majesty has so many constitutional

duties, swearing in the members of the new government . . .'
He sighed, as if to express regret.

'So basically you are saying there is no hope?'

'Perhaps if you were to return later in the year,' he suggested, 'when His Majesty is not so busy.'

Right then I decided to get on the first available flight out of Kathmandu.

Chapter Six

MUSTANG – KINGDOMS WITHIN KINGDOMS

Within the territorial boundaries of Nepal lies another kingdom. Technically, it has been attached to the Kingdom of Nepal ever since its ruler accepted Gorkha overlordship in 1789. But it is so difficult to reach, lying on the far side of the Great Himalaya, that until recently not even Nepalese officials bothered to visit, leaving the local kings to rule over their subjects with the unquestioned authority of a highland laird.

So isolated was the Kingdom of Mustang that it remained locked within a time-capsule. No Western explorer is known to have entered there before the 1950s, and apart from a handful of royal guests, scholars and mountaineers who gained special permission, it remained completely closed to foreigners until 1992.

Its very inaccessibility has always been to me a powerful attraction. More to the point, there is still living a King of Mustang whose lineage can be traced directly back to the fifteenth century. To journey into this long-forbidden kingdom and meet its ruler would, I was sure, provide valuable insights into the earlier type of personal kingship that once existed right across the Himalayan region. It would also be the fulfilment of a lifetime's ambition.

I had known about Mustang's existence since the very first time I visited Nepal with my family when I was eleven. That was in January 1965. We flew up to Pokhara in an ancient DC-3 Dakota with no proper seating, just metal benches facing each other as used by parachutists in World War II films. The next day, while my family were wandering around Pokhara's main bazaar, I must have gone off on my own. Anyway, neither of my parents were there when I spotted a string of Tibetan ponies tethered to a rail. I was fond of horses and, imagining these must be for hire, I mounted a friendly looking palomino and prepared for the usual round of bargaining.

The next thing I knew I had been bucked off and was lying in the dust, surrounded by the men in charge of the horses. They reminded me of Tibetans, only they were much bigger and more fierce-looking than any I had run into before. They picked me up off the ground and marched me over to a wayside shop. While sitting there, waiting for my parents to turn up, I learned that these big men who walked with a swagger were Khampas, that they were fighting some kind of war against the Chinese, and that they and their ponies were heading off on a long journey, maybe six or seven days, to a land called Mustang where they now lived. Then my father arrived and scolded me for running off like that.

My curiosity about Mustang was aroused, and over the next few days I added to my store of knowledge by listening in to various conversations at the hotel we were staying in. The Sun and Snows (Proprietor: A Tibetan) was then the only hotel in Pokhara, and what it lacked in amenities – the roof was of corrugated iron and hot water was carried around in basins – it more than made up for by its atmosphere of intrigue. The anonymous Tibetan owner, I learned, was somehow involved in helping get supplies to the Khampas who were fighting on behalf of the Dalai Lama. One of the other hotel guests, an American, was rumoured to be working for the CIA. I remember my father saying this to my mother in hushed tones, along with something about gun-running. When I asked about Mustang I was told there was a king up there; also that nobody from outside was allowed to go in. All of which made going there a very desirable thing to do.

Not long afterwards I picked up a copy of *National Geographic* which contained photographs and excerpts from Michel Peissel's *Mustang, A Lost Tibetan Kingdom*. Peissel was a Frenchman of the adventurous sort who succeeded, through connections within the Nepalese royal family, in gaining permission to spend several months in Mustang during the spring of 1964. He was the first European to make more than a cursory visit, and his account of this hidden kingdom where Tibetan customs remained intact, completely undisturbed by outside influences, had me longing to make such a journey myself. And that initial fascination did not fade. If anything, the wholesale destruction of Tibetan monasteries during the Cultural Revolution and the creeping sinification of Tibet made this outpost of traditional civilization, this rare survivor among Himalayan monarchies, seem all the more fascinating.

The more I learned about Mustang, the more extraordinary it appeared that any sort of civilization – let alone a once flourishing and independent kingdom – could have established itself in such inhospitable terrain. For Mustang is almost entirely high-altitude desert – a barren, treeless, windswept wasteland that is a daunting prospect even to Tibetans. On the map, Mustang is a thumb-like protrusion sticking upwards from the main body of Nepal into the Tibetan plateau. It is so arid because it lies in the rain-shadow of the main Himalayan range. Rising up immedi-ately to the south of Mustang are two of its highest peaks, the Annapurna Massif and Dhaulagiri, and together they form a near impenetrable barrier to the moisture-laden monsoon. Lesser mountains — though many of these rise above 20,000 feet — hem the land in both west and east, the easiest access being from Tibet over the 15,500-foot Kare-La pass.

Because it is geographically part of the Tibetan plateau, its terrain and climate having more in common with western Tibet or Ladakh than with the foothills south of the Himalayas, Upper Mustang was settled by people of Tibetan stock. They called this desolate country 'The Land of Lo', and still refer to themselves as Lobas. The name Mustang, by which it is commonly known, is probably a Nepalese corruption of the capital's name, Lo Manthang. It is cor-rectly pronounced 'moo-stang', though nowadays foreigners and even Nepalese in Kathmandu use a novel pronunciation which fails to distinguish between the Himalayan kingdom and the wild horse of the American West.

Although very short on rainfall, pockets of agriculture are made possible by taking water from snow-fed streams and feeding it through irrigation channels. The early settlers, some of whom were cave-dwellers, combined growing such high-altitude crops as buckwheat and barley with the more pastoral life of rearing livestock — principally yaks, sheep and goats. That was sufficient to support isolated village communities. But for a more complex civilization to arise something else was needed, the surplus wealth that could be derived from trade.

And here the Land of Lo enjoyed a natural advantage, for it controlled the upper reaches of the Kali Gandaki – one of the relatively few rivers in Nepal whose headwaters rise on the Tibetan plateau and then cut their way through a gap in the Himalayas. Over millions of years they have carved out terrific ravines, and where the Kali Gandaki runs between the snow-capped peaks of Annapurna and Dhaula-giri it has formed the world's deepest gorge. In some places, the vertical cliffs would seem to prevent any passage; yet this river gorge offered an easier route for trans-Himalayan traders and pilgrims than tackling the higher snow-bound passes. It became a major trade route, with yak caravans bringing salt and raw wool down from Tibet to be exchanged for rice and other grains which grow only at lower altitudes. Whoever controlled the choke-points along the Kali Gandaki and the relatively easy passes into Tibet could grow rich on this trade, either by imposing tolls on all traffic or by participating directly as middlemen.

That the Kingdom of Mustang emerged as a distinct entity, separate both from the Tibetan heartlands and from the various principalities that ruled over the more fertile foothills to the south, is entirely due to its commanding position astride one of the main trans-Himalayan trade routes. And it was not just traders who journeyed up and down the Kali Gandaki. Hindu pilgrims on their way to the holy spring and eternal flame at Muktinath passed through Lower Mustang, while those heading onwards to Lord Siva's abode in Mount Kailash and Lake Mansovar continued upstream and over the passes into Tibet. Going in the opposite direction, Buddhist pilgrims from western Tibet used the same road to reach the Gautama's birthplace at Lumbini before proceeding to Bodh Gaya, Sarnath and other holy places down in the plains of India. Mustang stood at the crossover-point between two cultures, and drew other benefits from its position as an entrepôt. Tibetan traders were generally unwilling to venture too far down into the foothills, for at lower altitudes both they and their yaks contracted illnesses. So somewhere along the trail they drew a halt and exchanged salt for grain, the salt being carried onwards by pack ponies or porters.

Mustang was well placed to profit from this. Like fabled Timbuktu, it stood between a salt-rich desert and a rice-growing belt, at the very point beyond which long-distance caravans from the north dared not venture for fear of tropical diseases. And like Timbuktu, it grew fat on the proceeds of trade.

By all accounts, the fifteenth century was a 'Golden Age' for the people of Mustang. It was when most of the larger monasteries were founded — usually an indication of surplus wealth as well as piety. And it was then that the son of a Tibetan regional governor, Ame Pal, subdued all the feudal lords who had been fighting among themselves over control of the trade route and in 1440 established himself as the first Lo Gyalpo or King of Mustang, protector of religion and absolute ruler over a wealthy and now fully independent trans-Himalayan state.

The present Lo Gyalpo, Jigme Dorje Palbar Bista, is a direct descendant of Ame Pal and the twenty-fifth King of Mustang. Sometimes the title was passed temporarily to a brother, so by strict calculation the living ruler belongs to the twenty-first generation of the royal line. Few monarchies in the world can claim so ancient a lineage. By comparison, most of the royal families of Europe are positively nouveaux. Even within the Himalayan region, the royal house of Mustang predates the first Dalai Lama (sixteenth century), the first Chogyal of Sikkim and the founding Shabdrung of Bhutan (both early seventeenth century). The Shah dynasty is more recent still – at least as rulers of Nepal, though their ancestry is traced back to Rajput princes who fled to the hills during the fourteenth century. When Mustang was at its peak, various branches of the Shah family were still establishing themselves as petty hill rajas to the west of Kathmandu.

But with the present king, Jigme Dorje Palbar, the direct succession comes to an end. Having no children of his own, he has adopted his brother's son – a common practice among peoples of Tibetan culture. It was to this adopted son, whose name I was told was Ashok Bista, that I first applied to see whether I might be granted a royal audience. He lives in Kathmandu for most of the year, so while I was waiting to see King Birendra I contacted him at his house near the great white stupa at Boudhanath.

His initial response was not promising. For one thing, Ashok Bista is the Nepali version of his name. In Tibetan he is Jigme Singe Palbar, and his title is Gyalchung or crown prince. (I later learned that the royal family has only recently added the Nepali word Bista to their names as a token of their integration into the mainstream of Nepal's multi-ethnic society, though the kings have been commonly known as the 'Mustang Raja' or 'Raja Sahib' for much longer.) I probably committed numerous other breaches of etiquette.

Whether this affected the outcome of our conversation I do not know, but the response was still negative. Although the king was then staying in Kathmandu, I was told he was unable to see me at such short notice. Perhaps if I returned during the summer months, when the king would be residing in Lo Manthang, something could be arranged.

Once again, I was disappointed. Yet, in another sense, I was deeply relieved. To have interviewed the King of Mustang in Kathmandu would not be the same as meeting him in his ancestral palace. Besides, I really wanted to make the journey into Mustang. I would be coming back to Nepal anyway, in the hope of securing an audience with King Birendra. Why not combine this with a trekking expedition beyond the Himalayas? And I was quietly confident that Jigme Bista could arrange things. For apart from being heir-presumptive to the royal title, Jigme was a businessman. He had a Tibetan carpet factory just outside Kathmandu. He also ran a trekking agency called Royal Mustang Excursions. If I booked the trek through them, then of course it might be possible to see his father. 'All very Nepalese,' I thought, and kept my counsel. But it was the best guarantee I could find of meeting the king.

Four months later I was on another plane bound for Kathmandu. This time Sarah was with me. When I had told her of my plan of going to Mustang, she nearly exploded. 'No way are you gallivanting around up there on your own. I'm coming too.'

'But it's a high-altitude trek. What about your asthma?'
'I'll get all the drugs. Besides, we'll be riding horses.'
'And the slipped disc?'

'Riding'll be good for it.'

'And the vertigo? It's all bare slopes and gorges up there. Some of the drops are horrendous.'

'I'll get there,' she replied, steadfastly.

In fact I needed her. A party of two is the minimum required to obtain entry permits for Mustang, this being a restricted area under Nepalese regulations. The relevant pages of our passports had to be photocopied and faxed to Kathmandu in advance, and also a bankers' draft for a frighteningly large sum in US dollars. The Nepalese government charges a hefty royalty on all foreigners entering Mustang: a minimum $700 for the first ten days and an additional $70 per day thereafter. They also require that all groups be accompanied by a liaison officer, whose travel and living expenses must be met in full. And to minimize the demands of visitors on the region's scarce supplies of firewood and foodstuffs, every expedition must carry in enough rations and Calor gas to make it virtually self-sufficient. Which means having to hire a large number of porters and pack animals.

I can see the point of this last provision (though it also excludes most of the local population from making any money out of tourism). But the entry fee is just a government fundraising scam, especially since only a tiny percentage of the royalties paid to visit Mustang are channelled back into the region, the remainder disappearing into some black hole in Kathmandu. The only possible justification is that by making it so expensive to get into Mustang, the system keeps out mass tourism and all its unwanted side-effects. As for the liaison officer, I could not really understand what he would be there for. After all, Mustang is not populated by heavily armed and potentially hostile tribesmen. It is not like heading off into the anarchy and lawlessness of Pakistan's North-West Frontier Province. Who was he expected to 'liaise' with? The only role I could imagine was that he was meant to spy on us, the outsiders.

As soon as we arrived in Kathmandu I contacted Jigme. 'All the arrangements are in place,' he assured me. 'The horses, yes . . . even now they are coming down from Lo Manthang. And my father is there, yes . . . But first I need your passports to be stamped. I will call at your hotel, the Manaslu, yes? Also, if it is convenient, to collect the balance outstanding? Oh, and I nearly forgot. We have had a stroke of luck. The liaison officer who is to go with you – he is good friend of mine, truly an exceptional man. I will bring him to meet you tomorrow.'

I still harboured doubts about this liaison officer, and when Jigme came round the following evening I was more taken by the second person he had brought with him. This was Gyatso, a rangy youth with strongly Tibetan features, who turned out to be the son of the Mustang Raja's personal bodyguard. Although only nineteen, there was a calm assurance about him which made me feel good that he was coming with us.

The liaison officer's name was Ganga Sakar Dhakal, and he worked in the Home Ministry. A slight man even by Nepali standards, the regulation moustache failed to divert attention from his eyes, which were large, inquisitive, almost doe-like in their shape and the luxuriance of the lashes, and oddly compelling. He was a strict Brahmin and would not take any meat, eggs or alcoholic drink; but he followed these rules without fuss and, unlike other Brahmins I have met, never made others feel guilty about indulging. On that first evening he hardly spoke, and I failed to register that in Mr

Dhakal's neat person we had been landed with a Brahmin beyond compare.

We arranged to meet up the next day to go out to the airport in good time for the Kathmandu-Pokhara flight. Waiting to be checked in, I discovered an unexpected addition to our party. This was a Tibetan monk-artist called Likche Dukta. Apparently he would be travelling with us up to Lo Manthang, where he was to repaint the king's chapel and sacred statues. Finding his Tibetan name hard to pronounce, Sarah and I gave him the nickname of Leonardo.

Leonardo looked rather baffled by what was going on around him at the airport. I found out that until only a few months previously he had been in a Lhasa monastery and had never flown before. Otherwise the flight to Pokhara was uneventful, the snow-peaks being entirely obscured by cloud. On arrival we were met by Pema, a mountain-man from Dolpo, who was to combine the roles of guide and sirdar – or, to give it a more modern title, head of logistics. With our entourage still swelling, I reckoned he would have a tricky job on his hands.

The onward flight from Pokhara to the high-altitude airstrip at Jomsom is scheduled to leave at dawn, this generally being the time when there is less cloud cover. For five days, however, the clouds had not parted and no planes had got through to Jomsom. We were lucky to get out on the first morning, though I did not feel that way mid-flight when the mountains seemed to press in on either side. We were in a Twin Otter, a small enough plane for me to look over the pilot's shoulder and see what was up ahead. What I saw was a solid bank of cloud merging into mountains. I was aware that a similar aircraft had crashed the previous year flying this same route. There had been no survivors.

I began to think maybe it would have been better to trek all the way from Pokhara. But then I looked out at the rain-lashed hills and imagined what it would be like down there — five days of slogging uphill through leech-infested forests, slithering across fresh landslides, struggling to keep your footing along precipitous trails made slick by the monsoon. I had been there before. Far better to go quickly, I decided.

As I was reaching this morbid conclusion, the landscape changed before my eyes. Gone were the dense forests and paddy terraces, the wooden houses with their pitched roofs of thatch or rusted metal, and in their place was bare earth the colour of sand, a thin scattering of fir trees, and flat-roofed houses made of stone and beaten earth. We had swung around behind the Himalayan divide, and in just five minutes' flying time passed from a wet zone to a very dry one. Already the dun-coloured hills, the low-built houses with their parapets of winter firewood and prayer flags, reminded me of Tibet.

The airstrip at Jomsom was crowded with people desperate to get out after waiting five days for a plane. Amidst the general frenzy there stood one man who radiated calm. Pema and the liaison officer went over and shook hands with him, before calling to me. 'Please meet the king's private secretary, Chandra Bahadur Thakali.'

This was the man who was to be my interpreter when I met the King of Mustang. He had sharp features and seemed to be perpetually smiling behind his thin moustache. His name confirmed that he was a Thakali, a distinct ethnic group who live mostly in Lower Mustang. Their religion is a peculiar amalgam of Buddhism, animism and Hinduism. But throughout Nepal they are best known as resourceful —

some say unscrupulous – traders and businessmen. On account of these worldly skills, Thakalis have often risen to high office within the Kingdom of Mustang. In this respect, Chandra stood in a long tradition.

He told us there was a shortage of horses at the moment. There would be only three between us. These were on the way down, but had not yet arrived in Jomsom. Perhaps if we started walking we could meet our mounts on the road. He himself would be accompanying us to the capital, Lo Manthang, on foot – the first time he had walked up in many years. This left me feeling embarrassed about doing the journey on horse-back.

The horses arrived at a gallop before we had even cleared the straggling collection of shops and government insti-tutions – administrative offices, schools, the army's moun-tain training centre – that is Jomsom. When I saw them I realized 'horses' was a misnomer. They were Tibetan ponies – hardy, sure-footed, but smaller than anything I had ridden since I was a child. Initially I was allocated a little bay which was a real trier, but so small that if I extended my legs they almost touched the ground. Sarah took the grey, clearly the best of the batch. The liaison officer was given the third pony, a palomino, but then nobly offered it to the monk-artist 'because he is not so accustomed to walking'. All the horses had wooden saddles covered over with a brightly coloured Tibetan rug. Their harness was of cloth, not leather, and around each horse's neck there hung a bell. So we rode off to the jingling of bells – a sound I was to grow very familiar with.

Above Jomsom, the Kali Gandaki spreads across a flood plain, the river dividing into many channels that run between sandbanks strewn with boulders and rounded pebbles. There were people sifting through these pebbles, searching out ones containing fossils of prehistoric marine creatures. For what is now Mustang once lay at the bottom of the Sea of Tethys. The fold mountains that hemmed us in are composed of soft rocks or sand mixed with pebbles, ready-worn deposits that had lined the bed of a vast inland sea.

Such soft stuff is easily eroded by wind and water, and as we progressed up the gorge we encountered cliffs and pinnacles worn into ever more fantastic shapes. It was more like a dream landscape – or, at least, something dreamt up by Max Ernst or Salvador Dali – than anything I could connect with 'reality'. The unremitting clarity of light, the enormity of the sky, the creeping realization that these contorted land-forms repeated themselves, ridge after ridge, all combined to instil in me a sense of foreboding. What kind of country had we ventured into? Even the Tibetan monk-artist looked bewildered by such desolation.

Rainfall is rare in these parts, though when rain does come it runs straight off the parched earth, carving deep furrows in the landscape. But the wind is always there, building up in intensity from noon onwards – the reason being that the Kali Gandaki gorge acts as a pressure valve between the very different weather systems of South and Central Asia. By late afternoon, dust storms came surging up the valley. I began to understand why our liaison officer wore wrap-around shades and a scarf tied over his face like the baddies in a Western movie. He had done this trip twice before and knew what to expect.

We were heading for Kagbeni, which stands at the junction of the old trade route into Tibet and the pilgrims' path up to the holy places at Muktinath. There we would have our papers stamped and enter the restricted area of Mustang. But to reach Kagbeni we first had to ford a swollen tributary which had recently washed away the bridge. Pema found a likely crossing place and stripped down to his underwear before leading the first horse through the fast-flowing waters. The others followed nose-to-tail, and we reached the far bank with only our boots wet. We dismounted and Pema, who was by now soaked up to his chest, led our horses back across the stream so that the others could ride through the water. 'This crossing is not too difficult,' he commented. 'Sometimes the horses have to swim. Sometimes, they are washed away.'

Soon afterwards we sighted the red-painted tower of Kagbeni's monastery perched on a cliff above the Kali Gandaki; then the flat-roofed, white-washed houses of the village itself, which are built so close together that they create the impression of a city wall rising above orchards and willow trees. We made for a large house that was painted in monastic red, and unsaddled the horses in its central courtyard. There was a strong smell of fermentation.

'They are making chang,' said Pema, and pointed to jerry cans full of the cloudy Tibetan-style beer. 'This place is called The Red House and we stay here tonight.'

Hardly the most original of names, but then it fitted a pattern. When I had asked what our horses were called, I was told the palomino's name was 'Yellow Horse', the bay's 'Brown Horse', and the grey's 'White Horse'.

The Red House was full of hidden wonders. We ate in a room decorated with finely executed though now faded wall-paintings. It had once been the library, but the former owner had drunk his way through his inheritance and sold off the books. Next door was a private chapel with a ten-foot Buddha and smaller statues of local deities and lamas. The chapel walls were cracked and bowed; the air was dusty and smelled of old butter lamps; and scattered around were piles of threadbare tangkas and a strange collection of ancient weaponry – bows and arrows, spears, a long-barrelled musket. I learned that the house had been occupied by senior Khampa guerillas during the 1960s.

Equally curious were the two little boys who chased each other through the house. One was a local kid, our landlady's nephew. The other behaved just like a native highlander, right down to the muddy smudges all over his face, but his hair was ash blond. When I first saw that shock of matted hair I thought he must be an albino. Then I discovered he belonged to an odd couple also staying in the house. She was Dutch, he from Northern Ireland, and together with their young son they had spent the past year living in a nearby village where she was conducting anthropological field-work.

The original idea had been to see how local beliefs about holy mountains or sacred streams influenced farming prac-tices and the way people used natural resources. But the preconceived theory had been thrown out, and she had settled down to study how such a community worked in practice. They spoke of the terrible cold in mid-winter, the hard life of the villagers (especially the women), of how when a man died his closest friends carved up the body before throwing the pieces in the river. We sat up late drinking the local apple brandy. The candlelight made all the painted bodhisattvas on the library wall assume an unnatural radiance, and I wondered if this effect had been intended by the artist.

I was still suffering from a hangover when we went to

the monastery next morning. The main prayer hall was locked, but we were offered tea by an artist who had been repainting the upper gallery. He was a Tibetan refugee, originally from Amdo, and his work incorporated some modern elements like having defenders of the Buddhist faith armed with machine guns. But the execution was crude, and I left him and Leonardo discussing art while I wandered around the monastery precincts, peering occasionally over the parapet. The drop was close to vertical, and at the cliff's base the Kali Gandaki seethed like an angry brown snake.

Back at The Red House, mules were being loaded and horses saddled up. Our party was now at full strength. Besides Sarah and me, there was our Brahmin liaison officer, the Tibetan lama, and the king's private secretary. Looking after us was a team of seven: Pema as guide, Gyatso in charge of provisions, one cook and three assistant cookboys to help carry all the utensils, and one muleman. We had the three riding ponies between us, and nine mules.

Since Sarah had packed all our possessions into one army surplus kitbag, nine mules seemed rather excessive. But then there were two tents, a table and chairs (used only once), enough provisions to feed the entire party several times over, gas cylinders for cooking, and two large jerry cans which I later discovered contained rakshi liquor and chang respectively. These were the property of the muleman, who claimed he was taking the rakshi to sell in the capital – though he was not averse to dipping into his supplies en route. He usually started on the chang at breakfast and sang away merrily as he chased his mules along the trail. I reckoned we made up a larger expedition than the one my father had led into Tibet in 1939. As we left Kagbeni it seemed that an entire caravan was on the move.

All morning we stuck close to the Kali Gandaki, sometimes climbing onto a barren plain, at others skirting cliffs that rose vertically above the silt-laden river. We had to negotiate several landslides where one wrong step would have had you down in the raging torrent. Crossing over to the west bank by a new steel bridge below the village of Chele, we started climbing out of the gorge. The little bay pony could not take my weight over such a long ascent and kept stopping for a breather. Since the lama's palomino was larger and sturdier, we decided to swap mounts. But the climb continued all afternoon, and to rest the horses we dismounted and walked from there on.

By now the altitude was beginning to affect us. 'Couldn't we stop at that village just ahead?' asked Sarah.

'Not possible,' I puffed.

'Why not?' she asked crossly, and then froze. For suddenly it was apparent why we could not enter that village. We had reached the lip of a canyon more than six hundred feet deep, and the village stood on the far side. Worse still, we could see the path we would have to take. It zigzagged up a perpendicular rock-face and was very narrow. In some places the road – if that is the appropriate term – had been built out over the void. Elsewhere it had been carved out beneath overhanging cliffs.

'Oh my God,' she said very slowly. 'That's my worst nightmare.'

Even for those who do not suffer from vertigo, the trail ahead was intimidating. Sarah has had vertigo since she was a child. When there's nothing but a void she gets the full-blown symptoms – the shakes, legs turn to jelly, sudden switches between feeling rooted to the spot and wanting to run, to hurl herself over the edge.

'There's no other way up to Mustang?' she pleaded.

'Sorry. This is it.'

'Then there's nothing for it,' she said, summoning all her reserves of bloody-mindedness. 'Let's get moving before I change my mind.'

There were moments when I thought she wouldn't make it. After a particularly nasty section we had to stop to let the shakes subside, assisted by a large slug of Nepali rum from the hip flask. Then we rounded a corner, and Sarah declared she would be all right from here on.

I looked at the narrow path ahead and the near-vertical drops to our left. If anything, this section was more danger-ous than the last. But such rational calculations have nothing to do with how vertigo works on you. The cliffs now sloped slightly away from the perpendicular. Sarah no longer felt surrounded by the void.

'You made it,' I said, hugely relieved.

'What do you mean?' she replied. 'Of course I made it up that bloody precipice. But I know for certain that I'll have to go down it again to get out of this country. And going down is always worse.'

At the top of the pass there was a chorten and a mound of stones thrown by travellers seeking good fortune. We added ours to the pile before continuing on our way. The land hardly fell away, for we had now entered what Ganga called 'the high country'. From here on we would be traversing the broad shoulders of the mountain range that separates Mustang from Dolpo. It was much colder, and as we entered the hamlet of Samar I noticed that poplar trees grew here rather than the willows of the lower valleys. We pitched our tents and tried to eat something before turning in. It was our first night above 12,000 feet. My appetite had gone and, although exhausted, I could hardly sleep – both possible symptoms of altitude sickness.

Next morning we found that a fox or jackal had been at our food supplies. This high country obviously attracted more rainfall than the Kali Gandaki gorge. During the brief summer there are wild flowers everywhere. Whole stretches of upland plain were touched with their blue and purple tints. Mostly they were of the ground-hugging, dwarf variety, capable of withstanding the long and bitter winters. For a while we passed through a stunted forest of cypress and juniper, their ancient and contorted trunks split open by frost, their spread roots clutching desperately at inadequate soil.

Wherever snow-fed streams came down from the mountains they had carved deep gashes in the landscape. These had to be negotiated carefully, dismounting and walking downhill while relying on horse-power to get us up the other side. But sometimes the ascent was too steep for riding, and then we followed local custom and hung onto our ponies' tails. It is highly effective, as you are pulled uphill very rapidly and with minimal effort; but being attached to the horse you have to take the same leaps and bounds as it does. By the time I reached the top my lungs were gasping for oxygen.

The wayside hamlets we passed through were small, isolated communities of just two or three families. Their houses were made of rough stone and beaten earth, low-built and with narrow windows to cheat the mountain winds. Mothers and daughters were busy adding to the store of firewood heaped up on their flat roofs. One girl was collecting wild leaves which Gyatso said are used to make a winter curry. Usually these isolated homesteads were guarded by huge Tibetan mastiffs which greeted any stranger with much barking and growling. If they were not already tied up to a stake, our muleman threw stones to keep them at bay.

At Sangbochen, where we stopped for lunch, I saw two birds of prey circling overhead. Pema identified them as eagles, though they bore a closer resemblance to vultures. He was corrected by Ganga, our liaison officer, who spoke rarely but always with authority. 'Lammergeyer,' he pronounced, as the great birds floated effortlessly on the thermals.

A long but gradual ascent led up towards Nya-La, at nearly 14,000 feet the highest pass along the main route to the capital. I rode beside Ganga, chatting to him and trying to keep his spirits up, for I could see the altitude was beginning to get to him. He had nobly given up his horse and walked all the way from Kagbeni – 'slowly but surely', as he liked to say. Even on the steepest sections he never paused between fixed rest-stops, preferring to keep trudging onwards, talking all the while about village life in Nepal or Hindu philosophy or, as now, about how he had read the Bible cover-to-cover in both Nepali and English.

'In places', he observed, his legs maintaining the same measured pace, 'this book is most illuminating; but some parts I found most obscure.'

This habit of conversing on philosophical topics in the most trying of circumstances reminded me of the fictionalized Bengali pundit, Hurree Chunder Mookerjee, in Rudyard Kipling's novel *Kim*. And although Ganga's slight frame – not to mention his wrap-around shades and baseball cap – were all very different from the portly, umbrella-toting Bengali's, he was equally resilient and imbued with much the same spirit of enquiry.

Among our party, it was not the government officer but the lama who wandered through the High Himalaya holding an umbrella aloft. Many times I looked back to see the monk-artist beneath his black umbrella. He held it high, for better balance, while skipping down scree slopes. It was always there, tucked over one shoulder, even when he was riding the small bay pony at a brisk trot. Leonardo used it more as a parasol than to keep off rain, for he was unused to such strong sunlight, having spent most of his life within the confines of a monastery in Lhasa. Again, there was something Kiplingesque about this solitary maroon-clad figure, parasol held aloft, moving through such an empty wilderness. Of course he was much younger than the lama in Kim; and, strictly speaking, he was just a monk and not a lama at all – though the local people always referred to him as such.

After the long climb we all stopped at the top of Nya-La to rest. A strong wind rattled through the line of prayer flags and Leonardo almost lost his precious umbrella, so Sarah leant him some of her sun-cream.

'From here', Ganga said, 'you can see nearly all of Upper Mustang. Those distant mountains mark the border with Tibet.'

I looked out and saw nothing but range upon range of bare, contorted mountains. They were bleached out, the colour of a dead man's bones. Some ravens were squabbling noisily among themselves. Otherwise nothing moved out there. And it was difficult to imagine how any life form could survive in such an environment. We might as well have landed on the moon.

'Where exactly do you think you have brought us?' asked Sarah.

'I'm told we are looking over Mustang,' I replied, my heart sinking.

'That's obvious enough. But what are we doing in the middle of this?' and she waved an arm at several hundred square miles of lunar mountains.

'I know it looks bad, but . . .'

'No buts. Even Leonardo is freaked out by this, and with good reason. He has to stay up here and paint for months on end.'

And it was true: the monk-artist did look worried. I asked Pema to question him about his first impressions of Mustang. 'It is not like Lhasa,' was his curt response.

'I'm sure there's a lovely green valley just around the corner,' I announced, and started walking.

Of course there wasn't. Even from the top of the next pass, all that could be seen was more bare mountains. Only this time they were painted in Technicolor hues, as though the gods had gone mad with some child's colouring set. In the distance, the rocks glowed pink and gold. But the mountain straight ahead of us was blue shading to purple, and the cliffs on our left a deep red.

Upon closer inspection, the blue mountain was composed of many different layers of rock which formed horizontal stripes, some grey, some almost black, but with plenty of blue and purple tones in there. The red cliffs were more uniform in colour, but had been eroded into such bizarre shapes that they could have been the setting for *The Chronicles of Narnia*.

'Where do we go from here?' asked Sarah.

'Oh, no problem,' said Pema. 'We have not far to go now.'

'I was worried you'd say that,' she replied, still staring at the landscape in disbelief.

But less than ten minutes later we rounded a spur and there, directly below us, was a large village surrounded by sparkling green fields of barley and wheat.

'Ghemi,' announced Pema.

Ghemi was the largest settlement since we had left Kagbeni. As with most villages in Upper Mustang, it existed for two reasons: its position astride the trade route, and having sufficient reasonably flat land around it which could be irrigated by waters drawn off a mountain stream. The road into Ghemi was awash with surplus water from the fields, so we rode right into the village centre, dismounting in front of a large chorten. It was painted with vertical stripes of orange, grey and white, the colours of the Sakya Order of Buddhists, and covered by an umbrella-like structure of thatch supported by wooden poles. All these features, I was to learn, are typical of Upper Mustang, where most people follow one of the Sakya schools.

We took a wrong turning and walked past a Mani Wall made up of hundreds of slabs inscribed with Om Mane Padme Om or other Buddhist prayers. The large house where I thought we would be staying the night turned out to be an abandoned royal palace. We retraced our footsteps and found the mules being unloaded in front of a newly whitewashed house scarcely smaller than the ruined palace.

It belonged to one of the king's cousins and it was here we stayed, in a guest room built on top of the flat roof. The clouds parted and we had a fine view of the now distant Himalayan snows over a parapet of winter firewood. Sparrows were nesting among the dried and contorted branches.

Ghemi resembles a reasonably prosperous village in Tibet. Or rather, what a Tibetan village was like up until around fifty years ago. It has its Big House where the local aristocracy live, a monastic-temple or *gompa*, chortens large and small, and its Mani Walls (there is a really long one across the valley, beside the main road to Lo Manthang). In Ghemi, prayer flags fly from every rooftop. It is as filthy as any Tibetan village, but the cold dry air keeps excessive odours and diseases at bay. The people speak a Tibetan dialect, and their culture remains almost wholly Tibetan. So it is hardly surprising that when the first Westerners entered Upper Mustang they thought they had discovered a lost Tibetan kingdom.

Virtually nothing was then known about Mustang's history or its relations with neighbouring powers. Its monarchy could be traced through an unbroken line back to the fifteenth century. Beyond that, things became uncertain. Early Tibetan chronicles refer to its being a part of the domain of King Songsten Gampo, who ruled over an immense Tibetan Empire during the ninth century. Local tradition has it that the eighth-century Buddhist saint Padmasambhava visited Mustang. The region was probably settled by people of Tibetan stock even earlier than that. But what happened during the 400 years following the break-up of the Tibetan Empire remained a mystery.

The first European to spend any time in Mustang, Michel Peissel, thought he was on the right track when he

discovered texts known as Mollas in various monastic libraries in Upper Mustang. The Mollas appeared to carry the
genealogy of the royal house back to Tibet's Yarlung dynasty
and beyond, to the divine kings who came down from the
sky to rule on earth. Such mythical genealogies are common
to many of the lesser dynasties which ruled over portions of
the Tibetan plateau after the break-up of the Yarlung
Empire. Moreover, the Mollas are not historical chronicles
as such, but praise-giving speeches that were recited before
patrons and benefactors of a monastery. Their purpose was
flattery, not impartial history.

The political fragmentation that followed the demise of
the Yarlung dynasty allowed local rulers – especially those
on the fringe of the Tibetan world – to rule more or less
independently. Mustang appears to have been part of Ngari,
the name given to the far western region of Tibet. But Ngari
was not so much a unified kingdom as a loose collection of
feudal principalities. Outlying regions such as Dolpo and
Mustang maintained relations with other, non-Tibetan principalities to the south. And it was there, during the twelfth
century, that a new trans-Himalayan power arose – the
Empire of the Khasa Mallas.

The Khasas were a warlike Aryan tribe who came from
the west. They are briefly mentioned by classical scholars
such as Ptolemy and Pliny. They probably entered what is
now far western Nepal around the sixth century AD. But the
Khasas have left few physical traces, and the very existence
of a medieval Malla Empire was not suspected until Giuseppe Tucci, the Italian Tibetologist and Himalayan
explorer, and the Nepalese scholar Yogi Naraharinath, began
publishing their research in the 1950s. The most important
discovery was the Dullu Pillar, whose stone inscriptions list

the kings of the Malla dynasty. From these inscriptions, and references to the same kings in Tibetan chronicles, it has been possible to reconstruct the history of a trans-Himalayan kingdom whose capital was at Sinja, near the Nepalese town of Jumla, but which ruled over the western Tibetan regions of Guge and Purang, large parts of Ladakh, all of Garwhal and Kumaon, as well as what is now western Nepal – including Dolpo and Mustang.

The Malla Empire flourished on both sides of the Himalayan divide between the twelfth and the late fourteenth centuries. Its rulers observed Hindu caste rules and began the gradual assimilation of the Mongoloid hill peoples, mainly the Magar and Gurung tribes, into the caste system. But the Khasas practised a mixed religion, combining Hindu, Buddhist and animist elements. Some Malla kings sent their sons to monasteries in Tibet so that they could become powerful lamas. This first Malla kingdom (not to be confused with the later Malla dynasties of Jumla or the Kathmandu Valley) extended its influence from Ladakh and central Tibet down to the low-lying Terai.

It was a power to be reckoned with. During the thirteenth and early fourteenth centuries, Khasa armies invaded the wealthy Kathmandu Valley on six occasions. But the Khasas never established permanent rule over the valley. Nor did they attempt direct rule over most of their far-flung domains. The Malla Empire was not so much a centralized state as a confederation of local feudatories who owed allegiance or had to pay a tribute to their Malla lords at Sinja.

The reunification of western Tibet under King Changchub Gyaltsen (c.1350), the loss of Kumaon and Garwhal to the west, and repeated revolts by vassals closer to home, all contributed to the break-up of this trans-Himalayan empire. The rediscovery of its two hundred-year existence should not, however, be taken as evidence that regions like Mustang 'were always part of Nepal'. On the other hand, it certainly proves that such border regions were not 'lost Tibetan kingdoms' — despite their predominantly Tibetan culture. Rather, they stood in between two worlds, maintaining contact with both Tibet and the central Himalayan valleys, quietly profiting from their trade, and accepting the overlordship of whichever was the dominant power at the time.

The collapse of the Mallas left a power vacuum, into which stepped local lords. By the late fourteenth century there were many such 'one-castle kings' fighting it out for control of the Kali Gandaki trade route. Among them were the ancestors of the Mustang kings. The founding monarch, Ame Pal, conquered all of his rivals and declared his independence from the Tibetan governor of Gungthang. Moreover, by building the 'iron-walled' city of Lo Manthang, Ame Pal consolidated his hold over the entire length of the trade route. He and his successors were able to impose customs dues on the caravans passing up and down it. They also conquered a broad swathe of highland territory beyond the Himalayas. The extent to which this independent Loba kingdom amassed enormous wealth in the fifteenth century can still be seen in the number of monasteries founded during that period, and in the richness of their decoration.

But Mustang's 'Golden Age' lasted only a hundred years or so. By the late sixteenth century, the neighbouring Kingdom of Jumla had gained control over the salt monopoly. Although permitted to retain the royal title, the kings of Mustang had to pay a heavy tribute to their overlords in Jumla. And the Jumlis were harsh masters, launching punitive raids when the full quota was not met. Looting and kidnapping were commonplace. A princess from Ladakh on her way to marry the Mustang Raja was arrested and held to ransom. Similarly, some forty dignitaries from Lo were 'detained' by the Jumlis in Kagbeni until their demands were met. As a result of these depredations, Upper Mustang was gradually impoverished. No wonder their kings sought alliances with Ladakh or any other power that might help free them from Jumla's domination.

The rise of the House of Gorkha offered a golden opportunity to throw off the overlordship of Jumla. And the Shah dynasty also saw advantages in detatching Mustang from their Malla rivals to the west. Even before they attacked Jumla, the Gorkhalis wooed the King of Mustang by granting him lands they held in the Nubri region beyond the Himalayas. And once Jumla had been conquered, the Gorkhalis accepted Mustang as a dependent state, allowing its kings to rule as they wished within their domains provided they paid a nominal tribute. The formal treaty of dependency dates from 1789, and the terms were confirmed the following year by King Rana Bahadur Shah.

To Raja Wangyal Dorje of Mustang

We hereby confirm your rule over the territories occupied by you from the time of your forefathers, adding thereto the territories situated north-east of Banadaphat, along with Barbung Khola, Tarap Khola, etc, which had been encroached upon and occupied by Jumla. We also confirm the customary payments you have been collecting in Thak, Thini, Barhagaun, Manang and other areas. Jumla, when it occupied your country, used to collect forcibly the

Chhyakpol tax from those who visited it for trade. We hereby grant you authority to collect this tax.

Do not create obstructions when our troops or nobles visit your country on any business. When we commence military campaigns in the north and west, send wholeheartedly your troops and supplies to join our troops. Attack the territories that are to be attacked, and guard those that are to be guarded. Formerly you used to make Sirto and Mamuli payments to Lhasa and Jumla. Continue paying Rupees 71 to Lhasa as before. A sum of Rupees 929, along with five horses, which you used to pay to Jumla, should now be submitted to us at Kantipur

Be faithful to us and comply with our orders. Rule over and enjoy your territories within the prescribed boundaries from generation to generation.

The terms were generous, as was customary when an allied raja voluntarily accepted Gorkha overlordship. For Mustang was never invaded by Gorkhali troops. Significantly, traditional payments to Lhasa were to continue, so links with Tibet were retained. Although Mustang technically became part of the Kingdom of Nepal, in practice its kings enjoyed greater autonomy than when it had been subject to Jumla. Nepalese officials rarely visited so distant a region, and the payment of tribute was more than offset by the right to tax the salt trade. Upon the whole, Mustang was left by its Shah overlords in a state of benign neglect. And so it continued through the nineteenth century, long after the Ranas ruled Nepal as hereditary prime ministers.

But the wily Thakalis of Lower Mustang cultivated closer relations with their Rana overlords in Kathmandu, hoping to re-establish their hegemony over the region. Unlike the Tibetan-speaking nobility of Upper Mustang, the Thakalis learned the Nepali language and became indispensable as intermediaries. By the early twentieth century, the Thakali subba or chief official for the region enjoyed a very close relationship with the Rana prime minister Chandra Shumsher, and it was proposed that a customs house and administrative offices be set up in Jomsom. These were staffed by Thakalis, some of whom pressed for the abolition of the Kingdom of Mustang. In its place they wanted to set themselves up as hereditary feudal chiefs. So powerful were these Thakali subbas that they arrested the Mustang Raja himself and kept him in their custody at the customs office in Jomsom for thirteen days.

The balance shifted back in favour of Mustang's kings after the Ranas were overthrown in 1951 and the Shah dynasty returned to power in Nepal. Monarchs tend to be sympathetic towards other monarchs. True, Mustang's special status as a dependent principality was amended in 1961, so that legally it became part of a more integrated Kingdom of Nepal. But in practice, King Mahendra allowed the Mustang Raja to rule over his domains just as before. The real threat to his authority came not from distant Kathmandu but from the Thakalis around Jomsom, which was then being built up into an important administrative and military base.

This ancient rivalry between Upper and Lower Mustang, between Lobas and Thakalis, continues to this day. The more worldly and cosmopolitan Thakalis have always had an advantage, and this has become far more pronounced since Nepal became a multi-party democracy in 1990. They have extensive business interests in Kathmandu and much better connections within the main political parties. The king has tradition on his side, and this counts for much among the Loba people. But the Thakalis have greater influence in Kathmandu, where it really counts.

The woman who sold me two bottles of Chinese beer in Ghemi was a Thakali. At first I was surprised that the beer was Chinese, brought down by mules from the Tibetan border, rather than Nepalese. But the further we travelled into Upper Mustang, the more Chinese goods were in evidence. Not just luxury items like beer or Chinese brandy, or manufactured goods like soap or plastic combs, but basic foodstuffs such as sacks of Chinese rice. Pema explained that it was all to do with transport costs. Apparently it was cheaper to truck such goods 3,000 miles across China and Tibet, right up to Mustang's northern border, than it was to bring up their Nepalese equivalents by mule from Pokhara. And while the border with Tibet is officially closed, this does not prevent Lobas from bringing in whatever they need.

Having stocked up on provisions, Sarah and I spent the rest of the morning looking around Ghemi. Hidden behind a high wall we found a small but charming gompa with a tall prayer flag in its courtyard but no monks in residence. The wall paintings in the main prayer hall were darkened with age and had been damaged in places by water seepage. Clearly, the roof had once leaked badly. It had been replaced quite recently and the whole upper floor redecorated using modern chemical-based paints; so, while the Buddhist iconography was traditional, the execution was garish in the extreme.

A little further down the same lane was the back of the king's palace. It had once been attached to a much older fortress, now completely in ruins, though its commanding position on the lip of a steep ravine helped explain why Ghemi had grown into an important staging post along the trade route. The king's palace was scarcely in a better state of repair. The back wall had fallen down, leaving massive wooden beams exposed to the elements; and where there had once been a courtyard there was now a pile of rubble upon which half a dozen stray goats were playing a goatish version of 'who's the king of the castle?'.

The palace fronted onto the main road leading to the capital, and on this side at least some of its thirty or more rooms were still inhabited. Pema pointed out the royal stables, which were large enough to cope with a sizeable entourage. Across the way was a walled garden which I was told also belonged to the king. It had been turned into an orchard, full of apple and apricot trees, while the patches of open ground were densely planted with sweet peas.

We returned to our lodgings to find the liaison officer and the king's secretary preparing to set off by themselves for the capital. Since they were travelling on foot, they had quite sensibly decided to take the most direct route. It was a long walk but they reckoned they could do it in a day. The mule train and those on horses would continue at a gentler pace up the old Tibet trade route, stopping at the monastery of Lo Ghekar for the night. So the party split up, and we turned our horses west towards the high mountains.

Initially the way followed a river valley, and we climbed gently through water meadows where brood mares and their foals had been let out to graze on the lush summer grass. It is wonderful how a little water can transform so austere a landscape. The meadows were studded with wild flowers, while the irrigated fields sparkled with the yellow of mustard and the pink of flowering buckwheat. And yet, all the while we were running parallel to a series of sharply eroded cliffs that glowed the colour of dried blood.

Each of the villages we passed through had its own Mani Wall, its diminutive gompa and neatly white-washed houses (some of them quite substantial) with prayer flags sprouting from their flat roofs. It was all so enchanting that I did not notice there was something missing.

Until, that is, Sarah reined in her horse and shouted back 'Where are all the people?'

'I don't know,' I replied, suddenly aware that we had been riding through ghost villages. 'Maybe they're out working in the fields,' I suggested.

'Only the women,' she retorted, 'and not that many of them. We've been riding nearly two hours and I haven't seen one able-bodied man — just young kids in the villages and the occasional woman out in the fields.'

I decided to ask Pema why the villages seemed to be deserted. 'So many people go off trading or to work in the cities,' he explained. 'Also, some are in the mountains with their animals. When it is harvest, then they will come back.'

This fitted with what I had heard about the Lobas' tendency to seasonal migration. But I had not expected to see flourishing villages left almost deserted.

We stopped beside a stream to water the horses before the big climb that lay ahead. As I dismounted, my foot caught in the stirrup and I landed on my back. I must have looked rather comical with one leg stuck up in the air, as everyone burst out laughing. But I had hit the earth quite hard and didn't see the funny side — at least not at first.

While I was pulling myself back together, a village woman approached us shyly. At first she tried to interest us in some fossils she had collected. She had some exceptional specimens, but with a steep climb ahead of me I did not feel like weighing my pockets down with rocks. Then she asked us if we had any medicines.

'What for?' asked Sarah.

In answer, the woman gave out a high-pitched whistle and up ran her son. He was about eight years old and he had an evil-looking gash over one eye. Nothing had been done to clean up the caked blood and dirt around the wound. Left like that, infection would soon set in and he might even lose the use of his eye.

'How on earth did this happen?' Sarah exclaimed.

'Older boys throwing stones,' Pema translated. 'Can you help him?'

'Well, first of all this blood must be cleaned off.' This was done in the stream, revealing a deep cut above the eyelid.

'He needs stitches,' Sarah commented. 'He should really be taken to hospital.'

'Soon there will be a new hospital at Ghemi,' Pema replied, 'but now we have nothing.'

So Sarah put together an antiseptic dressing, showing the mother how it was done, and bandaged it in place. The boy did not flinch once. We gave her more dressing and antiseptic cream; otherwise there was nothing we could do. I had my doubts whether the wound would heal. Life in such isolated villages may seem idyllic; the reality is extremely harsh.

The climb up to the next pass was the toughest yet. No sooner had we left the green valley behind than we entered a parched and broken country where even the hardiest plants failed to take hold. These truly were badlands. I noticed the muleteers heading the other way hurried to get through them. Our horses hadn't the strength to to carry us all the way, so we dismounted and climbed the final stretch on foot – Leonardo scrabbling up the scree like a true Tibetan, his black umbrella unfurled as always to shield him from the burning sun.

We all needed a breather at the top of the pass. Far to the south, the ice-bound Dhaulagiri Range reared up above the clouds. The afternoon winds were picking up, so we kept moving through a high plain where herds of cattle and goats grazed on sparse tufts of grass that grow in between the omnipresent thorn bushes. Our horses needed resting and we walked most of the way to Lo Ghekar. Only when we reached the final ridge overlooking the monastery did we mount up again. This time Pema borrowed the monk's bay pony and led us on a wild downhill gallop past a row of chortens and right into the monastic courtyard, so as to make a fine entry.

The cookboys had walked ahead and already set up camp on a grassy slope beyond the monastery. There is no village at Lo Ghekar, and the surrounding meadows are home to a large colony of hares. I watched them scampering for cover whenever one of the monastery's guard dogs came too close. A brood mare was whinnying frantically, trying to call back a foal that had wandered too far. Beyond, a mountain stream plunged into a ravine where some of its waters were diverted along dry-stone irrigation channels that led eventually to the fields around Marang, a village far down the valley.

The guardian-monk who kept the keys could not be

found, so we left visiting the prayer hall to the following morning. The interior is very dark and, most unusually, the walls are decorated not with paintings but with stone slabs carved in bas relief, each of them set within a wooden frame. The inner chapel is presided over by a large statue of the eighth-century Buddhist missionary Padmasambhava, who is believed to have stopped here on his way to Tibet. Pema and Gyatso lit a row of butter lamps and placed them on an assemblage of steel trunks that served as a temporary altar. By their flickering light I tried to see what kind of wall-paintings adorned this sanctum sanctorum. To my surprise, I found no painting visible at all. The walls appeared to be completely black. Either the shrine had been gutted by fire (which might explain the absence of a proper altar) or the walls had been so blackened by the smoke from countless butter lamps that nothing was to be seen.

Neither Pema nor Gyatso could explain this mystery. For them it was enough to have prayed at the shrine of Guru Rinpoche – as Padmasambhava is known throughout the Tibetan world. 'If the high lama was present,' Pema said, 'maybe he could tell us. But now he is very old and his health is not good.' As if to prove his point, he showed me a brightly painted sedan chair that had last been used to carry the head lama down the valley to Tsarang, from where he had been helicoptered out to hospital in Pokhara. To me, it seemed bizarre that this dignitary be carried on the shoulders of villagers to catch a helicopter flight. To them it was just switching from one mode of transport to another.

We saddled up in the courtyard and set off on our final day's march to Lo Manthang. There was an air of expectancy as we packed up camp. Everyone knew that our long journey was nearly over. And this time we all travelled together, mule-train, cookboys and riders. The lead mule — a bossy grey with a huge bell around its neck — set a furious pace as we tackled the long but gradual ascent to the last high pass. The descent was even more rapid, and soon we entered a desolate country of bare rock and earth that looked like it had been scooped out by some diabolical mining operation.

I found it hard to believe we were approaching Lo Manthang, the seat of kings and capital of Mustang, but Gyastso assured me we would be there within the hour.

'Look,' he said, as a streak of greenery appeared from behind another knuckle-white range, 'that is Thingkar, my home village. That red house on top of the hill is Namgyal Monastery. And there', he pointed to the east, 'is Lo Manthang.'

Arriving from this direction, the walled city appeared to rise straight out of the desert. The walls ran in straight lines, punctuated here and there by slightly protruding, rectangular towers. These hid most of the buildings within; but two large structures poked their heads above the parapets. One was painted red, suggesting it was a monastic foundation, though its form was that of a massive tower, without windows or any other means of access. The other was mainly white and seemed to occupy half the town. Gyatso confirmed that this was the king's palace.

Just then, Sarah came trotting up on her lively grey. 'Is that it?' she queried.

'Yes, Lo Manthang,' I replied, scarcely able to control my excitement. 'And what a remarkable sight it is. A medieval city, perfectly preserved, its walls still intact . . .'

'It's rather smaller than I imagined.'

'Walled cities are like that. They have to cram a lot into a small space. Think of San Gimignano.'

At which she dug her heels into the grey's flanks, leaving me to follow at an awkward trot. It did not look like being the joyful arrival that I had imagined.

The final approach to Lo Manthang revealed a softer side. Here, on the slopes beneath the city, waters channelled from a mountain stream had worked their customary miracle. We rode through walled fields of flowering buckwheat and mustard, a patchwork of intense pinks and yellows that would have delighted any painter of the Impressionist school. In places the irrigation overflowed and turned the path into a fast-flowing stream. Upon reaching the city's only gate we all dismounted.

'Nobody can enter the city on a horse,' explained Gyatso, 'except the king.'

Above this entrance through the city walls, supported by beams that still resembled tree-trunks, was what I thought at first was a gatehouse. I later discovered it was a chapel whose dark interior is almost entirely filled by a drum-shaped prayer wheel.

A group of women coming the other way had head-straps across their foreheads to help bear the weight of wicker baskets on their backs. I peered into one of these baskets. It contained animal dung mixed with straw – excellent manure, no doubt, and very good for spreading on the fields. But what were these women doing carrying it *out* from the city?

The mystery was soon resolved when a goatherd cajoled his bleating charges through the main gate and into the city. I followed them in, leading my own palomino by the reins, and found the square in front of the king's palace was alive with domestic animals of every sort – donkeys, goats, mules, cattle, pack ponies. Most of them didn't need to be driven on. They knew their way home and meekly disappeared through the doors left open for them.

I now realized that the citizens of Lo Manthang still bring their livestock in from the fields each evening, that the ground floors of most houses are in fact barns or stables, and that such practices naturally result in a rapid build-up of animal droppings that need to be taken out from the city. As there is no wheeled transport – let alone motor vehicles – anywhere in Upper Mustang, the only way to remove all that manure is to carry it out on a donkey or, as I had seen, on a human back.

And it was not just cow shit that was being carried out of the city. There are no sewers or water mains in Lo Manthang and lavatories are fairly primitive – basically a hole in the floor. For all that, there is an element of class distinction in the Lobas' sanitary arrangements. Commoners generally squat on the second floor, the nobility on the third, while there is a five-storey drop from the spacious cubicle in the king's palace.

It was all very medieval. Indeed, it dawned on me that living for a while in Lo Manthang might be just a little more 'medieval' than I had bargained for.

'We are staying in the house of the king's cousin,' announced Pema, as if to reassure me. He led the way down a narrow alley just beyond the royal palace and opened a door in the blank wall. It gave onto a narrow courtyard where one of our pack mules was being unloaded. I climbed a wooden ladder up to an open gallery, where I was greeted by the lady of the house, Yanji Maya Bista. I had already spotted her from down in the courtyard, for she was a striking woman. She wore a heavy striped apron and kept her long hair tied up in a tight bun. But it was the way she stood at the top of the stairs, hands on hips and a wry smile playing across her lips, that made me aware that here was a woman of authority.

She ordered her keys to be brought and opened the padlock to what was to become 'our room'. I had to duck my head to get through the doorway, but once inside I realized what privileged guests we were. For she had offered us the family shrine room. In the far corner was a glass-fronted cabinet containing statues of the Buddha Maitreya and holy lamas. Silver bowls for water offerings and incense were lined up before it, and to one side hung a framed print of Guru Rinpoche.

'But we can't possibly stay here,' I protested.

Yanji insisted it was also a guest room, and to prove her point lifted the Tibetan rugs that covered what I had supposed were low-slung divans. They turned out to be narrow iron-framed beds, and there were four of them in the room. Two had already been made up with coloured sheets and pillowcases of Chinese manufacture that must have been intended for children. One set was adorned with bunny rabbits, while the other was printed with the message 'welcome'.

She left us with one of her quizzical smiles and we set about unpacking our kit-bag. The more I looked around this room, the more curiosities I discovered. An ancient muzzle-loader hung from one of the wooden pillars that helped support the roof. There was a fine tangka hidden in one of the corners. But what I found most fascinating was the collection of photographs and pictures. Apart from the sacred images around the shrine, these included a wedding portrait of the King and Queen of Mustang, a black-and-white photograph of the young King Birendra and his queen wearing a fur hat, another of Yanji's husband, Gyanendra Bista, out trekking with the crown prince of Denmark, and a privately taken group shot in which the Dalai Lama featured prominently. I could detect a certain consistency so far. But how did the torn poster of George Michael fit in beside these worthies?

Our presence in the shrine room was not allowed to disturb the daily round of offerings. Each morning the water offerings were replaced, and each evening incense burnt and a single butter lamp lit (I soon grew used to nodding off in its flickering light). At meal-times we were joined by the liaison officer, the smoky kitchen where everybody else ate being deemed unsuitable for honoured guests.

Ganga's natural fastidiousness grew more pronounced in such an easy-going household. He complained about the smoke and dirt, and once sent back a plate that had been placed over a dish of eggs to keep them warm. But then some things did happen that were bound to upset a strict Brahmin – as when the local butcher came round and slaughtered a large white billy goat in the central courtyard. I remember seeing the tethered animal very much alive when I went out one morning. When I returned I found its newly skinned head dripping over the door mantle while the courtyard walls were hung with the four quarters. The butcher was still there, squatting beside a basin of fresh blood mixed with offal which he was laboriously squeezing into the large intestine in order to make chitterlings. Although I am not that squeamish I found myself hurrying past. As for poor Ganga, he took to his room until it was all over.

The kitchen was the real centre of activity in the

household, so Sarah and I took to dropping in for a cup of tea or to watch the menfolk gamble at dice and cards. Most Tibetans and Nepalis are compulsive gamblers, but never have I seen such marathon sessions as were played out in that kitchen. Everyone was at it: Pema, the cookboys, the master of the house and various friends of his – including a very cool, long-haired Khampa from a village beyond the Kali Gandaki. I was worried that Pema had gambled away the expedition's budget, but he claimed to be several hundred rupees up.

While these sessions continued, endless cups of tea and rakshi accompanied by little snacks of curried goat were served up by Yanji and her best friend, Tara Gurung, who worked in the offices of ACAP (the Annapurna Conservation Area Project, an environmental group responsible for Mustang) when she was not in the kitchen. The two women called each other sister, though they were not blood relations. Between them they cooked up a plan for a rather different kind of evening's entertainment.

This involved connecting a mobile cassette player up to a car battery, which had been charged up courtesy of a solar panel that someone had borrowed. (There is still no mains electricity in Lo Manthang because the micro-hydro project installed by the Nepalese government was built in the wrong place, where there is insufficient water flow to turn the turbines.) A single neon panel was fixed to a pillar and, when switched on, this cast an unnatural light over the habitually dark and grimy kitchen, revealing how the ceiling timbers had been blackened by wood smoke and turning the copper-banded barrels used for making butter tea and tsampa an electric blue. Further preparations included cooking vast mounds of rice and curry, and decanting rakshi into magnum-sized bottles that had originally contained Chinese brandy.

When all was prepared, Tara came over to invite us to the party. 'Sister-sister,' she called out – for by now Sarah had been included within this informal sisterhood. Indeed, Tara persuaded her to try on her best set of Tibetan clothes, which looked splendid even though they were several sizes too small. The same cannot be said of Tara's attempt at wearing Western clothes, for her small frame was swamped by the only dress that Sarah had brought to wear for our audience with the king.

'Sister-sister,' she repeated. 'Disco-disco. Come quickly.'

We followed her into the kitchen to find the room full of gyrating bodies. The decrepid ghettoblaster was pumping out Nepali pop songs at a volume that I thought must surely blow the speakers soon. Two of our cookboys were dancing with each other, while Mr Cool Khampa strutted his stuff before the lady of the house. When that song ended, Yanji grabbed my arm and led me onto the beaten earth that served as a dance-floor. I tried to follow her graceful arm movements (which reminded me more of Nepali rather than Tibetan dance) but was aware that my legs were stuck in a fixed shuffle that owed more to Tamla Motown than the music of these hills.

Tara, meanwhile, had coaxed Sarah onto the dance floor, where they were soon joined by Pema and the Cool Khampa. Gyatso did a star turn, suggesting that when in Kathmandu he often went out clubbing. Even the king's secretary had a whirl.

Apart from us two, everyone knew the words and sang along. More rakshi was brought and the dancing became ever more frenetic until, as I had anticipated, the tape player packed in. While Tara set to poking a screwdriver around its innards, Yanji organized an impromptu sing-along. Again, most of the songs chosen were Kathmandu chart-toppers, so everyone could join in.

Only the old muleman sang in Tibetan. Pema whispered that it was a song of the Brogpas, the nomads who used to move between Mustang and Tibet with their yaks and goats. The muleman had a deep, guttural voice, and he gave it his all. The effect on his audience was palpable: their eyes glowed as they listened with silent concentration. Then it was jollity time again, and our Gurung cookboy launched into another pop anthem.

When our turn came round, Sarah and I could think of nothing more original than 'Jerusalem'. Unfortunately, the rakshi must have gone to our heads and we were unable to agree on the correct order of the verses. Did the 'dark satanic mills' come before or after the bit about 'England's green and pleasant land'? In desperation, I gave an operatic rendering of 'The Masturbatory Intermezzo' – a spoof version of a Gilbert and Sullivan air – hoping that nobody would understand the words. At first, everyone looked on in amazement. But about halfway through I noticed that Chandra, the king's secretary, was giggling uncontrollably. He at least had caught on as to what the song was about.

The Lobas certainly knew how to party. They were still hard at it long after Sarah and I had retired to the shrine room. And the next day Tara was suggesting we have another 'disco-disco'. My rakshi hangover suggested that this might not be a good idea. Besides, I had other things to do while in Lo Manthang.

*

The fortress-monastery of Tashichodzong, Thimphu. Formerly Bhutan's winter capital, the dzong was rebuilt in the 1960s by the late king and now houses government ministries alongside the monastic body.

Tongsa Dzong, birthplace of Bhutan's monarchy.

Spiralling sound: two monks blow on *jalings* to announce the beginning of the day's teachings in a valley high above Drigung.

Tibetan nuns offering butter tea and tsampa during the Full Moon Festival, near Drigung, Central Tibet.

Right: Crowd-control, Tibetan-style. A discipline monk prepares to wield his big stick against the crush of pilgrims seeking a blessing from an incarnate lama, during the Drigung Festival.

Below: His Holiness the Dalai Lama with the author, Dharamsala.

Top left: Coronation Day: HM King Birendra of Nepal and Queen Aishwarya in Kathmandu, 1975.

Top right: Entrance to Hanuman Dhoka, the old royal palace, Kathmandu.

Below: Durbar Square, Patan – almost entirely built before its conquest by the Shah Kings.

Lo Manthang, the capital of Mustang, with the royal palace at its centre.

Kagbeni, the Gateway to Upper Mustang. Kagbeni clings to the cliff above the Kali Gandaki River.

The road to Lo Manthang, on the little bay pony.

King Jigme Dorje Palbar and Queen Ridol of Mustang.

Tarang Monastery, Upper Mustang, whose head lamas have traditionally been chosen from Mustang's royal family.

Left: Warrior-monk: Captain Yongda would have fought to preserve the Kingdom of Sikkim. Now he runs a school for orphans at Pemayangtse monastery.

Above: Tea pickers on the Temi Estate in West Sikkim. The British brought tea cultivation to the highlands and with it Nepali labourers, who soon outnumbered the indigenous population.

A chorten and prayer flags mark the spot where the first Buddhist king of Sikkim was enthroned in 1642.

Novice monks, Tashigang, East Bhutan. Traditionally, boys entered
the monkhood early, though now the age of entry is rising.

The King of Bhutan, HM Jigme Singye Wangchuck, seated on
the Golden Throne.

Chandra called round after breakfast to tell us that our audience with the king was 'imminent'. Meanwhile, why didn't we explore the sights of Lo Manthang? There were three monasteries within the walls. Attached to one of these was a new monastic school, where young boys destined for the monkhood were being given instuction in the Tibetan language. The king thought this an important development if Mustang was to retain its distinctive culture.

But first I wanted to see the Thubchhen Gompa, the great prayer hall that had enjoyed royal patronage through many generations. It was not far from where we were staying, but the alleyways of Lo Manthang are so narrow and twist so deceptively that Sarah and I lost our way at least twice. Down one cul-de-sac we came across a group of women practising a dance for a forthcoming festival – a much more restrained and traditional kind of dancing than what had gone on in the kitchen disco. We also saw several of the older inhabitants spinning goat's wool by hand to help supplement the family income (most households are home to three, if not four, generations). It is a sociable activity, and they huddled together on the rough-hewn steps to their houses, gossiping away as they spun the wool with the same automatic movement as is used in revolving a prayer wheel.

It was the noise from a generator that eventually drew us to the prayer hall. Electric cables snaked down the steps into the interior and the main entrance was sealed off with plastic sheeting. Obviously some major restoration was under way. Somewhat hesitantly, we walked down the steps, aware that we were flanked on either side by enormous terracotta figures of protective deities. I peered inside and found an exceptionally large and brightly lit hall. Straight ahead was a forest of pillars – massive enough to support the weight of the broad roof, and yet so finely proportioned and delicately carved that they appeared to perform this effortlessly. One glance at the wall paintings confirmed that this was an exceptional temple.

In its current state, however, the place looked more like a building site than a temple. Half the walls were covered in scaffolding, and where the roof had caved in yet more plastic sheeting was stretched as temporary protection against the elements. The floor was piled high with massive timbers, carpentry tools, coils of plastic hose and sealed pots containing paints and chemicals. There was a lot of activity. Workmen perched high on the scaffolding were scraping away at the walls or injecting them with chemicals through plastic tubes. I needed to know what was going on.

My wish was fulfilled, and in the most unexpected manner, by Rodolfo Lujan. When I first entered the temple he had been up on the scaffolding, his face hidden by a respiratory mask, inserting chemical stabilizer into a section of wall painting. I had to wait for him to complete this delicate task; but as soon as he pulled off that mask I knew I was in the hands of an expert.

Rodolfo explained he was a Guatemalan by birth but had lived in Rome for many years – whenever, that is, he was not busy restoring temple paintings in Burma, Cambodia and across the Himalayas. He was in Lo Manthang for the whole summer, part of an Italian team whose duties were both to lead the restoration work and teach local craftsmen how to continue the job in their absence. It was this aspect of his work that he liked best. 'They are very intelligent boys,' he smiled, 'very eager to learn.'

'It is a very big project', he said, 'with funding from the

American Himalaya Foundation. Of course, there is Nepalese involvement through the Annapurna Conservation Area Project. But the King of Mustang – he also has taken a great interest. These big timbers needed to make new pillars, he found them in Tibet. Also, as soon as this work is finished he wants this to be a living temple again. Already he has made provision for a monk body to return.'

Rodolfo invited us to climb the scaffolding to see how work was progressing. Sarah declined on account of her vertigo, but I followed him up to a section of wall that was being cleaned by a local artisan. 'Here you can see there has been overpainting, maybe from the eighteenth century when this wall collapsed. But here they have preserved the original work, as though they knew they had something very precious.'

I agreed that the original fifteenth-century paintings were exquisite. And it was not just that Rodolfo's enthusiasm was catching. Even before meeting him, I had been astounded by their gracefulness of line, their richness of colour.

'Yes, yes,' he enthused. 'They used only the most precious materials. I believe I have found traces of malachite and real vermilion – although by this time the Chinese had invented a substitute. Also, a little of lapis lazuli. The use of gold is quite profligate. But you must look also at the detail, the little flowers here. It is so fine that it is almost like the work of a miniaturist.

'Of course this is a royal foundation. But the king who ordered this must have had wealth beyond our dreams. Not only wealth, but taste. The style of painting is so distinctive that I think the master must have come from far away, possibly from India.'

We climbed back down to the ground, where Sarah joined us for a tour of the bronze and terracotta statues down the altar end. Although impressive in size, Rodolfo thought only one of this group – a bronze Buddha – showed true refinement in its execution. But it was for the wall paintings that he reserved his highest praise.

'Is it not a coincidence', he asked, 'that at the same time this building was decorated, in Europe there was also an artistic movement that valued gracefulness above all else? I am speaking of the style known as International Gothic. There is a quality to these paintings that makes me think of Gentile de Fabriano. And the richness of workmanship, the grandeur of conception? I can think of only one place to equal this, in Florence, and that is the Cappella Medici in the Palazzo Medici-Riccardi.' I made a mental note that if I ever found myself in Florence I would visit the Medici chapel.

We left Rodolfo to get on with his restoration work. But there was more to come. Just down the lane from Thubcchen Gompa stands the thick-set, red-painted tower that I had seen riding into Lo Manthang; and although from the outside it looks like a military structure, in fact it contains a gigantic Buddha.

We entered by the first floor, and still it towered above us. At first I was puzzled as to why such a monumental statue should be enclosed within a tower. Even from the upper storeys it was impossible to get a good view of it.

Then I realized that the statue was made of beaten earth and had to be protected from the wind and rain. I also noticed that the gallery around it was painted exclusively with mystic mandalas – abstract, symmetrical images that are often used as aids for meditation. This I had never seen in any other Buddhist temple. Obviously, the tower and the gigantic Buddha were intended to be a focus of intense spiritual power. For this it was not necessary to see or admire the statue within. It was enough to know that it was there, guarding over the city of Lo Manthang and its people.

When we returned home there was a message from the king's secretary. An audience had been arranged for the following morning, at ten o'clock. In the meantime, did we fancy another disco party?

Not wanting to turn up at the palace with a monstrous hangover, I declined the last part of the invitation. And while I was delighted that I would finally meet the Mustang Raja, I was aware that many things needed to be done beforehand. For one thing, we had forgotten to purchase a kadda, the white silk scarf that is always exchanged on such occasions. How could I buy one now that the few shops in Lo Manthang were shut? Thankfully the lady of the house, Yanji, came to our assistance, saying that she would find us both kaddas — and of good quality at that.

I tucked the little roll of silk into my pocket next morning as we marched the short distance to the king's palace. It is a massive structure, more like a fortress than what one normally associates with the word 'palace'. Its white-washed walls taper inwards slightly, reinforcing this impression of strength, and there are no windows at all on the lower storeys. I was told these lower floors served as storerooms and stables. Higher up, where the royal household lived, there were still only a few windows, and these were narrow and unevenly spaced. 'It must be very gloomy inside,' Sarah commented.

There is only one gateway, which is sealed by heavy wooden doors at night. Within is an entrance hall, its walls the colour of dried mud, its uneven floor lined with rough slabs. The air was heavy with dust.

Access to the palace's upper storeys is by a wooden staircase so steep that it resembles a ladder. Nobody was about, so we started climbing, only to be greeted on the first floor by the concerted roar of three Tibetan mastiffs. Two of them are kept chained up in the hallway, and these hurl themselves towards you with much barking and growling until they are pulled up by their chain. But the largest is kept separately in a guardroom over the palace entrance. Here he can roam around and, whenever he senses an intruder, propel his massive frame against a rickety stable door – this being the only barrier between his fine set of teeth and the visitor's throat.

'No need to worry,' commented Chandra, who had appeared from an upper level. 'It is only palace security.'

All very well for him to say that, I thought. He was used to this sort of thing. Besides, wasn't it cruel to the dogs? I asked, with typical Western sensitivities.

'They always stay here – they are guard dogs. They are used to it,' said the private secretary in the same tone that his predecessor, just one generation earlier, might have dismissed the grievances of serfs.

We kept climbing up to the fourth floor, where we entered an open courtyard sealed with beaten earth. It was here that Leonardo, the monk-artist, would sit in the sunshine while touching up the gilt and paintwork on half a dozen assorted Buddhas. With Chandra leading the way, we crossed the courtyard and ascended a final stairway to the palaces's fifth and topmost level. Here, an open gallery gave onto the royal apartments. We halted before an open door, screened off in the Tibetan fashion by a length of patterned cloth. The private secretary peered inside to check everything was in order, and then ushered us into the audience room. There was a shrine against the far wall, in front of which sat a dignified old man. He stood hurriedly and smiled a greeting, so the first thing I noticed about the King of Mustang was that he has a gold front tooth.

He also sported a single gold and turquoise earring, and on his 'marriage finger' a heavy signet ring. Otherwise, his dress was simple: a plain white shirt beneath a sleeveless cardigan, and grey trousers. He wore his hair long, in tightly bound tresses that formed a circle around the crown of his head.

The hair is still black, despite his having passed his seventieth birthday; but it had thinned and receded like the snows in summer. His face bore testimony of many days' out riding through harsh weather, for it is as deeply lined and indented as the eroded mountains of his kingdom, and his complexion is much darker than is usual among the Tibetan aristocracy. And while many foreigners have remarked upon the resemblance between peoples of Tibetan stock and the North American Indian, King Jigme Dorje Palbar really did look like a veteran of the Little Big Horn.

A voluminous black shawl was draped over one shoulder, like a scarf of office. It fell in heavy folds around his lap, where a little black-and-white kitten was playing without concern for royal dignity. The king would occasionally stroke its neck, to calm it down, and then resume clicking the beads of his rosary. Obviously the king was fond of animals, for there was also a pair of lapdogs – an Apso and a crossbreed with plenty of Apso in the mix – scurrying about the floor. For the most part, the king sat erect and unsmiling, a stern figure of authority. I guessed this was how he appeared to the people of Lo. But occasionally his face would break into a smile and, as the creases deepened, a hidden reserve of warmth seeped out.

Sarah and I presented the silk scarves we had brought and these were graciously accepted. Tibetan tea was served, but it was not too salty and I had no trouble drinking it. Since everything that was said had to be translated by Chandra, there were long pauses during which I could take in my surroundings.

The room was large enough to seat twenty people on low benches strewn with carpets, but it retained an informal, lived-in air about it. Across the far wall stood a pair of antique cupboards of the Tibetan sort, their wooden doors painted with intricate designs now faded with the years. I saw their open surfaces and glass-fronted cabinets were crammed with butter lamps and vases for religious offerings, a full tea service, assorted bric-a-brac of mainly Chinese manufacture, and numerous family photographs – including one of the young Prince Jigme Bista in school uniform and Nepali cap.

Looking around the other walls I spotted the standard portraits of King Birendra and Queen Aishwarya in full regalia, though here the picture frames were draped with white scarves as a token of respect. There was a photo of the Mustang Raja in the military uniform he is entitled to wear as an honorary colonel of the Nepalese army, and another of his wife bowing before the king and queen of Nepal during an investiture ceremony when she was honoured for nearly thirty years of public service. That was mainly during the Panchayat era, and I understood Queen Ridol has been less active in local politics under the new multi-party system. A black-and-white wedding photograph in which she was wearing the twin-horned headdress typical of the old Tibetan aristocracy hung in a far corner of the room. Traditionally the kings of Mustang had sought their queens in Lhasa, or sometimes in Ladakh, but Queen Ridol was born into one of the leading families of Shigatse. She had married at seventeen and, although there were no children, the marriage remains a happy one after almost fifty years.

The queen peered in a couple of times to see whether there was sufficient tea and biscuits to go round, but otherwise left her husband to do the talking. I asked him whether as a young man he had worried about becoming king. 'But I was not meant to be king,' he announced, before explaining how all through his boyhood he had enjoyed 'a very carefree life because both my older brother and father were still living'. So clear was the line of succession that, after twenty years on the throne, King Ahan Tenzin Jampal Dhadul had retired in order to devote himself to religious pursuits, appointing his elder son Wangdu as dungpa, the king's executive representative. But Prince Wangdu died unexpectedly in 1958, leaving two daughters but no male heir. So the old king resumed his duties until he too died in 1964.

Remembering how 'my unfortunate elder brother's death' entirely changed his life, King Jigme said that 'like thunder it came, all the responsibility of kingship came down to me'. But his father's resumption of powers provided a breathing space. 'Always my father insisted I should have some knowledge of how to govern, how to administer. So he kept me with him, and showed me how it should be done.'

None the less, it cannot have been easy taking over in late 1964. By then there were some 7,000 Khampa guerillas based in Mustang, and they were being trained and armed by the CIA. While under strict orders not to interfere with the local population, the Khampas remained a law unto themselves, beyond the king's jurisdiction. Some incidents did occur, usually involving Khampas seducing Loba women. And as the guerilla army mounted more raids into Tibet, the opposing Chinese forces began patrolling the border more aggressively. What was left of the old trade with Tibet dried up. The seasonal migrations of Loba herdsmen with their yaks and goats became a thing of the past.

Both the king and people of Mustang were sympathetic to the Khampas' cause. As he now told me, 'When Tibet was free, we had good relations with them.' So many aspects of their lives– their Buddhist culture, their language, their family and commercial ties – depended on free access to Tibet, that the Lobas were only too ready to believe the Chinese would soon go away and the Old Order be restored. How could they know that the Khampas' struggle to liberate Tibet was just a side-show in the game of global brinkmanship known as the Cold War, and that it was never taken seriously by the Americans? Or that, for all the Khampas' claims about successful raids, their operations never amounted to more than a minor irritant to the Chinese army in Tibet? And whatever clandestine funds received by the Khampas trickled through to their Loba 'hosts', such pay-offs provided only a temporary respite. The closure of the border meant that Mustang was no longer on a trade route. It was on a road to nowhere, and the entire economy suffered accordingly.

The royal government of Nepal found it convenient to close its eyes to what was happening in Mustang. It did not want to accept responsibility for the Khampas' presence there, since to do so would undermine Nepal's new friendship with China. Nor did it wish to antagonize those powers, principally America and India, which supported the guerilla movement. So it did virtually nothing to assert its authority within Mustang. This unusual situation left the king in charge. Even after America withdrew its support and the Khampas finally surrendered in 1974, King Jigme continued to exercise real power throughout Upper Mustang.

Further down the Kali Gandaki, the Nepalese had established a major military post and administrative headquarters at Jomsom, and the Thakali people of that region were only too happy to cooperate with the new authorities and do whatever they could to erode the Mustang Raja's authority. This was an ancient rivalry, but now they could produce legal documents to prove that King Jigme should no longer be wielding such powers, that he was not really a king any more. Armed with such papers, Thakalis tried to spread disaffection among the Loba population. They had little success, probably because there was no alternative source of authority. The absence of any Nepalese officials on the ground meant that the king continued to collect taxes and dispense justice through the 1980s. In theory, serious criminal cases ought to have gone before the District Court in Jomsom. In practice, not a single case from Upper Mustang was heard there. King Jigme gave judgement in open session, just as his ancestors had done. Mostly these concerned family disputes over property. But on the rare occasions that a Loba was found guilty of theft or violent crime, such traditional punishments as being beaten with a knotted rope were meted out.

The past decade has seen far greater changes. The king acknowledges that 'before we had power in this area. But now there is a new movement, a changing situation, in which the royal government of Nepal is taking on more activities. So I am ruling through an era of change.' It was said without regret, although sometimes he can become frustrated because he still feels responsible for 'his' people but is no longer able to do much on their behalf.

'Another great change is this. In the time of my ancestors, people had to come from all over to work here in the palace. They received no salary. It was their duty. But now,' he said, staring meaningfully at his private secretary, 'I give salaries to everyone.'

'Only a very little one,' said Chandra, making everyone laugh. Then he explained to me that 'basically we have moved on from a feudal set-up'. He uttered the word 'feudal' as though it gave off a bad smell. Clearly he was embarrassed by it. And it is true, as a concept feudalism has few positive connotations in this day and age. But he was right to do so, for Mustang is an unusually well-preserved example of a feudal principality.

Until the 1960s, its formal relationship with the Kingdom of Nepal was that of a 'Dependent State'. The Mustang Raja was required to send an annual tribute to the King of Nepal at Kantipur. Otherwise, the kings of Mustang were to 'rule over and enjoy your territories within the prescribed boundaries from generation to generation'. The relationship was similar to that of a feudal client or vassal and his liege-lord. Even after the special status of the four Dependent States as 'kingdoms within the greater kingdom' was dissolved in 1961, the Mustang Rajas retained virtual autonomy and ruled over their subjects just as before.

When King Jigme observed that before 'people had to come from all over to work here in the palace', he was referring to a system of feudal obligations that continued until well within living memory. At the top of the pyramid, noble families were required to provide counsellors and personal attendants. At the bottom, the king's serfs had to till and harvest the king's fields. In between, specified households had to provide for all of the palace's needs without payment. These obligations were hereditary.

A local man called Jabyang, who reckoned he was fifty-seven years old, could still recall how the old system operated. 'For collecting firewood – eighteen houses had this duty. To look after the king's palace, for drawing water, for doing the cooking, again eighteen houses. For cleaning the rooms and looking after the king's dogs, eight or nine households. The same number of houses were responsible for the horses. My own father was in charge of the king's horses, and for this he was paid nothing.' Jabyang did not look like he remembered this with pleasure. Horses are expensive to look after properly, and their owners tend to fuss over them more than just about anything else.

He explained how families with special skills were assigned to particular duties. Besides looking after the royal yaks, the tent-dwelling nomads of the highlands had to make strong threads from yak's hair which were used for horse harnesses and tying up dogs. Other families inherited more spiritual duties. Eight households were responsible for prayers in the king's chapels. But the most curious of these feudal obligations was that of staging Tibetan operas. Six households had to bear the costs. 'All these duties fell on families from Lo Manthang or villages nearby,' said Jabyang. 'In Ghemi and other places there was the same system, though maybe the obligations were less because the king went there less often.'

Very similar patterns of feudal service were to be found throughout the Himalayan region – in Tibet, Bhutan, the various principalities of Nepal – until around 1950. Obligations fell upon family households and were hereditary. Some honour was attached to serving the king in this way, and families who performed such direct service were often exempted from other dues and taxes. As a means of providing for the basic needs of government it was less than efficient. But in a pre-cash economy there was no real alternative. Rulers did not have the ready money to pay salaries to their officials and servants. Taxes were paid in kind – mostly in grain or livestock – through the village headman. If the quota was not fulfilled, their property went to the king.

The only unusual thing about Mustang is that the system remained unchanged for so long. Jabyang remembered that 'it began to be replaced about fifty years ago, but only very slowly'. The king was still collecting land taxes and the duty payable whenever landed property is transferred during the 1980s. By rights the Government of Nepal should have collected such revenues, but they had no officers based in Mustang. The exercise of justice also remained with the king, partly because the nearest government court was several days' ride distant, but mostly because the Loba people seem to have preferred it that way.

Nowadays, local disputes over land or irrigation rights

are normally settled by the elected members of a Village Development Commitee. But appeals can still be made to the king's judgement, and some Lobas prefer to go directly to the palace for arbitration.

Only in the last decade of the twentieth century did central government make its presence felt in this bastion of traditional monarchy. The king has sold off some of his lands, but still there is a shortfall in revenues. So today, more than half of the hundred or so rooms in the palace are left unoccupied. The fabric is in dire need of repair. And nowadays the royal household has to get by with a staff of between ten and fifteen paid retainers.

The pattern of service is well illustrated by the career of the king's bodyguard, Pema Ngutuk. His mother was in royal service before him, and he was actually born within the palace. 'I went straight into service at the age of five or six, looking after the king's calves up in the mountains. From the age of fourteen I walked with the mules carrying supplies down to Pokhara and back. Not once did I lose a mule or a horse,' he added with some pride.

'Then, when I was about twenty-five, I was put in charge of the palace stables. The king keeps about forty horses there. And for the last twenty-one years I have been the king's bodyguard and house-master in charge of palace security.' At which he pulled out the ancient sten gun he always carries with him. 'Fortunately the king has never been in any dangerous situation, so I have not had to use this.'

Pema has been well rewarded. His family live in a substantial house right next to the king's summer palace in the village of Thingkar. But then he is more than just a bodyguard; he has become the king's right-hand man.

Whenever he is unable to attend on the royal family, his brother stands in. And his son, Gyatso, who accompanied our expedition, is already working for Crown Prince Jigme and looks like becoming his right-hand man. Such personal loyalties remain one of the monarchy's strengths – provided, that is, they can recruit people of the same calibre in future.

But there is more than self-interest in this network of patronage and service. How else can one explain why King Jigme adopted a young Indian boy who had been on a pilgrimage with his father to one of the lakes in Mustang that is sacred to Hindus? In the course of this journey his father died, and the boy was brought to Lo Manthang, where the king decided to take him into the palace. Now he is a trusted royal servant. When I met him on the road he was escorting an incarnate lama whom the king had decided to send down to Kathmandu. Apart from its fairytale quality, the story of this orphaned child being taken into the royal household illustrates a strongly philanthropic streak in King Jigme's character. Certainly, all those gathered together in that wayside inn, when they heard what the king had done, agreed that it was a meritorious act.

I had been told that King Jigme is a deeply religious man. Every morning he rises before dawn and completes three koras, walking in a clockwise direction around the walls of his capital, counting his prayer beads and chatting to any of his subjects who care to join him. When I raised this with him, he laughed. 'Oh that is not just religious. My doctor advises me to take the exercise because I have high blood pressure.'

But he does take very seriously his duties as a Buddhist

king. Among his titles is 'protector of religion', and not only does he preside over public ceremonies such as the prayers and masked dances performed during the Tizi Festival every spring, he attends to private requests when there is a death in the family or when someone is suffering from an illness thought to be caused by malevolent spirits. His very presence is believed to be beneficial – not, he insists, on account of his personal merit, but because of the merits of his ancestors. And it is in this light that he sees his own role as Lo Gyalpo.

'My ancestors', he said, 'had great respect for the Buddhist religion. I also have responsibility to promote the Buddhist religion here. In practice, I do this by worshipping together with the people, the lamas and monks of the different Buddhist sects who are present in Mustang. But I am also aware of the loss of Buddhist culture and am trying to find the best way to preserve it for future generations.

'In my opinion, we must combine modernization and cultural development. The most important thing is that our children are taught in their local language. Some years ago, most people had the opportunity to learn the Tibetan language. Now there are many more schools in the villages, but instruction is in the Nepali language only. If we had a good local language school, that would help both our traditional culture and, by raising standards in all subjects, assist in our development.'

This was not the first time I had heard such a call to do something to protect the local language and culture before it is too late. It is something one encounters among minority language groups throughout the Himalayas – whether it be

Sherpas or Gurungs in Nepal, Bhotias and Lepchas in Sikkim, or even Tibetans within Tibet. The setting up of government-funded schools in more remote regions is a recent development, and while the availability of 'modern' education is generally welcomed, when instruction is given only in the national language there is inevitably an erosion of local language and culture.

The Lobas are at least fortunate in that they speak a dialect of Tibetan, a written language with a rich literature that is being actively fostered by the exiled community in Nepal and India. The Sherpas, although widely admired for their rich folklore as well as their mountaineering skills, have only an oral tradition to fall back on. Sadly, the tendency of central governments to use standardized schooling as an instrument of 'nation-building' means that many distinctive hill cultures are likely to vanish.

In Mustang's case, the closure of the border with Tibet has left it cut off from its religious and cultural roots. In his youth, King Jigme was sent to Shigatse and Lhasa for a traditional Tibetan education, just as his ancestors had done with their children for hundreds of years. His adopted son was schooled in Jomsom before going on to college in Kathmandu. Similarly, the mainly Sakya monks of Mustang used to be sent to complete their religious education in Tibetan monasteries. Now they go down to Kathmandu or to Dehra Dun, the headquarters of the exiled Sakya Lama in northern India.

'It is good that we can maintain some of our religious traditions this way,' commented the king. 'Also that we now have a monastic school here in Lo Manthang' – referring here to the Tsechen Shedrubling Mon Gon Lobdra, a school established in 1994 for instructing novice monks in Tibetan as well as Nepali. But he also wants the local language to be taught to all children, not just those intended for the monkhood.

He would welcome closer relations with Tibet, but believes this would only be possible when Tibetans gain some form of independence or autonomy. 'If they have freedom', he said, 'we can renew our relationship. Now it is not possible to maintain our cultural or family ties with people inside Tibet. We cannot go, and they cannot come here.'

'What about the impact of foreign visitors?' I asked, changing the subject. After all, Upper Mustang had only been opened up to foreigners for seven years. Surely contact with outsiders had brought unforeseen changes?

'I had been trying for years to open the country', he said, 'working with His Majesty's Government of Nepal. Before, people thought their living standards would rise. But now we are open to foreigners I do not see any real change. Only a very few people who can speak English draw some benefit. Most people have no contact, and therefore gain nothing from this change.

'Also, there is the matter of the royalties paid by visitors. To begin with, sixty per cent of royalties was invested here. Many projects were started through the good offices of ACAP – the conservation of our monasteries, teaching and cultural programmes, tree plantings, bringing in solar energy and small hydro-electric schemes. But now the money is not coming back. As chairman of Upper Mustang Conservation and Development Project, I have made representations in person to Kathmandu. We try, but I am not hopeful that we'll get back to sixty per cent.'

*

It is not so much the impact of limited tourism that worries King Jigme as the growing trend, particularly among young people, to abandon their native land and move down to Pokhara or Kathmandu in search of easier ways of making a living. Seasonal migrations have always been a part of Loba life, with much of the population moving down to lower altitudes for the winter months. The royal family follows this custom, seeing out the winter in Kathmandu. But whereas Lobas used to be traders, moving around from place to place until spring came and they could return to their villages, now more of them are settling down in urban areas and only occasionally going home on family visits.

'I have this anxiety', said the king, 'that they will forget their own ways and take up other people's. And this also will bring changes here in Mustang.'

He would like to see the living standards of his people improve. He is pressing for a hospital to be built in Lo Manthang, so that the sick can be treated locally rather than having to travel for days. 'I am in favour of development. But I also think people should follow their own culture. If we can combine these two things, then they will have a good life. That is my personal opinion. But it is very difficult to achieve this balance.'

'But does your heir also share these hopes?' I asked. This must have touched a nerve, for the king looked very solemn.

'Jigme has a good knowledge of the Tibetan language and knows something of our traditions. If he can follow our culture, then he will be a worthy successor. But if he does not follow our traditions it will be very difficult for him also to be king.'

'And which of the previous kings of Mustang do you yourself most admire?'

'I have great respect for all my ancestors,' he declared, 'but most of all for King Wangyul Dorje. He was a visionary man, almost like a genius. His rule brought much good to this land. And he was always successful in battle.'

A very diplomatic choice, I thought. For it was Wangyul Dorje (1789–95) who allied himself to the rising power of Gorkha. In doing so, he freed his people from the depredations of the Jumlis and greatly increased the territorial limits of his kingdom. By bringing Mustang within the ambit of the Nepalese state, freely rather than by compulsion, he ensured that his successors could rule over their domains in peace, with virtually no interference from outside. It was he who forged the link with the Shah kings of Nepal – a special relationship which, to judge from all the royal photographs on the walls, continues to this day. And the ordinary people of Mustang also benefited from being under the protection of the Gorkha state. After centuries of intermittent warfare, they entered an era of peace. That counts a great deal among a society of farmers and traders.

There have probably been greater changes in Mustang during King Jigme's reign than during the previous two centuries. These he has accepted with grace, although his own status and wealth have declined. When I asked him what had been the most difficult period, he simply replied that 'by the blessings of God I haven't had to face any problems in my time'. I sensed the curtains were coming down. Maybe I had pried too closely. But as we took our leave, the king asked us both to have dinner with him the following night. Then he returned to his seat and took up his rosary.

*

The next morning I saw the king come out of his palace, mount a fine-looking grey gelding, and ride off through the city gate. He was followed by his armed bodyguard and three other riders. Only the king and those with his special permission can ride within the city walls.

'Where is the king going?' I asked Gyatso.

'To the Tibetan border. He is going there for discussions about the new road. The border is three hours' distance, if you ride fast. Hurry, our horses are ready and we are taking the same road. We can follow them part of the way.'

We mounted up outside the walls. The liaison officer was on the little bay, and extra horses had been found for both Pema and Gyatso.

But although we were all on horseback, there was not a chance of catching up with the king's party. We were cantering, but they were going like the wind. I mentioned that the king had a good horse. 'Yes, its value is more than one lakh rupees,' said Gyatso. This is roughly three times what the average Nepali earns in a year.

The road to the Tibetan border follows the upper reaches of the Kali Gandaki. Mostly it is quite flat and on horseback makes easy going. After an hour we turned off towards some villages on the far bank and forded the river. Each village had its own monastery or temple, a Mani Wall and a string of chortens. One of the monasteries was built out from a natural cave, and the surrounding cliffs were full of old troglodyte dwellings. The liaison officer and I explored an abandoned network of galleries and storerooms carved out of the rock. Ganga kicked aside some feathers and said: 'Now only the eagles nest in such caves, but in former times the ancestors of these Loba people lived here.' And not only in former times. The next village had been quite recently hit by a flash flood, and the inhabitants had moved back into caves up in the cliffs where they felt safer.

One of them, an old woman with matted hair, might easily have been mistaken for a witch. She spat when Sarah first approached, and then covered her face with both hands.

'Don't worry,' shouted Pema, 'she is only afraid of the camera. These people believe it can steal away their souls.'

He got to talking with her and eventually she invited us into her cave-dwelling. Access was by an open gallery piled high with firewood and the coarse wool she was spinning. Inside, the cave had been turned into a single room, where the old lady both ate and slept. The roof above the hearth was encrusted with soot and the only light came through a single aperture into which a glass window had been fitted. This may have helped keep out the winter gales, but it did not improve the ventilation. Everything in the room was impregnated with woodsmoke. The woman said she had raised six children in that cave, but now they were all married and she lived alone.

On the way back to Lo Manthang we rode past one of the king's country residences. Though described as a 'palace', it was no more than a large farmhouse with a row of prayer flags outside. It had an abandoned air, and Gyatso confirmed that the king no longer came here often.

We had been riding quite hard that day and still did not return to the capital until late afternoon. I wondered whether the king would be able to make it all the way from the border in time for our dinner. Sarah and I sat by the main gate and watched as herdsmen and livestock returned within the city walls for the night. Still no sign of the king.

*

I needn't have worried. At eight sharp we were summoned to the palace. Other guests had arrived before us. The director of the American Himalayan Foundation, Broughton Coburn, was discussing the restoration work his people were doing, while his wife sat silent and his young daughter, Phoebe, complained loudly about the fruit juice she had been given and demanded why she couldn't have Pepsi. The king is fond of children and wanted to give her a hug, but she clung to her mother. When plates of food were brought, I noticed the Americans stuck to the biscuits and prawn crackers imported from China. Meanwhile Sarah and I fell upon a plate of goat's liver and lung fried up with cumin – a local delicacy prepared, I was told, by Queen Ridol herself.

We decamped to the dining room – a large, sparsely furnished hall where a Nepali-style buffet of various curries and rice had been laid out. The king chatted about the monastic school, which is also partly funded by the Americans, and a planned centre for traditional Tibetan medicine. But he seemed worn down by worries. His sister, who lived half a day's journey away at Tsarang, had been robbed of her jewellery. It was a serious loss, their value being estimated at around $70,000. Then there was this question of the new motor road from Tibet. Work on it was due to start very soon, with the formal ground-breaking ceremony at the border scheduled for the next day. But the king did not look happy about so important a development, and I soon discovered why.

The first section of the road would allow trucks to drive down to Nheyjung, one of the villages we had visited that same day. The trade-mart would move there from the border, making it much easier and cheaper to buy Chinese rice and manufactured goods. But it would be strictly a one-way trade, for the Lobas produce nothing worth exporting to China.

The only way they could pay for more Chinese imports would be to leave Mustang and find paid jobs in Pokhara or Kathmandu. Loba society would be further disrupted without drawing any real benefit. And yet the Lobas themselves – or at least their Village Development Committees – have been persuaded to pay for the road. The brains behind the scheme, however, were Thakali businessmen – the head of the planning committee being a 'notorious contractor with connections into the ruling Congress Party'. In Nepal, big infrastructure schemes rarely get the go-ahead unless deals are done – whether in cash or in 'delivering' enough votes to ensure that the Congress representative for Mustang keeps his seat at the next election. So building a road is likely to bring more corruption into Mustang as well as cheap Chinese goods. It has become a politically charged and socially divisive issue. Which explains why King Jigme is unhappy, though he no longer has the power to put a stop to things.

Once road construction is started, it would be hard to prevent its being extended further south. Such projects tend to gain a momentum of their own. I heard of plans to run the new road all the way down to Thakali country in southern Mustang, where there are large apple orchards producing prime-quality fruit. And it is the Thakalis who would benefit from such a road. Their current problem is in getting their apple crop to Nepal's urban markets before it perishes. The mule track down the Kali Gandaki is simply not good enough, and proposals to build a motor road up from Pokhara have been turned down by the World Bank and other multi-lateral backers as too expensive.

To drive a road through the world's deepest gorge certainly presents some serious engineering problems. An alternative scheme, to build a ropeway over the mountains, has also been turned down. So the only option left is to push a new road north to the Tibet border and then use existing roads to drive across the Tibetan Plateau and back down to Kathmandu. It is a roundabout route, and special transit arrangements would have to be agreed with the Chinese authorities. None the less, a truck loaded with Marpha apples could make the journey in two days. The Thakali owners of those orchards stood to make enormous profits. As for Upper Mustang, Broughton Coburn foresees it becoming 'just a truck stop on the way from Marpha to Kathmandu'.

I wondered what Indian military intelligence would think about another road coming down from China through the Himalayas. And how could Mustang retain its special status as a conservation area – or, for that matter, charge $700 for an entry permit – once the trucks were rolling through? A motor road would change things beyond recognition. It was madness, and I said as much.

The king let his own feelings be known the next day by not turning up for the ground-breaking ceremony at the border. His excuse was that he felt unwell. Strangely, he seemed no less active than usual. Sarah and I bumped into him several times around town and when he was performing his afternoon circumambulations. The head lama also stayed away from the ceremony.

We made one more journey out from the capital, to see the king's summer palace at Thingkar and the big Namgyal

Monastery perched high on its hill. Gyatso was pleased we were visiting his home village and invited us to the family house for butter tea and tsampa.

The palace was locked up and looked like it hadn't been lived in for years. A pair of *dzos* – strange beasts that are half-cow, half-yak – occupied the muddy courtyard. We were able to visit only the royal chapel, which contains some very unusual wall paintings of the former kings of Mustang. Then we climbed up to Namgyal Monastery, impressively situated on a hill overlooking the capital. Again there were some fine paintings, but not a single monk was in residence. Both palace and monastery told a similar story of decline and fall.

The time had come for leave-taking. The king presented all of us with kaddas, which we kept around our necks until reaching the first pass. Lo Manthang lay far below, nestling between the bare-sided mountains, a vision of timelessness that seemed to me no less surreal than when I first clapped eyes on it. Then we kicked our horses on, traversing a high plain where herds of donkeys were grazing. The plain narrowed, with steep gorges dropping away towards the Kali Gandaki.

From the top of the next pass we could look across another tributary to Tsarang, the second town in Upper Mustang. An ancient castle seemed to grow out of the sheer cliff, and attached to this was a more recent building which I learned was another of the king's palaces. But first we had to make a steep descent to cross the intervening river. It was a hot afternoon, and we stopped to water the horses and splash our faces by a water-mill. A jovial monk accompanied by an attendant, both of them on horseback, stopped to enquire who we were before galloping up the hill to Tsarang. We plodded along behind them, drawing up eventually before a large white-washed house built around a courtyard. 'We are staying here,' said Pema as he began to unsaddle the horses.

It belonged to the king's sister, and the entire household was in turmoil over the theft of her jewels. Best not to get involved, I thought. So Sarah and I set out for the gompa, an imposing, red-walled building that looked more like a fortress than a monastery until you noticed the gold, pagoda-shaped lantern sticking up from its roof.

By tradition it is the most important of Mustang's monasteries, the Tsarang Lama usually being chosen from the royal family. The present incumbent, the king's middle brother, had given up his monastic vows and married. But when his young wife died, he had been driven almost mad with grief. He fled the country, living for many years in Dolpo. Their son was left in the care of the king, who, having no children of his own, adopted his brother's and declared the boy to be his own rightful successor. Which is how Jigme-la came to be crown prince of Mustang.

His natural father is still alive and normally resides in Thingkar, but that summer he had gone into Tibet. Having renounced his monastic vows, he no longer held office in Tsarang Gompa. But until his death nobody else can be recognized as the Tsarang Lama. For more than thirty years, therefore, the monks have been without a resident lama. Instead, they are ruled over by a chief-monk, who turned out to be none other than the jovial lama we had met down by the river.

We found him in the monastery's main prayer hall,

preparing a special puja for a recently deceased villager. His name was Thubten Chophel and he sat cross-legged as the rest of the resident monks filed in and arranged themselves in two rows facing each other. 'It would be good', he told me, 'if we had a monastic school here, like the one in Lo Manthang. Now, our monks must go to study in Kathmandu or to Dehra Dun in India, and some do not return to Tsarang.'

But things were greatly improved, he said, since the years immediately after the king's brother had given up his duties as Tsarang Lama. 'Then the monks didn't care and just stayed in their villages. Now more of them live in the monastery and every day they make pujas.' And while he admitted that the prayer hall needed restoration, he pointed to the building works going on out in the courtyard. 'We are making new residences for the monks, that is our first priority.'

Sarah and I stayed on to listen to the puja. It began with deeply intoned prayers punctuated by reverberating crescendos of trumpets and drums. The head of the dead person's family entered and distributed offerings – a large wad of rupees to the acting abbot and smaller amounts to each of the other monks present. At regular intervals one of the younger monks came round with butter tea and tsampa. Then three monks arose, advanced towards the altar, and began singing a sort of plainsong in which sadness and joy were inextricably combined. It was strange music – saddest when most melodious, and joyful when it shifted towards abstraction. 'Tibetan music,' whispered the young monk beside me.

There were other signs of renewal in Tsarang. One of the large chortens beneath the monastery had caved in; but

I saw workmen carrying away the rubble and bringing new materials for its repair. The king's palace, however, is a deserted shell, all its windows broken and the interior thick with dust. Only one room is vaguely inhabitable, and this serves as a combined shrine room and library. An entire wall is stacked up to the roof with Buddhist scriptures, the most precious being a complete set of the *Kanjur* written in gold leaf on black paper. Tragically, one of these volumes had recently been stolen.

I was surprised on returning to our lodgings to find King Jigme had turned up. He was on his way to attend the opening of the new hospital at Ghemi, and had broken his journey to comfort his sister over the loss of her jewellery. Having just seen the condition of the royal palace, I could see why he preferred to stay in this well-ordered household. So, for this night, we slept under the same roof, and I kept on bumping into him down narrow hallways. 'It's funny, isn't it?' commented Sarah. 'We spend ages trying to see this elusive king, and now we can't get away from him.'

From Tsarang we rode to Gilling, a lovely village surrounded by water meadows and meandering streams. The next morning I climbed up to the monastery only to find it locked, the caretaker monk having gone off to Ghemi to attend the opening ceremonies for the new hospital there. Not long after Gilling we rejoined the same road we had come up on, and from there it was two days' hard travelling down to the Kali Gandaki gorge and Jomsom.

This time, Sarah made it down the stretch of ravine she had been so dreading without stopping once. I walked ahead on the outside, and at certain points was pretty scared myself;

but what she said helped most was Pema following just behind, clicking his rosary and chanting softly all the way. When we finally got through that ravine, Ganga turned to me and said: 'Now we have left the high country behind us.' Although not a highlander himself, he spoke with some regret.

Our troubles were not all behind us, however. From high above Chele village, we looked down to find the Kali Gandaki swollen with snow-melt and the recent rains. We could plainly see that all the ant-like figures trying to cross it were having real difficulties. Some were up to their chests in the raging flood. Sarah was worried about her cameras and wanted to stop for the night in Chele, the river usually being lower in the mornings before the snow-melt feeds through. Pema insisted we continued, claiming that he knew of a safe place to cross. This involved riding the horses through fast-flowing water for half an hour, but by sticking to the hidden sandbanks we made it to the far bank without even our boots getting wet.

From there it was straight down the Kali Gandaki valley to Jomsom. On the way, we were joined by a young incarnate lama who had only recently left Tibet. He looked to be only about fourteen, though he claimed to be nineteen years old. The reason for this upwards revision of his age, it transpired, is that to obtain the visa required to leave Tibet you have to be at least eighteen. Regardless of age, as an incarnate lama he was shown deep respect by the villagers we met. His attendant was a dark-skinned Indian, the same orphaned boy who King Jigme had taken in. Both were on horses, so it was quite a cavalcade that rode into Jomsom just as it began to rain.

This was the end of our land journey. We parted with

our horses and bade farewell to the muleman, who was going back to Mustang, and to the cookboys who still had to walk down to Pokhara. Then we started praying that the weather would be clear enough for the planes to fly in. I asked the lama to say a Buddhist puja, and our Brahmin liaison officer was in charge of the Hindu side, so I reckoned we were well covered. And early next morning, down at the airport I thought it had worked. Two helicopters came in and the radio tower announced our flight had taken off from Pokhara. The helicopters left and still no plane had arrived. Then it was announced that due to bad weather all flights had turned back. There was nothing for it but to sit back and wait.

And wait, and wait, and wait. Four days in a row the weather was too bad for flying. You knew it as soon as you looked out of the window each morning. But still you hoped that maybe a helicopter could get through. Everyone waiting to fly out was slowly going mad. Several had already missed their long-haul flights back home. A pair of Spaniards who had a satellite phone with them spent hours talking to Madrid. I thought their behaviour unusual until I discovered they were both policemen. One was a security officer to the Spanish royal family, the other a specialist in mountaineering and scuba-diving, and together they were supposed to be in charge of arrangements for the crown prince's trekking expedition. But the same bad weather meant his trekking holiday had to be cancelled, and the Spanish royal party had flown on to Bali while their official scuba instructor was still stranded in the Himalayas.

By the fourth day, things were looking bad for Sarah and me. Less than twenty-four hours remained before her flight back to London, and by rights I should have been waiting in Kathmandu to see King Birendra. I made a couple of calls to the Palace Secretariat to warn them I might be late. And we both made friends with a blond-haired Russian boy called Anton who looked like a storm-trooper and bragged that his family were Mafia. More importantly, his father piloted the big MI-17 helicopter that right then was our best hope of getting out of Jomsom.

And that is how we finally flew out, with Anton and the Spanish policemen aboard, and Anton's father up front weaving the big chopper through gaps between the clouds. At Pokhara we had to hustle to get onto the first flight to Kathmandu. Only when we touched down at King Tribhu-van Airport could I relax and let out five days' of accumu-lated madness. 'Shit, that was a close-run thing,' I said to nobody in particular.

Chapter Seven

NEPAL II – MONARCHY
AND DEMOCRACY

Back in Kathmandu I contacted the king's principal press secretary, Mohan Bahadur Panday. He was a very different character from Mr N.R. Pandey, his predecessor in that office. In fact, he had been extremely helpful. Many letters had been exchanged between us. Various drafts of what questions I could (or could not) ask King Birendra had been discussed and refined.

'Where are you now, Mr Gregson?' he enquired.

'Roughly five minutes' walk from the palace. We flew out from Jomsom this morning.'

'Then everything is in hand. I suggest we meet tomorrow, by which time I will know whether the green light has been given. Also, it would be best if you left Thursday evening free.'

I was beginning to get the hang of interpreting such cryptic messages. By the sound of it, final permission for an audience had not yet been granted. But the last part was definitely promising. I was tantalizingly close to meeting King Birendra Bir Bikram Shah Dev, the only ruling Hindu monarch in the world.

*

There was no time for celebration. More mundane tasks needed attention. Sarah was taking the evening flight out of Kathmandu for London. The army kit-bag had not been unpacked since it came off a mule at Jomsom and our combined belongings needed sorting. As I picked through pairs of dirty socks I could not stop myself from speculating about what meetings were being held just down the road at the palace. I had learned from long experience not to expect anything from this quarter until it was definitely confirmed.

I saw Sarah off at the airport and then took a taxi to nearby Durbar Square. It dropped me off at the top of Jhocchen, the area once known as 'Freak Street' because back in the sixties it was colonized by dope-smoking hippies. I walked past the handful of lodging houses and cafes that still trade on its former notoriety. Nowadays they are filled with thirty-something design consultants trying to recapture their lost youth; and though the whiff of pachouli still hangs heavy upon the air, the truth about Freak Street is that it has been turned into a museum. This was confirmed by a banner that the local tourism authority had stretched across its entrance, welcoming visitors to this 'once hippies' haven'. Only those on a serious nostalgia trip actually stay in Jhocchen these days, it being far more convenient to be based in Thamel along with everyone else and make a half-day's excursion down to Freak Street.

I kept walking past the serried ranks of souvenir sales-men who now fill Basantpur Square to bursting, before turning right below the grilled window from which the Kumari, the living child-goddess of Kathmandu, is some-times allowed to look at the world outside. This brought me into Durbar Square, where the air was rent by the cries of yet more souvenir-hawkers and clouds of pigeons rose with a great fluttering of wings from one pagoda before settling on the one next door. I approached one of the smaller temples in front of the old royal palace. Its steps were occupied by a group of Hindu holy men, including a couple of bearded sadhus whose bright orange robes were proving a magnet to tourists. One of these 'rent-a-sadhus' offered me the opportunity of taking his picture for a mere five dollars (US). I declined, and kept moving until I reached the palace entrance. This time the museum was open, so I paid for my ticket and eagerly entered this shrine to the memory of King Tribhuvan, the present king's grandfather.

For the first forty years of his life, King Tribhuvan had been little more than a figurehead. His father, King Prithvi Bir Bikram Shah Dev, died in the same year he was born, and the infant king was brought up in the massive mock-Palladian pile that was Narayanhitti Palace before it was rebuilt. The Shumsher branch of the Rana family were firmly in control, and while the king attended public ceremonies he exercized no real power. As Nepal established diplomatic relations with more foreign countries, their envoys were ushered into the royal presence; but for the most part the king remained silent, all matters of substance being discussed with the hereditary prime ministers rather than the monarch.

But the Rana oligarchy's hold on Nepal began to slip after the British left India in 1947. With their staunchest allies gone, the Ranas now had to contend with a democratically elected Congress government in Delhi whose sympathies naturally tended towards the outlawed Nepali National

Congress Party. There was also discontent among the Rana establishment itself. The inflexible 'Roll of Succession', which reserved all top government posts for the sons of 'A' class Ranas, left many educated and progressive 'B' and 'C' class Ranas without hope of office simply because one of their ancestors had married outside the highest Hindu caste.

King Tribhuvan was secretly in contact with some of these exiles in India. In September 1950 a conspiracy to assassinate the Rana prime minister was nipped in the bud. Whether the king was involved in any way remains unclear. Certainly, he felt his position was increasingly precarious. What he chose to do next was to change the course of Nepal's history.

It was all very carefully planned. First, the king obtained the prime minister's permission to go out on a family picnic. It was a large convoy that left the royal palace that morning, for besides Tribhuvan and his two queens, all three of his sons and his senior grandson, Prince Birendra, were aboard. As the motorcade approached the Indian Embassy, the gates suddenly swung open and the royal family were driven through. Once inside the diplomatic compound, King Tribhuvan claimed political asylum.

For a reigning monarch to seek safety in a foreign embassy was dramatic enough to focus the world's attention on this sleepy Himalayan kingdom. There followed a war of nerves. Since the Rana government did not dare storm India's embassy, the king and other members of the royal family who had sought asylum were formally dispossessed. At first the crown was offered to the five-year-old Prince Birendra. But since he too refused to leave the embassy, the younger of King Tribhuvan's grandsons, Prince Gyanendra, was discovered within the royal palace and duly installed on the throne of Nepal. His coronation was a farcical attempt to restore some legitimacy to the Rana regime.

Meanwhile, Tribhuvan and the rest of his family were still holed up in the Indian Embassy. After long negotiations they were allowed to fly out of Kathmandu aboard an Indian Air Force plane, on condition that they should not be permitted to engage in any political activities on Indian soil. This did not prevent the Nepali Congress from immediately launching a war of liberation from their bases in India. Large areas of the lowland Terai, including the key town of Biratnagar, were captured. Within Nepal, support from the Rana regime was crumbling. Under Indian guidance, a compromise was reached whereby Tribhuvan would return as king, Mohan Shumsher Rana would remain prime minister, and an interim government be formed with half the seats reserved for 'democratic' Nepali Congressmen.

It was the strangest kind of revolution – half-populist, half-royalist. But the crowds came out to cheer King Tribhuvan as he descended from a DC-3 Dakota at Kathmandu's airstrip, accompanied by the top Nepali Congress leaders. The king received a hero's welcome. That much was plain from faded photographs and news clippings on display in the old palace's museum. The date was 15 February 1951, and it marks the first time in 104 years that any king of Nepal exercised any real authority in his own country. The Rana oligarchy was finished. And the presence of Nepali Congressmen in those photos provided the basis for another powerful myth: that the restoration of monarchy was indissolubly linked with introducing some form of democracy into Nepal. Despite what has happened over the last half-century, that myth lives on.

The King Tribhuvan Museum does its bit to perpetuate the myth. The restored monarch is shown as 'a man of the people'. The photographs selected include the charismatic Congress leader B.P. Koirala rather than his Rana ministers; but the fact remains that no democratic elections were held during the next four years. Instead, government was conducted by the king-in-council, which retained the forms of a constitutional monarchy. He ran through a succession of short-lived coalition cabinets, the different parties involved finding it impossible to work together. Perhaps having been isolated for so long, the Nepalese lacked the experience to form governments that were both representative and reasonably stable. For one year, King Tribhuvan tried to rule directly; but his health was failing and he found such duties burdensome.

The other exhibits were intended to provide a glimpse of his personal life and character. There was a section given over to the king's hobbies – especially the more 'progressive' ones. His interest in chemistry is exemplified by various test tubes; photography by antique cameras and a home cine machine; painting by some uninspiring landscapes; music by his personal violin. The more traditional pleasures of the hunt fill an entire room of stuffed animals he had bagged, together with pictures of the king with his favourite horse and dog, a large portrait in oils with a dead tiger, and his gold-plated revolver.

His son, King Mahendra, was even keener on shikar or big-game hunting, and had far broader opportunities to prove his skill as a marksman. He is remembered chiefly for his determination to put Nepal 'on the map' in international affairs. The kingdom joined the United Nations in the first year of his reign and became a committed member of the

Non-Aligned Movement. One of Mahendra's aims was to counterbalance the predominant influence of India, and to this end he opened diplomatic relations with both China and the USSR. He travelled frequently, attending international conferences and visiting other heads of state.

The section of the museum devoted to him has endless photographs of King Mahendra with world leaders – with US presidents Eisenhower and Johnson, with the Soviet leader Kosygin, with President Tito of Yugoslavia and Prince Sihanouk of Cambodia.

Judging from the room crammed with his hunting trophies, he profited from these overseas trips to add to the already impressive 'bag' of Nepal's native species. In 1960 he shot a mountain lion in the United States; the next year a red deer in Scotland. Other countries he visited – West Germany, Spain, Yugoslavia, Mongolia, Ethiopia, India, Ceylon – all offered their different opportunities, though East Africa (giraffe, lion, leopard, rhino, wild dog, etc.) provided the richest haul. Quite a few of these trophies took pride of place in the Cabinet Room: the standard lamps are supported by stuffed giraffe legs, while zebra hocks and antelope legs serve for table lighting and rhino feet are scattered about, to no apparent purpose. Regardless of one's views on hunting, this display of personal trophies around the table where government policy was supposed to be decided reveals a rather tasteless strain of machismo.

I remembered how Kirthinidi Bista, who served both Mahendra and his son as the most compliant of prime ministers, spoke of the late king's enthusiasm for shikar. 'He was so passionate about hunting that whenever he saw wild animals, he couldn't resist. It was a tremendous temptation, even after he had his heart attack. Actually, that happened when I was with him in a hunting hide. But even then he didn't give up his sport. He died during a hunting expedition in Chitwan.' The former prime minister obviously shared his king's sporting instincts, for he had a large tiger skin mounted on the wall.

I had the impression that King Mahendra liked to be thought of as a man of action in the Hemingway mould. From early on he had shown himself to be fiercely independent. When his first wife and mother of his children, Indra Rajya Laxmi, died young, he defied the opposition of King Tribhuvan and married her elder sister, Ratna Rajya Laxmi. As a statesman, he took upon himself the mantle of a fervent nationalist (which in Nepal generally means running down India's influence over the country). His frequent visits abroad were part of a sustained diplomatic offensive to raise Nepal's profile on the international stage, and thereby reduce the likelihood of Indian intervention in her internal affairs. All of his diplomatic skills were needed to keep Nepal securely neutral though the Sino-Indian conflict of 1962, and the following year he achieved what had never been done before – an agreed demarcation of the Himalayan border with China.

On the home front, he ruled with an iron fist, pushing through land reforms and development programmes from above. He did believe, however, that the promise of democracy implicit in the 1951 'revolution' should be fulfilled, and on the eighth anniversary of the overthrow of the Rana regime the people of Nepal went to the polls for the first time.

The outcome was a massive victory for Nepali Congress, and B.P. Koirala was appointed prime minister. But this experiment with democracy was short-lived. In December

1960 the king dismissed the elected government. The Congress ministers were arrested and the parliament dissolved.

From then on, King Mahendra moved towards a system of 'guided democracy' in which political parties were banned and members of parliament were elected indirectly through intermediate bodies representing the different classes and occupations in Nepal. This Panchayat system was justified as being 'indigenous', more in keeping with Nepal's social and political traditions. In fact it concentrated all power in the hands of the monarch. The Panchayat Raj was formally introduced through the new constitution of 16 December 1962. It was to remain in place, a fig leaf that barely disguised the workings of an absolute monarchy, for the next twenty-seven years.

When King Birendra succeeded to the throne in 1972, hopes ran high that this young, energetic, foreign-educated monarch would introduce sweeping changes. But although he was by nature less autocratic than his father, the new king had grown up with the Panchayat system and decided to stick with it. His early initiatives were in the field of foreign policy, notably his declaration that Nepal should become the centre of a 'Zone of Peace' in the Himalayan region. At home, he and his charming young wife, Queen Aishwarya Rajya Laxmi, went on frequent tours of the different regions of Nepal, addressing mass audiences in the hope of forging a direct link between the people and an overtly populist monarchy. A political culture was nurtured in which national unity and the public good was closely identified with the person of the sovereign, while anything labelled 'private' – whether political parties or business interests – was associated with narrow self-interest.

The rationale of the Panchayat system was that it gave the Nepalese the right to elect their representatives at village level or through local organizations that could express their particular interests – whether they be peasants, youth, women, workers or ex-servicemen. New initiatives, such as the 'Back to the Village' campaign, were introduced to reinforce the local base of the Panchayat regime. All-powerful commissions of inspection were despatched to root out corruption. Complaints could be taken directly to the Investigation and Enquiry Centre rather than through the normal judicial and administrative channels. Everything tended to concentrate more power in the hands of the king – or, more accurately, the Palace Secretariat, which filtered all information and access to the king himself.

There grew up a multi-layered system of government in which it was impossible to tell where the real centre of power lay. The national legislature continued to sit, but was not invited to debate key issues. The king continued to appoint ministers, including choosing his favourite, Kirthinidi Bista, as prime minister on more than one occasion. Despite Bista's claim that King Birendra 'would not unnecessarily interfere in the functioning of his governments', it is widely recognized that the Palace was involved in decision-making at every level. As one of his former private secretaries admitted: 'We used to run this country.' There was no accountability upwards, except up to the king. While the fear of intervention from on high probably held corruption in check, the Panchayat system failed in most of its representative functions.

And yet, when a referendum was held in 1980 to decide whether Nepal should have a multi-party democracy or continue with a 'reformed' version of the Panchayat system, the panchas won the vote by a narrow margin. It was sufficient for the king to claim popular legitimacy for his regime, even though in practice it had to be maintained by imprisoning political activists and harsh censorship of the press. But by the later 1980s, private newspapers were revealing corruption in high places and cover-ups. The royal family, however, could not be criticized directly, there being no real distinction between any criticism of the monarch and treason against the state. There was no give in the system, no way that legitimate complaints could reach the king's ear.

After the Berlin Wall came down in 1989 and autocratic regimes tumbled across Eastern Europe, a new feeling of hope emerged among the pro-democracy groups in Kathmandu. The toppling of Ceauçescu in Romania was particularly encouraging. He had been an 'old friend' of the Nepalese monarchy. But the main impetus for change came from a different quarter.

The governments of India and Nepal had failed to agree on terms for renewing their treaty governing trade and commerce. Or rather, Prime Minister Rajiv Gandhi insisted there be no agreement, so that he could punish his upstart neighbour. So India imposed what amounted to an economic blockade on land-locked Nepal. King Birendra chose to brazen it out, counting on popular support for an assertively nationalist policy. To begin with it worked; but then vital imports such as petrol and kerosene grew scarce. Black-market prices went through the roof, and there was real economic hardship.

With India's encouragement, the main political parties in Nepal set aside their differences and formed a United Front. Although still technically banned, political rallies held in Kathmandu drew thousands of supporters. In nearby

Bhaktapur, police fired on demonstrators; in Patan, angry crowds took control of the Old City and erected barricades. A General Strike was called for 2 April 1990. Residents of Kathmandu expressed their dissatisfaction with the existing regime by switching off their lights and plunging the city into darkness.

The king broadcast on Radio Nepal that he had appointed a new cabinet, which was to enter talks with the leaders of the political parties. The popular response was to assemble en masse on Tundikhel, the huge parade ground at the centre of Kathmandu. They were in a celebratory mood. But then the atmosphere changed, and some groups in the crowd began chanting slogans. For the first time, these were directed against the king and queen rather than their palace cronies. The crowd moved up Durbar Marg towards the royal palace. Security forces opened fire and several demonstrators were killed or wounded. That evening the ban on political parties was lifted and the following day, 9 April 1990, King Birendra declared the Panchayat system dissolved. The way was open for a multi-party democracy to take power in Nepal. These events are known as Jana Andolan or the 'Spring Uprising'. They mark the end of nearly forty years during which the Shah kings ruled their country as absolute monarchs.

There were many other exhibits of interest in the Tribhuvan Museum: the snake-headed golden thone of Nepal and other regalia; the bejewelled fans and elephant trappings that are brought out for coronations and other ceremonies of state. But there was one section of the museum which was definitely closed off from public view – the one that was dedicated to the living monarch, King Birendra. The doors to this gallery were double bolted and I was unable to discover whether this was because the exhibition was being restored or, as I strongly suspected, that their contents were still deemed to be too controversial now that Nepal has settled down to being a constitutional monarchy.

King Birendra had been inside Narayanhitti Palace when the crowds surged up Durbar Marg towards the high-security steel bars that protected the front gate. I doubt they would have ever breached that line, for the Nepalese army's loyalties lie first and foremost with their king, and there were elite units ready to intervene had Birendra given the order. That he did not is entirely to his credit. Not only did he prevent enormous loss of life, his willingness to give in gracefully got the monarchy out of a head-on confrontation, as much with India as with local democrats. If he had tried to force the issue and lost, the Kingdom of Nepal might well have become a republic.

Having done my utmost to gain access to Narayanhitti Palace, I was annoyed to discover rather late in the day that anyone can buy a ticket to visit the State Rooms. Now that Buckingham Palace has opened its doors to tourists, so too has Narayanhitti. Nepalese citizens can visit one day a week, foreigners on another. So on the appointed day I just turned up at the front gate, handed over my camera (photography is strictly forbidden) and underwent a perfunctory body search. Then I was escorted by a royal guard up to the foot of the main staircase where a palace official took over.

The ornate nineteenth-century palace, built by the Ranas for their nominal sovereigns, was almost completely rebuilt by King Mahendra during the 1960s as part of his programme to give the Nepalese monarchy a more modern and progressive image. All of the main façade dates from this period. It is a peculiar combination of traditional and modern.

The central tower above the main staircase has a double pagoda roof, and much of the other roofing is in traditional tiles. But beside the pagoda-like structure rises a needle-thin and very modernist spire. The grand entrance is lined with outsized statues of peacocks, fish, elephants and other auspicious creatures; the rest of the south front is left unadorned, according to the architectural strictures of those times. The overall effect is that of a building designed by committee; though, curiously enough, the mixing of different styles and materials anticipates what has since become known as postmodernism.

Apart from two Japanese girls, I was the only visitor that morning. My guide was reverential in the extreme, a committed royalist. He almost bowed before the life-size portraits of Prithvi Narayan Shah and his immediate successors which adorn the reception hall and the double staircase.

I was ushered into a room lined with glass-fronted cabinets containing all manner of gifts – mostly very ornate crystal and gilded Sèvres-style porcelain – which had been presented to Their Majesties. Some were from visiting dignitaries, though the more ostentatious items came mainly from other royal relatives (over the last six generations the Shah dynasty has consistently married senior members of the Rana family). More wealth than taste was on display, and I was grateful to be led up the grand staircase to the Throne Room.

This lofty room occupies the space underneath the pagoda-shaped tower. Its interior is loosely modelled on that of a Hindu temple, and the elaborately carved columns and paintings are heavily symbolic of the divine nature of kingship. The throne itself is very tall and upright. Lions and elephants support its front pedestals, while golden snakes with a single head cover its arms. All the symbols of Hindu kingship, religious banners, the sacred umbrella, the royal emblem flanked by Jaya and Vijaya (the personal guards of Lord Vishnu and therefore of his royal incarnation), are present. The Royal Standard hung from a flagpole beyond the plate glass window.

Next door is a much more modest room filled with some of the most bizarre furniture I have ever seen. Tables, chairs, everything is made of frosted glass, including a huge collection of Lalique pieces assembled by King Tribhuvan. Then it was down the stairs again, a brief look into the banqueting hall (I was told its endlessly long table can seat more than a hundred guests) and back out into the grounds, my mind still reeling from the strange juxtaposition of images just received.

If Narayanhitti Palace is meant to convey how a traditional Hindu monarchy is trying to embrace modernity, I suppose it more or less succeeds on the symbolic level. But it also conveys confusion, uncertainty, an inability to achieve any genuine fusion between ancient and modern. The overall effect was profoundly unsettling. Of course, I had not seen the private apartments where the royal family spend most of their lives. But the State Rooms managed to impart a sense of megalomania and insecurity at the same time. This was the setting for important state functions, the swearing-in of ministers and the king's receiving foreign heads of state or ambassadors. It was not an atmosphere that I could live in without gradually losing my sanity.

*

I put in another call to Mr M.B. Panday. He was delighted to tell me that this time the 'green light' had been given. My audience with His Majesty would take place the next evening, at 7 p.m. sharp. I was immensely relieved. Only later was I informed that this was the first royal audience granted to a non-Nepalese writer since multi-party democracy replaced the king's direct rule in 1990.

And this time, rather than being kept waiting outside the palace gates, I was immediately ushered in and saluted by the Gurkha guards. Once inside, instead of turning left to the secretariat buildings, I was escorted up the broad avenue lined with heavily cropped firs that leads to the west wing of Narayanhitti Palace. This I knew from my previous 'unofficial' visit is where royal guests are usually lodged.

A door opened and I entered a small, functional ante-room where my photograph was taken. It was like being inside an airlock between the palace interior and the outer world. The king's ADC, his khaki uniform weighed down by medals and decorations, engaged me in light conversation while I awaited my summons. Mr Panday returned through the inner door. 'Please come with me. His Majesty is expecting you now.'

The king rose from his seat and advanced to shake my hand. He was dressed in white, the loose shirting and tight cotton trousers or *suruwal* worn by most Nepalese men. On his head was a typical Nepali topi, again mainly white with a muted grey-and-pink pattern. His heavy, dark-rimmed spectacles were as in all the official photographs I had seen, but his face was thinner than it had once been and his moustache was trimmed to a shadow of its former, more luxuriant self. I wondered whether the weight loss was connected with the king's recent heart problems.

I was asked to sit on an upright, white upholstered chair, while King Birendra returned to his black leather armchair opposite me. The room was large and rather impersonal, its furnishings dating from the 1960s or 70s when Narayanhitti Palace had been refurbished. A leopard skin half-hidden beneath a glass-topped table and a pair of elephant tusks above the book case were the only hints of oriental exoticism. Otherwise all was plain and functional. The king put his hands together in front of him, forming a bridge with his fingers.

'So what do want to ask me?' He smiled.

And so began a long and broad-ranging conversation, the main theme of which – whether one liked it or not – was the limitations of what King Birendra can speak out on in his role as constitutional monarch. We touched on many topics: the changing role of monarchy; Nepal's delicate position wedged in between India and China, which the king's ancestor Prithvi Narayan Shah bluntly described as being like 'a yam between two boulders'; Birendra's own proposals that Nepal and the Himalayan region generally be declared a 'Zone of Peace'. But every time we seemed to be getting somewhere the trail went cold and we entered an indeterminate region of possibilities and options, with the king proposing any number of alternative ways of looking at the question without coming up with any clear opinions of his own.

To begin with I found all this rather baffling. The whole conversation had an Alice in Wonderland quality to it. For just as it seemed that the king was on the point of reaching a firm conclusion, he would introduce two other points of view; and, like Alice, I was left wondering which hole the White Rabbit had run down.

On the other hand, I was left in no doubt that Nepal's ruling monarch has an agile mind with a strongly analytical bent – an approach which, like the slightest trace of an American accent, may well go back to the time he spent at Harvard. As he worked his way around a subject his whole body shifted from side to side, as though this would facilitate his acquiring a fresh viewpoint on the matter at hand. The large square glasses which he always wears swivelled like TV monitors that seemed to focus upon some mid-point in the air where he could best conceptualize his latest argument. In his mannerisms he reminded me more of an academic than a power-broker. And yet I was very much aware that for nearly two decades King Birendra had exercised close to absolute power over his twenty million subjects.

I must confess to experiencing real difficulties in following some of the king's arguments. Maybe this is because I am not sufficiently quick-witted to appreciate all the subtle nuances. Or maybe it is because he has adopted a new rhetoric to fit in with his new position as constitutional monarch within a multi-party democracy.

One of the cardinal rules of this 'palace-speak' is the avoidance of any statement that might be construed as an official line on policy, since this could be taken as infringing on the domain of the duly elected government. And given how recently the Palace was effectively running the country, locking up pro-democracy leaders and shutting down opposition newspapers, it is only natural that the current generation of politicians remains highly sensitive to anything that smacks of royal intervention in policy-making. The end result is that King Birendra is unable – or unwilling – to make an unequivocal statement on just about anything. For if he were to do so, he would almost certainly be criticized for acting unconstitutionally.

To give some idea of how palace-speak has evolved during the 1990s, here are some of the king's formal replies to my questions.

Q. What were your overriding thoughts at the time of your coronation?

A. I have always endeavoured to abide by the aspirations of the people in the best interest and welfare of the nation. Some of my primary concerns during that time were consolidating the sovereign integrity of Nepal and safeguarding the liberty of every Nepali while enhancing their welfare and building the necessary institutions so that all Nepalese could live in justice, peace, security, happiness and freedom.

Q. Shortly thereafter you proposed that Nepal and/or the Himalayan region become a Zone of Peace. Do you think the concept still has validity? Or given the proliferation of nuclear weapons in the region, is it an idea whose time has now come?

A. There is a wide consensus on the fact that the need to institutionalize peace is even greater today than ever before. There can, of course, be differences of opinion on how best to go about achieving it.

Q. What do you consider the principal benefits conferred by the monarchical system, as opposed to republican or other forms of government?

A. Every nation has to evolve a political system which is best suited to meet its requirements. In Nepal, the monarch has always been guided by popular will and the relationship between the monarchy and the people is traditionally based on mutual trust and confidence in each other.

I could go on, though I doubt one would be any the

wiser about what the King of Nepal actually thinks on such weighty matters. His replies, both formal and informal, more closely resemble an elaborate kind of verbal fencing, the main purpose of which is to avoid making any statement that could be judged unconstitutional rather than an attempt at a 'full and frank response'.

That King Birendra does have strongly held views on all these issues is certain. The role of monarchy, the direction of the country, foreign policy issues, the importance of traditional culture – all of these were expounded in extenso during the eighteen years he presided over the Panchayat system of government. Then came Jana Andolan and the country's adoption of multi-party democracy. Since when there has been a resounding silence from the Palace. And although, through persistence and luck, I became the first foreign writer to be granted an audience with the king under the new dispensation, I cannot claim to have penetrated the palace's in-depth defences whose very purpose is to shield from public scrutiny what are the king's real views on matters of public interest.

Such self-imposed restraint applies to all constitutional monarchs. Imagine the public outcry in Britain if Queen Elizabeth II were to make any statement that clearly favoured one political party over another, or even seemed to endorse a policy other than that approved by the elected government of the day. It is almost unthinkable precisely because Britain has had a constitutional monarchy for so long. And although left unwritten, the basic ground-rules of what may or may not be said have been observed punctiliously from one generation to the next.

This is not the case in Nepal, where less than a decade has elapsed since the monarchy stood at the very centre of government. True, the 1991 constitution redefines the king's role with some precision. But there has not been sufficient time for its provisions to become accepted norms, nor for their observance to be taken for granted. And some areas remain rather loosely demarcated. For instance, while I was waiting in Kathmandu to see the king a controversy arose over whether the three royal appointees to the Upper House could vote as they deemed fit, or whether they should always support the elected government. Some members of the majority Nepal Congress Party went so far as to accuse the Palace of acting unconstitutionally because the royal appointees voted against their party.

A residue of suspicion remains between the Palace and the main political parties. Sensitivities are such that even the slightest issue might spark off accusations that the king has exceeded his constitutional role. Which is why the king does not normally talk to the media, and when he does is careful to steer clear of any contentious issues.

Even when I asked about the ceremonial aspects of Nepal's monarchy – the use of regalia and other aspects of court protocol, things which I assumed belonged in the realm of traditional practice rather than the political arena – I could sense the shutters coming down. 'In a democracy', the king replied, 'it is vital that everyone plays a responsible role within the constitutional framework. Our constitution is quite clear on the provisions relating to constitutional monarchy and its role. The decorum needed for formal and ceremonial functions have symbolic significance, touching upon our cultural and historical values. It is maintained to a certain extent while adjusting to changing times.'

Not exactly the most transparent of answers. But then I realized that in Nepal these ceremonial aspects of monarchy still have political connotations which have been largely forgotten among the monarchies of Europe, where long usage has dulled sensitivities to the point where ceremony becomes purely a matter of accepted form.

Among the Nepalese – or at least among the political classes – the detail still matters. As in whether, during the swearing-in of a new prime minister, the king should be standing (as he does) or seated, and how he should be dressed. Such is the concern to demonstrate absolute parity between monarch and minister that when Mr Bhattarai was sworn in both he and King Birendra wore nearly identical black topis, grey jackets and tight white trousers. So they ended up looking like Tweedle Dum and Tweedle Dee.

The same applies to the order of ceremony during royal investitures when honours and decorations are handed out, ostensibly for loyal public service. Again this is an area of sensitivity, for it can be viewed as a surviving mechanism of royal patronage in which the king has some say as to who receives such honours, and is therefore vulnerable to accusations of palace favouritism.

On the other hand, if the politicians have it too much their own way over who gets on the list (especially if these include some of the more dubious contributors to party funds) then the whole system is devalued and the monarchy becomes partner – albeit unwillingly – to a new breed of cronyism built around party political ties. Even among the longest established of Europe's constitutional monarchies, the conferring of honours can occasionally provoke charges of political cronyism. In Nepal, where traditional patronage systems have survived largely intact but have had to accommodate themselves to newer and brasher methods of rewarding party henchmen, the pressures are that much greater.

When a constitutional settlement is as recent as that of Nepal's, there are bound to be some grey areas where it is not entirely clear how the various powers and mechanisms should function in practice. Only time can iron out these points of friction and provide its sanction to whatever compromises are reached. I was made aware that this process continues, but that it is conducted behind closed doors. King Birendra observed that, 'transparency means different things for different institutions – monarchy, governmental and financial institutions. For each there is an appropriate level of transparency.' In other words, whatever deals are being cut in private, the Palace is not going to be the first to reveal them.

If discretion is, as far as the Palace is concerned, the better part of valour, there is one message which is constantly stressed. This is that the king is a constitutional monarch who has faithfully abided by its provisions in every detail. So when I asked him what were the main challenges he has faced since 1990, he tactfully replied that, 'in a multiparty democracy everyone is expected to play a responsible role in keeping with the spirit and norms of the constitution. Then there should be no problem.'

Whether the main political parties have, in their eagerness to construct improbable coalitions so that they can take office, themselves abided by the spirit and norms of the constitution is another matter altogether. As one admirer of King Birendra put it: 'Our king is possibly the only person in authority who has always respected the constitution.' That this should be regarded as exceptional is a sad reflection on Nepalese politics, both past and present. But in gradually building up this image of being a safe and conscientious constitutional monarch, King Birendra has done much to consolidate the Shah dynasty's position within a democratic framework.

Given the latent hostility to monarchy revealed during the popular uprising of 1990, this is no mean achievement. True, the leaders of the democratic parties have unwittingly assisted in the royal family's rehabilitation by bringing the new democracy into disrepute. This began almost on Day One when, amidst the euphoria of the first open elections, they made expansive promises to the people of Nepal – promises on which they have almost without exception failed to deliver.

Instead, they ushered in a new era of political infighting. Both the main parties, the Nepal Congress and the Communists, split into warring factions. The end result was chronic instability. Six changes of government over nine years is a pitiful record, even by South Asian standards. And corruption, always a part of the political scene, has assumed epidemic proportions as the new party bosses scrabble to pay off their supporters during the brief term they expect to hold office. Some ministries, I was told, which had the power to grant or withhold licences for lucrative logging and construction contracts, changed hands on a monthly basis.

Everywhere I went in Kathmandu I heard the same embittered denunciations of corrupt politicians. Taxi-drivers, who have to pay all manner of kickbacks and bribe the police in order to ply their trade, were particularly vocal. One of them made a striking comparison of how corruption worked under the Panchayat system and the new democratic set-up.

'Before', he said, 'we had corruption, but it was like those big birds.' I looked up and saw a pair of kites circling above the city, looking for something to scavenge. 'But now these elected politicians, they are eating us up like those other birds, there—' And he pointed to a refuse dump out beyond the ring road where maybe a hundred crows were picking over the spoils. 'All politicians are the same – Mr Fifty Per Cent!' At which he spat out of the car window.

It is not only the Nepalese who are growing disillusioned with the local variant of multi-party democracy. Kathmandu is home to hundreds of international aid agencies which, taken together, pump billions of dollars into much-needed development programmes. Normally, such organizations prefer to work with democratic governments. Indeed, most of them hailed the arrival of democracy in Nepal as the dawn of a new era. Less than a decade later, 'donor fatigue' has become the buzzword among this community. For the simple reason that many such organizations have had enough of seeing their money and resources 'diverted' from where they were supposed to go.

'The only thing which keeps us here,' said one harassed aid-worker, 'is the thought of what would happen at the village level if we pulled out completely.'

It would be wrong, however, to say that democracy itself has been discredited. The younger generations of Nepalis see it as their birthright and appreciate the other freedoms of speech and assembly which come with it. Despite the frequency of general elections, voter turn-out remains high. It is more the functioning of the main political parties, their deliberate avoidance of economic and other concrete issues in preference for personality-based politics, and above all the relentless spread of corruption at every level of public life, that has caused such widespread disenchantment.

And what of the monarchy? If anything, there has been

a resurgence of sentiment in its favour. Many of the older generation look back longingly to the Panchayat era, to the sense of order and security it once provided. I listened to several of them in Kathmandu's leafier suburbs, though in some cases I suspect they were former panchas who had since re-invented themselves as democrats of a conservative or nationalist hue. More to the point, I witnessed an old man on a public bus shouting 'Bring back the king' slogans. And when King Birendra returned from a trip to London where he had been treated for his heart condition, the people of Kathmandu turned out in crowds to welcome him home.

The passage of time may by itself have healed the rift between monarchy and people that opened up during Jana Andolan. A lot can be forgotten over ten years. But equally important has been the transference of esteem from party political leaders – who back then were venerated as selfless heroes of the pro-democracy movement, but whose reputations have since been tarnished by crude political deal-making and allegations of corruption – to an institution that is ancient, almost intuitively respected, and has been virtually untouched by the many political scandals that have marred the first decade of multi-party democracy in Nepal.

The new-style constitutional monarchy has emerged unscathed because it can no longer be held responsible for the political mess – the failure to implement very basic development programmes, all the charges and counter-charges of corruption and impropriety. Monarchy has taken a step back from the political arena. It is no longer held to account, as it was in the Panchayat years. It is altogether less controversial. And perhaps for these very reasons, it is better loved.

King Birendra has re-invented himself as the model constitutional monarch. Although he has the unquestioned loyalty of the Nepalese army, there has never been the faintest suggestion of a military coup d'état.

The royal family goes about its public duties – the formal opening of university buildings, receiving the credentials of newly appointed ambassadors – with a minimum of fanfare. They have deliberately avoided the intense media attention that accompanies some of Europe's royal families. The kind of coverage they receive in the Nepalese press is reminiscent of the 1950s – formal statements that Their Majesties or His Royal Highness graced such-and-such a function, perhaps accompanied by a stilted photograph. There is none of the media courting game, the attempts to personify 'family values' or deliberately win popular esteem, that characterize the 'modernizing' monarchies of the West.

King Birendra explained this in terms of there not being the same pressures from the media – and especially television – in Nepal. But there has also been a conscious decision to keep a low profile. The royal family does not want to be portrayed as glamorous or fabulously wealthy, this being deemed inappropriate in such a poor country as Nepal. Their private visits abroad are kept out of the public eye. Since 1990 they have retreated behind their palace walls, becoming almost as invisible as the many generations of royal ancestors who survived as prisoners in their own palaces during the 104 years of Rana domination.

What must it be like, I wondered, for this king who inherited real power and virtually ran the country for eighteen years, to adapt to this new role as benign constitutional monarch? The very fact that the king was willing to see me implies that the transformation has been accomplished. And although he conscientiously refrained from commenting on any policy issues, King Birendra made it clear that 'behind the scenes' he remains very much involved in public life.

I was left in no doubt that the king is exceptionally well briefed. Not only does he hold regular meetings with the prime minister and other members of government; he is also served by a Palace Secretariat which, although scaled down since the Panchayat era, remains a well-oiled machine for gathering and processing information.

But now that he no longer exercises executive power, what does he do with all this information? The answer, as far as I could perceive through the elaborate obfuscations of palace-speak, is that he applies his knowledge and residual authority to influence events – especially when, as he puts it, 'things get bogged down'. And there have been many such occasions when this has happened since multi-party democracy was introduced. As when it was necessary to put together a viable coalition where no single party held a majority; and, once such a coalition government was in place, to persuade its fractious members to continue working together. These discussions require a fine sense of 'the art of the possible'. By undertaking such mediating or conciliatory roles, the new monarchy can claim to have assisted Nepal's fledgling democracy through several potential crises.

All this struck me as being very different from the way King Birendra was portrayed as a power-hungry dictator in writings published shortly after the 'Popular Uprising'. But then the Palace has evolved its own version of recent history in which certain episodes, like the Panchayat years and Jana Andolan, are generally passed over in silence. According to this perspective, the king has always been a constitutional monarch – or at least since 1951, when King Tribhuvan overturned the Rana regime. His son and grandson have equally been constitutional monarchs, in that they ruled according to the constitutions of those times. The fact that for most of this period the constitution banned all political parties has no bearing upon the matter. Now there is another constitution, the fifth since the monarchy reassumed its rightful place in Nepal, and King Birendra continues to abide by its provisions.

Another strand in palace historiography is the intimate link between the monarchy and the people. As King Birendra puts it: 'Nepal's history and tradition have bound monarchy and her people in an enduring and intimate relationship, and the Institution has always been guided by the desire and aspirations of the people as a whole.' This special relationship can be traced back to King Prithvi Narayan Shah, whom the present king especially admires for unifying the country and, 'thereby laying the foundations of modern Nepal. For us Nepalese, no achievement could be greater.'

The close identification of monarchy and popular will was again stressed when he described his grandfather's triumphant return to Kathmandu in 1951. 'King Tribhuvan, in keeping with the people's aspirations, inspired and led the Nepalese people in their struggle for a democratic set-up against the Rana oligarchy. He also introduced a democratic polity in Nepal.'

The insistently populist note of this palace rhetoric reminded me of the official outpourings of China's Communist Party. Certainly, it seemed strange to be receiving such formulaic material from a ruling monarch. It was unbefitting. But then I remembered that there are other models of kingship very different from those we have grown accustomed to in the West. Prince Sihanouk of Cambodia, for instance, who at various points in his career had to treat with the Pol Pot regime. I also recalled that King Birendra had made several visits to China and spoken warmly of the Communist leadership. And in one of his asides, he mentioned how Nepal's monarchy had 'always maintained close relations with the parties of the Left', namely the local Communist parties. In Nepal, it seems Communism and monarchy can co-exist quite happily. At times they have lined up together to limit the preponderant influence of the Nepal Congress Party.

But the most likely source for this populist strain in palace-speak lies closer to hand. Palace rhetoric has simply taken on board the same formulaic language, with its tendency to repetition and fixed slogans, used by the democratic parties for their election manifestos or when addressing mass rallies. Everything has to be spelled out in the simplest terms. There is little room for subtlety. It is the lingua franca of a democracy that has not yet reached maturity.

It was supposedly to allow the Nepalese people time to achieve this political maturity, through advances in education and economic development, that King Mahendra set up the 'partyless' Panchayat system. This remains a delicate subject in palace circles, for the present king stuck with the increasingly discredited Panchayat regime until being obliged to assent to its dissolution after the 1990 Uprising. So when I asked what he thought were his father's greatest achievements, I was not surprised that he chose to begin with international relations – Nepal's joining the United Nations in 1955 and the Non-Aligned Movement six years later – through which 'King Mahendra promoted our national interest and projected it internationally'. He also pointed out that 'the first general elections under the multi-party polity were held during his reign'.

Only then did he move on to the Panchayat system, which he said 'was introduced to consolidate the people's right to elect their representatives, from the village to the national level, and also to strengthen the administrative division and structure of the country'.

Scarcely the stoutest defence of a system so intimately connected with the Shah dynasty over three decades. But since then, the Palace has done what it can to dissociate itself from the failures of the Panchayat era and project a new image of a constitutional monarchy that 'has always been guided by the desire and aspirations of the people as a whole'. The stress on continuity, on monarchy's natural tendency to take the long view, helps paper over any past mistakes; though the king did observe that, 'sometimes there are different views on what is right in particular circumstances. Sometimes we have to go back and re-think, and then go forward another way.'

One aspect of the monarchy that is obviously still alive and well in Nepal is its embodiment of traditional values. As a Hindu king, Birendra continues the tradition of bestowing the *tika* on the foreheads of the multitudes who gather in front of Narayanhitti Palace during the Badha Dasain Festival. Among many Nepalese, and particularly those of the older generation, he is venerated as an incarnation of the god Vishnu. His public addresses often end with the invocation of Nepal's patron deity, 'May Lord Pashupatinath bless us all!' But he also attends Buddhist ceremonies, and insists that 'Nepal's monarchy does not discriminate against any Nepali citizen on linguistic, ethnic or any other grounds'.

Nor is he an unthinking traditionalist, ready to support anything and everything simply because it is sanctioned by age. 'The Nepalese', he observed, 'are sensitive about safeguarding their culture and traditions, and through time monarchy has also played an important role in this regard.' But modernization, and the inevitable change in cultural values that goes with it, is accelerating, and the king argues 'we should welcome and even initiate change'. However, 'wisdom lies in managing change, by introducing values and processes which complement the best of our heritage. One should move with the times, but with roots firmly embedded in a country's soil and the best of its legacies.'

This quest for a 'middle way', which allows for modernization while safeguarding a people's heritage, is subscribed to by most developing nations these days. The dilemmas posed have been particularly acute among the Himalayan kingdoms, which until fifty years ago preserved their traditional cultures by maintaining a deliberate policy of isolation from the outside world. Some countries, like Bhutan, have been more thoroughgoing in their defence of traditional values than others. Just looking at what has happened in the Kathmandu Valley, with its uncontrolled urban sprawl and pollution, its westernized shops and hotels and Internet cafes, it is hard to find much balance between the headlong rush for 'development' and preserving the nation's heritage.

King Birendra is very much aware that these changes are happening, and that in many cases they cannot be reversed.

But he believes that 'culture and religion give a country and its people their identity, to which our varied terrain, in Nepal's case, gives specific meaning'. One must therefore 'hang on to what is basic to our cultural identity' rather than try to maintain the entire panoply of inherited beliefs and customs simply because they are sanctioned by age.

Some of these usages he defines as being 'peripheral'; though he also noted that with any attempt to change or reform them 'one comes up against what are, to be quite frank, vested interests'. And there are many age-old customs in Nepal, from social inequalities justified by the caste system through to wholesale corruption among temple officials, which could be reformed or discarded without losing anything that contributes to Nepalese culture.

That such reforms are needed was brought home to me just days after I had interviewed the king. The chief guardian of Pashupatinath Temple, the holiest and most visited shrine in Nepal, was accused of siphoning off millions of rupees donated by pious pilgrims. I noted that before the scandal broke, various long-serving trustees of the temple complex – including Queen Aishwarya Pajya Laxmi – had resigned from their duties, thereby distancing themselves from the public outcry that inevitably followed.

A note of caution permeated all of King Birendra's utterances. Perhaps this is only to be expected. These days he is an ardent disciple of gradualism. As he put it, 'taking a snap decision may seem the more attractive option, but it is better to get there slowly'.

His natural tendency to examine a topic from every point of view, to seek a balance, fits him well for his new constitutional role. In due course, this might be extended so that the king fulfils a function closer to that of the President of India, assisting in the formation of democratically elected governments and stepping in publicly when 'things get bogged down'.

But for the time being he is still unsure of what he can or cannot do, and prefers to err on the side of caution. As for the future of the monarchy in Nepal, he believes that 'each one of us must make a step, and be sure that it is solid enough to build the next one'. Crown Prince Dipendra has been carefully groomed to take up the royal succession. He has been exposed to all the analytical and decision-making processes. 'It is a role he knows he has to take on,' commented his father. 'But in the end, each individual must make his own job of it.'

I could have asked more questions, but I was aware that the audience had already continued far beyond its allotted span. King Birendra rose and shook my hand. 'I hope all this has been of some use,' he said modestly. And while I did feel somewhat frustrated by the artful ambiguities of palace-speak, I was also aware that on some of the more sensitive subjects he had been seeking an understanding without actually expressing it in words. Then, still accompanied by the press secretary, I went through the air-lock of the ante-room and out into the palace grounds. The rain had held off, but the night air was heavy with the monsoon.

'Now you have seen what a simple king we have,' observed Mr Panday. To which I muttered assent, thinking all the while that though his dress and manners were informal enough, King Birendra's mental processes appeared to be far from straightforward.

That was the least perplexing part. What really puzzled

me was how to reconcile the benign, ever-smiling monarch I had just met with the bogeyman depicted in so many accounts of the 1990 Revolution – and not just those written by Nepalese activists, but also by supposedly impartial foreign observers. Was this the same man who held the reins of power during the decadent, final years of the Panchayat regime? The man subsequently branded as a dictator, on whose orders practically all the pro-democracy leaders had been imprisoned, whose security forces repeatedly fired on unarmed crowds of protesters, leaving hundreds of dead and wounded in the streets of Kathmandu? Could this same individual have re-invented himself so effectively that within a decade he has become a benevolent father figure to the nation, respected even by his former enemies? These two images of Birendra are so diametrically opposed that it becomes hard to believe in either of them.

What seems to have happened is the creation of contradictory myths – one of which might be called 'the demonization of Birendra'. Around the time of Jana Andolan there were plenty of good reasons why party activists should hate Nepal's ruling family. For almost thirty years their party organizations had been banned and persecuted. Many of them had been jailed for political activities. The Panchayat system sustained a self-serving elite from which they were automatically excluded. Moreover, the blacker things seemed under the former regime, the brighter they now appeared in the dawn of multi-party democracy.

Politicians who had been in prison made the most of their new status as revolutionary heroes. Even those who had been actively involved in the Panchayat system were so busy re-inventing themselves as good democrats that they readily joined in the chorus of condemnation. In the aftermath of the so-called People's Revolution, nobody had a good word to say about corrupt old panchas or, for that matter, the institution of monarchy.

Amidst the euphoria that accompanied Jana Andolan, a number of other myths emerged. The scale of the popular uprising was itself exaggerated. In reality, the demonstrations and strikes were almost entirely confined to the Kathmandu Valley. It was by no stretch of the imagination a nationwide uprising. Nor is it clear precisely when and why the crowd moved from protesting against the Panchayat system in general or the faceless functionaries of the Palace Secretariat, and began instead to chant anti-monarchist slogans — first against Queen Aishwarya and then finally attacking King Birendra himself. This was previously unheard of, and even witnesses sympathetic to the pro-democracy movement suspect this escalation of sloganizing was carefully orchestrated, as it often is in India. Similarly, much was made of the heroic intensity of the revolutionary struggle during those crucial days of April 1990. Yet compared to most other popular revolutions, Jana Andolan was a pushover.

It was almost too easy a victory. If King Birendra had been the cold-blooded dictator he is often depicted as being, then he would have called in the army at the first sign of trouble. Instead he gave in gracefully, dissolving the Panchayat system and immediately recognizing the legality of political parties. But events in Kathmandu had to be moulded to fit pre-existing models of the people's revolution overthrowing the evil dictator. The more repressive the ancien régime could be shown to be, the greater the glory of the populist leaders who were now in charge. And since it was to these same politicians that foreign journalists and academics turned for first-hand accounts of such momentous events, it is hardly surprising that they all tell one side of the story. Nobody bothered to talk to the Palace, then deemed to have been discredited. And sensing which way the wind was blowing, the Palace decided it was best to stay quiet for the time being.

As I had recently discovered, the Palace's version of these same events is somewhat different. The king had been ruling according to the existing constitution, whose validity had been re-endorsed by the people's vote only ten years previously. Both he and Queen Aishwarya had been staying in Pokhara, away from the capital, and were not fully apprised of the level of popular discontent. Once he had himself witnessed the crowds surging up Durbar Marg, King Birendra set in motion the process of consultations which led to the appointment of a new government and, eventually, the adoption of a new constitution whereby he could continue to reign in accordance with the aspirations and wishes of the people. Of course, this version also glosses over some unpalatable truths. But it has served its purpose in enabling the Shah dynasty to ride out the storm and wait for better times.

Most Nepalese I met agreed that the king's standing and popularity have grown in recent years. Whether this is due to the reverence in which the institution of monarchy is still held by most Nepalese, or because they have grown disillusioned with all the political jerrymandering and corruption that has become the hallmark of democracy Nepalese-style, it is hard to say. What is clear is that the system of monarchy is so deeply entrenched that it would take a far greater upheaval than Jana Andolan to turn most Nepalese into republicans. Meanwhile, the king is quietly consolidating his role as a constitutional monarch, seeking new ways in which he can make himself indispensable and, in doing so, enhancing the long-term security of the Shah dynasty. But he is no longer his own man.

There remained one last thing I wanted to do before leaving Nepal, and that was to visit the hill town of Gorkha. It was there that the remarkable story of the Shah dynasty had its beginnings. Although it is only a six-hour drive from Kathmandu, I had not yet had time to make that particular journey.

For most of the way you follow the appropriately named Prithvi Highway towards Pokhara. Even in the middle of the monsoon, when the country is at its greenest, the bare hillsides west of Kathmandu showed how far deforestation has gone. The road descended through a succession of hairpin bends down to the Trisuli River. At this season it was in full spate, and we followed the angry flood down to its confluence with the Narayani before turning up a side valley towards the Great Himalaya. Until this side road was built by the Chinese seventeen years ago, the only way to reach Gorkha was on foot.

The road climbed through a gorge and into a broad valley which once formed the hub of the Kingdom of Gorkha. The soil is a deep red and the rice crop was already well advanced. Then the town appeared to the right, clinging to the side of a spur, above which I could just see the ancestral palace of the Shah dynasty upon a much higher ridge.

Much of the lower town has been built since the new road came through using the usual mix of concrete and brick, so the approaches to Gorkha are not that attractive. But all that changes just beyond the bus stop. There is a sacred tank where local kids were gleefully splashing, and a park filled with temples – some pagoda-roofed, others with rounded domes that are a distant echo of Mughal architecture. All of them were built by Prithvi Narayan's ancestors.

There are two royal palaces in Gorkha, one within the town and the other perched on the commanding heights above it. The lower palace, Tallo Durbar, is the larger of the two; but while it was used in the nineteenth century to house exiled royalty, it fell into disrepair under the later Ranas and was left empty until after 1951. Since then it has been used firstly as a school, then as a district office, until finally it was handed over to the Department of Archaeology, who have carried out extensive repairs. Most of the woodcarving and even the brickwork is new. Upstairs is a gallery with ancient inscriptions and faded photographs which show what Gorkha looked like before the coming of motor traffic – a small, deeply provincial hill town whose stone-built, shingle-roofed houses had obviously seen better days.

The Gorkha Durbar, or hill-top palace, had been shrouded in mists when I arrived. This was my true goal, for it was here that Prithvi Narayan Shah was born. I waited until the weather cleared before setting out on the steep ascent, accompanied by a pair of extremely street-wise village boys. A well-paved path led through terraced fields planted with maize, each plot of land surrounded by rough stone walls that harboured a bewildering variety of ferns and wild flowers. The humidity at this lower altitude slowed me down and I was happy to rest about halfway beside the stone platform where the early Gorkha kings had dispensed justice. The final approach to the palace takes you past two helicopter landing pads – the first one is for royal guests and servants, while the higher one, nearest the palace, is reserved exclusively for members of the royal family visiting their ancestral home.

I removed my shoes before entering the palace precincts, since there are numerous temples within. The buildings are of faded brick, their roofs pagoda-shaped, their latticed windows surrounded by exquisite Newari woodcarvings of peacocks, lions and other auspicious creatures. I was shown the courtyard where buffalo are ritually slaughtered with a kukri. Finally, I peered into the small room beside the palace gate where Prithvi Narayan Shah was born. Inside, a flame is always kept burning in his memory.

The workmanship on the temples, the diminutive guest house and the palace itself is of the highest order. The setting, looking out towards the main Himalayan range to the north and endless forested ridges to the south and west, is spectacular. But what struck me about Gorkha Durbar is how tiny it is — especially when compared to the royal palaces of the Kathmandu Valley.

It seemed highly improbable that any hill raja who called this place home could possibly conquer the whole of Nepal and found a dynasty that is still very much in place some 250 years later. And now, having gone back to its roots, the very survival of an independent Kingdom of Nepal appeared to be built on a series of improbabilities. That it has survived against the odds, and is still home to some of the most fascinating cultures in the world, is something to be thankful for. Whether those cultures will still be there in another fifty years, or whether by then there will even be a Kingdom of Nepal, is another matter. As I walked down the hill from Gorkha Durbar, I felt that I had been looking into a vanishing world.

Chapter Eight

SIKKIM – THE KINGDOM
THAT DISAPPEARED

Sikkim was the first Himalayan kingdom I ever visited. I was just seven years old, and my family was spending some time in Kalimpong when the invitation arrived. We were to go up to Gangtok to see the Buddhist mask-dances, before taking tea with the Chogyal or King of Sikkim.

Entry to this tiny country was less difficult than the other Himalayan kingdoms, because Sikkim was then a protectorate of India. It had an Indian-appointed Dewan or chief executive, and there were plenty of other Indian advisers and army officers present at the ceremonial dances. Their wives had put on their best saris and shawls for the occasion, though mostly they stayed inside the large tent where tea was served.

It was Tibetan-style tea, made with salt and slightly rancid yak butter, and I had to get rid of mine by emptying my cup into a flowerpot. No sooner than I put the cup back on the table, however, it was filled again to the brim. 'Try to drink it slowly,' suggested my mother, 'and do stop pulling faces.' Much later I learned that even hardened explorers have found butter tea 'an acquired taste'.

I was much more impressed by the masked dancers' acrobatic leaps – so much so that I tried to learn some of the basic steps. Their vivid costumes of red and gold silks caught my fancy, and for some reason I was not at all frightened by their demon-masks. The dancing took place in the palace grounds, near the royal chapel. The king presided over the celebrations, a rather lonely figure since at that point his Tibetan wife had recently died and he had not yet met the young American graduate, Hope Cooke, whom he was to marry. I recall that he looked very dignified in his long Sikkimese robes of very pale yellow frosted silk – until, that is, he went out into the bright sunlight and put on a pair of dark glasses. Then he looked slightly sinister.

The next time I went to Sikkim, it was by default. By then I was at university, and I had travelled out along 'The Hippy Trail' to India with the intention of meeting up with my old school friend, the crown prince of Bhutan. His father's untimely death meant that these plans had to be cancelled; so instead I arranged to visit the neighbouring Kingdom of Sikkim, taking the Darjeeling Mail up from Calcutta and then continuing by jeep-taxi to Gangtok.

I stayed in the Green Hotel, a cheap place down by the main jeep stand. That evening I fell into conversation with the proprietor's son, who proved to have an encyclopaedic knowledge of football. The conversation was rather one-sided. Whereas football has never been one of my stronger passions, this Sikkimese teenager was a fanatic. He was able to run through the names of half the players in my 'home team' (Brighton and Hove Albion) and then give a measured judgement on the club's chances of promotion next season.

Just as I was about to give up the unequal struggle on Second Division statistics, my quizmaster suggested we went to a 'charity dance' – at which, he assured me, there would be a 'beat group'. Visions of Cliff Richard lookalikes crooning away while the drummer tried to catch up rose before my eyes. I tried polite excuses, but there was no way out. Before I knew it I was being frog-marched towards the Norkhill Hotel, by far the grandest establishment in town.

Then, to my complete incredulity, I heard drifting across the thin mountain air some extremely feisty guitar licks. Somebody down there was turning out a highly charged version of Carlos Santana's 'Soul Sacrifice'. My amazement was complete when, having purchased my ticket from a pair of ravishingly beautiful Sikkimese girls, I entered the Norkhill Palace to discover that the band was largely a royal affair – the crown prince on lead guitar and his cousin on drums. It was explained to me that this was an informal occasion, and no one batted an eyelid when a door opened and the king danced into the room, his American wife in his arms.

I had not expected to find such sophisticated, westernized society in a small and remote kingdom like Sikkim. I guessed that this was mainly due to Queen Hope's influence. She was wearing a long silk dress that looked as though it had been self-consciously designed to make use of Sikkimese material and motifs. The Chogyal also wore silk, but in the traditional style. As for the royalist rock band, I knew that the princes had been educated at an English public school, Harrow, and that during the early seventies just about every public schoolboy wanted to play in a rock band. The only unusual thing about the crown prince was that, unlike most, he had learned to play his instrument.

There was a surreal quality to the evening. I became aware that this 'charity dance' was crammed with Sikkim's highest families, that half of the people I talked to were minor royals, and that they mainly wanted to talk to me in order to learn about 'the latest London fashions'. I was introduced to the Chogyal and his wife, who asked about my travels. They seemed charming and still deeply attached to each other. But there was something I could not figure out — namely how this very cosmopolitan elite fitted in with what I understood to be a traditional Buddhist monarchy. And there was a frenetic, enjoy-life-while-you-can element to the festivities that I found slightly disturbing. For some reason it made me think of a Grand Ball in St Petersburg, circa 1916. Everything seemed to continue as before; but there was a nasty surprise lurking just around the corner.

For the Chogyal of Sikkim, that nasty surprise was timed for his next birthday — 4 April 1973. As the hereditary monarch sat in a raised chair, his family and courtiers to his right, the Indian Political Officer and army generals to his left, an angry crowd was gathering down the hill in Gangtok. They were mainly Nepali-speakers, including large contingents which had been bused in with Indian assistance from outside Sikkim, from Darjeeling and Kalimpong, to boost their numbers. They wanted to assert their majority rights to bring an end to the 'dictatorship' of the Chogyal and the dominance of the Bhotia and Lepcha peoples.

These ethnic rivalries go back to the nineteenth century. Similar demands had been made by the Nepali population of Sikkim since the early 1950s. But this time the political leaders who were stirring up protest knew that the advantage was on their side, for they knew the highest Indian authorities were behind them. All this had been quietly arranged through Lhendup Dorji Kazi, president of the largest pro-democracy party, the Sikkim National Congress. Certainly, the Indian police and army stationed in Sikkim were not going to intervene to protect the Chogyal. So when the angry crowds swarmed out of the Kazi's petrol station and started marching into Gangtok, it was left to the poorly equipped Sikkim constabulary to restore order. They tried tear-gas, but half of the canisters failed to go off and were hurled back into the police lines. As bricks and stones rained down and the mob demolished barriers, the police opened fire. Nobody was killed, and only two were wounded. But this was enough for reports of 'ruthless firing' and 'the collapse of law and order' to be broadcast.

That was the excuse that India needed to intervene. The Research and Analysis Wing (RAW) of India's intelligence services had been prepared well in advance. When loyal Bhotia volunteers from northern Sikkim came down to defend their Chogyal, they were turned back by the Indian army. The Chogyal himself ordered them to return home so as to prevent fighting between his Buddhist supporters and the mainly Hindu and Nepali-speaking opponents. That, he believed, would only lead to a 'communal holocaust' in which one ethnic group was pitted against the other. Rather than resist, he sat down with L.D. Kazi, K.C. Pradhan and other opposition leaders, to try to work out a new deal. They got most of what they wanted – a new 'one-man one-vote' constitution which would give the descendants of Nepali immigrants a guaranteed majority; a closer relation-ship with India, which resulted in Sikkim's separate status as a protectorate being changed to that of an associate state; and the reduction of the Chogyal's powers to that of a mere figurehead, though he was still accorded the title of constitutional head of government.

All of this was too much for Queen Hope. She had entered a fairytale romance with an exotic eastern ruler. Her marriage had been fêted by the world press, though the more conservative Sikkimese always had their reservations. None the less, she had done a lot to help restore Sikkim's sense of identity, by encouraging the publication of schoolbooks in Sikkimese and championing the new national anthem. For all this, she is still widely respected by Sikkimese today. But because she was an American, because her presence in Sikkim drew US ambassadors and congressmen and other high-ranking visitors, stories began to circulate in the Indian press that Hope Cooke was in fact a CIA agent.

There is nothing to substantiate such claims. Indeed, as her son Prince Palden points out: 'Anyone who knows my mother will say that she'd make the world's worst spy.' But the mud stuck, and it suited New Delhi that her well-meaning efforts to bolster Sikkim's identity be seen as part of a plot to install a US base in India's backyard. It pandered to the strongly anti-American streak of Indian politics at that time, and it helped prepare public opinion for the final takeover of Sikkim. Having been vilified in the Indian press, Hope now found herself married to a monarch who seemed content to sign his country away. She packed her bags and left for New York, taking the young Prince Palden and Princess Hope Leezum with her. If it was not quite yet the end of the monarchy, it was certainly the end of a marriage.

*

I next returned to Sikkim, this time with Sarah, in the winter of 1992. By then the Chogyal was dead, the monarchy in abeyance, and this ancient Himalayan kingdom had been a full member state of the Indian Union for nearly two decades.

We returned again in October 1998. By then the situation in Sikkim had changed out of recognition. But the long drive up the Teesta Valley was much as I remembered it. Dense tropical jungle cascaded down to the river's bed. Monkeys crouched by the roadside in the hope of being fed by passing travellers. Convoys of military and civilian trucks lumbered up this slender lifeline, there being no other road access to Sikkim and the strongly defended border with Chinese-occupied Tibet. And just as before, the road had been washed away in places during the monsoon, and we had to slither across a nasty landslide or two.

Our passports were inspected at the Rangpo checkpoint to make sure we had the special permits still required for foreigners entering Sikkim. Then we left the Teesta Valley and started climbing through densely cultivated country – the terraced paddy fields shining golden green in the afternoon light. We passed commercial nurseries that specialize in growing orchids (Sikkim has more than six hundred native species) and newly built hotels and restaurants which cater mainly for the growing number of Indian tourists.

Even before we reached Ranipaul, I was aware that there had been a great deal of construction going on. But I was quite unprepared for the final climb up to Gangtok. Not so long ago this had been open country. Now the entire road was lined with shoddily constructed shops and houses, some of them already sliding down the hill because they had been built in landslide areas.

There were half-finished 'English-medium-schools' and cheap hotels with metal rods protruding from their flat roofs, dingy godowns and wholesale merchants who all offered exactly the same goods. Gangtok, which had once stood aloof on its hill, now slithered down to the valley floor thanks to this ugly, unplanned string of half-empty concrete shells. Obviously, there was a construction boom in progress; but it was hard to see how this kind of speculative strip development could bring any long-term benefits.

I was glad to leave the lower town behind and climb up though the main bazaar towards the Old Tibet Road. There we were greeted by Pema Namgyal, who runs Netuk House – a traditional Sikkimese household which takes in paying guests. Prayer flags lined the entrance. The rooms were filled with brightly painted furniture in the Tibetan style.

We were invited to drink chang. Here it is served in cylindrical containers resembling a pint-sized wooden barrel which have been filled in advance with the dark fermented barley or millet. Hot water from a kettle is poured over this mash, which is then left to infuse for a few minutes before the warm and mildly alcoholic brew is sucked up through a bamboo straw. When all the liquid has been drunk some more hot water is added to make a second 'round'. And so it continues, a deliciously alcoholic variant of the tea ceremony, until the fermented grain begins to lose its potency.

At dinner we were joined by our host, who apologized for all the noise emanating from the upper storeys, an odd mixture of monkish droning and the scamper of tiny feet. 'I have seventeen relatives staying', he said, 'for a house blessing ceremony. This is an auspicious time, as declared by the astrologer who is also in attendance, and I hope the sounds do not disturb your peace.'

Namgyal's courtesy was matched by his fine, sensitive features which, though resembling the Tibetan in some respects, were more delicate – the skin paler and lacking the apple-red cheeks typical of people who live in the unremitting winds of the high plateau. He was of slight build, around 5 feet 8 inches tall, and sported a neatly trimmed moustache. In all his movements there was what I first took to be insurmountable shyness, but was later to recognize as good manners. I asked him where he had learned his excellent English.

'I was educated by the Jesuit fathers at St Joseph's College – do you know it, near Kalimpong?'

Yes, I did. But I was more interested in asking him about the black-and-white photographs hung around the dining room. 'Ah, that is the late Chogyal together with his councillors, including my father. He was president of the Sikkim National Party, which stood for the old constitution and preserving Sikkimese culture. When I was a boy I used to drive him to political meetings. But after 1974 he retired from politics.'

When he heard of my previously meeting the last King of Sikkim, Pema agreed to try to contact the royal palace in Gangtok to see if an audience could be arranged with the present Chogyal. He is the younger son of the last ruler of Sikkim and his first wife, who was Tibetan by birth.

'But it may prove difficult,' he warned. 'Prince Wangchuck is a very retiring person.' In the meantime he suggested we make a tour of West Sikkim, to see the throne where the first Chogyal of Sikkim was installed and to visit some of the ancient monasteries there. Then, after dinner, he showed us a video made up of ancient cine films of the Dalai Lama's passing through Sikkim in 1956 on his way to

India, where he attended the Buddha Jyanti celebrating the 2,500th anniversary of Lord Buddha's birth. There was some remarkable footage of the Dalai Lama's retinue and hundreds of pack mules descending the Old Tibet Road.

'Many of the mules were carrying gold and religious treasures', Pema said, 'just in case things turned bad with the Chinese inside Tibet. His Holiness entrusted so much treasure to the Chogyal of Sikkim, who hid it all in the palace grounds for safekeeping.'

Special permits had to be obtained to go into West Sikkim, even though it is nowhere near the sensitive border with Chinese-occupied Tibet. After a day's delay we finally set out for Yuksom, dropping back down to the Teesta and then turning upstream.

I had never been to West Sikkim before, and marvelled at the lushness of the country we were passing through. The terraced fields marched up the mountainside in even steps, as though some giant had thought to build a stairway to the snow-bound peaks. The rice crop was turning a shade of pale gold that indicated it was almost ready for harvesting. Then we entered a broadleaf forest where bromeliads sprouted from every branch and the ground was carpeted with ferns and iridescent mosses. We climbed up through a belt of cloud to a ridge-top village inhabited mainly by Tibetan refugees, before plunging down into another valley. As always in the Himalayas, a journey of twenty miles as the crow flies can easily take half a day.

It was dark by the time we reached Yuksom, but the next morning revealed Kanchenjunga's southern flanks at close quarters. It was only a short walk to the white chorten which marks the spot where, in 1642, three high lamas came together and chose to crown Phuntsog Namgyal as the first Chogyal of Sikkim. The carved stone throne is still there, sheltered by a grove of dark pines. Prayer flags drooped motionless from their poles. The morning air was full of birdsong and I sat down to contemplate how a monarchy that had endured for more than three hundred years could have been extinguished in less than three.

The distant origins of Sikkim's royal family may be traced back to the Minyuk dynasty, which once ruled over parts of Kham in eastern Tibet. Early migrations of Tibetan peoples into Sikkim probably began in the thirteenth century, but the exodus of Nyingmapa lamas and their followers grew after the reformist Gelugpa sect gained the ascendancy within Tibet and in due course produced a line of Dalai Lamas. The Bhotia population of Sikkim were, in a sense, political refugees. But the Chogyals subsequently made their peace with Lhasa, accepting a loose form of Tibetan suzerainty, and took to marrying into the Tibetan aristocracy. Sikkim became one of the more compliant of Tibet's 'satellite states' on the southern side of the Himalayas, and whenever the Chogyals were threatened by their Bhutanese or Nepali neighbours they invariably appealed to Lhasa for military assistance.

In earlier days, the Kingdom of Sikkim was far larger than it is now. It encompassed all of Darjeeling and Kalimpong hill districts to the south and spilled over the Himalayan divide into the Chumbi Valley – where the Chogyals still retained estates until the 1950s and to which they often withdrew to safety when threatened from the south.

The first two hundred years of the kingdom's history

saw the gradual assimilation of the indigenous Lepcha people, most of whom adopted Buddhism alongside their own animist beliefs. This process was not always peaceful, and Lepcha chieftains often led revolts against the king and the Tibetan-style feudal hierarchy which supported him. But during the eighteenth century most of the Lepcha chiefs were co-opted into the feudal aristocracy. In more recent times, Bhotias and Lepchas have combined together in the face of more serious threats to their traditional way of life.

The Bhutanese were the first to make serious inroads into Sikkimese territory by conquering the hill area around Kalimpong. But it was the Gorkha invasions of the late eighteenth century, their pillaging of monasteries and annexation of all lands west of the River Teesta, that marks the beginning of Sikkim's long decline. A reprieve was granted by the British, whose peace terms after winning the Britain-Nepal War (1814–16) included the restoration of territories between the Mechi and Teesta rivers to Sikkim.

But there was a price to pay. The British wanted access to Sikkim in order to open up a trade route to Tibet and Central Asia. They also coveted the cool hills around Darjeeling, and in 1835 the Chogyal 'gifted' this thinly populated region to them in return for an annual pension of 3,000 rupees.

Darjeeling soon became a boom-town. Sanitoriums and boarding schools were founded, tea gardens planted, and before long the entire Government of Bengal was moving up during the hot weather. To build and service this model hill station the British required labour, and this they found in the thousands of land-hungry Nepalese who walked over the border to find gainful employment. The imperial masters found the Nepalese industrious and loyal, so they were not averse to their migrating further afield to the tea gardens of the Duars or up towards the heartlands of Sikkim.

By the late nineteenth century there were more Nepalese settlers in Sikkim than Bhotias and Lepchas combined. The newcomers were industrious, and besides planting paddy they developed new cash crops such as cardamom and oranges. They were also more aggressive than the Lepchas, who were soon driven out of their native lands or made do with less productive, marginal farms.

The British authorities approved of these developments, which tended to reinforce their hold over the frontier region. When the Chogyal protested or, worse still, when he called on Tibet for assistance, their response was to launch a punitive expedition. A Political Officer was installed in Gangtok to oversee the workings of the Chogyal's government and Sikkim was reduced to protectorate status, with Britain taking responsibility for all matters pertaining to foreign relations and defence. The Chogyal was treated as just another Indian princely ruler when he attended the imperial Durbar in Delhi. When Chogyal Thobden proved uncooperative, the Political Officer had him removed from Gangtok to Kurseong, a stopping point on the Darjeeling Railway, where he and his wife were kept under house arrest until he mended his ways.

Although Britain never tried to incorporate Sikkim into India, the Himalayan kingdom was definitely regarded as falling within her 'sphere of influence' and treated as a client state. So when the British finally quit India in 1947 they left two rather dubious legacies for the Kingdom of Sikkim. One was its indeterminate status as a protectorate, neither wholly independent nor part of India. The other was the

Nepali-speaking majority. With the dawn of democracy in India, they now started demanding democratic reforms in Sikkim.

As I gazed upon the throne of the first Chogyal, I realized that Sikkim's sudden disappearance as a distinct kingdom did not happen overnight. Its history over the previous century had been one long decline into ever deeper dependence. Still, there were other reminders of its ancient glories around Yoksum, so I picked myself up and asked a village boy for directions to Dhumri Monastery.

The path up to Sikkim's oldest monastery meandered through a shady wood whose floor was planted with mature cardamom bushes. Their spreading fronds and reddish, tightly clustered seed pods make this one of the world's more attractive cash crops. We crossed a wooden bridge over a swift-flowing stream before beginning the final ascent, which took us through flower-studded meadows and forests of Himalayan cypress. Just one of these giants is supposed to have provided sufficient timber to build the original monastery at Dhumri, and there are still some mighty specimens nearby, their branches crowded with wild orchids and hanging moss. The monastery itself was locked up and no one knew where the monk-guardian had gone off to. But I was happy enough to sit in the sunshine beside a crumbling, fern-encrusted chorten, and look out at the green valleys and ice-bound peaks. It made me appreciate why the oldest inhabitants of this land, the Lepchas, believed they lived in an earthly paradise. But I was also very much aware that, in recent years at least, there had been much trouble in this natural paradise.

Across the valley from Yuksom stands Pemayangtse Monastery. The direct road to it was impassable because the last monsoon's landslides had not yet been cleared, so we had to take a long detour via the 'holy mountain' of Tashiding.

Pemayangtse prides itself on being a 'royal monastery'. It was founded in the early eighteenth century by the third Chogyal of Sikkim, since when it has enjoyed the patronage of successive rulers. As a result, its monk body has been mainly recruited from among the old Bhotia-Lepcha aristocracy, who continue the practice of entering their second son for monastic training at an early age. As with most other monasteries in Sikkim, the monks are members of the Nyingmapa sect, the oldest tradition of Tibetan Buddhism, and are allowed to marry. Pemayangtse sits astride a high ridge, and as we climbed past a chorten and lines of prayer flags towards the monastery's entrance, I looked back to see the white mass of Kanchenjunga filling the horizon.

A thick-set man awaited us at the top of the steps. His head was tonsured and he wore the maroon robes of an ordained monk, though his erect, unbending posture was more that of a military man. I guessed that this was Pema's father-in-law, Captain Yongda. Just looking at him, it was impossible to tell his age. He could have been anything from thirty-five to sixty. Only the knowledge that he was already a grandfather made me veer towards the further end of the scale.

We were invited to have breakfast with him before being shown both the monastery and the nearby school which he had founded for orphans and what he called 'near-orphans' – the children of very poor or landless villagers. They came from all over Sikkim, he explained, and this school was unusual in that instruction was given in the Sikkimese language and Buddhist traditions followed. State schools used Nepali as the medium of instruction, this having been adopted as the official language of Sikkim since the monarchy was overthrown. I had the impression that for Captain Yongda this project was about more than educating poor children. It was a last-ditch attempt to preserve Sikkim's cultural inheritance.

The main prayer hall in the monastery was crowded with young novices who peered round eagerly to look at the strange visitors. Some burst into giggles, but mostly they kept up their rhythmic chanting without missing a beat. We climbed up stairs to another temple which housed Pemayangtse's greatest treasure – an intricately carved representation of Guru Rinpoche's heavenly mansion. There are many holy sites in Sikkim associated with this ubiquitous eighth-century missionary. In fact, if you give credence to all the legends about where he has meditated, there is scarcely a corner of the Himalayas that he did not visit.

I learned that Yapo Yongda, as he preferred to be called, had entered the monastery when he was four and completed all his studies by the age of eleven (normally these require a further six years). The youthful prodigy was called Yapo, a title normally reserved for senior monks, and continued his education at secular schools. His talents were noticed by the Chogyal, who asked him to join the palace establishment as a security guard. He was sent to an Indian military academy and was attached to a Gurkha regiment before returning to Gangtok. 'With these different experiences', he said, 'I was able to choose my future path – monk or soldier.' He chose to serve his king and was made Captain of the Sikkim Guards, a small, Indian-trained unit charged with internal security.

Captain Yongda's loyalty to his king was beyond question. He was unusual in that he understood the importance of monarchy as being the focus of national unity. Its strength, he said, was the key to Sikkim's separate identity. And Yongda served the Chogyal not just as an ADC in charge of security but also in a religious capacity, assisting in arrangements on days when special ceremonies were called for. 'I would sit with him for one or sometimes two hours, always learning so much from him. And during the crisis of 1975 I acted as his personal secretary. I had to prepare all the briefs and submit them to him.'

It was his unfortunate duty to inform the Chogyal that Indian combat units with heavy mortars and artillery support had taken up position around Enchey Monastery and ridges overlooking the palace. The king could not believe that Indian troops would attack. He pointed to the solemn treaty signed by Nehru and his father, wherein India had promised to defend Sikkim's sovereignty. Moreover, the Indian political officer in Gangtok had assured him it was 'only a military exercise'. The officers of the Sikkim Guards saw things differently. 'We advised a build-up of defensive measures in advance', said Yongda, 'and that we should distribute rations and ammunition to troops stationed at the palace.'

It fell to Captain Yongda to convey this to the Chogyal. 'It was 11.30 p.m. and I had to wake him up. We talked until two in the morning. I reported the views of his senior advisers. Either he must escape in secret from the palace, or some defensive measures should be put in place. The Sikkim Guards had light machine guns and mortars; and though our full strength was only 300 men, we could have resisted for for three to four hours. In that time we could inform

China or Pakistan of the situation and request their assistance.'

I sat up at this mention of intervention by the two regional powers most consistently hostile to India. 'I should have mentioned', Captain Yongda added, 'that during the King of Nepal's coronation in Kathmandu, Chinese and Pakistani representatives had advised that the Chogyal shouldn't return to Sikkim unless he first obtained clear guarantees from India. The Chinese made this offer: that if anything was to go wrong they were ready to help Sikkim. But the Chogyal wouldn't listen. He had complete faith in the Government of India.

'I discussed this with him until two a.m. But he still said no. "India is a peace-loving nation," he assured me. "They would not do such a thing. And even if they do attack, I am a Buddhist king. I cannot order you or any other soldiers to fire on Indian troops."

'Then he asked me this question. "Do you think the Indian soldiers joined the army with the intent of protecting India's sovereignty, or just because they had to earn their livelihood? They come from very poor families. Is it right they lose their lives just because joining the army was their way to earn a livelihood?"

'You see, the Chogyal was a very religious man. As a truly Buddhist ruler, he couldn't order anyone to shoot to kill. Not just because of some policy decision taken in Delhi. And I tell you, I really learned a lot from our late Chogyal.'

That conversation took place in the early hours of 7 April 1975. Soon after he left the palace, Captain Yongda was arrested by the Indian Central Reserve Police (CRP) and thrown into jail. He petitioned the Central Court in

Gangtok for immediate release, but before the case could be heard he was taken to another jurisdiction in West Sikkim and then down south to Namche.

His CRP guards claimed to be acting under the Chogyal's orders. They told Yongda that he had been arrested for planning to assassinate Kazi and the president of the Youth Congress. Meanwhile, back in Gangtok, India's top man in Sikkim was briefing reporters on how Yongda had signed a confession that implicated the Chogyal in the plot. Strangely, this document never materialized. As for Captain Yongda, he says he was never even questioned about this alleged conspiracy. The only documents he signed were two petitions against unlawful arrest. Moreover, he knew nothing about any 'confession' implicating his monarch until he was released on bail, and that was fifteen days after he was first arrested.

The reason for this frame-up is simple. Captain Yongda needed to be got rid of. He was the only officer in the Sikkim Guards who might have organized an effective defence of the royal palace. Besides which, the Indian authorities could circulate another lurid anti-Chogyal story in the press. As a 'dirty tricks campaign', it was simple but highly effective.

The Indian army made its move on 9 April. They were taking no chances and committed an entire brigade to a three-pronged assault on the diminutive royal palace. Only a handful of Sikkim Guards were on duty and there was no officer present. The two sentries guarding the gate were cut down before they had a chance to fire. That was the end of any 'resistance', for the Sikkim Guards did not even have live ammunition. It was like smashing a nut with a sledgehammer.

When the Chogyal heard the sound of gunfire, he immediately phoned the Political Officer at India House to ask what was going on. After all, the Chogyal was himself an honorary colonel in the Indian army. The Sikkim Guards had been trained by the Indian army; most of their officers were Indians; they thought of Indian soldiers as comrades-in-arms, not enemies.

His call was passed to the general-in-command, who told the Chogyal to order his men to surrender. And that is precisely what happened. The remainder of the Sikkim Guards were rounded up, made to listen to a tape-recording of Chief Minister Kazi urging them to surrender, and then bundled into trucks and driven to an internment camp. Their escort could not prevent them from defiantly singing Sikkim's national anthem as they went.

'And so', explained Captain Yongda, 'this ancient Kingdom of Sikkim ceased to exist without a single drop of Indian blood being spilt.' The last part, at least, accorded with the Chogyal's wishes.

The Chogyal was unharmed. He was still accorded a modicum of respect. But all telephone lines were cut and he was completely isolated, a prisoner in his own palace. He was kept in ignorance of moves towards the formal merger of Sikkim with India. His letters of protest to Indira Gandhi were left unanswered.

The Kazi and four other ministers sworn in by India's representative, B.S. Das, moved swiftly. The day after the army stormed the palace a resolution was passed demanding the removal of the Chogyal and full merger with India. A popular referendum was called just four days later. It was all orchestrated from Delhi. The local press was crammed with anti-Chogyal stories and, with the Kazi and other political leaders urging their followers to approve, the outcome of the referendum was never in doubt.

The Chogyal heard on All-India Radio that India's constitution was being amended to allow Sikkim to become a fully fledged State of the Indian Union. Henceforth it would be entitled to send one elected representative to the Lok Sabha, the lower house of India's parliament in New Delhi. The new State would also have one representative in the upper house.

The Chogyal protested to Mrs Gandhi that all these changes amounted to a unilateral abrogation of India's 1950 treaty with Sikkim. He pinned his hopes on personal intercession by the Indian Prime Minister. But Mrs Gandhi would not be robbed of the glory of having brought Sikkim into the fold. The merger was justified as being an extension of democracy. It was deemed necessary to defend India's legitimate security concerns. The Chogyal was portrayed as a relic of feudalism or an autocratic monster in most Indian newspapers. Only a few brave voices queried the morality of the takeover.

As to the legality of the process, one of India's most prominent jurists, Chief Justice Hidayatullah, declared it was so obviously deficient that it should not affect the kingdom's legal status at all. 'The status of Sikkim in international law', he concluded, 'before and after the constitutional amendment in India remains exactly the same. Sikkim's international distinct personality is unaffected, and it is a protectorate as before.' Because the whole process was invalid, he declared, 'Sikkim has not become an Indian state or union territory.' He described the merger to be 'a journey towards becoming a colony,' whereas, 'India made its journey the other way.'

I learned of other shortcomings in the way the merger

was pushed through from K.C. Pradhan, one of the cabinet ministers present when the resolution was passed. He had with him a copy of Justice Hidayatullah's learned opinions, and pointed out that the Chogyal's prior assent, though required by law, was lacking. To which he added that the normal constitutional procedures had been ignored. The resolution calling for merger with India and a referendum should have been moved by the Speaker of the Sikkim Assembly; in fact it was introduced by B.B. Lal, the Indian civil servant appointed to the Government of Sikkim as adviser on administration.

'When this resolution came before the cabinet I challenged its legality,' said Pradhan, 'and the very next day I resigned as Agriculture Minister. So then there were just four ministers left to approve it as a Bill. It was steamrollered through.' He also pointed out that the 'urgent situation' which was supposed to justify the swift removal of the Chogyal was a total fabrication.

What had happened was this. After attending the King of Nepal's coronation, the Chogyal and his entourage were driving back when they were stopped by a crowd at Rangpo checkpoint, on the border with West Bengal. A Sikkimese legislator was wounded by a man armed with a kukri, the curved dagger made famous by the Gurkhas. He was wearing the uniform of the Sikkim Guards, so B.B. Lal pointed the finger at the Chogyal. If his own guards were attacking members of the legislature, clearly the Chogyal had to be removed immediately.

'I challenged this in cabinet,' declared K.C. Pradhan. 'Who used the kukri? I asked. The Sikkim Guards were just two hundred young boys. They were not even issued with *kukris*. The legislator could not identify his assailant. Even four months later, after identity parades, he was never recognized. Therefore, I tell you it was a deliberate plot. Some West Bengal constable wearing the Sikkim Guards' uniform attacked this legislator. And why should the Indians do this? So they could blame the Chogyal and demand his immediate removal.'

Whatever the truth behind such allegations, it is clear that the vast intelligence and military resources available to the Government of India were called in to ensure that the merger went as smoothly as possible. No sooner than he was released on bail from police custody, Captain Yongda was re-arrested by the military and sent to the same internment camp as the other Sikkim Guards. When permitted to return to Sikkim, he was kept under house-arrest. Anyone who might upset the kingdom's merger with India was placed under surveillance.

The Chogyal lived on for another six years. He was very much alone in the palace, shunned by the same people who had once sought his ear. He had forfeited the throne and all the royal privileges that went with it. He lived now as a private citizen of India and, when he could scrape together sufficient foreign exchange, travelled on a standard Indian passport. His refusal to recognize his own overthrow and so bestow any legitimacy on the act of annexation meant that the Indian authorities kept a close watch on him. But he held out, despite the knowledge that he would have been richly rewarded for giving his seal of approval to the merger with India.

Those who visited him during those twilight years recall how he would sink into long silences. He no longer showed any interest in what was happening in the world. He also drank too much. His second wife, Queen Hope, had moved with the younger children to New York, where she dragged him through the courts over custody and her financial settlement before their 'fairytale marriage' finally ended in divorce.

The Chogyal's eldest son, Crown Prince Tenzing, was killed in a car accident in 1978. (Some say it was no accident, and that the truck involved deliberately forced Tenzing's Mercedes off the road and down a steep ravine.) He was just twenty-eight years old, and his death left the Chogyal utterly distraught.

Towards the end, the Chogyal complained of a painful throat, but could not be bothered to have it treated. Eventually he was persuaded to travel to America, where he was found to have throat cancer. He underwent chemotherapy first, and accepted an operation that would leave him unable to speak. But it was too late to halt the cancer, and the last kingly ruler of Sikkim died in a New York hospital.

The body of Palden Thondup Namgyal, twelfth Chogyal of Sikkim, returned to Gangtok in an upright coffin wrapped in the national flag. The corpse within had been embalmed and was sitting in the lotus position, with a bell in one hand and a dorje dagger in the other, as befits an incarnate lama. People from all over Sikkim, Nepalis as well as Bhotias and Lepchas, flocked to the royal chapel to pay their respects. A funeral chorten was prepared up on Luksh-yama ridge, the pyre was lit, and the faithful mourners observed that seven vultures circled above. Fittingly enough, since the vulture is traditionally the Chogyal's guardian bird.

*

It may have been the end of an era; but it was not the end of the Chogyal's lineage. His second son, Prince Wangchuck, was immediately recognized as the thirteenth Chogyal of Sikkim. He chose to dispense with a coronation, but still his people came to pay homage, presenting silken kaddas to him and prostrating themselves full length three times before their hereditary ruler.

Prince Wangchuck had been educated at Harrow and the Ealing School of Business in London. But he found within himself a strongly religious bent, and after becoming Chogyal he went into a lengthy retreat in Nepal. Since then he has stayed out of politics, living quietly within the palace and channelling his energies into religious works. I tried to contact him while I was in Gangtok, but the palace is strictly out of bounds to visitors these days. My letters remained unanswered: and when Pema Namgyal did get through on the telephone to the Chogyal's private secretary, the response was hardly encouraging. Prince Wangchuck was extremely busy with his religious duties, we were told. Most unfortunately, he was unable to receive any visitors.

I understood that the Government of India preferred the Chogyal not to see foreigners, especially if they might report on the current situation in Sikkim. I also heard that permission to sell off some of the family estate was being sought. Unnecessary complications were therefore to be avoided. But I still felt as though I had been given the brush off. It was small consolation to discover that this was the standard response from the palace – even if you were Sikkimese.

'Prince Wangchuck doesn't seem to be bothered about the people of Sikkim,' said the editor of the *Sikkim Observer*,

Jigme N. Kazi. 'For the last two decades our monarchy hasn't been able to do anything constructive. Instead, they have built a wall between the palace and the people.

'Even religious functions, like the lama dances that used to be held up there: the people want these traditions to continue, but the palace doesn't show much interest. Prince Wangchuck has completely withdrawn from public life. I think it's to do with his personal attitude. But now the younger generation of Sikkimese cannot see a future in which the monarchy will play a role. The link between the royal family and our sense of separate identity that used to be there, that has been allowed to die from neglect.'

Over the last decade, Jigme N. Kazi has been an embattled editor, struggling to get his paper out without accepting the kind of self-censorship that is commonplace amongst India's provincial press. Issues that carried stories critical of the ruling party in Sikkim were mysteriously held up at the printers. Both he and his wife received thinly veiled threats. 'People say that freedom of expression was suppressed during the monarchy's time,' he said. 'From my own experience, I know that there is still not any real freedom of expression in Sikkim.'

He also pointed to a mounting sense of frustration among Sikkimese. 'Since the merger we have had three different political parties in power. Before the elections they all made promises that they would call for Sikkim's special status to be restored, that even though we are part of India our separate identity should be preserved. They played upon the deep-seated fear among many Sikkimese that we are slowly being submerged, and they won plenty of votes for taking this stand. But once in power they forgot all about it. And the reason is this: that where corruption is concerned, our politicians are as bad or worse than the mainstream of Indian politics.'

And there is plenty of money available to oil the wheels. Jigme estimated that India pumped some 400 crores of rupees (roughly £60 million) into Sikkim every year. Given the total population is only around half a million, I calculated that every man, woman and child should receive subsidies worth £120 – a huge sum anywhere in South Asia.

'But if you look for any real economic development', he said, 'you won't find much around here. Most of the money disappears through corruption. And all this assistance from India has just made us more dependent. This country used to be called Denzong, the Valley of Rice; but now we have to buy it in from outside even though eighty-five per cent of the population are farmers. Where I come from in North Sikkim nobody bothers to grow rice any more. It's easier just to take government handouts.'

Indian subsidies may keep the population quiet and ensure their elected representatives tow the line. But there are other issues that cannot be so easily smoothed over. Most critical is the flood of 'outsiders' – economic migrants from other parts of India and Nepal who have moved into Sikkim since the merger. The older established families who have lived in Sikkim for several generations – regardless of whether they are of Lepcha, Bhotia or Nepali stock – fear that they will be swamped by outsiders. They also resent the fact that these newcomers very rapidly established a stranglehold on trade and commerce.

'Look around the bazaar here in Gangtok,' Jigme suggested. 'You will find ninety-nine per cent of shops are owned by outside traders.'

'But hasn't that always been true?' I countered. 'Even in the old days, most of the traders were Marwaris or Tibetans.'

'In the old days that was okay,' he said. 'Then the Sikkimese were either farmers or worked in government service. But now they are better educated and there aren't enough government jobs to go round. So more of them want to set up shops, but there's no room for them in the market. And not just here in Gangtok. Most of the smaller towns in Sikkim have been taken over by outsiders. The same is true of tourism, since most of the hotels and lodges are run by outsiders – some even by people from Bangladesh. They stand to benefit from the beauty of our country, not us. But there must be no excuses. We allowed this to happen because we're too lazy.'

What he found most worrying was how rapidly these outsiders managed to buy influence and could even ensure their candidates were put up for election. 'There exists a nexus between bureaucrats, businessmen and politicians. The rich Marwaris and Biharis get their way through bribes and extortion. They tend to be more aggressive than we are. So we Sikkimese are left to fight over the scraps. What has happened since our merger with India is simply a form of economic colonialism.'

I asked him about the large military presence. 'There were 20,000 Indian troops stationed in Sikkim from long before the merger,' he said. 'They say they are here for strategic reasons, and that I understand. But I think it is wrong that they prevent even Sikkimese people from moving freely around their own country. I am from North Sikkim, and still I need a special permit to go there. Also, I cannot understand how they justify taking away our separate identity on so-called strategic grounds. Why? Because they didn't trust us? Or the Chogyal? That is no justification for what has happened in Sikkim.'

In his view, the merger had been a mistake because it was storing up more trouble for the Indian government in future. 'Unless there is a change for the better, the political situation may get out of hand. The Sikkimese people feel threatened– Bhotias, Nepalis, Lepchas, all of them. They need to feel secure, to know that they can retain their own separate identity. Unless these very basic aspirations are met, I think there will be turmoil in this State. A secessionist insurgency might creep in, and that would be a direct challenge to the Government of India. The situation could spin out of control. I believe that stage is not so very far away.'

Jigme N. Kazi is an outspoken critic of the cronyism that has taken hold in Sikkim under the guise of democracy. But he does not see a return to the royalist past as a practical alternative. He wants a democratic system, but one where politicians are responsible to the Sikkimese people and not just to their paymasters in Delhi. And like many others I spoke to, he wants safeguards to prevent the influx of new settlers from swamping the original inhabitants of Sikkim, undermining their distinct culture and marginalizing them in their own land.

There are obvious parallels to be drawn with the Tibetans' fears of being swamped by Chinese settlers or Bhutan's reaction to 'illegal immigrants'. The eastern Himalayas and the high plateau beyond, closed off from outsiders for centuries, are now a magnet to economic migrants, virgin territory ripe for exploitation. But in the case of Sikkim, it becomes difficult to define who are 'outsiders' and who are

Sikkimese. Even before 1950, more than half the population were Nepali-speaking settlers who had entered Sikkim over the previous century. Now these older immigrants are complaining of Sikkim being a 'dumping ground' for new waves of migrants. Where do you draw the line? And since Sikkim is now part of India, how can any restrictions on internal migration be enforced?

As I left the *Sikkim Observer*'s tiny offices, Jigme N. Kazi turned to his computer screen. He needed to file an article for a newspaper in Calcutta. I returned to Netuk House, where Captain Yongda announced that we had both been invited to a meeting at K.C. Pradhan's residence. There was some move afoot. So we went down to his spacious but cheaply furnished flat below the main bazaar, where the indefatigable ringmaster proffered tea and biscuits before getting down to business.

He was planning to form yet another political party to fight the forthcoming elections. To this end, he wanted to sound out Captain Yongda as a candidate. He could stand on two possible 'tickets' – either a constituency in West Sikkim or as representative of the sangha, the Buddhist monk body. The Captain listened carefully but declined the offer, saying he was too involved in running the school in Pemayangtse to enter politics. But the wily old politician did his best to persuade the monk-soldier, whose support would help bring in the Bhotia–Lepcha vote.

'Don't you know', he said, turning to me, 'that these people who used to be the ruling class in Sikkim are now classified as tribals?' He then explained how the Bhotias, Lepchas, Tsongs and other indigenous peoples of Sikkim had in 1978 been lumped together with primitive forest-dwellers as 'Scheduled Tribes', and this had been approved by the Indian parliament in Delhi. I noticed how Yapo Yongda, himself a monk-scholar and heir to a sophisticated culture, winced at the word 'tribal'.

And Pradhan was not through with baiting him yet. He outlined a thoroughly 'Sikkimese' programme that would appeal to conservatives like Yongda. Further immigration might be stopped by resuscitating the Sikkim Subjects Law from the Chogyal's time. More seats should be reserved for ethnic minorities like the Bhotias and Lepchas. Sikkim's special status should be reinforced.

'A return to protectorate or associated status would be acceptable to us', he declared, 'as long as we have internal autonomy. Our relationship with India would remain friendly. They would look after external affairs and defence, as per the 1950 treaty. But internal autonomy should be ours.'

I was astounded to be hearing such proposals from this wiry politician who proudly asserted 'my grandfather was a Nepali immigrant'. After all, he had been responsible for whipping up anti-monarchist feelings among his mainly Nepali-speaking followers back in the 1970s. Now he was invoking the same laws and treaties as the last Chogyal had done in the defence of Sikkim's separate identity and status. But then twenty-five years is a long time in politics, and the same followers who had voted for him as a champion of democracy now found themselves being marginalized by new immigrants. Democracy in South Asia is very much a numbers game, and the numbers were swinging inexorably in favour of the newcomers.

'Today, almost fifty per cent of those in Sikkim are outsiders,' observed Pradhan. What he proposed was a 'nationalist' alliance of Bhotias, Lepchas and the older

Nepali population. It was a last chance to stem the tide of this new colonialism which, he claimed, had been carefully planned in New Delhi as far back as 1966. 'It's all there in the official gazette,' he declared. 'They did forward projections from existing electoral rolls. Their target was to swamp us by the year 2000.' After that there would be new rulers, with the indigenous population reduced to tribal status.

I had the impression that Captain Yongda did not entirely trust K.C. Pradhan. For all his fine talk, the primary purpose of his new political party was to split the vote in the forthcoming elections. It was with great excitement, therefore, that Pradhan communicated to me that Kazi Sahib was in town. We could both drive down to see him.

Old Kazi Lhendup Dorji, the man who led the attack on the monarchy and pushed through the deal whereby Sikkim was merged with India. For which he was rewarded with the honour of being Sikkim's first democratically elected Chief Minister and, I was given to understand, much else besides. Yes, I wanted to meet this godfather of Sikkimese politics, and see how he might defend his legacy.

Pradhan's jeep was low on fuel, and on the way out of Gangtok we had to stop at a filling station. When he tried to pull back onto the road, the way was blocked by an endless convoy of jeeps and minibuses that were honking their horns and flying the flag of the current chief minister's party, the Sikkim Democratic Front. A big political rally was being held in Gangtok, and supporters were being bused in from all over the state – all expenses paid, naturally.

Pradhan glared with ill-conceived envy at this demonstration of the new political patronage at work. These were not 'his people', and he clearly disliked the triumphalism of this motorized procession. Back in his political heyday there had not been as many vehicles in all of Sikkim as were now parading up the hill towards the state capital. He revved the engine and inched forward, trying to force a gap in the endless column. But the SDF convoy would not have their unity broken, and Pradhan had to give way. It took twenty minutes to get out of that petrol station, and it was an embittered old politician who drove the remaining half-mile to the large house where Kazi Sahib was staying.

We were met by his son and daughter-in-law, who look after Kazi Sahib's interests in Sikkim. He himself normally lives in Kalimpong, the hill station just across the border in West Bengal. 'I went there in 1953,' he told me, 'because there were some problems in Sikkim.' Another way of putting it is that he was declared persona non grata by the Sikkimese government.

The Kazi Sahib limped out of the gloom like a Galapagos tortoise. He proudly declared that he was ninety-six years old – though these days he is much troubled by lumbago and neither his hearing nor his eyesight are what they were. And yet he had not surrendered his position as the kingmaker in Sikkimese politics. He claimed to have 'made the present government', and now he was being courted by India's Congress Party, which was planning a big campaign for the next state elections. No wonder K.C. Pradhan wanted to be here. The two of them disappeared into a room together to broker a deal in private.

Pradhan was smiling from ear to ear when they emerged. 'You have been present at the birth of a new political movement,' he whispered.

I remained sceptical of any meaningful exchange coming

out of a political party that required the blessing of these two godfathers. None the less, I wanted to ask Kazi Sahib why he had done away with the monarchy.

'The last Maharaja of Sikkim', he declared, using the Hindu term for the Chogyal and scowling darkly, 'was ruling as a dictator. He took all powers into his hands. You must understand that from the time of our first kings, Sikkim was always run as a religious state. But the political and religious authority was kept separate.

'That practice continued until the time of Sir Tashi Namgyal, the eleventh Maharaja. But then his eldest son died in an air crash. So his second son, Palden Thondup Namgyal, took over both the administration and as the Dharma Raja, the head of religion. For this reason he exercised greater powers than previous Chogyals. That is why I always refer to him as a dictator.'

Kazi Sahib's hostility to the monarchy is all the more remarkable since he came from an old Sikkimese family. But he chose to climb the ladder through democratic politics, emerging as president of the Sikkim State Congress. 'I wanted justice,' he said, 'political and religious justice.' For this to happen (and for his own party to seize power) the complicated system of elections in which a number of seats were reserved for the Bhotias, the Lepchas and so on, had to be removed. He argued that 'all this communalism was not necessary'. It should be 'one man one vote'.

But the ethnic minorities disagreed. They wanted to retain the system of reservations which prevented them being swamped in the polls by the Nepali-speaking majority. This stand was supported by the Sikkim National Party, whose president was none other than Pema's father, Netyuk Tsering. The Chogyal also favoured this arrangement as it reinforced the Buddhist monarchy. And the Chogyal was adept at frustrating Kazi's ambitions, offering him a place in his government but no real power. All of which might explain Kazi Sahib's relentless hostility to the last king of Sikkim.

So Kazi Sahib turned to the Government of India, which took a dim view of the communal nature of Sikkimese politics and suspected the Chogyal of encouraging anti-Indian sentiments. From his base in Kalimpong, Kazi cultivated top-level contacts in Delhi while at the same time ensuring that his party activists kept things on the boil inside Sikkim. In this he was greatly assisted by the Kazini, his rather mysterious Belgian wife. (She called herself Elisa-Maria Langford-Rae and claimed, amongst other things, that her father was Marshal Carl Gustaf Mannerheim of Finland while her mother was alternatively 'a dear little German baroness' or a French countess settled in Geneva.) A natural conspirator and social climber, she dreamt of becoming 'the first lady of Sikkim'. Any such hopes were dashed when the Chogyal married Hope Cook, towards whom the Kazini developed a very personal animosity. If anyone worked tirelessly towards the destruction of Sikkim's monarchy, it was this embittered woman.

'I have been a widower these nine years,' the Kazi Sahib told me, fondly adding that Elisa-Maria had been a great journalist, holding both MA and PhD degrees besides having practised as a barrister-at-law. But when I asked about her part in the Chogyal's downfall, he rapidly returned to such broad concepts as 'justice' and 'democracy'. He complained that under the monarchy there had been no economic or political progress. He was proud to have been Sikkim's first

Chief Minister, hinting that although he had been in the political wilderness for nearly twenty years, he remained an éminence grise, working quietly behind the scenes.

'And has there been any real progress in Sikkim?' I asked.

'The problems are the same,' he said. 'There has been no progress – only more corruption, communalism, anti-nationalism.'

Such is the political legacy of the man who brought down the monarchy and handed Sikkim over to India – lock, stock and barrel.

It is impossible to ignore the presence of the Indian army in Sikkim. The road up to Gangtok was clogged with convoys of drab green eight-ton trucks bringing up supplies for the Seventeenth Mountain Division, which is permanently stationed up by the border with China. It is known as the 'Black Cat' division, and Sikkim's main distillery down by Rangpo produces 'Black Cat Rum' to keep the *jawans*, the poor freezing infantry, more or less happy. Army staff cars and jeeps go speeding through the streets of the capital. Military despatch riders roar about on Enfield Bullet motorcycles that have been de-tuned so that they don't stall at high altitudes. Most of the roads in Sikkim were built and are still maintained by the army's pioneer corps. When it comes to repairing or bridging the many landslides that occur with every monsoon, it is the military roads that receive priority.

The military authorities have declared all areas adjoining the border out of bounds. Until recently, all foreigners needed a special permit to go beyond Gangtok. The whole of North Sikkim was the military's preserve, and even local people needed authorization to travel to their native villages.

Previously, the road up towards the Nathu-La was categorized as a restricted area. It shadows the old trade route between Gangtok and Lhasa, following more or less the same route that my father took when he walked into Tibet in 1939. So I was pleased to hear that the restrictions had been partly lifted. Provided one obtained a special permit and was accompanied by an official guide, the road was open to foreign visitors as far as a holy lake that the Sikkimese call Tsomgo and the Indians Changu Lake.

Pema fixed all the arrangements for us, and on a sunlit morning we drove out of town. Once through the check-post (where our pass was carefully examined and all names entered in a register) we began climbing in earnest. I asked the jeep-driver to pull over so that we could look down on Gangtok and the vast sweep of foothills stretching away towards Darjeeling and the Nepal border. The royal palace was in clear view, standing on an open ridge above the town. From this distance it looked like a doll's house, defenceless and exposed, and I realized how easy it must have been for the Indian assault troops to come down from the surrounding heights and overwhelm the token force of Sikkim Guards. The last Chogyal had been right; any resistance would have been futile.

Continuing our ascent, we passed through villages wreathed in prayer flags until the land became too steep for cultivation. Wild ferns and creepers clung to the rockface, the drops became more precipitous, and waterfalls plunged down the mountainside and over the road. The driver stopped beside one such torrent to top up the water level in the jeep's radiator. A group of off-duty soldiers had been swimming in a rock-pool and were now sunning themselves on a flat boulder. Some of them looked as though they came from South India. For them a tour of duty in Sikkim must have been the first time they ever experienced ice and snow.

The road passed over several landslides and climbed through a series of sharp bends before reaching what had once been an open meadow and was now a large army camp. Signposts showed the way to the Officers' Mess or warned transport drivers: 'Fuel is scarce. Petrol is precious. Save it.' A Sikh regiment was doing a tour of duty here, and turbaned heads had to duck as they went in and out of the camouflaged Nissen huts that served as their temporary barracks.

'No photography,' warned our official guide, 'nowhere in military areas.' I wouldn't have dreamt of it, knowing how paranoid India's military can be about 'foreign spies'. I was sorely tempted, however, by a sign that boasted 'This Road leads to Lhasa, Glory and Beyond.' I wondered how Chinese diplomats might react to this, for it suggests that India's high command does not see the 'Black Cat' division as fulfilling a purely defensive role. I was also surprised by the number of field guns in the artillery park just below Tsomgo Lake – especially since these were being held in reserve, the front-line units being stationed in the final 20 kilometres up to the border where people like me were most definitely not allowed to venture.

The seasons were changing as we climbed ever higher, the lush greenery of the lower Rangpo Valley gradually taking on more autumnal colours. We passed through forests of pine and rhododendron. Towards the top of the pass the country opened up into alpine pasture which, as my father recalled, are covered with a mass of wild primulas and Himalayan poppies in springtime. But now the meadows had been burned by frost, and all that remained were the shrivelled stems of irises and countless other species which, in their present state, I could not identify. Then we turned a corner and the dark green waters of Tsomgo lay before us in a natural bowl. We were now above 12,000 feet and an icy wind was whipping up the lake surface. Prayer flags snapped angrily in the breeze.

Local legend has it that the lake originally filled another valley a little further on, and that when its natural dam collapsed and the waters rushed down to where they now rest, a couple of yak herders and all their animals were drowned in the flood. The line of prayer flags signified that this was a holy lake, and the message was reinforced by signs urging non-Buddhist visitors to use the toilet facilities provided and to refrain from throwing rubbish into the water. It was obvious these instructions were not always observed, and any sense of peace or sanctity has been banished by the ramshackle bazaar that has sprouted up between the road and the shoreline.

I learned that no sooner than the area was opened up to Indian tourists, makeshift stalls selling snacks and souvenirs suddenly appeared. These continued to spread along the roadside until they formed an unsightly bazaar. Whoever granted the licences must have made a good deal of money; but by allowing such uncontrolled exploitation of a famous beauty spot there was not much beauty left. Most of the stall-holders were outsiders who could speak some Hindi and understood the requirements of Indian visitors better than local people.

The one exception was the rent-a-yak business. This was

run by weather-beaten Bhotia or Tibetan herdsmen, and they worked the crowd nicely. They paraded their small and unusually docile yaks through the bazaar, pointing to their brightly coloured and obviously comfortable carpet saddles, to the scarlet sheaths which covered the beasts' horns like pointed tea-cosies, smiling all the while and assuring nervous tourists that it was all perfectly safe.

Most of their customers were content to be hoisted into the saddle for a few seconds so that their picture could be taken. Others were more adventurous and went for the 'full tour'. This started sedately enough, though once clear of the bazaar the herdsmen urged their yaks into a lumbering canter. Usually, the customers would start shrieking, which caused the yaks to go even faster; and when the herdsmen could not keep up, there was no one left in charge. I know, because I had to jump out of the way as an out-of-control tourist yak went charging down the lakeside path.

I marched off alone towards a spur that came down to the lake. Maybe from that ridge I would be able to see the main Himalayan range or the Nathu-La. But I had only just started climbing when there was a great shouting and waving of arms from down by the lakeside. Then Sarah called out that I should stop. I had been spotted by our guide, who was yelling that foreigners had to stay down by the lake. If I kept going they would send a search party after me. So I never did get to look upon Nathu-La, the trans-Himalayan pass which my father had crossed nearly sixty years earlier.

Like so many other restrictions in Sikkim, it seemed absurd that I could not walk up a hill — presumably because this might pose a risk to national security. Another absurdity was that the Old Tibet Road, which I had seen curling off to the north, had originally been built to carry trade; but no trade had passed this way for forty years. Nowadays the only traffic that continues north is military convoys carrying men and munitions towards the front line.

Long after the Iron Curtain has faded into history, the 'Ice Curtain' between India and China remains very much intact. The troops who sit it out on either side of this geopolitical fault line have to endure terrible hardship in subzero temperatures. And for what? So that both sides can assure themselves that their national security is being well looked after?

It occurred to me that if China had not invaded Tibet, Indian troops wouldn't need to be here in such force. But both sides have pushed their territorial claims to the utmost, swallowing up the peaceful nations that had once performed a very useful role as buffer states. Now the two Asian superpowers stared at each other down the barrel of a gun. Did that enhance their security? As for the moral arguments, did China's colonizing of Tibet justify India's doing much the same thing in Sikkim? For that is what has happened. And there is a bitter irony in the fact that both China and India, two great nations which suffered so at the hands of European colonialism and led the struggle for freedom, should end up acting as colonial powers on the Roof of the World.

Chapter Nine

BHUTAN II – THE KING AT LAST

I never gave up on my hope that one day I might return to Bhutan and finally meet up with King Jigme. It would take time, I knew, for the necessary permissions to come through. But in early 1996 I spent three months in India on a motorcycle expedition. There would be plenty of time then to arrange things; or so I thought, until once again I ran into an impenetrable curtain of officialdom. I pestered the Bhutanese Embassy in Delhi, to no avail. The weeks slipped past. Sarah and I had already booked a flight back to London when I decided to make one last call from a rat-infested booth in Calcutta.

'Thank goodness you phoned,' exclaimed the diplomat on the other end. 'His Majesty has altered his plans and will be able to see you next week. Please ensure you are in Thimphu by Monday.' Since this was Friday night, it looked like a tall order. But as I marched homewards in the twilight I knew this would be third time lucky.

On this visit there was no possibility of our being 'non-persons' – not even for a few days. Sarah and I qualified as 'guests of His Majesty', no less. As we stepped off the plane at Paro Airport a smiling protocol officer rushed forward. We were taken directly to Thimphu and installed at the

Druk Hotel, right in the middle of town, where I was to await the king's summons.

Thimphu had by then grown up into something more closely resembling a capital city. There were more offices and houses, more shops – even a convention centre – practically all of them built according to modern construction techniques but none the less decorated with traditional Bhutanese woodcarvings and paintwork. It still had the feel of an overgrown village; but I was aware that most of what I saw was very recent.

Apart from the monasteries and a few old farmhouses, everything has been built in the past fifty years. I have seen photographs taken in the 1950s, before King Jigme Dorje decided to make Thimphu the country's permanent capital. Tashichodzong, the seat of royal government, was then surrounded by rice fields, with scarcely another building in sight. And although the dzong is still there, it was almost completely rebuilt during the 1960s to house the fast-expanding royal administration.

It was King Jigme Dorje who pushed Bhutan out of its medieval seclusion and at least halfway into the modern world. His reign lasted just two decades, but during that time roads were built linking both the capital and eastern provinces with India. Schools, hospitals, hydro-electric stations, factories – all the basic infrastructure of twentieth-century living – were introduced for the first time to Bhutan.

In 1953 he established a National Assembly. Serfdom was abolished three years later, and other traditional duties such as conscripted labour and paying taxes in kind were gradually phased out. Bhutan's traditional legal code, the Trimshung, was adapted to the needs of a more modern society. But perhaps King Jigme Dorje's greatest achievement was to secure international recognition of Bhutan as a sovereign and independent state. In this he had to move slowly, winning India's confidence and approval at each stage. Finally, in 1971, Bhutan was admitted to full membership of the United Nations.

King Jigme Dorje's memory is still venerated by the Bhutanese people. He is considered to be 'the founder of modern Bhutan'. Some go so far as to claim he was a hidden bodhisattva – a living Buddha who had forsaken nirvana to help living beings on earth. Others argue that his son, the present king, has done no more than carry through his policies to a further stage.

I never met the late king, my introduction having been through Queen Ashi Kesang Choden at a time when the royal couple were living separately. I knew that this had been a difficult time both for her and the crown prince, and could not help wondering whether those events had a lasting effect on the schoolboy who was to become king. I remembered how withdrawn Jigme had been at school. He had not had a carefree childhood. Now, more than thirty years later, I would be meeting him again.

This time, Sarah and I were free to roam about town unescorted, dropping into any local eating houses we liked for a plate of steaming momos or a glass of fiery Bhutanese liquor. I noticed that in nearly every bar or shop there was a portrait of the king, either by himself or with the chief abbot. Was this just traditional respect? I wondered. Or had Jigme adopted a 'cult of personality'? If so, it was hard not to draw comparisons with autocratic regimes elsewhere in the world.

And there were other matters I wished to discuss with my old school friend. Many things had changed since I had last visited his kingdom. There had been serious trouble in the south of Bhutan. Tens of thousands of Nepali-speaking people had been evicted as 'illegal immigrants'. The royal Bhutanese army had been called in to deal with groups of terrorists (or 'freedom fighters', depending on your point of view). International human rights agencies were talking about 'ethnic cleansing'. At one point, the king had threatened to abdicate. I had followed these events from a distance, reading any reports I could lay my hands on. And I grew increasingly perplexed, for the events described did not in the least fit with Bhutan's peaceful 'Shangri-La' image.

One has to be carefully vetted before being granted audience with an absolute monarch. From the moment I arrived in Thimphu I shuffled between government offices, always aware while I was conducting an interview that in fact it was me who was being checked out. I had just finished talking to Dawa Tsering, who then enjoyed the distinction of being the longest-serving foreign minister in the world, and was about to be briefed by members of the Planning Commission, when a messenger entered the room bowing continuously. Instructions had been received from the king's secretary. Both Mr Gregson and his wife were to await an audience with His Majesty at two o'clock. Obviously my chat with Dawa Tsering had gone well.

There was only just time to go back to the hotel and collect Sarah. Then we were off again, rushing through the streets of Thimphu towards Tashichodzong. As we pulled up outside the main gate, two sentries of the Royal Guard snapped to attention. We were escorted into the dzong's central courtyard by an aide-de-camp who chatted amiably, as if to put us at our ease. By the time we had climbed halfway up a steep wooden staircase I was short of breath.

'Take your time', said the ADC. 'You probably haven't adjusted to the altitude yet.'

At the top of the stairs was an antechamber. It was hung with silks and painted in glowing primary colours. Here we were asked to wait, surrounded by half a dozen of the king's personal retainers. Then the curtains leading to the audience hall were pulled back. 'You lead on,' whispered Sarah. 'After all, he's your schoolmate.'

King Jigme Singye Wangchuck was smiling broadly as we advanced across the polished floorboards. He wore a brightly striped silken kho above woollen knee socks, and over his shoulder was folded a broad scarf of saffron – a colour worn only by the king and the Je Khempo or chief abbot. Instinctively I stuck out my hand, which he duly shook before enveloping me in a bear-hug. 'It has been many years', he said, 'since I last saw you.'

As we crossed the audience hall, I commented on the splendour of the silken wall hangings and tangkas depicting Buddhas in their various emanations. 'Ah, but I don't live here,' he said. 'Much of what you see here in the Tashichod-zong was built by my father and now serves as government offices. But I've never really lived in a palace. I prefer to live in a log cabin.'

He sat down next to me on an embroidered couch and smiled conspiratorially. 'Do you remember the first time we met', he asked, 'when we played tag together in the garden at Government House in Calcutta?' So we talked for a while about our schooldays and exchanged news about mutual friends.

'Those four years spent studying in England were a tremendous experience for me,' he began. 'I have very happy memories of those times, playing football and rugby.' He reminded me of his school companion Dodo, before moving into what was for me uncharted territory. 'My mother was very keen that I continued my education abroad. But my father was not well: he had his first heart attack when he was only thirty-six years old, and from then on he was determined to keep me in Bhutan.'

We talked of the time just after his father died, and his face grew solemn. 'I was just seventeen years old,' he began. 'Those first few years after becoming king – that was a very difficult time for me. All the policy decisions, all the problems, the issues, they all came up to me. And I wasn't prepared for it. I didn't have the experience and the knowledge. A lot of people thought I must have been groomed to be king. But the truth of the matter is that I was totally unprepared.'

I was hearing the rough side of being a king, of what it is like to become the lynchpin of government when still just a teenager. 'Nevertheless,' he continued, 'the tremendous confidence and faith the Bhutanese people had in me – that was what made it possible for me to take on the job.'

He broke off while tea was being served, and I took the opportunity to look at him more closely. The youthful shock of blue-black hair I remembered was now trimmed close to the head and had begun to recede from the front. His face had filled out a good deal, and when he smiled his lips formed a cherubic bow which reminded me of an incarnate lama I once met in Sikkim. He had all the ease and polish one imagines in a ruling monarch; and yet he struck me as still being rather shy. I wondered whether this childhood trait had been reinforced by the isolation which goes with being an absolute monarch.

I soon discovered he wanted to talk about Bhutan rather

than himself. The country's GDP had almost quadrupled in the last decade, he told me, sounding more like a chief executive than a king. Infant mortality had been halved and average life expectancy had risen from 47 to 66. Free health facilities were now available to 90 per cent of the population – 'and we plan to have universal coverage by the beginning of the twenty-first century'. It was a tour de force. But then Jigme is a working monarch – as opposed to a constitutional figurehead – and has all the facts and figures at his fingertips.

I sensed a strong undercurrent of caution, both in his character and how he approaches what he calls 'the job'. For instance, he has always been reluctant to take on large foreign loans. 'Standing on our own feet' and 'self-reliance' are central to his philosophy: and Bhutan retains sufficient reserves of foreign exchange to carry it through two years of anticipated spending on imports. I commented that this is almost unheard of among less developed countries, which usually borrow all that they can and more.

'It has not been easy,' he confided. 'You'll never know the pressure we came under in the 1970s and '80s to take out large loans from financial institutions. And there was tremendous domestic pressure as well. A lot of government officials wanted to take them. Our sticking to a conservative policy was not a popular decision.' I noticed that when Jigme used the word 'we' it was impossible to tell whether he was referring to himself, his government, or the country as a whole.

'Also,' he continued, 'there was tremendous pressure after I became king to cut down our forests and sell the timber to India and the Middle East. People argued that this was the easiest way to earn revenue, and the logging operators had a very strong lobby within Bhutan. Only with great difficulty did we refuse them, with the result that we now have 72.5 per cent forest coverage – one of the highest in the world.'

The young king resisted these pressures by a mixture of innate caution and stubbornness, and by working extremely hard. 'But,' he declared, 'I don't think anyone's naturally a workaholic. I certainly don't enjoy working long and hard hours. But the job and responsibility I hold are heavy. A never-ending stream of problems and issues crop up which must be addressed; decisions need to be taken.'

Much of his time is spent touring the more remote parts of this mountainous kingdom where, even since modern roads were built from the 1960s onwards, it normally takes at least two days to travel between the capital and the eastern provinces. Jigme regularly does this trip by car rather than going to the expense of maintaining a helicopter. He rarely travels abroad, and then mainly within South Asia to attend regional summits, preferring to go walking out to remote villages to consult with his people.

His is a very 'hands-on' approach to kingship. Yet he says he does not allow the pressures of work to affect his family life. Of this he is fiercely protective. When I asked him why he had not married until quite late in life, he gave me a look that was a clear warning to tread gently from here on. 'I was officially married in 1986', he explained, 'to four sisters, but unofficially my marriage goes back five years earlier.'

To take four wives is fairly rare, although Tibetan Buddhism accepts that a man may marry several sisters; though the reverse situation, where several brothers share the same wife, is more usual.

Despite this unusual arrangement (each of the four

queens has her own house in a shared compound above Thimphu, while the king's log cabin is several miles away), Jigme says he has a 'very happy family life'. When out on tour in the provinces, the four queens sometimes accompany him in a separate land cruiser.

'I have five sons and five daughters,' he added (two of the sisters have three children, the others two each), 'and I love my children very much.' But that doesn't mean they get special treatment. 'My children go to an ordinary local school, where they have to mow the lawn just like other students. I insisted they have no special privileges. Only when they have finished school, then perhaps they may go abroad to university' – an opportunity which he himself was denied.

Jigme may not have had a university education like King Birendra, but he is obviously well read and keen to discuss broad issues like the nature of monarchy and democracy. 'I don't believe monarchy is the best system of government', he told me, 'because the person who reaches very high office does so not on merit but by birth. Here in Bhutan, if there's a very good and competent king, then he can do much good; if not, then he can do a lot of harm. I tell this to school children and university students. I try to impress upon them that you cannot depend just on one individual, and that the future of Bhutan can only be secure if it is in the hands of the Bhutanese people.'

Monarchy may not necessarily be the best form of government, but Jigme does not believe Western-style democracy is the only alternative. 'When you look at supposedly multi-party democracy in Africa, Latin America, the former Soviet Union, or even in our own region of South Asia, it's hard to find many good examples. The essence of democracy, I don't question at all. The essence of democracy is very, very good. But I think it would only function in a perfect society – or at least where there are the traditions and spread of wealth to prevent it from being distorted and corrupted in practice.

'So many so-called democratic governments borrow as much money as possible for political reasons,' he continued, getting into his stride. 'Their leaders aren't that concerned with repayment because they know they won't be in power when rescheduling comes around. Their decisions are based not on what's best for the country but what's best for winning votes. They make a lot of promises and have to repay favours when they get into power; while the opposition parties' main aim is to obstruct the plans of government – even if they're in the best interests of the country. That may be irresponsible, but it's built into the system. As is rampant corruption. It's a vicious cycle. There's corruption in every form of government, everywhere in the world; but I think it's accurate to say that in Bhutan it is far lower than in most developing countries.'

Instead of trying to transplant Western democracy, the king is seeking to broaden the political base through a pyramid of representative institutions. At its apex is the National Assembly, initiated by his father in 1953, where more than two-thirds of members are elected by secret ballot. Then there are elected representatives at the district and village or 'bloc' level. Spreading political participation and responsibility down to the local level is something which the present king has championed – sometimes against the wishes of his advisers (he had also shortened the terms of officeholders to ensure they don't become 'bureaucratic'). 'We must have very close consultation with all our people', he declares, 'so that in all our discussions they decide their own priorities. Sometimes, five or ten thousand people come to discuss issues or to put questions to government.'

It is a process of consensus-building which accords with the country's Buddhist traditions rather better than adversarial politics. 'Some people complain that we aren't a democracy. But they don't realize – or they don't seem to care – that in Bhutan there are 3,254 representatives of the people elected by secret ballot.' Such criticism stings all the more since it is on his own initiative that power is being decentralized. And the king hinted strongly there was more to come. 'Whatever changes I bring about in the near future, the most important factor is that it should be indigenous – something that can function in the conditions which exist in Bhutan.

'I have no reservations about further political changes', he declared, 'provided they are in the country's best interests.' And first priority goes to defending Bhutan's status as a sovereign and independent state. Given that it is a small, landlocked country sandwiched between the two Asian superpowers, China and India, this requires tact and delicacy. 'You can choose your friends', Jigme laughed, 'but you can't choose your neighbours.'

There is also the problem of having some 450 miles of jungle-covered and unguarded border across which thousands of immigrants have entered Bhutan. Some have been there for generations and have Bhutanese nationality. Others arrived more recently, hoping to find jobs and settle in southern Bhutan. Their presence sparked a crisis which pushed the king to threaten abdication.

'The scale of the problem became evident from the first proper census in our history,' he said, 'which revealed large numbers of non-nationals were living illegally in Bhutan. They had grabbed hundreds of thousands of acres of forest. Many were contract labourers from Nepal, and we wanted to reduce their number when their contracts finished. But they objected strongly, demanding automatically the right to Bhutanese citizenship. The problem was complicated when some of our own people of South Bhutan (Nepali-speakers and Hindus, like more recent immigrants) supported them.'

Pamphlets calling on the southern Bhutanese to revolt against the royal government started appearing in 1989. By the following year there was rioting right across the south. Local government offices were attacked by mobs which specifically targeted census and immigration records. Armed bands began terrorizing the region. Atrocities were committed and arrests made. Those found to be either 'anti-nationals' or 'illegal immigrants' were trucked across the border.

In October 1991 the National Assembly lost patience and voted to freeze development activities in the south. This the king objected to, since it would deepen the divide between the mainly Buddhist highlanders and the Nepali-speaking southerners. He gave his pledge to abdicate rather than cancel development plans. It was brinkmanship; but it paid off. The Assembly members relented; the crisis in the south passed; and, as Jigme told me, 'that's where I am going on my next tour'.

There remains the question of some 95,000 'Bhutanese refugees' living in camps set up by UNHCR in eastern Nepal from 1991 onwards. The king accepted that some may be bona fide Bhutanese citizens. But the vast majority, he said, were previously illegal immigrants, while others still have never set foot inside Bhutan. They are either part of the Nepalese diaspora which affects all of north-eastern India (more than 70,000 Nepali 'infiltrators' had been detected and deported from Assam); or they are simply poor people from Nepal itself, attracted to the camps by the free food, health services and education being provided by inter-national agencies.

Bhutan had been criticized quite recently by the Euro-pean Parliament for its handling of the situation, which called for the return of all those claiming to be Bhutanese refugees. It also recommended that Bhutan's nationality laws be amended so they could be granted full citizenship. Jigme is sensitive to such criticism, but argued that the correct way of finding a solution was through bilateral discussions with the Nepalese government.

'Some solution is necessary', he said, 'because we can never become "Fortress Bhutan". We have neither the manpower nor logistics to patrol 450 miles of very porous border.' Moreover, he sees Bhutan's dilemma as part of a much broader trend. 'Looking around the world today, there are millions of economic migrants moving from less developed to more affluent countries. We in Bhutan are experiencing it now, but I think this will be a global problem in the twenty-first century.'

Domestically, the king explained that he was pursuing a policy of economic self-reliance, privatizing enterprises set up with foreign aid so that 'they pay their own way and don't become a drain on public finances'. At the same time Bhutan is developing new sources of revenue, the most important being hydro-electricity. 'Just as the Middle East has oil – which is a depleting resource – we in Bhutan have water. So long as the snow falls on the Himalayas, and our rivers flow swiftly from north to south, then we have a natural resource for all time to come. We can generate cheaper power than anywhere in the world, while our neighbour India is an almost limitless export market. And cheap electricity will reduce our use of firewood for heating and cooking, so pressure on our forests will be reduced.' I was reminded that Jigme was committed to conservation even before it became fashionable in the West.

The Bhutanese system of government has been condemned as 'autocratic' or 'dictatorial', because political parties are banned and it is not a democracy in the Western sense. 'Paternalistic' would probably be more accurate. King Jigme is trying in a single lifetime to build a bridge between the Middle Ages and the twenty-first century. He is a relentless modernizer when it comes to health and education, but is wary of changing everything too rapidly. In particular, he believes Bhutan should retain its distinct identity and culture.

And here the dangers are more insidious. For Bhutan adopted English as the medium of instruction in its schools as far back as 1962. Most younger Bhutanese speak some English and are therefore more open to Western influences than elsewhere in South Asia. Walking around Thimphu, I noticed young people were wearing jeans and sweat shirts, though traditional national dress is technically required by law and still prevails in the countryside. I also noticed how many shops were selling videos – both Hollywood and Bollywood (as Bombay's Hindi film industry is known) – there then being no television service in Bhutan. At that point, satellite dishes were officially banned.

I asked the king why this was so. He smiled resignedly, as though he had answered similar questions many times before. 'The main reason', he said, 'is to preserve our unique Buddhist culture. And the reason we attach so much importance to our traditions is not that Bhutan is an orthodox society; not that we expect our culture to be practised by the younger generation without any changes; but because we are a small, landlocked country, and the only factor which strengthens our status as a sovereign and independent state comes from our distinct culture.

'As we modernize it is inevitable that some of our traditions will be affected. I believe that any culture which is not practised won't live long. What we're trying to do is to blend development with our traditions, to preserve our culture and our identity as Bhutanese.' Then, looking very serious, he added: 'Whether Bhutanese culture will survive – that really depends on the younger generation. Basically, it's in their hands.'

The king rose, signalling our meeting was at an end. 'I have to get on with my work,' he said simply. He gave me another bear-hug, during which my arms got tangled up in the folds of his saffron scarf. I silently cursed my clumsiness, thinking that in this respect things hadn't improved much since our first meeting in Calcutta. But Jigme just laughed, and for a moment I saw behind the royal mask to something like the schoolboy I had once known. Then he switched gears again, reverting to his role as head of state, asking me what I thought would be the outcome of the forthcoming election in India. He must do this a hundred times a day. And it must be lonely, I thought, to be such a king.

Sarah had been present throughout the audience. As we walked across Tashichodzong's great courtyard, I asked her what she thought of my old friend who was now the king.

She was looking unusually serious and did not answer until we were out of the gates.

'It's difficult to say', she said, 'because you hear so many contradictory stories about what's going on in Bhutan. But from what I've just heard, all I can say is this: your friend Jigme is a good man.'

We left Thimphu the following day, heading eastwards to Tongsa and Bumthang. I chose these regions beyond the Black Mountains because it was from here that the Wang-chuck dynasty emerged to become the supreme power in the land. It was the cradle of Bhutan's monarchy, homeland of the royal ancestors, where the first two kings preferred to spend their days.

It is all too easy to forget how recently the institution of monarchy was adopted in Bhutan. The first king was only installed in 1907. Compared with most royal dynasties, this is very recent indeed. For two generations before that the family included the most powerful lords in the land. And before that? Their ancestors were members of the religious nobility, being one of the Choejey families whose head of household enjoyed the title of 'Lord of Religion'.

The Dungkar Choejey family held lands in Kurtoe, a remote region of north-eastern Bhutan; but from very early on they were closely associated with the Bumthang Valley. For it was there that the most celebrated royal ancestor, the Buddhist saint Pemalingpa, was born and spent much of his life, founding monasteries and discovering religious treasures.

The role of the treasure discoverer or terton has a very special place in Bhutan, especially among the followers of the Nyingmapa tradition. The concept goes back to the great Buddhist missionary Padmasambhava, who is believed to have concealed religious treasures in lakes and caves and clefts in cliff faces wherever he went. These treasures might be statues or other ceremonial objects containing spiritual power, though more often they are sacred teachings written in a coded short-hand that only the predestined discoverer can unravel. Since the transmission of these teachings across time occurs on a metaphysical plane, even a few leaves of script might contain the keys words for a terton to receive sufficient teachings to fill many volumes. The treasure-discoverer is guided first to the secret places of concealment, and then in understanding the true meaning of the treasures, by trances and dreams in which Padmasambhava himself might appear. In this way, the terton is a living link with the distant past, bringing to light esoteric teachings from the Golden Age of Buddhism.

Even today, it is commonly believed that religious treasures lie waiting to be discovered. I have listened to sophisticated, Western-educated Bhutanese discuss the possibility in all seriousness. Some religious treasures were found in 1990 near Taktsang, the 'Tiger's Lair' high above Paro Valley where Padmasambhava meditated. But, while there have been many tertons across the ages, the most famous and, within Bhutan, the best loved, is Pemalingpa.

This might be because Pemalingpa was not a learned lama — as is the case with most other tertons — but a man of the people. He was a blacksmith by trade, without any formal education. Some of his exploits, as when he drank an entire village dry and still remained sober, have become legendary. He did not go quite as far as his contemporary and occasional disciple, the 'Divine Madman'

Drukpa Kunley, who was given to waving his penis in the air. But both blacksmith and madman are held to have been divinely inspired, their eccentricities carrying the Buddhist message that external behaviour counts for nothing beside spiritual truth. They remain two of the most popular saints in Bhutan. The fact that the Wangchucks are direct descendants of one of Pemalingpa's sons certainly contributes to the royal dynasty's lustre. It is like former kings of France being able to point to Saint Louis.

From Thimphu to Bumthang, where Pemalingpa lived and died, is a solid day's drive – even when travelling as a royal guest in an efficient Japanese vehicle. 'We have a tight schedule,' said Jamba Gyeltsen, the protocol officer who looked after us throughout our stay in Bhutan. So there was only time for a brief glimpse of the fortess-monastery at Wangdiphodrang while the driver filled up with petrol before the long climb up into the Black Mountains.

Rhododendron and magnolia trees were coming into bloom, the scarlet and white varieties predominating. And it was amongst a flowering rhododendron forest, just short of the Pele-La pass, that I saw yaks for the first time in Bhutan. They were smaller than the lumbering beasts that roam the Tibetan plateau, and were feeding on a species of dwarf bamboo. Then we passed into cloud, only to re-emerge in a steep and virtually uninhabited valley where the road clung to the rockface and all one could see was endless forest.

Just as I began to think that this road was leading us to the middle of nowhere we rounded a bend and there, across a precipitous gorge, stood the most imposing fortress I had seen anywhere in the Himalayas. Its massive red-and-white-painted walls looked impregnable, and above these rose a profusion of golden-roofed towers and temples. It was like coming upon the stronghold of a Japanese Shogun in the middle of a deserted forest.

'Tongsa Dzong,' announced Jamba with satisfaction. 'We can stop to look, but only for a brief time. You are taking lunch with the *dzongda*. He is a most important officer, like a district commissioner, responsible for the whole of Tongsa district. We must not keep him waiting.'

'But surely we have plenty of time,' I protested. 'The dzong is only just across the way.'

'Ah, that is true if you are a bird. But to reach there by vehicle we must cross the bridge much higher up the valley, maybe another fifteen kilometres. Also there is a landslide.' Then, smiling mischievously, he added: 'If you want to, you can take the old mule road. It is much more direct. But you will have to run very fast, both downhill and uphill. Do you see how this road goes?'

I stared at what seemed like unbroken jungle until I saw a faint line zigzagging its way up the near vertical slope opposite. That, apparently, had been the main road linking western and eastern Bhutan until quite recently. I saw how the road entered through one of the dzong's great gates and exited through another, ensuring that all travellers had to be checked by the authorities and pay any dues levied on their merchandise. The strategic importance of Tongsa Dzong – and the reason why it became the power base of the ruling Wangchuck dynasty – were readily apparent.

'Thanks for the offer,' I replied, 'but I think I'll stick with you and go the long way round.'

And so, half-an-hour later, we reached Tongsa and drove up the hill to the government rest-house where the Dzongda awaited us.

His name was Dasho Tobgye Tshering, and the combination of dark glasses and the finely striped kho he wore made him look extremely cool. As we stood on the terrace overlooking Tongsa Dzong's jumble of golden roofs, he explained in his low, unhurried voice that there would not be time to make a full visit today. 'But when you return this way from Bumthang, then all will be arranged. Perhaps you would also like to meet the Abbot of Tongsa?'

Although soft-spoken, Dasho Tobgye gave the impression of being accustomed to command. The guest-house servants approached with eyes lowered respectfully as they laid out bowls of sweet yellow rice and butter tea. I attacked the rice, which had dried fruits in it, too eagerly; for just as I finished my second helping the dasho suggested 'we now go in for luncheon'.

It turned out that the yellow rice was just a welcoming snack. It was followed by mounds of plainly cooked rice, both white and the locally grown red variety, with half a dozen plates of boar-meat, beef, spicy vegetables and *hema-datse* (an explosive combination of chillies and soft cheese). Each time I managed to finish my plate more food was brought in. So it was with heaving bellies we continued our journey eastward.

It was dark by the time we arrived in Bumthang. Apparently, Sarah and I were to stay in the royal guest house. It had been built in 1972 to house foreign dignitaries attending the funeral of the late king. There we were met by a thick-set man obviously used to exercising authority. This was Dasho Pem Dorji, the Dzongda of Bumthang, who had been entrusted with showing us around 'his' district. He began by explaining why there were two double beds in the room we were to sleep in. The older one, of heavy carved wood, was tucked away in a corner. Two generations of the Gandhi dynasty – first Indira and then her son, Rajiv – had slept in it. Since when both had been assassinated.

'But there is no need to worry,' smiled Dasho Pem. 'There have been no reports of ghosts, and you may sleep in this second bed.' Otherwise the room was delightful, its walls painted in bright primary colours and hung with beautiful tangkas depicting the Buddha and innumerable saints and protective deities. I drew some comfort from the latter; but it was eery, none the less, spending the night in that room.

Dasho Pem came early next morning. 'Shall we be going now?' he beamed. 'We have a busy schedule.' It seemed somewhat excessive that so high-ranking an officer should be our guide; but then this was apparently standard procedure for 'a Guest of His Majesty'. I felt we ought to act the part. There would be people to meet. So instead of my travel-worn jeans and sweater, I put on a jacket and tie. And just as well, for as we drove up the valley the dasho strapped on the silver sword and rearranged the broad white scarf denoting his rank. 'In the old days you got the red scarf of a high official automatically, but now you have to earn it,' he laughed, before explaining that he needed to be correctly dressed to visit Kurjey, a complex of temples and royal funerary chortens further up the valley.

The Dasho was a stickler over cleanliness. As we approached the oldest of the three temples he stooped down to pick up sweet wrappers and other waste paper left by pilgrims. Next he tried out the hand water pump to check it was in perfect working order. Only then did we mount the steep steps to the most sacred temple, accompanied by a monk-guardian. It is built over a cave where Padmasambhava is said to have meditated, leaving the imprint of his body in the rock. A stately cypress rises out of the living stone where he is supposed to have struck the rock with his pilgrim's staff.

The temple building was constructed by the Penlop or regional governor of Tongsa, Ugyen Wangchuck, before he ascended to the throne of Bhutan. And there are other signs of royal patronage. A wall covered in high reliefs showing Padmasambhava in different manifestations along with his disciples was commissioned by the Ashi Phuntso Choegron, the royal grandmother. The flat ground in front of these temples is occupied by three chortens dedicated to the first three kings of Bhutan – that of the late King Jigme Dorje being simply a conical pile of black stones. The third and newest temple was consecrated only in 1990. Its chief patron is the Queen Mother, Ashi Kesang, and although newly built it is so similar in style to the other two temples that it is difficult to tell ancient from modern.

I soon discovered other ways in which traditional and modern overlap in Bhutan. Dasho Pem had to 'drop into the office for a few minutes'. By which he meant Jakar Dzong, the sixteenth-century fortress which still serves as the seat of regional government. 'It is known as the Castle of the White Bird', Dasho Pem told me, 'because when a monastery was first founded here by the Shabdrung's ancestor, Ngagi Wangchuck, a white bird was staying here and this was taken as an auspicious sign. Also, when seen from the pass at the head of the valley it can – with a little imagination – look rather like a white bird.'

Before entering the dzong he again put on his ceremonial scarf of office and his sword, encased in a silver and snakeskin scabbard. Then we climbed the steep hill from his house, past a disused water prayer wheel, up to his office in the dzong. 'This is the Bumthang way of commuting,' he laughed. The dzong's outer walls are constructed of rough-hewn stone, much of what we see today having been rebuilt by Ugyen Wangchuck after the earthquake of 1897. The courtyards inside are surrounded by brightly painted wooden balconies.

'We keep our computers in a separate building', the dzongda told me, 'since we decided not to install electricity in the historic dzong because of the potential fire hazard.' All very modern and conservation-minded. 'But who are those people?' I asked, pointing to an old man and two women standing by the gate.

'Ah, they are peons waiting to carry messages to outlying villages which do not yet have a radio-telephone link. Very often the community will send old people to do this duty because they are not so useful in working the fields.' The same considerations apply to labourers conscripted for repairing the roads. Again, the village headman or head of the family will send 'less valuable' members – usually women or teenagers – to fulfil their quota. This system of conscripted labour for government works has survived the abolition of serfdom in Bhutan.

While most dzongs have a resident monastic community, at Jakar the handful of monks present only came over occasionally from Tongsa Dzong. Feeling deprived in this respect, the people of Bumthang petitioned the royal government for a permanent body of monks to be installed. Their request has since been granted, and the last time I passed through Bumthang I met Lam Karma Gyeltsen, a venerated lama who had spent fourteen years in retreat before assuming leadership of the community.

Dasho Pem showed me the district law courts with their bright-yellow patterned walls. Sessions are held every day, much of the law being based upon the code established in the seventeenth-century by the Great Shabdrung himself. And while there is an independent judiciary in Bhutan, there are no professional lawyers – the Western-style adversarial approach being considered foreign to Buddhist principles of justice. Normally litigants plead their own cases, though trained legal advisers known as *jambis* are available to the community, and their competence has been upgraded since international human rights organizations expressed concern over Bhutan's legal system. A new centre for training jambis has opened in Thimphu, so that in future they may better advise individuals as to their legal rights. And in the last resort, any Bhutanese citizen may appeal directly to the king, in whose person is vested supreme judicial authority.

Western-trained lawyers may detect certain shortcomings in Bhutanese law, especially in its safeguards of individual rights, compared with their own experience. But here they run up against local custom, such as the acceptance of communal responsibility – whether it be the village or the extended family – for the misdeeds or obligations of one of its members. Such habits of mind are deeply ingrained in

Bhutan's traditional society. So should the country's laws be changed to make them more 'acceptable' to Western jurists and human rights campaigners? Or should they be left as an expression of indigenous values and a different way of the people seeing justice done?

Another wing of the dzong housed the district adminis-tration, including Dasho Pem's own offices. We walked in to find four section heads gathered together over a pot of tea. 'Aha!' he boomed. 'You lot must be plotting something.' He left the room abruptly, before he started shaking with laughter. Dasho Pem, it seemed, had a capricious sense of humour.

I would not have normally volunteered for the next part of our schedule. But Dasho Pem wanted to show me some of the many development projects around the Bumthang Valley set up with foreign funding. Since this is a broad alpine valley, it is easy to see why it proved attractive to 'development experts' from half a dozen different donor countries. So we did the rounds of the dairy and cheese factory (set up with Swiss assistance) and the sheep-breeding and wool-processing centre (Australians started up this proj-ect by crossing Merino and local sheep). The dairy makes cottage cheese used in the *hemadatse* – the fiery dish laced with chillies which the Bhutanese eat even at breakfast – but also excellent versions of Emmental, Gouda and Gruyère that are much appreciated by the royal household. I later discovered our protocol officer carried some cheeses back to Thimphu for one of the queens.

'It is all part of a programme to diversify farming practices,' explained the dzongda. 'In Bumthang, previously the farmers grew only buckwheat. Livestock was mainly yaks and sheep and horses. But the valley prospered because up until the 1950s the king made this his summer residence. All the royal household accompanied him, so it became the summer capital. When Thimphu was made the permanent capital, Bumthang lost out. So we are trying to introduce more cash crops and process them here for sale in the main markets. You see, transportation costs from Bumthang are high because it is so isolated.'

Some of these development projects have been more successful than others. Orchards of apple, peach and pear have been planted, so that in springtime the valley is carpeted with white blossom. Some of the fruit is processed locally into apple juice or cider, or distilled into various flavoured schnapps which keep out the cold on frosty nights. The cultivation of potatoes – well suited to these higher altitudes – is encouraged by a former German aid worker, Heiko Deneka, who has settled permanently in Bumthang. But the Austrian-sponsored stud for breeding Haflinger ponies has been less of a success. I saw plenty of these handsome, cream-and-gold creatures grazing in meadows around Bumthang. The only problem is that they are not so sure-footed on steep mountain tracks, and traders going up to remote valleys prefer to use the hardy native breeds.

'But how does all this affect the lives of ordinary farmers?' I asked.

'You want to see now? Then we shall drop in on the next household on this road.'

We pulled up in front of a farmhouse which looked as if it had stood there for centuries, though in fact it was only four years old. But like all houses in Bhutan, it had been built in the traditional style, which would resemble an alpine chalet if beam ends and window frames were not painted with Buddhist symbols in vibrant primary colours. Four generations of the Darjong family lived under its broad roof, the shingles held down by boulders against the mountain winds. I had the impression they were rather overwhelmed by this unexpected visit from the dzongda, though the mother-of-the-house bade us welcome and asked me to follow her up the wooden ladder to the upper floor, where all the family lived, ate and slept.

Like most Bhutanese, the Darjongs practise mixed farming – barley, maize, cattle, and apple orchards. The son-in-law brings in cash as head mechanic at the local Agro-Industry Centre. Dried maize and strips of yak meat hung from the kitchen ceiling; embroidered quilts were unrolled for us to sit on in the living room, which also contained a chapel for the family's religious observances. The altar was of wood, richly worked and gilded, with statues of the Buddha and saints placed in its recesses. Before this were placed the daily offerings – a silver bowl of fresh water and some puffed grain. Within the chapel I noticed the same framed photograph of the king and the chief abbot I had seen in shops and public places.

We were offered tea – thankfully without the usual dollop of yak butter in it. The Dasho proudly pointed out some of the new features introduced during the five years he had been in office: electrification, fuel-saving stoves, piped water, and separating the livestock (traditionally they were kept on the ground floor), which has helped reduce the incidence of parasitical diseases. Basic measures, but ones which are having a dramatic effect on Bhutan's overwhelmingly rural population. They also bring other changes with them. Electricity brings light first, but probably the next priority is a video recorder. The handful of bar-cum-shops I visited in Bumthang were well stocked with video films, mainly Hollywood action movies and Hindi-language musicals from Bollywood. Even before television was introduced in Bhutan, the video cassette had carried in the detritus of alien cultures.

'What else do you want to see in Bumthang?' asked Dasho Pem as we stood in the farmyard surrounded by chickens, a sow and piglets, and a rather sad-looking mule.

'Well, there is Pemalingpa,' I ventured.

'Ah! Here in Bumthang there are so many places where Pemalingpa discovered religious treasures. But to reach most of them you will have to walk for many hours.' Then, consulting his heavy wrist-watch, he added: 'We could go now to Mebartshu, the burning lake. You have heard of this place?'

Indeed I had. Mebartshu is one of the holiest pilgrimage sites in Bhutan. For it was here that the king's distant ancestor Pemalingpa began his long career as a terton or discoverer of religious treasures. So we drove down the road towards Ura to just short of the Tang River, from where we started climbing a well-worn trail through the conifer forest.

'There has been much reforestation,' said Dasho Pem, still very much in the present day. 'And all through natural regeneration, not by making plantations.'

When I pointed out a clump of fungi resembling Japanese oyster mushrooms that were pushing through the bed of pine needles, he declared this an auspicious sign. 'Do you know that Pemalingpa had also gone to look for mushrooms when he received instructions from a mysterious stranger to go and seek treasures in this place? Ah, definitely an auspicious sign.'

As we climbed, Dasho Pem recounted the story of how Pemalingpa came to this gorge with five companions to look for hidden treasures; how he fell into a trance and dived into the river; and how, to everyone's astonishment, he returned bearing religious texts concealed seven centuries earlier by Padmasambhava. Then later in that same year, 1475, he returned with a great crowd of people and plunged into the pool with a burning lamp in his hand. When he resurfaced carrying yet more religious treasures including a statue of the Buddha, and with the lamp still miraculously burning, his claim to be the spiritual heir of Guru Rinpoche was accepted throughout Bumthang.

'This is the very place,' he said. We ventured out over a bare rock overhanging the river gorge. Below us the waters had carved out a rock pool. This, apparently, was 'the burning lake'.

'Devout persons coming here sometimes place floating lamps on the water,' the Dasho informed me.

'But you are an educated man. Do you believe in all this?'

Dasho Pem stared down into the depths, rubbing is chin, before answering. 'It is true,' he said, 'I was sent for schooling at Dr Graham's Homes in Kalimpong. The royal government paid for everything, providing scholarships. But in those days Bhutanese families did not want their children to be sent away for education. They made protests. Sometimes they hid their children. Now I see I was lucky to be sent abroad for education. It is because of that chance I am now Bumthang Dzongda.

'Now, your question about Pemalingpa . . . Yes, as a Buddhist, I do believe he was a great terton. I also believe in good management and the country's development. In Bhutan, there is no contradiction in this. People believe in many things they hear — foreigners as much as Bhutanese.

'You know,' he smiled mischievously, 'once I brought some French people to Mebartshu. I heard them say among themselves that the pool below was like a piscine, a swimming pool. So I walked out to where that rock sticks out and bent over, like I was going to dive in. Then I told them very seriously that this place was Pemalingpa's swimming pool, that he used to dive from this rock. And they believed me. People are always ready to believe what accords with their experience – Westerners as much as Bhutanese. Really! A swimming pool!' The very idea of it made the dasho break out in uncontrollable laughter.

Dasho Pem invited me to his house for dinner that evening. Children scurried around or hid their faces in mother's skirts before being told to go off to bed. Other guests arrived, mainly high officials and their wives. The men talked mostly about development plans, while the women quizzed Sarah about the British royal family. A mighty quantity of rice was produced together with side dishes. We drank a local version of arra, a slightly cloudy distillation of grain that reminded me of Japanese sake.

The conversation grew more animated, and we were told of many other monasteries and temples and abandoned royal palaces I should visit during my stay in Bumthang. Dasho Pem excused himself for not being able to show me everything. 'Tomorrow I really must spend in the office.' I agreed readily. He was a knowledgeable if rather unconventional guide; but we wanted to wander around the beautiful Bumthang valleys on our own. I was thankful that not only did he recognize this, but could come up with such a tactful solution.

The next day we walked up the main valley to Tamshing Monastery. It was founded by Pemalingpa in 1501 and its outer vestibule contains the oldest cycle of wall paintings in Bhutan. The main prayer hall was being repaired but the monk-guardian beckoned I should enter, leading me past piles of building materials to one of the central pillars from which there hung a length of chain-mail armour. Pemalingpa is reputed to have forged the links, being a skilled blacksmith as well as a predestined treasure-discoverer. The coat-of-mail is enormously heavy to carry, as I found out when I was offered the chance to circumambulate the shrine with it draped over my shoulder. The Bhutanese believe that to do this three times helps wash away some of your earthly sins. All I know is that, having carried it, I immediately heard a cat yowling and was able to free it from beneath a pile of timber. Perhaps my karma had already improved.

The return journey from Bumthang was at a less frantic pace. I wanted to see some of the abandoned palaces I had heard about. One of these, Wangduchoeling Palace, was only a short distance from the guest house; so the morning of our departure, Sarah and I walked there through the early morning mist.

A line of chortens loomed out of the gloom. Prayer flags hung motionless, merging into the grey-white background. We were stumbling across the archery range when the sun nudged its way over the mountains to the east, and the blanket of mist was pierced with shafts of golden light. Only then did I see the row of red-and-white chortens, each of them a miniature water-mill that kept a prayer wheel the size of an oil drum in perpetual motion. Behind these stood a temple that looked deserted, though from its interior came the sound of Tibetan trumpets or jalings being blown to greet the dawn. A little further on, I saw a square house of at least three storeys emerging through the gold-tinged mist.

It looked to me more like an outsized version of typical Bhutanese farmhouse than a palace. But a caretaker confirmed that this indeed was Wangduchoeling Palace, the summer residence of three generations of the Wangchuck dynasty.

It was built in 1856 by Jigme Namgyel, the real founder of the Wangchuck family's fortunes. As the younger son of a noble but not particularly powerful family, he was expected to make his own way in the world, and in his youth he worked as an ordinary herdsman in the hills around Bumthang.

It was there that he met a lama who recommended him to one of the most powerful lords in the land, the Tongsa Penlop, in whose service he rose rapidly from common menial to chamberlain and ultimately to *dronyer* or 'guest-master'. He led successful military campaigns against rebellious fort governors, uniting all the forces of eastern and central Bhutan behind the Tongsa Penlop, whose official champion-at-arms he became. At a meeting of rival feudal lords at Punakha in 1849 he saved his master from assassination, drawing his sword and covering the retreat. For this he was promised the governorship of Tongsa when his master retired. This was to become his impregnable power base for decades to come, giving him a decisive advantage when he intervened in the political struggles in the western 'capital dzongs' over who should be appointed Regent of Bhutan.

By twenty-first-century standards, Jigme Namgyel's methods may appear somewhat brutal. Quite early on in his career, he organized an ambush in which a rival champion who had insulted him was stabbed to death. Later on he preferred to use his superior military strength to reduce rival lords to submission; though even then he was not averse to political assassination – as when he had an untrustworthy official decapitated and the head thrown out of the tower of Paro Dzong. Even towards the end of his life, he had rebel leaders at Wangdiphodrang bound hand and foot, led them onto the bridge to the accompaniment of music, offered them a final meal, and then tipped them into the river so that they died by drowning – thereby avoiding any bloodshed, which Buddhists believe generates more negative karma.

But given the almost constant vendettas and civil wars which plagued Bhutan throughout the nineteenth century, there was nothing unusual in this. One luckless regent met an untimely end when he was given a fine silken kho which had been deliberately contaminated with smallpox.

Jigme Namgyal was also adept at placing loyal men in key positions, including the regency – most of them bound to him by ties of kinship. But besides these 'conventional' means of securing power, he also relied on the prophecies of two venerated lamas that both he and his heirs would attain greatness and benefit the kingdom. To this end he erected great statues of protective deities in Bumthang and Tongsa Dzong, for supernatural powers remained as important in warfare as in the Shabdrung's time. He also assumed the first Raven Crown, more as a magical battle helmet rather than as a symbol of royalty, though the image of the raven-headed deity Mahakala is the same as that adopted by the first unifier of Bhutan, the Great Shabdrung. A less warlike version of the Raven Crown is still worn by the present monarch on state occasions.

Although he was himself regent for only three years, Jigme Namgyal passed on the office to a trusted cousin and made sure that he remained the real power behind the throne. Thereafter he was known as 'Black Regent' because he usually rode a black horse. Having unified the country he installed himself at Simtokha Dzong (close to Thimphu) so he need not journey so far to suppress any further revolts in western Bhutan. He died there in 1881 from head injuries sustained after falling off a riding-yak. By then his son Ugyen Wangchuck – who had been born at Wangduchoeling Palace – held the most important post in the west as Paro Penlop. Practically all other key fortresses in Bhutan were in safe hands.

This was the inheritance of Ugyen Wangchuck, who was to become the first king of Bhutan. He grew up mainly in Bumthang and Tongsa, but although he received some formal education from his maternal uncle, who was also the eighth incarnation of Pemalingpa, he was expected to rise up through the ranks as his father had done – collecting firewood, eating with the servants, working on roads. By the age of sixteen he was assisting in a military expedition to subjugate the Paro Valley. When the young Ugyen was captured by the enemy, his father held an entire noble family hostage to secure his release. The tradition of a tough boyhood training – or, at least, not granting any special privileges to the heir apparent – continued once the Wangchucks became the royal dynasty.

Although he was in a position to make himself Tongsa Penlop and control appointments to the regency, Ugyen Wangchuck still had to put down two insurrections. The second revolt, precipitated by the dzong commanders of Thimphu and Punakha installing their own candidate as

Regent, resulted in Bhutan's last civil war. While raising troops in his home province, the Tongsa Penlop would stop at each temple and swear an oath to the guardian deities. 'If my enemies are destined to bring benefit not only to the teachings of the Lord Buddha in general and in particular to those of the Glorious Drukpa but also to all subjects of Bhutan, and if on the other hand I am doomed to cause them injury, then may my own vital organs come into their hands. If, on the other hand, I am the one destined to bring benefit and my enemies doomed to cause injury, then may their vital organs come into my hands.' Such was the conception of the common good, and the very personal nature of loyalty, in late nineteenth-century Bhutan.

The last battle fought on Bhutanese soil took place on the level ground where the Saturday market is now held in Thimphu. One of the rebel leaders was killed by the Paro Penlop during a parley before battle was joined; the other fled to Tibet after his troops were routed. The year was 1886. For more than a hundred years beforehand, Bhutan had been wracked by civil wars. Since then, ordinary Bhutanese have known nothing but peace – at least until the 1990s, when violence erupted in the south. The pacification of so warlike and fractious a nation is no mean achievement, and it is still constantly referred to in public orations – usually expressing thanks to the Wangchuck dynasty who made it all possible, first by force and later through growing consensus.

Ugyen Wangchuck was to live for another forty years, most of which he spent amidst his hereditary estates in Tongsa and Bumthang. Whereas his father had fought the British (there is a memorial to the officers who fell during the Anglo-Bhutan War of 1864–6 in the church where I was christened, St Paul's Cathedral, Calcutta), Ugyen befriended the dominant power in South Asia. In 1904 he accompanied Colonel Younghusband's expeditionary force into Tibet, where he won much thanks for mediating with the Tibetan authorities. His reward was to be made Knight Commander of the Indian Empire and – equally important – a doubling of the annual subsidy paid in silver rupees. And it was with British approval that Sir Ugyen Wangchuck became the first king of Bhutan. John Claude White, the Political Officer for Sikkim and Bhutan, made the difficult journey to Punakha for the coronation, where he represented the British government. Such obvious support from the greatest power in Asia could only add to the new monarchy's prestige.

Whenever possible, Ugyen Wangchuck passed the summer months at Wangduchoeling Palace. It is difficult to imagine now that this fortified manor house was the real seat of government, with all its court officials and scribes and visiting petitioners, for nearly a century. In those days the royal household included perhaps a hundred *zingaps* or menial servants, even more butlers and men-in-waiting, a royal bodyguard forty strong, stable grooms, cooks, blacksmiths, silversmiths and weavers who provided for many of the court's needs. Above them were the royal family's personal assistants, the king's conversation companions, the royal secretaries and counsellors. Only a few of these could be accommodated within the palace, the remainder living in nearby villages or in tents.

The estate subsequently passed down through the female line, as is quite common in the Bumthang region, and belonged to a succession of royal aunts. Nowadays it has an abandoned air that reminded me of a decaying Jacobean mansion. The paint-work needed renewing, and some of the exceptionally well-carved window surrounds were cracked in places. Its doors were chained and bolted, so we were unable to explore inside. But Wangduchoeling's modest and essentially domestic proportions speak not of pomp and circumstance, but of a very personal style of governing. Even after he became king, Ugyen Wangchuck liked to go around barefoot.

His son and heir, Jigme Wangchuck, spent much of his youth in Bumthang, where he was educated at the Palace School, acquiring fluent Hindi and some English besides being well versed in traditional Bhutanese studies. From an early age he was required to wait upon his father, rising rapidly through the ranks to chief guest-master. At the age of eighteen he was made Tongsa Penlop, by now a largely honorific title retained within the royal family. His assumption of this title confirmed his position as heir to the throne in much the same way as the investiture of the Prince of Wales — beginning a tradition that continues to this day.

Although not so fond of Bumthang's cold climate as his father, King Jigme habitually spent the summer months there and had a new palace constructed in the Chumey Valley near the village of Domkhar. Since we had to pass nearby on our way back to Tongsa, I asked the protocol officer whether we could take a look at it.

Domkhar Tashichoeling, as it is known, stands within a raised and partly walled compound above the village. It was built in the 1930s on a lower, broader plan than the ancestral home; but it is still more a large country manor house than what one normally thinks of as a palace. If anything, disused Domkhar Tashichoeling presented an even sadder aspect — its windows boarded up and the line of prayer flags hanging limp in the fine rain. I was told there are plans to make this a centre of Buddhist studies, though these had not yet come to fruition.

We took the journey back to Tongsa at a leisurely pace. Possibly because I had enquired whether the king was still keen on fishing, word had gone out that the royal guest was a passionate angler. In fact, I am pretty useless. But we had to stop at every trout stream along the way and, to maintain honour, I had to try my hand at casting (I never caught anything, which is just as well since many Buddhists consider it sinful to hook a fish). So it was afternoon before we reached Tongsa.

The third former royal palace I managed to visit, Kunga Rabden, is down a winding road south of Tongsa Dzong. Initially this passes through a steep gorge cloaked in subtropical forest, where I was told a troop of golden langur – a species found only in Bhutan – could often be seen. Then the valley broadened out and we entered Mangdelung, a country of stepped rice fields whose temperate winter climate and deliciously soft spring water were much appreciated by the second king. It was his favourite place in Bhutan and he had three palaces built here. Of these only Kunga Rabden is still standing, just below the new paved road. It was built in 1928 and served as the winter capital until King Jigme's death in 1952.

The habit of moving the entire household to warmer valleys in winter probably goes back to the transhumance of early settlers who led their yaks and cattle down from the high alpine pastures each autumn. In time, it became one of the signs of a well-to-do family that they held lands in the lower country where they could pass the winter.

When the royal household made the journey down from Bumthang it required a hundred pack ponies and five hundred porters. A grand cavalcade set out from Tongsa, led by trumpets and drums, the king surrounded by his armed retinue and supported on particularly steep sections of track by *chashumi* – especially tall men, often more than six feet, who helped to hold him in his saddle. The journey took three days and was punctuated by tea and lunch ceremonies put on by the local aristocracy. It was customary to arrange these halts at the top of a high pass; and in some respects the tradition continues today. Whenever a government minister or high official is journeying through Bhutan, the dzongda of that region will go out to the pass giving entry to his jurisdiction and greet them ceremoniously with tea and food.

In King Jigme's day, the whole area around Kunga Rabden would have been crowded with makeshift dwellings made out of bamboo. These provided shelter for most of the royal household, there being sufficient space within the palace itself only for the royal family and a few favoured courtiers. Across the courtyard is a kitchen range, and out front a grassy terrace where the king's troops would parade and his band play a strange medley of military airs they had learned from their British instructors.

It is a remote spot to have a winter capital. But then King Jigme was fond of the Mangdelung region, and in those days that was reason enough. Here he could indulge in his favourite pastime, the breeding and riding of fine horses, and take part in archery contests that often continued for three weeks at a time. Apart from his quarrel with the Shabdrung he faced no serious challenges to his power. His only possible rival, the Paro Penlop, was allowed to raise his own revenues in western Bhutan but presented no political challenge (it helped that he remained a bachelor).

Otherwise, the king stuck to the traditional Bhutanese policy of self-imposed isolation from the outside world as being the best guarantee of independence. Towards the end of his life this became more difficult to maintain. The British withdrawal from the subcontinent in 1947 raised the spectre of newly independent India claiming Bhutan should be treated as any other 'princely state' and be incorporated within it. But Prime Minister Nehru thought otherwise, and respected Britain's previous treaty arrangements. These provided that Bhutan be guided in its foreign relations by the Government of India, while retaining full independence in its internal affairs. Then, in 1950, the Chinese invasion of Tibet completely changed Bhutan's traditional relationship with its spiritual and cultural heartland. The ageing monarch rode out these storms and passed on his kingdom, its independence intact, to his son.

Little had changed within Bhutan. Serfdom remained in place, the nobility and larger monasteries being supported by hundreds of landless labourers, some of them technically still slaves. All taxes were collected in kind: foodgrains like rice and buckwheat, yak-meat and butter, woven cloth and bamboo, animal fodder and firewood. The king and high officials could requisition porters, horses and food from the local population whenever they went on journeys. There were no motorable roads linking Bhutan to the outside world, no electricity, and no modern medical facilities. Diseases such as leprosy and goitres, that now seem 'medieval', were commonplace.

And yet King Jigme did make a start in modernizing his

kingdom. Young officials were sent off to India for training – as were a number of army officers and recruits who formed the core of a new standing army. The king spent much time in simplifying the system of taxation, making it less arbitrary and abolishing numerous offices below the level of dzongda whose incumbents had previously taken a sizeable cut for themselves.

But the machinery of government remained unchanged. Officials and retainers were recruited from well-established families on a hereditary basis. The provision of a son to enter royal service was expected of them, and if they could not provide such from within the family then a substitute had to be found. Their education was strongly monastic in character. And given the very personal nature of Bhutan's monarchy, the distinction between courtier and government official was blurred. A promising personal retainer would be sent out to oversee a sub-district or conduct a census of the king's yaks, returning to palace service as a secretary before being appointed to a regional governorship.

Much has changed since then, with today's government officials usually being educated abroad and following a logical career path. But I was constantly surprised at how many different jobs most senior officials had done. One dzongda I met had qualified as a doctor and practised medicine before joining government service – first as a zonal medical officer, then with the planning department in Thimphu, and finally as a regional governor.

As usual, we had to wait for someone to fetch the guardian. Seen from the outside, Kunga Rabden is a handsome structure, rising through four storeys to a slightly pitched roof. I was particularly taken by the intricately carved and painted surrounds to the windows on its upper levels – fine examples of Bhutanese craftsmanship. Nowadays, the palace is the property of the National Library and is used to store a large collection of manuscripts, woodblocks and printed works. Among these I spotted the *Epic of Gesar* – one of King Jigme's favourites, which he had read out to him by his conversation companions before retiring for the night. For reasons of security, he wore to bed a gown of tightly stuffed silk which might protect him from a stab wound, and he always kept his sword beside him.

Eventually the guardian brought his keys and showed us into the shrine room. It was unusually large for a private house and still had its heavy silver-encrusted altar in place, while the walls were brightly painted with boddhisattvas and protective deities. Then we proceeded to the royal apartments. Most of the furnishings have gone; but the walls are painted in vivid pinks and yellows and subtly decorated with stylized cloud patterns. The rooms were well lit by oriel windows looking out over the Mangde Valley.

'This is the room in which His Majesty passed away,' announced the guardian. 'The year was 1952. There, you can see his bed.'

I looked at a simple, iron-framed cot. It had a modern pink blanket strewn across it. If this was the royal death bed, then somebody had been sleeping in it quite recently. 'Rather them than me,' I thought, for the room had acquired a sinister aspect.

The king's death in 1952 was not entirely unexpected. There had been strange and inauspicious omens. The pole of his archery tent had broken, as did the prayer flag outside the palace. The Mangde River had changed colour and was full of unnatural creatures. He had, in many respects, been the last medieval ruler of Bhutan; for his son and grandson were to be great modernizers.

My footsteps echoed as I walked the bare boards of this deserted palace, avoiding the loose feathers and droppings left by pigeons roosting in the upper floor. Although sound enough structurally, nothing had been done to restore it to its former glory. I knew that other royal palaces of this period had fallen into decay and were dismantled. It would be sad if Kunga Rabden were to go the same way.

There was a reception committee waiting for us at the gate to Tongsa Dzong. The regional governor, Dasho Tobgye, was there with his sword and scarf of office, as was a representative of the monk body. True to his word, Tobgye had arranged for us to meet the chief abbot, Lama Dorje Neten, a very dignified prelate who stood head and shoulders above the monkish officials clustered around him. His complexion was exceptionally pale, his tonsured hair silver, and he seemed to float on a sea of calm. I was told we had been invited to take tea with him.

This involved first descending to the central courtyard and then climbing many wooden stairways as steep as ladders. Tongsa Dzong is built on many different levels, and there is no simple way of moving between the dozens of temples, monastic halls and dormitories enclosed within its massive walls. Eventually we reached a very ornate temple, and sat in a row before a huge statue of a Buddhist deity in its most terrifying form. It was here that tea was served — English-style, with milk and sugar and biscuits on the side. Sat between the abbot and the dzongda, I tried to make polite conversation; but I felt completely overawed in this room, for everywhere I looked there were images of deities in their most fearsome manifestations, many of them engaged in a tantric sexual embrace with their consorts. The evening light was fading and I had this terrifying image of what it would be like to be shut in here for the night.

In fact, we spent the night in the government guest house, in the same room the king normally stays in whenever he stops over in Tongsa. We huddled around a wood stove sipping Bumthang apple brandy, for the night was cold. But the sun shone bright and clear next morning, and we walked down to the dzong, where Dasho Tobgye was already tapping away at his computer. 'Every night I take away the keys to the dzong', he explained, 'so every morning the doorkeeper comes at 5.30 to collect it. Work is work, and at least it makes me wake up early.'

As in other dzongs, one wing of the building houses the district administration. But Tongsa is a large and active monastery, with some three hundred monks (including those who go to Bumthang during the summer), and the contrast between these civil servants at their computers and the arcane rites being performed by venerated lamas just across the courtyard is more striking than elsewhere. The dzong is still the embodiment of power, both temporal and spiritual, just as the Great Shabdrung intended. I was reminded that in Bhutan it is difficult to separate the two.

Dasho Tobgye was preparing an engineer's report on structural damage to the dzong. Huge cracks had appeared, possibly caused by installing running water and modern lavatories without providing adequate drainage. Precious altars had been removed to safety from the main tower, which looked like it needed to be completely rebuilt. Foreign assistance in this huge task of restoration had been requested;

otherwise Tongsa Dzong was in danger of sliding down the hill.

I had no doubts that this remarkable fortress-monastery would be rebuilt from the ground up, if necessary, for it holds a very special place in Bhutan's history. It was from Tongsa Dzong that the king's ancestors set out to unify this mountain kingdom. Both his father and grandfather were born here — not within the dzong itself, for even the most illustrious births cannot take place inside a monastery, but in a manor house on the way up to the watchtower. Moreover, it is customary for the heir to the throne to be installed as Tongsa Penlop in a ceremony that has many parallels to the investiture of the Prince of Wales in Caerna-von Castle. Whatever the costs, Tongsa Dzong will be saved.

The dasho arranged for a young monk to show us round some of the twenty-six temples. His name was Gaylong Pema Dendup. Unlike most novice monks, who are brought to the monastery when they are only five or six years old, Gaylong completed his college studies — in commerce of all things — and was twenty-two when he chose the monastic life.

'That must have been a radical change,' commented Sarah.

'Not really,' he replied, 'in Bhutan it is usual for lay people to enter the contemplative life at any stage in their lives.'

'But most of the novices here are still young boys,' she said, pointing to a group of diminutive maroon-clad figures who appeared to be playing some kind of game.

'That is so. But now the early entry is usually at ten or eleven years. Before, it was much younger.'

*

We walked up to the parapet where the young monks were playing under the watchful eye of a discipline monk. They were squeezing spoiled rice into little discs and hurling them into the void. The trick was to get them spinning like a frisbee, so that they floated far into the distance. The discipline monk decided to give us a demonstration. Clearly, he had honed his technique, for the disc seemed to hover in the air as it curled around a distant pine tree before slowly descending to the river valley several hundred feet below. He then insisted I try my hand; but my attempt was so dismal that the young monks burst out giggling.

'How long have the monks being playing this game?' I asked the discipline monk.

'Oh, for many years before I came,' he replied. 'Many hundreds, maybe.'

I left Tongsa Dzong thoroughly convinced that the monks here had invented something very like the game of frisbee long before it became a craze in the West. It was a most unexpected discovery.

We had a long drive ahead and there would be few opportunities to break the journey if we were to make Thimphu before nightfall. This time the skies were clear, and the Black Mountains reared up majestically on either side of us. I asked Jamba why they were called 'Black', for their slopes were so densely forested that we seemed to be zigzagging our way through a sea of green.

'I think because they are very high, but do not have snows like the Himalaya,' was his response. Then he jammed a cassette of Bhutanese folk songs into the tape-player, possibly to avoid having to answer any other awkward questions.

We did persuade him to stop at Chendebji Chorten, a

large white stupa of the Nepalese kind with stylized eyes
staring out in the four cardinal directions. It stands beside a
mountain torrent and is surrounded by rhododendron
bushes which, during this season, were heavy with scarlet
blooms. A blue-and-white Tibetan-style tent had been set
up beside the chorten to provide refreshments for a high-
ranking Indian army officer who was travelling the same
way as us.

I had spotted him by the roadside earlier that day,
scanning the mountainous terrain through a pair of binocu-
lars. I knew this road had been built by Indian engineers,
and that should another war between India and China spill
over into Bhutanese territory, it would assume immense
strategic importance. But I couldn't help smiling because he
reminded me of earlier generations of Indian army officers,
men like Captain Younghusband, who trained their field-
glasses across other Himalayan passes, trying to assess which
route an invasion force might take. In this respect, the
'Great Game' is far from over.

Darkness had fallen long before we were anywhere near
Thimphu. Then I noticed how the sky ahead was lit up by
street lamps. 'Only twenty more minutes,' said Jamba, who
was looking forward to seeing his family again.

We scarcely had a chance to take another look around
Thimphu. Our flight to Calcutta left from Paro Airport the
following morning. I penned a letter to Jigme, thanking him
for the audience and for letting us see something of Bhutan.
It is a bizarre country, quite unlike any others I had visited in
South Asia. I now understood that this is so not only because
of its long isolation from the outside world, but because its
last two kings have steered a very different – some might
say idiosyncratic – course towards modernization. That they

have been able to do so is due to Bhutan's monarchy remaining firmly in control. For nearly a quarter of a century King Jigme had exercised absolute powers and, to an unusual degree, the country is of his own making.

I was aware that we had still seen only around half of Bhutan. The entire eastern part of the country, the troubled south – these areas remained a mystery to me. But the king had invited us back. He had also hinted of further political changes to come. Perhaps when these were in place, we would be able to get a more balanced view of Bhutan and of its monarchy. I needed little persuasion.

Chapter Ten

Bhutan III – A Retiring Monarch

The changes that Jigme had promised were announced in June 1998. They came like a thunderbolt from the blue. Many Bhutanese felt that their king had deserted them. For what he proposed was that he ceased being an absolute monarch.

Ever since he acceded to the throne in 1972, King Jigme Singye Wangchuck had exercised the highest executive powers as Head of Government. He held absolute powers without any constitutional limitations – for the simple reason that Bhutan had no written constitution. All government policies, all disagreements between ministers, were referred up to him. His was the final decision; his the ultimate responsibility. And from what I had seen of Jigme, he was a very 'hands-on' chief executive who ran the entire country like a family firm.

All that changed during the extraordinary session of the National Assembly over the summer of 1998. To the astonishment of the assembled representatives, the Speaker read out a resolution whereby the king voluntarily renounced his position as head of government. In future, all ministers would be responsible to the National Assembly rather than the king. Furthermore, King Jigme had insisted that the National Assembly be empowered to hold a motion of confidence in the ruling monarch if he was seen to have acted against the national interest, a simple two-thirds majority against him being sufficient to require his abdication.

This last announcement caused profound shock throughout Bhutan. Many felt that it spelled the end of a very personal type of kingship that had brought them peaceful progress. In fact, in the unlikely event of a forced abdication, the Raven Crown of Bhutan would pass to the next in line of succession. But simple villagers, long accustomed to a patriarchal system, did not see it like that. Some broke down crying when they heard the news.

The National Assembly initially refused to countenance such changes. This created the very unusual situation in which the king himself had to force them through by threatening to use the *kasho* or royal edict if the assembled representatives did not accept their new powers and responsibilities. The king would remain head of state, and keep special responsibility for Bhutan's sovereignty and security; but he would step back from direct involvement in the country's internal affairs.

Thus ended the last absolute monarchy in the Himalayas – not through revolution or political pressure, but because the king willed it so. He had greatly reduced his own powers, while making himself and his heirs accountable for their actions to elected representatives of the people. Bhutan was still a kingdom, and even this new political settlement fell short of full multi-party democracy. None the less, seen from afar, it appeared that a 'top-down' revolution had taken place.

When I requested permission to return to Bhutan,

expressing my interest in how these events might affect the future of the monarchy, I received a curt reply to the effect that 'the role of monarchy was the last thing on His Majesty's mind at this moment in time'. My request would, however, be considered.

I was aware of other changes that had supposedly happened in Bhutan. The 'refugee problem' rumbled on, and in the east there had apparently been 'an uprising' against the royal government. That, at least, is how it was portrayed in a report sent to me by Amnesty International, which claimed human rights abuses had been committed in suppressing this revolt. I needed to get to the bottom of this. So when planning my next visit to Bhutan, I requested we be allowed to visit both southern and eastern districts.

The initial response was negative. I was told such lengthy journeys could not be fitted into our schedule. But I was persistent, and eventually it was agreed that we enter the country overland through Phuntsholing, the main road entry point in south-west Bhutan. This fitted well with our travel plans. Sarah and I had already arranged to be in Sikkim during the autumn of 1998. From there we could go overland via Kalimpong to the Bhutanese border.

As for visiting the easternmost districts of Tashigang and Tashi Yangste, we were advised against it. To do this and then return to the capital for another audience with the king would entail almost two weeks of constant travelling. Again I was insistent. It might entail a punishing schedule, but for most of the time we would be in uncharted territory.

Sarah and I were waiting in Kalimpong when the letter confirming these arrangements came through. Sarah was delighted, but soon turned to the practicalities. 'How do you propose we get from here to Phuntsholing?' she asked, staring at a map of north-eastern India. 'It's a real cross-country journey.'

So off I went to Kalimpong's bazaar to make some enquiries. It was feasible by public transport, but only if we changed buses twice. That might lose us a day inside Bhutan; so I asked around until I found a jeep-driver willing to take us to Phuntsholing for a half-reasonable fee.

As we pored over various maps after dinner, plotting and planning, I realized that practically all the territory we would be crossing to reach Phuntsholing had once been part of Bhutan. Kalimpong itself, and all the hill country east of the Teesta River, had originally belonged to the Chogyals of Sikkim. But during the eighteenth century the Bhutanese had conquered these hill tracts. They also controlled a broad swathe of jungle-infested plain stretching down from their mountain fortress towards the lands of the Maharaja of Cooch Behar.

Border disputes were frequent, and the Maharaja claimed the protection of his British overlords. A diplomatic mission led by Ashley Eden was despatched to Bhutan, where they complained of receiving barbaric and insolent treatment at the hands of local officials. The outcome was the Anglo-Bhutan War (1864–6) which, despite fierce resistance by Bhutanese troops armed only with bows and arrows, ended in a British victory. By the Treaty of Sinchula (1865), both Kalimpong district and the flatlands at the foot of the mountains passed into the hands of the British, who promptly cleared the forests and began planting tea. Kalimpong was built up into a hill station, its 'healthy climate' encouraging the foundation of private schools and sanitoriums. The labour needed to build this and to work the tea gardens down in the Duars was mostly of Nepalese origin. As in Sikkim, the British actively encouraged the eastward migration of Nepali-speaking peoples to help them tame the virgin lands that had come under their control.

The Bhutanese were pushed back behind their mountain ramparts. Very probably, this was a blessing in disguise, for the possibilities of further disputes with British India were greatly reduced. Although Britain exercised 'guidance' over Bhutan's foreign relations, the country was never colonized and retained full control over its internal affairs. The main contact with the British was through a Bhutanese trader in Kalimpong called Ugyen Dorji, who became the first king's most trusted confidant. He was also appointed 'Bhutan Agent' by the British in 1898. As such, he was an indispensable intermediary between the Imperial Power and a strategically important frontier kingdom. He was also made responsible for bringing in Nepali labourers to clear the forests of southern Bhutan. This was in 1900 and marks the beginnings of Nepali immigration into the south. Ugyen Dorji's family continued to play an important role in the opening up of Bhutan. His grandson became the country's first and only Prime Minister, while his granddaughter married the third king, Jigme Dorje Wangchuck. The present King of Bhutan is the fruit of that union.

We set off early from Kalimpong, descending through mist-filled forests to the plains of north Bengal. It was a round-about route, but it is usually much quicker to go down into India and travel on the flat than attempt to traverse the endless ridges and river gorges of the Himalayan foothills.

Simple geography dictates that the different Himalayan kingdoms have far more contact with India than with each other.

Soon we were rattling through the Bengal Duars. The name Duars literally means 'gates' and refers to the flood-plains that open up wherever fast-flowing torrents pour out of the mountains. Every ten minutes or so the road climbed up to another long bridge that carried us over the next Duar. I knew that some of these bridges got washed away during the monsoon; but in late autumn there was scarcely any water left – only sandbanks and great piles of boulders. Most of the land in between is taken up with tea gardens, some of the estates retaining the same names as when my father used to go on tour through the Duars in the 1930s.

The men walking beside the road sported brightly coloured Nepali topis on their heads, while the women – who do most of the tea-picking – had heavy earrings and nose jewellery. In the roadside towns, however, most of the people were Bengalis.

As we moved eastwards, the country flattened out and there was less tea and more rice paddy. The road was lined with gul mohur trees in full bloom, their flowers falling in golden cascades. But the road surface was a nerve-jangling succession of pot-holes that had me clinging to the jeep's dashboard, and the sheer volume of heavy traffic (this being the only main road linking most of India to Assam and the eastern hill states) meant that things could only get worse. I was grateful when the driver turned off down a side road towards the foothills of Bhutan – until, that is, the paved surface gave out completely and we were all choking on the dust thrown up by convoys of Tata trucks. A lot of them now had red Bhutanese license plates, and it occurred to me that practically everything imported into Bhutan has to come along this terrible road.

After grinding along in low gear we eventually arrived in Jaigaon, the town on the Indian side of the border. There was a well-ordered army camp on the outskirts where Indian instructors help train the royal Bhutanese army; but, apart from that, Jaigaon was the kind of messy frontier town that makes me desperate to get across to the other side. The jeep driver appeared to share this sentiment, because he drove straight through the lavishly decorated gateway that welcomes overland travellers to Bhutan. Without anybody even trying to stop us, we had left one country and entered another.

'Wait a minute,' Sarah said suddenly, 'we haven't had our passports stamped on the Indian side. Unless we can prove we've left the country they'll never let us back.'

'No problem,' the driver shrugged, and roared back across the international border.

Back in India again, we found a man in a dingy office who made us fill in forms before eventually locating the appropriate rubber stamp. We then tried to register with Bhutanese immigration, but the guard just waved us on. I was worried because we hadn't been issued with Bhutanese visas in advance. We had no choice but to go to our hotel and try again later. I began to understand what King Jigme meant when he talked about 'permeable borders'.

Phuntsholing was more orderly and better built than its twin across the way, but it is still basically a transit depot. The population seemed to be mostly Lhotsampas, as Bhutanese citizens of Nepali stock are known; though there were several hot-looking highlanders in the national dress of khos or *kiras* down by the vegetable market, as well as a sprinkling of Bengali traders and travelling salesmen from further afield. There is a Buddhist temple in the main square, where a few elderly women were turning the prayer wheels while youngsters in Western dress looked on. Then a crowd surged into the square. I was told they had just come from 'a political meeting'. None of them looked too pleased about what they had just heard.

I found it difficult not to cross back into India by mistake, since one of the main shopping streets is Indian down one side and Bhutanese along the other. I noticed there were more booze shops on the Bhutanese side, and stopped off in one to buy a bottle of local whisky. As I was clanking back towards the hotel a very glamorous Bhutanese woman ran up. She wore her hair long, as do an increasing number of the more sophisticated younger generation, rather than the traditional pudding bowl crop. Her slim, slightly gawky frame was encased in a light silk kira.

'You are Mr Gregson-la?' she queried, adding the customary honorific to my name.

'Ahem, yes,' I replied, trying to conceal the bottle.

'Ah, good. My name is Pema and I am your protocol officer. So sorry not to have greeted you upon your arrival.'

It had not taken long for our 'minder' to catch up with us. At that point I thought she had been assigned simply to take us up to Thimphu. Little did I imagine she would be our constant companion for the next three weeks.

We set off for the capital next morning, Pema beside the driver up front, Sarah and I in the back. The road started climbing even before we had left Phuntsholing. To begin with our progress was slow since Pema kept asking the driver to stop by roadside vendors so that she could make various purchases. She returned after one long bargaining session with a sackful of oranges – which together with cardamom are the main cash crops grown in the south. 'Here, they are much cheaper than in Thimphu,' she said, smiling.

This first range of foothills were so densely settled that I found it hard to imagine how recently there had been no one living here – only malarial forests where herds of elephant roamed. Now, most of the lower slopes had been cleared and terraced for growing rice and maize. On either side of the road were small villages and hamlets, the houses roofed with corrugated iron and generally of a much lighter construction than the stout alpine farmhouses of central Bhutan. I realized the task of clearing this land had been mostly done by Nepali-speaking immigrants, the Lhotsampas; but there was also much evidence of government-sponsored development. Unpaved tracks leading off to villages bore signposts to primary schools, BHUs (basic health units) and local police stations. I also noticed that the steeper hills were scarred by landslides – usually a sign of excessive deforestation.

The road climbed ever higher until the plains of North Bengal vanished in the heat-haze. Signs of human habitation grew scarcer and we entered a dense subtropical forest. At times we travelled along the spine of a ridge with sheer drops on either side; but mostly the road hugged the rising contours of the hills, describing huge semi-circles rather than ever losing altitude. We passed several heavily laden trucks grinding along in bottom gear, and I understood why the engineers who built this road strove to maintain a gentle gradient. Then we crossed a 7,000-foot pass marked by prayer flags and followed the lower reaches of the Wang Chu – the same river that flows past Thimphu. Down in the gorge I saw power lines carrying electricity from the big Chukha hydro-project to India. This was King Jigme's vision of Bhutan's future – a clean, almost invisible export industry, rather than factories and all their attendant problems.

We stopped for a late lunch in Bunakha (I would have happily continued to Thimphu, but the Bhutanese insist on a large midday meal – even if it's just rice). From the wayside restaurant, which was deserted apart from ourselves and an extremely bold cat, we looked down a pine-covered slope to the shingle roofs of Bunakha village. By now we had left the troubled south behind, though at frequent intervals along this road we had to pass through checkpoints. For many years the movement of southerners into central Bhutan has been strictly controlled.

It seemed that we had passed through several distinct seasons since leaving the cloying heat of Phuntsholing. Above 7,000 feet, the air had an autumnal sharpness to it, and there were splashes of orange and gold in the forest where the occasional broadleaf grew among the dark mass of conifers. And whereas flowers were just coming into bloom down in the foothills, here they had withered and the wild grasses had been touched by frost. At Chuzom we joined the main east-west highway after a long wait at the checkpoint. I walked down to the confluence of the rivers that run down from Paro and Thimphu. On the far side was a small temple and a group of chortens; behind me a cacaphony of motor vehicles. Eventually the log-jam at the checkpoint cleared, and we continued through the evening gloom to the capital.

This time we scarcely saw anything of Thimphu. Our guest house was on a hill above the town, and next morning we headed on to Bumthang. It was best to keep travelling, we were told, because everything would be closed over the next few days to celebrate first the king's birthday and then the Descending of Lord Buddha. As she was only a junior protocol officer, Pema would have to work on through this festive season. She arrived next morning in a different vehicle – an elderly, square-bodied Land Cruiser. 'It is not so comfortable as the car,' she confessed, 'but it is better for this journey. Sometimes the roads in the east are not so good.'

And so we drove on, ever eastward. The skies were overcast, and this time there was no chance of seeing the Himalayas from the pass at Dochu-La. What I did learn was that the chorten there had been broken into at night by 'criminal elements' hoping to steal the treasures buried within. In this case, they had been frightened off by an approaching truck. But just recently there had been other thefts from temples and chortens that had always been left unguarded. Previously such desecration was unthinkable in Bhutan.

It was evening before we reached Bumthang. The main Choekhar Valley was hidden in mist, and it was cold enough to justify a blazing fire in our room. Rather than keep on heading east, it was suggested that we stay in Bumthang to see the celebrations for the king's birthday. The emphasis would be very much on youth, with schoolchildren from all over the country taking part in parades. Besides, it would be a good opportunity to meet the new dzongda and other local dignitaries.

Sarah and I arrived early next morning to find the broad *maidan* below Jakar Town already crowded with local people in their best clothes. In the centre of the parade ground, pupils from two schools were lined up in rows. The boys wore khos of uniform colour and design, the girls Western-style skirts and blouses. They were being drilled by an Indian PE instructor who blew a whistle to signal the next move. Tweet, went the instructor, and six hundred hands were raised above heads; another tweet, and they all snapped backed to attention. The kids were taking it seriously enough, but there was none of that regimentation which makes such mass displays of callisthenics somewhat sinister – especially under totalitarian regimes.

We were content to mingle in the crowd, but Pema had other ideas. 'Please, you are invited to sit in the officials' tent,' she announced.

Sarah excused herself, saying she needed to take photographs. I had no such excuse, so somewhat reluctantly I joined the row of local worthies. I was sat next to a headmaster who proudly ran through the statistics on how educational facilities had expanded in Bumthang. 'And all thanks to the good leadership of His Majesty,' he added. I saw that a sort of shrine had been erected to one side of the tent. At its centre was a large portrait of the king, and around this were hung tangkas and white scarves.

The next part of the performance was traditional dancing. I looked down the official programme and noticed that these were split into three categories – Dzongkha, Bumtanghka and Lotshampa.

'Oh, these are referring to the different languages of the songs and the style of dancing,' explained the headmaster, before proceeding to a scholarly digression on Bhutan's ethnic and linguistic diversity.

'Dzongkha is our national language,' he declared. 'It is closest to the dialects spoken in the west, around Thimphu and Paro. Here, the ordinary people speak Bumthangka – a different language, but still it is possible for them to understand Dzongka. In the east, they speak Tsangla and other languages [he made the east seem very far away]. In the south, the Lotshampas have a language like Nepali. Also, you will see now that each region has its own kinds of dance.'

As if on cue, taped music burst from the public address system and a group of senior students, the girls now wearing kiras, ran onto the field. I found it hard to distinguish between the Dzongkha and Bumthangkha dancing, since in both cases the body remains fairly stiff and upright throughout the slow and dignified movements. The Lotshampa performance was a complete contrast. The girls wore headscarves and flowing skirts, the boys tight trousers and multicoloured caps. But it was the exuberance of the dance, the sweeping movements, that delighted the eye while at the same time revealing how they drew on Nepali rather than Tibetan roots.

'The music is also quite different,' commented the headmaster. In truth, it was hard to tell, so distorted was the sound coming from the speakers. But I did notice that some of the younger students performing Lotshampa dances were of local parentage. When I mentioned this, the headmaster admitted, 'perhaps in one or two cases; though of course we have students here from all over Bhutan'.

Later on I was able to pursue the matter in Thimphu, where a specially formed Cultural Commission is charged with developing Dzongkha – literally, the language of the dzongs – as the national language. I saw scholars and technicians refining the script to be installed onto computer programs. I went to the teacher-training centre at Simtokha which helps make it possible for Dzongkha to be taught in schools right across Bhutan. But I was also made aware of how recent this all is, the promotion of a national language having only begun in the 1960s.

Of all the languages spoken in Bhutan, Dzongkha is most closely related to Tibetan or 'Central Bodish'. As a mother tongue, variants of Dzongkha are spoken throughout the highlands as far east as the Black Mountains. Beyond, in what is now central Bhutan, various 'East Bodish' dialects – Bumthangka, Kurtoeka, Kyengkha – are spoken. Their similarities probably go back to the settlement of this region by clans from eastern Tibet or Kham. But as elsewhere in the Himalayas, these local dialects developed in mountain-bound isolation and are mutually incomprehensible. However, as the headmaster noted, it is easier for a Bumthangka-speaker to understand the standardized version of Dzongkha than it is for those Bhutanese whose mother-tongue has no Tibetan roots.

That is the case in eastern Bhutan, where the majority of Sarchops speak Tsangla – a quite distinct member of the Tibeto-Burman family of languages. As for the Nepali-speaking Lhotsampas of the south, Dzongkha may as well be a foreign language that must be learned from scratch at school.

Such linguistic diversity in a country with a total population of less than a million obviously contains the potential for separatist movements – especially since there is a fairly even demographic split between the three main language groups. Which is why the choice of Dzongkha as the national language has as much to do with 'nation building', or at least reinforcing the distinctiveness of Bhutanese culture, as with practicality.

A new and standardized form of writing had to be developed since previously only those with a monastic education were able to write. The language of the monasteries is Choekye, a variant of classical Tibetan. A very similar script has been adapted for writing in Dzongkha, thereby strengthening the links between religious and secular culture. But the main advantages are that it is the language of the traditional elite, and practically all who speak it as a mother tongue are Buddhists. As such it is the natural choice for a country ruled by a monarchy where the state religion is the Drukpa school of Mahayana Buddhism. But did this not accentuate the position of other groups – the mainly Nyingmapa Buddhists in the east, and the Nepali-speaking Hindus from the south – as second-class citizens?

I was very much aware that this celebration of the king's birthday, with its emphasis on youth ('the future of the nation') and its self-conscious inclusiveness ('we are all one nation') was part and parcel of the royal government's efforts to foster a sense of national unity. What I did not suspect was that I would soon become part of this. After the dance performance was over, the dzongda and his 'honoured guests' all rose and marched out onto the parade ground. Imagining that the usual speeches of thanks were in order, I followed along. But no, we all had to form a circle and perform a traditional dance. I tried my best to follow the movements of the others, but to no avail.

When finally allowed to quit the field, Sarah was waiting for me. And she was grinning from ear to ear.

'You looked perfectly ridiculous,' she announced. 'I was in among the crowd, and half of them were weeping with laughter.'

'I didn't exactly plan it that way,' I said, still smarting with embarrassment.

'Serves you right for hobnobbing with the great and the good.'

'And it's not over yet,' I countered. 'The dasho has invited us to lunch.'

The new dzongda, Jigme Zangbo, was of a less authoritarian stamp than his predecessor, the formidable Dasho Pem. But then the role of these regional governors is changing as the king's policy of decentralization, of encouraging villagers to take decisions themselves rather than waiting for orders from on high, takes effect. 'Now they are thinking much more among themselves,' he said. 'For example, last winter we had very heavy snow and the roof of a temple collapsed. Before they would have gone to the village headman. But what could he do, if not then come to me? This time they took their own decision and fixed the roof the next day.'

I learned much from the dasho over that lunch. As usual, he was preoccupied with development programmes – how to build more community schools and provide a safe water supply to all the population. Such basic issues are what really matter in isolated villages, not abstract rights. And questions such as which villages are connected to the main road or who gets electricity first are highly political. If these decisions are taken on a partisan basis, in order to win votes, then it opens up a whole new system of patronage – and with it, the possibility of corruption.

Across the table sat a very ethereal lama. He was afflicted

by some nervous complaint that caused one side of his face to twitch, but his hands moved like birds in flight. He had returned from a long retreat to lead the newly installed monk body in Jakar Dzong. Lam Karma Gyeltsen spoke no English, but he wanted to know whether I had heard of the fertility blessings for which the Bumthang region is famous.

'Have you seen how so many of the houses here are painted with rude images?' the dasho translated.

I replied that, yes, I had noticed the very large and brightly painted phallic symbols on some houses, especially around the Chumey Valley. 'Well, there is a reason for this,' he continued. 'Here in Bumthang there is a special ceremony for childless women. News of this got out, and an American lady came here and was blessed by the lamas. She had a baby in America and was so pleased that she came back with a large group of women who also wanted babies.'

He saw nothing unusual in this. 'Blessings for babies,' as he called the ceremony, were commonplace in Bhutan. 'Perhaps we should start a new kind of tourism,' he added mischievously. 'We could call it "baby tourism".'

Another kind of blessing ceremony was to be held the following day. This was for the 'guest of honour' at the parade, Dasho Jambay Ngedup, who had recently been awarded the blue ceremonial scarf of a royal councillor. Before lunch was over, Sarah and I had been invited to attend. I knew we had a long day's journey ahead of us, but it was impossible to refuse before the assembled company. So the next morning we watched the blessing conducted by Lam Karma Gyeltsen in one of Bhutan's oldest temples and then drove in convoy to the newly elevated royal councillor's house.

He was obviously a man of importance, for hundreds of

villagers were queueing up to pay their respects. Dasho Jambay had donned a striped kho of positively electric brightness for the occasion, and his feet were encased in equally colourful felt boots. But from his bull-neck upwards he looked like a hitman, and I thought he inspired as much fear as affection in the villagers, who presented him with ritual gifts of chang, arra, and hard cash. These he received in the family shrine room, which was hung with a new set of rather garish tangkas that had been sealed in plastic sheeting to prevent them being spoiled. His hospitality, however, was generous, and a great feast had been prepared in tents set up in his garden. The other guests were already downing mugfuls of *chang* when we took our leave. They seemed happy enough, though I suspect I had just witnessed the new patronage system – which so many fear will lead to corruption – at work. I had also noticed that, although still technically banned, there was a satellite television dish up on the roof.

The route from Bumthang to Mongar is the most spectacular road journey I have taken anywhere in the Himalayas. It crosses the Thumsing-La, at nearly 12,500 feet the highest pass along the east-west highway. Although a distance of only 120 miles, the road is so steep and tortuous that it took us eight hours to reach Mongar.

Even before we had left the main Bumthang valley, something unusual happened. Our driver started shouting and pointing to the side of the road, where I saw a mass of shiny black birds. At first I took them for crows. In fact they were black grouse, and to see them in such numbers is rare. From there we climbed through unusually open country, high grasslands where sheep and the occasional yak were still grazing. It was one of those autumnal days when you can see for miles, and the white ramparts of the Himalayas stood out clearly to the north — amongst them the massive cone of Gankar Pusam, the highest peak in Bhutan.

The road dropped only slightly before reaching Ura, a densely packed village whose loyal service to successive kings of Bhutan means that a disproportionate number of high officials call these stark uplands 'home'. Then we started climbing in earnest, mixed conifers gradually giving way to a primeval forest of Himalayan pines. They rose like dark sentinels, their massive trunks split open by frost or lightning. Many had simply collapsed from old age. Around their roots grew rhododendron bushes, which flower spectacularly in spring. Apart from a few huts built for road gangs, there were no signs of human habitation. We had entered a true wilderness.

Pema decided we should stop for lunch at the top of Thumsing-La. While she busied herself with metal containers of rice and chillied pork, Sarah and I walked up to a line of prayer flags. The eastern ranges of the High Himalaya marched in an unbroken line, far beyond the confines of Bhutan and into the Indian state of Arunachal Pradesh. We were so absorbed by this spectacle that we barely touched our plates of rice and curry. Pema said we should eat more. We still had far to go.

Not long after the pass we turned a corner and the world dropped away into nothingness. 'Oh my God,' shrieked Sarah, 'I can't look.' I realized vertigo was taking hold of her, and I fully understood why. For the road now clung to a vertical rock face, while on the outside only a low parpapet stood between us and the void.

I could look straight down nearly 10,000 feet to the valley floor, where a pencil-thin river snaked its way through tropical forests. It was like looking out from an aircraft, though the vehicle's bumping and swerving reminded me that we were still attached to terra firma – though only just. Sarah shut her eyes; but I could not stop myself from staring at the incredible drops and the endless mountain ranges stretching away into the distance. I was completely mesmerized.

'See there,' said Pema, 'that is Mongar, where we stay tonight.' I could pick out only the silvery reflections of sunlight off metal roofs, but it did not seem so very far. In fact, it took us another four hours. The road was mostly single track and in places we had to drive across landslides. We stopped briefly at a memorial to the 247 men who died building this road, most of them Indians or Nepalese. I did not feel inclined to tell the driver to go any faster.

Besides, we were descending through a wondrously wet and vertical landscape. Waterfalls cascaded from high above; moisture seeped from every rock; ferns and creepers clung to every crevice. For half an hour we were forced to stop by a waterfall where a bus had plunged into the gorge. 'All were killed,' said Pema, 'except one small baby.' Now a recovery truck was trying to winch the wreckage back onto the road, but it would not budge. Eventually they gave up and slackened off the hawsers, allowing us to pass.

The air was growing noticeably warmer, the vegetation more luxuriant, as we plunged through the deepening twilight towards the valley floor. We entered a forest where giant bamboo competed with moss-encrusted evergreens, a sinister jungle in which liana hung from every branch. At the edge of a clearing, an animal suddenly leapt onto the road. It was a barking deer, and it was so terrified that it stood transfixed for twenty seconds before bounding off into the underbrush. I began to speculate what else was out there in the jungle.

It was dark by the time we reached the river crossing, where we all had a much-needed mug of tea. Then we started climbing again, up towards Mongar.

I wondered whether we would ever reach our destination in daylight.

Our late arrival at the guest house caused a flurry of excitement. Firstly, there was a power-cut and we had to stumble around the cavernous rooms allotted to us, bumping into antique furniture until the guardian rustled up some candles. But, more urgently, we were invited to dinner with the dzongda and must hurry, since other guests had already departed.

Sarah sighed resignedly while I searched for a torch. A formal dinner was the last thing we felt like after that journey. But having dinner with the Mongar Dzongda had certain advantages. For one thing, his residence was equipped with a generator. Moreover, Dasho Jigme Tshultrim had arranged a very informal evening with just three other guests – an Englishwoman and two Canadians who had taught at schools in eastern Bhutan during the 1970s and '80s. They had just spent some time there, visiting former colleagues and pupils, and were now on their way back to Thimphu.

Dasho Jigme lost no time in announcing he was an easterner, his village being Radi in the district of Tashigang. 'Now that I am serving in my own region, where the people can understand my language, I feel I can do a lot of good.' He said that when Dzongkha-speaking officials came from West Bhutan, very often they could not be understood. 'There was a communications gap,' he admitted, 'but now all speeches are in our own language.'

He took special pride in his native village, claiming that it produced the best rice in Bhutan. A steaming mound was served with our dinner, and it was indeed very good.

'I come from a farming background,' he explained. 'We were not big shots, so I had to study hard under Father Mackey [the Jesuit who set up the first schools in eastern Bhutan] to win scholarships – first a BA in India and then postgraduate studies in adminstration at Manchester. I very much liked Scotland. You know, I have climbed Ben Nevis.'

His relatively modest background and foreign education are typical of the new meritocracy which administers Bhutan. 'We were all classmates,' he said with pride. But when I tried to move the conversation to broader issues, he cast a sidelong glance at the other guests. 'Best to talk about this in private,' he murmured. 'Come around before breakfast tomorrow.'

I did so, and soon discovered why he wanted a private conversation. For six years Jigme Tshultrim had been in charge of Samchi, one of the most troubled districts in South Bhutan. He wanted to 'put the record straight': but not in front of the Englishwoman, who now lived in Kathmandu and might well have supported 'the Nepalese side' of the argument.

'It was a special situation,' he said. 'We had a problem with illegal immigrants. It is the same in many countries. But, when we tried to address this problem, they put up armed resistance. There was a serious terrorism problem from 1990 to 1992, before I was posted to Samchi. Teachers were kidnapped, schools burned down. They used many methods, intimidation and false promises, to get people to join them. Even after I went there, many families were asking to leave Bhutan. We told them: "If you leave, you lose the right to come back again." We gave them special privileges and waived their taxes; but still they insisted on leaving. Why? Because they were given a false impression by their Nepali leaders that they were going into exile for only a short time, that very soon they would "return in victory".

'After they had left Bhutan, these people claimed they had been forced out at gunpoint. I know this was not so. But their leaders wanted publicity for their cause. So what began as a problem with illegal immigrants, they turned into an issue of human rights. But again they hid their real motives. There is clear-cut proof that the Nepalese government and people from the Gorkhaland Movement were involved in this. They thought they could repeat what happened in Sikkim. Their leaders in Nepal wanted to take over Bhutan – or at least to divide it up. We are talking about survival here. You can't compromise with people who want to take over your own country.'

Dasho Jigme's eyes had hardened. Disloyalty, ingratitude – these are unforgivable in Bhutan. I was aware that I was being told the 'authorized version'. But it was coming from an eye-witness, so I waited for him to continue.

'My job was to create some stability in that region, to prevent the terrorists from operating and do everything possible so that schools and health units that had been closed down were now reopened. It was important to build up the confidence of the people who stayed behind. I wouldn't say they have complete loyalty to Bhutan, but they realize now that any plan to divide the country cannot work. So I'd say they're sitting on the fence.'

'What about the people in the refugee camps?' I asked. Nearly ten years had passed since the first refugees had left for Nepal, and I knew that many had come from Samchi.

'I think we should continue a dialogue with them. If possible, there should be an agreed verification process carried out in the camps. If any genuine people are found, if they were threatened and forced out, then these people should be allowed to return to Bhutan.'

But there was something else that Dasho Jigme told me that makes their return increasingly unlikely. The Bhutanese government is pushing ahead with a resettlement pro-gramme, the main purpose being to reoccupy villages and farms in the south left vacant by departing refugees. Most of the 'volunteers' being resettled are landless peasants; and, as the dasho explained, are from East Bhutan.

'Here in Mongar we are holding a meeting about resettlement to the south,' he announced. 'I have 213 people ready to go. For them I have selected an area in Samchi where there is water supply, electricity and good grazing. Each household will be granted five acres of land, minimum. In December, on our National Day, thousands of settlers will travel to their new homes.'

I found this rather unsettling. I could understand why good farmland should not go to waste; similarly, that most of the settlers were Sarchops because there was a land shortage in eastern Bhutan. But there was a gloating trium-phalism about this mass population movement on National Day that I found sinister. It reminded me of China's sending Han settlers into Tibet and Turkestan, or Indonesia's notori-ous policy of 'transmigration'. I also realized that once these

Buddhist highlanders had taken over abandoned farms in the south, it effectively closed the door on people in the refugee camps ever coming back. The new settlers down by the border also had a vested interest in keeping out terrorists and other intruders. They could form local militias. It was all very logical. But was it ethical in any way?

'And what about anti-government demonstrations in the east?' I asked. Since he was both a Sarchop and a high-ranking official, I reckoned he should be well informed on this. 'Also, there have been reports of human rights abuses. What do you say?'

'I agree, there were some minor disturbances,' he said, completely unphased. 'Some Nepali people entered the country and tried to bring about an east–west rivalry. I'm happy to say they didn't succeed. Why? Because in their religion and culture, there is no difference. All are Buddhists. And from very far back, there has been intermarriage between east and west.

'It is true that in the old days, when a senior officer from the east served in west Bhutan, he was looked down on. But now all that has changed. When I was Paro Dzongda, that feeling was not there. And now, since the constitutional changes in Bhutan, you will find the majority of the National Assembly comes from the east. Tashigang sends thirteen representatives. Mongar eleven. Paro sends only three or four. The eastern block can make or break. Why then should we want to cause trouble?'

I left the dzongda's residence in low spirits. It was a radiant morning: sunshine glanced off scarlet poinsettias and late marigolds; but I felt very far from any Shangri-La. For while I was aware that Bhutan was groping towards some sense of national unity, I kept asking myself: 'At what cost?'

The rest of the morning I spent wandering around Mongar with Sarah. There is a row of general stores and boarding houses built in the Bhutanese style, with carved and gaily painted window frames. There are tin-roofed adminstrative offices, a large hospital and several schools that serve a huge area. All of them are of recent construction. And even though it looks several hundred years old, the dzong itself is a carefully crafted facsimile. We met an old carpenter who had helped build its foundations back in 1953. He was aged eighty-two, though he claimed to be twenty years younger so that he could keep on working. His latest project was a new pavilion on the edge of the sports ground.

From within the dzong's central courtyard came the sound of drums. A group of dance students were being put through their paces in preparation for the forthcoming *tsechu*. When they perform during that festival they must wear heavy robes and demon masks; but now they were practising in everyday khos, leaping and cartwheeling on the flagstones. A white-haired dance master called Ap Poktey demonstrated a special drumming dance peculiar to the region. He was remarkably agile for his seventy-seven years; but while the students danced barefoot, he rather incongruously wore a brand new pair of 'Campus' trainers beneath his blue kho. Finally, a troupe of women in kiras were practising their own dance routine, singing in a row as they shuffled rather self-consciously to and fro. One of them had a round badge, like a Mr Smiley button, pinned to her apron. When I looked more closely I saw that it bore the smiling features of King Jigme Singye Wangchuck superimposed upon the national flag.

*

It was time to get back on the road. At first we passed through a delightful broadleaf forest, before crossing a low pass and descending through an interminable series of hairpins down to a river crossing at around 2,000 feet. From there we followed the course of the Gamri all the way to Tashigang, the road clinging to the flatter ground high above the river gorge. We were now in the heart of East Bhutan, and both the countryside and the people were very different.

There are no broad upland valleys as in Bumthang, so most of the villages occupy the ridge tops where the ground is flat enough for cultivation. The houses are thatched and of lighter build than in the west, and maize is more often grown than rice paddy. The Sarchop people are of slighter build and darker skinned, and some of them wore conical straw hats. Where they originated a mystery, though most scholars think they migrated from further east through the Himalayan foothills. Certainly, they arrived in Bhutan long before the Tibetan migrants from the north and west.

Although too steep for cultivation, the river gorge had been stripped of most of its forest cover. Goats and cattle were grazing on these bare slopes, watched over by children. A form of lemon-grass grows in abundance – almost like a weed – and this was being collected and boiled up in rudimentary stills to produce a sweet-smelling concentrate that is said to possess numerous medicinal properties, including that of repelling mosquitoes. Since we were now down in the mosquito belt I bought a bottle. It seemed to be effective enough, for not once was I troubled by mosquitoes.

We passed the turn-off to Dametsi, the most important Nyingmapa monastery in East Bhutan. A gilded spire had recently been carried in procession all the way from

Thimphu, and thousands had gathered to witness its blessing. But Pema insisted we press on, arguing that Dametsi
was not listed on our schedule and that the road there was
'very bad'.

The fortress-monastery of Tashigang appeared up ahead,
sitting astride a narrow spur. It was built in 1659, shortly
after the Drukpas completed their conquest of eastern Bhutan, on the site of an earlier hill fort that had served many
generations of local kings. We had to stop in the gorge
directly beneath its walls because a truck had got stuck on
the Bailey bridge. From there it was obvious why this place
had been chosen to build a fortress on. The sides of the
ravine were so steep as to render it virtually impregnable,
and it commanded a choke point through which all traffic
from the north and east had to pass on its way into central
Bhutan or down to the Assam plain.

It was also clear that this spot had always been a river
crossing. A new concrete bridge was being built beside the
existing one, and a little further on stood two ancient, stone-
built towers that until quite recently supported the Chagzam
or 'iron bridge' constructed by the Tibetan lama Thangtom
Gyelpo in the fifteenth century. (We later saw some of the
massive iron links that carried this early version of a suspen-
sion bridge in the outer courtyard of the dzong.) The
lama was commonly known as Chagzampa, 'the builder of
iron bridges'. Quite apart from his metallurgical skills, he
founded a new school of Buddhism, which was also called
Chagzampa.

The modern road has to take a long and winding detour
before it climbs up to Tashigang. Along the way we encountered a group of Brogpa – a nomadic people from the high
country along the border with Arunachal Pradesh where

they keep great herds of yaks, trading the surplus butter and cheese they produce for rice and maize from the lowlands. They speak a distinct language, and in appearance were unlike any Bhutanese I had ever met. Their heads were covered by circular caps that might have resembled a French beret were it not that from the four corners of the headband there descended tightly knotted strands with pointy ends. Both cap and appendages are made of densely woven yak's hair. Apparently, this unusual headgear acts as a sort of umbrella, since rain runs down the strands and away from the wearer's face.

One of the men wore a jerkin of untrimmed deerskin with the fur facing out, while from his belt hung a large hunting knife with which he may well have skinned the unfortunate animal. The women wore long dresses of hand-woven cotton that were loosely gathered at the waist like a dressing gown. The coarse material had obviously been dyed and patterned by hand, and in colour ranged from faded reds to deep pink. Above this they wore woollen box jackets and shawls, both densely embroidered, and their necks were hung with heavy tribal jewellery. Since these necklaces incorporated much sought-after black-and-white striped zhi stones, I reckoned that — contrary to appearances — this must be quite a wealthy family. They said they were going to market in Tashigang and had been travelling three days already from their highland village.

It was good to reach Tashigang — and not just because it is the eastern terminus of the 'Lateral Road' across Bhutan (in fact, our travels were far from over). Tashigang would delight any visitor, for it is a lively market town where people from all over the east congregate in eating houses and liquor shops to exchange news and gossip. The town centre hangs on either side of a mountain stream, and there is even a square built around a large prayer wheel which the local children use as a merry-go-round. The streets were unusually crowded, both with villagers come to purchase manufactured goods and – since it was a holiday – with novice monks from the dzong and other nearby monasteries. In winter the climate is mild; bougainvillea and poinsettia add outrageous colour to the scene; and, from the very outset, the people were exceptionally friendly, displaying none of the reserve that is so characteristic of West Bhutanese.

Originally we had planned to spend three nights in Tashigang, but the dzongda dropped by to tell us that the Chief Justice of Bhutan and a group of judges were arriving on the third day so the guest house would be full. Dr Sonam Tenzin (he had qualified in medicine before joining government service) apologized for this, and for not being able to show us around his district in person. He was fairly new to this posting, and the next day was walking up the mountain opposite to meet two village development committees. 'One village is Sarchop, the other is mainly people from Khyeng, and there have been some differences between them.'

When I mentioned we had met some Brogpas, he said we had been most fortunate since they rarely came down from their mountain fastnesses. 'They have everything, these people. I have been up to their villages, to Merak and Sakteng, and on any special occasion – for a festival or when a soldier returns home from service – there is feasting and drinking all night. Now their children also have access to education. So far they have kept their culture and way of life. But they must be careful: one step more and they will lose everything.' I understood his concern better when he said that his family came from Ura – another highland community that has been far more assimilated into the mainstream.

It was not his first tour of duty in the east. Previously he had been zonal medical officer for the whole of eastern Bhutan, and he brought the same priorities – better health facilities, the need for safe drinking water – to his new job. But he also pointed out that enhanced life expectancy put new pressures on the environment. 'In the next twenty-three years our population will double, and thirteen years later it will double again. Already there is a problem, especially in the east, of slash-and-burn cultivation and overgrazing. I have to win over the villagers, to tell them that if their environment is abused, if they go on this way, then very soon they'll have to say goodbye to their village.'

With the dzongda occupied with his duties, Sarah and I were left to roam around Tashigang unescorted. We visited the dzong, where a young incarnate lama opened up a beautiful volume of the Buddhist scriptures copied in gold on black paper. He took me into the black-walled sanctuary of Mahakala (women are not permitted to enter) before showing us into a temple where the lineages of the highest Tibetan lamas are represented – the Dalai Lama's being conspicuously absent.

Pema had come down with a cold and excused herself from joining us at dinner. We ended up in a bar down by the main square where a local man kept buying rounds of drinks. When I protested he simply said, 'Why not?' In fact, as he got drunker, he added a giggling 'Why not?' to everything he said. But some of his friends remained a good deal more sober, and from them I heard a different version of what had been going on in the east.

They confirmed there had been meetings and demonstrations the previous year, mostly down towards the Indian border in Samdrup Jonkhar district, but also around Tashigang. Some of the ringleaders had come from outside Bhutan. The local people who turned up at these meetings came for a variety of reasons. Ironically, some thought they had been summoned by the dzongda. Others had specific grievances, about land or government regulations, that are normally sorted out at the village level. Others still supported a group of Nyingmapa lay-monks who had been denied permission to install new images of Guru Rinpoche that were deemed necessary to counteract adverse astrological influences – this being a 'black year' when marriages or new enterprises of any kind are best avoided. A Tibetan lama, now living in exile, had been involved in this. Moreover, he was known to have taken 'multiple consorts' – village girls offered up by their parents who believed that by having tantric sex with a Rinpoche they would be liberated.

'Actually, most of these people were only simple villagers,' commented one of Mr Why Not?'s friends. 'It is the same when they are advanced loans, for crop seeds and so forth, by the rural development bank. The money is all used up on wedding feasts, not for buying seed or a cow. Then they cannot understand that they must pay back the loan. They should be assisted in kind, not cash; otherwise more grievances will arise.'

From this rather muddled conversation, I gathered there had been disturbances the previous year, but they had to do with very specific local issues. The largest demonstration had mustered maybe two hundred people. It was by no stretch of the imagination a general 'uprising' of Sarchops against the dominance of West Bhutanese. Such stories, I was told, had been invented by people from outside who were in league with 'Nepalese terrorists'.

I might have learned more were it not for the appearance of a young man wearing a dark kho with immaculately laundered cuffs. Even I recognized him as a government official of some sort. He had a few words with our drinking companions, and suddenly the party was over. Whatever he had said, they looked distinctly worried. They downed their drinks and announced they needed to get home quickly. Sarah and I were left with the impression that 'Big Brother' had been watching our every move. It was not a pleasant sensation. As we climbed the hill to our guest house, I kept looking back to see if we were being tailed.

Just across the road was Tashigang Junior High School, one of the first schools opened in East Bhutan. The headmaster came over after breakfast and announced it was holding an open day. Would we like to see how the future generation of Bhutanese was being prepared? It was hard to refuse; and, looking back on it, I am happy that we followed him up the hill to the sports ground, where prize essays and poems and drawings had been laid out for inspection. Hundreds of schoolchildren, both girls and boys, were running around in the sunshine. And their pictures – mostly scenes of mountains and thatched cottages executed in bright crayons and entitled 'My Village' – helped restore my faith in the rural idyll.

'We have boarding students from all over Bhutan,' the

headmaster was telling me, 'and all of them learn our Sarchop language. Some speak four languages, which is an advantage in later life. But, as you see,' he added, pointing to some of his students' poems, 'instruction is also in the English medium.' Some of their writings expressed respect for teachers and elders in typically Bhutanese terms, as in:

> *School to me is like a temple,*
> *with the teacher as god*
> *and students, including me, as monks.*

But the poem that caught my eye was entitled 'Our Country Bhutan' and signed Orphan Girl, Whangzam Thinley. It began with the usual lyrical sentiments:

> *Surrounded by beautiful mountains, just like a paradise*
> *In mountain and village live the faithful people*

The last verses, however, showed some real insight:

> *But you are too small compared to other countries*
> *You are just like a doll*
> *If you were big you could have been hit by a sword.*

I asked the headmaster where she could have got such ideas. 'Oh, we teach them Bhutanese history up to Grade 6,' he replied, 'and then a little world history and geography. She has been a very good student.'

I found that visit to a junior school revealed more about how the next generation are taught to think about their country than our later excursion to Sherubtse College – even though this is the 'jewel in the crown' of Bhutan's education system, it being the only place where one can study for a university degree without leaving the country. In fact it mostly caters for the equivalent of Sixth Form students; but it is still a prestigious school, recruiting scholars from all over Bhutan. Many of the current elite were taught by its founder, the Canadian Jesuit Father Mackey. And it is significant that the government chose to raise a college in eastern Bhutan to university status, rather than one in the capital.

The imminent arrival of the Chief Justice's party meant that we had to leave Tashigang (I don't think the authorities would have appreciated my eavesdopping on private discussions about sentencing prisoners). So alternative arrangements were made.

We were to move on to Tashi Yangtse, right up by the border with Tibet and India. Few travellers go that way and I was curious to see the huge white chorten there, which draws as many pilgrims from among the tribal peoples of north-east India as from Bhutan. I learned that once a very devout nun from near Tawang Monastery had chosen to be buried alive within Chorten Kora. I also discovered that, as with other sacred places in Bhutan, some of its religious treasures had recently been stolen.

The road to Tashi Yangtse follows the Gamri River towards its Himalayan source. We stopped at Gom Kora, where the ubiquitous Padmasambhava is believed to have subdued a demon who dwelt within a massive black rock. The temple guardian was a gentle-natured monk, and when we arrived he was busy feeding a prodigious litter of puppies. He used a bamboo pole to knock down some long pods from a tree and opened them up for Pema. Inside the pod are transparent petals that are used for certain religious ceremonies. As we climbed back to the road I saw he was feeding the puppies again.

A little further upstream lies Duksom, a village renowned for its silk weaving. A girl of school age was sitting before a wooden frame, working on a gorgeous piece that would fetch several thousand dollars in Thimphu. I marvelled at her skill, while at the same time wondering whether it was right that a girl so young should be set to work in this way. Wasn't it a form of child labour? But seeing her practising her craft on the front steps of the family home, it seemed perfectly natural. Certainly it was a far cry from the sweat-shops I had seen in India where child weavers are used to make Kashmiri carpets – 'because their fingers are so nimble'. What might be condemned elsewhere seemed perfectly permissible in Bhutan, mainly because of the way in which it was being done.

We arrived in Tashi Yangtse to find an archery contest in progress. I scarcely had time to register the brand-new dzong and other building works going on, or the snow peaks that enclosed the valley to the north, before we were down by the archery butts. The contest was at a crucial stage, with the dzongda's team about to lose out to a roguish-looking lot from a remote village. Certainly the village team were doing most of the dancing and shouting the loudest abuse. The large crowd of onlookers seemed to be taking it very seriously. Then a whisper went around and they all decamped in a body, leaving the bowmen to continue in splendid isolation.

What had attracted the crowd was the spectacle of a huge cobra stretched out across the road. I was told that the snake had been rendered insensible by feeding it a mixture of milk and rum; but I was not going to get too close, the idea of a cobra with a hangover sending off all kinds of alarm bells. A young show-off was holding its neck down with a stick while the crowd shrieked and tried to make up their minds about what to do with it. A local magistrate suggested they did not kill it as this was contrary to Buddhist principles. Far better to put the cobra in a sack and release it in the forest beyond the river.

We left them still arguing and returned to the archery contest. The village team had just won, so we walked down to Kora Chorten. Pilgrims were turning prayer wheels as they performed their circumambulations around the white-washed stupa. Some looked very similar to Brogpas, though I was told they were tribal people from across the Indian border.

Then, as the light was fading, we settled down to tea and rum in one of the town's general stores-cum-liquor shops. Sarah made some purchases, for the region is famed for its handmade bark paper and beautifully carved wooden bowls (traditionally these were carried by travellers inside their khos and produced at mealtimes, so everyone had their own portable dinner service). Meanwhile I talked to an old-timer about how, during the Sino-Indian War of 1962, isolated detachments of Indian troops had been forced to retreat through here, even though Bhutanese territory was supposedly neutral. It was a vivid reminder of how close we now were to one of the more volatile international boundaries in the world, and how difficult it would be for Bhutan to stay out of any future conflict.

Tashi Yangtse marks the limits of the Drukpas' expansion eastwards in the seventeenth century. Beyond the next range of mountains lay tribal lands that owed their allegiance to the great monastery of Tawang which, being a Gelugpa foundation, could look to the Dalai Lamas in Lhasa for support. For us, too, it was the end of the line. From now on we would be retracing our steps all the way to Thimphu, for there is only one Lateral Road.

That first day's journey was a marathon drive. We hit the road at dawn and kept moving for twelve solid hours. The constant swerving motion as we tackled one bend after another produced a dream-like state in which mountain and forest, rivers and paddy, all melted together in a continuum whose predominant colour was deep green. The driver showed enormous stamina, plugging on for mile after tortuous mile without a break.

Our aim had been to reach Bumthang by nightfall, and we were more or less on schedule until we lost two hours getting a flat tyre fixed below Mongar. At least we made it through the most vertiginous stretch (where the recovery truck was still trying to drag the crashed bus out of the gorge) before daylight failed. But it was dark before we crossed the Thumsing-La, and the black pine forest seemed an even more terrible place to be stranded in. There were no lights to be seen until we reached Ura. Towards the end, I remember a big dog fox standing its ground in the middle of the road, eyes blazing in the full beam of our headlights.

And so it continued the next day, climbing yet another pass only to slither down the far side. I reflected that only thirty years earlier this same journey would have taken several weeks on horseback. On the other hand, I was told the king often reached Tashigang in just eighteen hours. But then he travelled in a more powerful vehicle, with outriders clearing the road ahead.

Having broken the back of the journey, we decided to

call on two of the dzongdas who had been so hospitable on our previous visit to Bhutan. Dasho Pem had been moved from Bumthang to the more populous district of Wangdi-phodrang. I saw immediately that he had at last been awarded the red scarf of high office; but he was still the same blustering character, for ever stooping to pick up litter as he charged around the dzong's spacious courtyard. A royalist of the old school, he described the king's decision to surrender absolute power as being a 'great shock'.

'You don't expect such things', he said, 'when everything in the country was going so well. But for us he's still the Boss.'

We also called on Dasho Tshering, who was still in charge of Tongsa District. Previously he had seemed some-what reserved. But this time he opened up — and on a subject that still burned within his soul.

'I was a sub-divisional officer down in Samchi when the real trouble started in the south,' he stated. 'I was there on 19 September 1990 and saw what happened.'

He paused to let this sink in. The date corresponded to the big demonstration which is supposed to have ended with Bhutanese security forces carrying out a general massacre of Nepali-speaking protestors. If he was in command, I could see why he took allegations of 'genocide' or 'ethnic cleansing' very personally.

'We received news of militant groups', he said, 'and went to check the situation. There were about eighty of them with guns. I counted seventy-seven. They went from village to village, calling on the people to join them. Some were reluctant; others welcomed them and brought out food.

'Our instructions from Thimphu were to do nothing.

Just observe. But by afternoon they had collected around 4,000 people and were moving towards Chengmari. It is down by the border, and in the tea gardens opposite were quite a number of non-nationals, either Nepalese or Indians. We asked them to stay where they were and not cause any problems. I went to talk to them.

'Ah, that was a field day for them,' he said with some bitterness. 'They were pointing their guns and wearing camouflage fatigues. Everyone who joined their demonstration was asked to take up arms – kukris or bows and arrows as well as the seventy or so with guns. They wanted to proceed to the district HQ at Samchi and approached a bridge that was protected by our policemen.

'Someone threw a hand grenade on the bridge and they started firing. Our policemen were firing in the air. I was on the spot, and can confirm that one policeman and two demonstrators only were injured. Imagine my surprise when the BBC reported that 334 people had been killed. I tell you, from childhood I had faith in their news reports. But I lost my faith in the BBC that day.'

I remembered being shocked by such reports at the time. But now it suddenly occurred to me that either the journalist concerned got it wrong or unquestioningly followed the line fed to him by Nepali activists, or . . .? The blunt alternative was that I was now in the presence of the very man who had overseen a brutal massacre of peaceful protest marchers. Moreover, he had subsequently been promoted by the royal government of Bhutan – the clear implication being that it had either ordered or at least approved such a course of action.

I decided to let him continue telling his story.

'We heard some days later that they [Nepali activists]

448

had killed some people from remote villages, well away from the border area. These were Lepcha people, not Nepalis, and they had refused to join in. So they were taken towards the border where two of them were beheaded, to set an example to others. On Demonstration Day, in my area, only that killing took place.'

I asked him if he had witnessed other killings, and he told me about an old man – one of the first settlers in that area – who had been kidnapped and taken to one of their camps across the border. 'They accused him of helping our census people, of telling the truth about who were illegal immigrants. Like most members of village committees, he had made enemies of the new settlers. After a week or so I heard this old man had been beheaded. They brought his head just inside Bhutan and I had to take it back it to his wife and seven children. Even now I feel the pain of having to present that head to his wife, and she with so many children.'

'But why did this conflict break out?'

'On their side, they say it was because of the census, because we wanted to stick to teaching Dzongkha in schools, because officials were forcing them to wear Bhutanese national dress. And yes, the census I conducted in Cheng-mari showed that sixty-three per cent of the population were non-nationals as per the citizenship law. This influx happened not long ago. Chengmari is on an open border, and between the 1960s and the 1980s the whole area was settled by non-nationals.

'Other issues, like their not wanting to wear the kho, these could be talked over. But on the problem with illegal immigrants, we had to try and safeguard the nation. There had to be a showdown: and it was better to act sooner than later, because then the problem would have been bigger. What their leaders were seeking was the Nepalization of my country. They wanted the whole of Bhutan to be opened for Nepali migrants to settle. They allied themselves with the Gorkha National Liberation Front. I tell you "Gorkha" has only one meaning. They wanted to achieve by stealth what their Shah kings could not do by force of arms two hundred years ago.'

The 'refugee question' was very much in the air when we returned to Thimphu. A senior UNHCR official had just been and gone; a Nepalese delegation about to arrive (as they were staying in the same guest house, I moved down into town); the regional director of Amnesty International was due shortly thereafter. The protocol division was working overtime. None the less, they had lined up a series of interviews with ministers and other officials while I awaited my audience with the king.

Sarah had to get back to England and flew out of Paro the next day. 'Be good,' she warned. 'Some of these Bhutanese women are just too damned attractive.'

But I had no time to appreciate the local beauties, so crammed was my diary with official engagements. My first call was on Lyonpon Jigme Y. Thinley. Until the previous June, he had been Bhutan's representative to the United Nations in Geneva. Now he was Foreign Minister and Chairman of the Council of Ministers. 'Not like a prime minister,' he insisted, 'more the first among equals.' But in the clean sweep of ministerial appointments, he had emerged on top.

He explained that each of five ministers would hold the

chairmanship for a year, the order having been decided by how many votes they had won in the National Assembly. After Thinley had served his year it would go to the Minister of Health and Education. Only later did I discover that this minister happens to be the brother of the four queens of Bhutan.

With his Western education and diplomatic background, it is hardly surprising that Lyonpon Thinley took a more conciliatory line on the 'refugee question' than the robust Dzongda of Tongsa had done. 'The new government attaches enormous importance to finding a speedy solution,' he declared. A new stage of bilateral talks with the Nepalese would begin next Monday. I smiled back, knowing full well that the Bhutanese are very adept at talking but, as a rule, prefer to play a waiting game.

As the days passed, winter gradually descended on Thimphu. The leaves which had just been turning a fortnight earlier were now a dull gold, and with each chill blast of wind coming down the valley more of them were scattered on the ground. I went up the valley to peer at Dechenchoeling Palace — now the Queen Mother's residence, though this was where Jigme spent much of his childhood. And far up a side valley, I caught a glimpse of the substantial log cabin where he prefers to live now he is king.

I visited the Saturday market, where everything from freshly slaughtered yak to tropical vegetables was for sale. It was busy enough, but there was none of the clamour of an Indian bazaar, the citizens of Thimphu preferring to fill up their shopping bags in near reverential silence as they moved between rows of neatly ordered stalls. I even poked my nose into a Bhutanese disco, which is like a disco anywhere else except that amongst those on the dance floor was the youngest sister of the four queens of Bhutan, a scion of the illustrious Dorji family, and various other young aristocrats.

But most of the time was spent shuffling between government offices. I called on the Home Minister, the head of the Special Commission on Cultural Affairs, the Speaker (who showed me round the deserted chamber where the National Assembly meets and pointed out the Golden Throne occupied by the king), and many others besides.

I was in the middle of interviewing the Finance Minister when the call came.

'So sorry we couldn't finish.' He smiled. 'But His Majesty will see you now'.

It was only a short walk around the inner gallery of Tashichodzong to the audience room, and before I knew it Jigme was standing there in a checked kho, smiling broadly and holding out his arms.

We sat in the same window seat as before and were soon discussing recent events. Prince Charles' visit to Bhutan had been 'very successful'.

'He charmed everybody, and was especially good when meeting younger people.'

When I asked after his family, Jigme again avoided the subject of his four wives and moved straight on to the crown prince, who was at school in Boston.

'He won a scholarship on merit, and now he's studying to get into college,' the king told me with some pride. 'He did very well academically and the teachers like him – probably because of his background here, where discipline and respect for teachers are deeply ingrained.' But he still had to pass his exams. 'He'd better score well,' was the king's only comment.

Now his eldest daughter and the next eldest son had completed high school in Thimphu, they too would be sent abroad for higher education. 'All the way through school they had no special privileges, but now they need exposure to ideas and experiences outside Bhutan.'

Less than two years had gone by since I last saw Jigme, but he seemed to have aged much more than that. He looked tired and care-worn – like a general who has fought and won many battles, but knows that all is not over yet. I guessed that pushing through all the constitutional changes over the summer had taken a lot out of him. So I asked him why had he done it? Why had he voluntarily – some would say unnecessarily – handed over power and ceased being an absolute monarch?

He smiled wearily. 'I think I told you this before, Jonathan. I never wanted to be king to begin with. It wasn't because of my merit or any personal desire, but because of my birth, that I became king.

'In the past, the king had complete powers. This situation has its disadvantages – regardless of whether it applies to a king, a president, a prime minister or a dictator. When an individual exercises tremendous powers, there is a great opportunity to do good. But what would happen if we didn't have a good king? I have always had great reservations about this. It's not something new.

'I would never deny that monarchy has played an important role in the history of Bhutan. In my great-grandfather's time and then under the second king, then monarchy had an important role. But at that time our literacy rate was in single digits. We had no schools or health facilities, no roads or economic development . . .

'We have come a long way in a very short time. I remember when I was eight, seeing the first jeep coming into Thimphu. It had been dismantled, carried across the mountains, and then reassembled and driven into town. Even after I became king, our priorities were to build a basic infrastructure and to strengthen Bhutan's status as a sovereign and independent country. Then I was very much in control, holding all the responsibilities of head of government. But just because kings have had an important role in the past, it doesn't mean that for all time to come we must continue in the same way as our forefathers.

'I always saw my role in terms of building up political institutions that could meet the needs and aspirations of the Bhutanese people rather than strengthening my own personal position. I have always tried to put the national well-being first, and I think these changes will contribute to that.'

'But why now?' I asked.

'I have been king now for twenty-six years. How can we then say there hasn't been time to bring about changes? That's a pretty lame excuse after two and a half decades of absolute power. For many years now I have been saying that the future should lie in the hands of the Bhutanese people. Now they can see that it's not just propaganda.

'Besides, the decision was taken long ago. For me, the process started in 1981 when we began decentralizing. We started by having elections by secret ballot at the district level. Then in 1991 we did the same at the village bloc level. For us it was a long process: ordinary villagers learning to elect their representative; and these representatives having to understand they are responsible to those who elected them.

It doesn't happen overnight. But because we started at the grass-roots level, building up the people's political consciousness, I am confident they are now able to shoulder that responsibility.'

'But why did you insist on there being a vote of confidence which, if it went against you, meant that you would have to abdicate?'

'Because without accountability the whole process wouldn't have much meaning. Accountability goes hand in hand with the delegation of power. You can't make people responsible without accountability. That should apply to the king as well as to government ministers and the people's representatives.'

'Then why did the people's representatives oppose it?'

'It's true that, to begin with, the National Assembly totally rejected it. I had to push it through the debate. But then I mentioned this to them: What if they don't agree with what the king is doing, if they think he is acting against the best interests of the country? To hold him accountable without having the constitutional means to back this up, that would be purely illusory. It is for that reason I wanted there to be a vote of confidence in the king. And unlike government ministers, who face a vote of confidence every five years, for the king there is no fixed time period. It can happen at any time – either through the Speaker or on the floor of the National Assembly. And if a motion against the king receives the support of two-thirds of members voting by secret ballot, then the king must abdicate.'

From the expression on his face, he appeared to accept this with perfect equanimity. For the time being, any such drastic measures are extremely unlikely since the king retains the support and admiration of the vast majority of his subjects. By any standards he is a 'popular monarch'. But things could change swiftly now that he is no longer in full control. I mentioned two negative aspects – increasing regionalism and corruption in politics – that many Bhutanese fear may prosper under the new regime.

'There is no perfect political system', he declared, back in philosopher-king mode, 'because of the fact that there is no perfect society. And yes, certain undesirable elements usually come to the surface when you have a democratic system. There is a tendency for those in power to do whatever is best for winning votes; and if they haven't built up a war-chest they think they'll have difficulties in winning the next election. Every country in the world faces these pressures. But in Bhutan, the level of corruption is very low compared to other countries in the region. I suppose that to a certain extent these factors will start to come in; though corruption is not really part of our culture as it is elsewhere.

'If by regionalism you are referring to stories about there being conspiracy and revolution in East Bhutan, outsiders saying they are a completely different people, then I think these foreigners' views must be influenced by tribal situations in Africa – not the reality in Bhutan. They even try to make out there are differences in religion between west and east, which isn't the case. It would be better if these people came and saw for themselves.'

Having just been through east Bhutan without seeing any signs of unrest, I tended to agree. And I subsequently became aware of certain misgivings within Amnesty International about a report they had published (timed to coincide with Prince Charles' visit to Bhutan for maximum impact) which asserted there had been an 'uprising' in the east. For such organizations, there is a fine line between trying to protect human rights and needlessly interfering in the internal affairs of another country — especially if this is likely to foment unrest which had not previously existed.

'We do our level best to show them the true situation in Bhutan,' he continued, a note of exasperation in his voice. 'Representatives of the Red Cross, Amnesty, UNHCR — they come and inspect all our jails and talk to the prisoners in private. We have organized many seminars for the judiciary, for government officials, the police and the army, and have a training programme for our *jambis* [lawyers] so that they are aware of human rights. I believe it is useful that foreign experts come — so long as they don't have a pre-determined agenda.'

The king was clearly sensitive to such criticism. All his adult life he had tried to put his country and his people first. And this was his reward.

'To be very frank,' he said, 'we have been criticized on practically everything we've done. Elsewhere, when they preserve culture and tradition, it's all very admirable. Here we are criticized. When we focus on economic development first, we are criticized for not being a Western-style democracy. We concentrate on putting in sanitation, electricity, water, roads, telephones; they want us to give priority to having television in Bhutan. Already we have TV dishes and there will be national television soon (the first broadcast was in June 1999, when Bhutan also launched its own Intranet). Even when we deliberately avoid mass tourism because we don't want to commercialize our culture and disrupt our monasteries, even for this we come under criticism.'

I might have added that he himself came in for criticism because outsiders see him as having 'this mission thing'. But Jigme looked cross enough already, so I thought better of it.

'For us', he declared, 'so long as we are able to get the job done, to have the right policies for the Bhutanese people and also safeguard our national security – that's far more important than any criticism from outside.'

'And what about the continuing refugee problem?'

'This so-called refugee problem is very different from others in the world. There is no war in Bhutan, no genocide. So why are they classified as refugees? They are not like Burmese or Cambodian refugees who have fled into Thailand. They are ethnic Nepalese living in Nepal; and yet they all claim to be Bhutanese refugees. That is enough, apparently, to give them refugee status.

'They claim to be a democratic movement because they know the West will give priority to such cases. What they didn't elaborate on is the fact that most of them are not Bhutanese nationals. So how are they supposed to represent the so-called democratic aspirations of the Bhutanese people? They accused us of ethnic cleansing. Where is their evidence?'

The king paused for a moment, if only to calm himself. 'Basically, we try to explain that the people claiming to be Bhutanese refugees are an admixture of ethnic Nepalese who have only this thing in common: that they all claim to have been persecuted by us and thrown out of the country. What's more, they do this with the full encouragement of the Government of Nepal, who for political reasons want to keep these people in the camps.'

He went on to explain that the very existence of these refugee camps in Nepal actually created a refugee problem. 'Before the Government of Nepal requested UN assistance', he said, 'only 234 people claimed to be refugees – and these are UNHCR figures.' Once the refugee camps got the go-

ahead, however, their number swelled rapidly to thousands
and tens of thousands. For many years now, the refugee
movement claimed there were 100,000 living in the camps
around Jhapa, in south-east Nepal. The Bhutanese government disputed these figures. Certainly they contested the
camp inmates' claims to be refugees from Bhutan. They had
been part of the Nepali diaspora that has spread right across
north-eastern India. Some had never even left Nepal. They
had gone to the camps for two reasons. Firstly, their political
leadership had promised they would be there for only a
short time before 'returning in victory' to Bhutan, when
they would be duly rewarded. But secondly, and more
immediately, the camps set up under the auspices of
UNHCR were among the best run in the world.

'They have free housing, education, healthcare, food
supplies, kerosene and stores. Any work they find outside
the camp is like pocket money. For people right at the
bottom of the employment ladder – those working on tea
gardens or road-workers and coolies – the standard of living
inside the camps is much higher than outside.'

As I was hearing the king out, I determined to go to
Jhapa and see for myself the situation in the camps there. I
did so four months later, and found entire townships had
been carved out of the steamy jungle – row upon row of
thatched cottages with communal standpipes and kitchen
gardens running between schools and assembly halls where
the camp committees held their meetings. Compared to
other refugee camps I have visited, these were very orderly
and well run (I was also told they are the most cost-effective
in the world). I saw sacks of rice being unloaded off trucks
and neatly stored.

All the basic necessities of life were attended to here; but there was a depressing permanence about these camps. For their 95,000 inhabitants, life has been put on hold. They are not officially allowed to find work outside the camps or integrate into Nepalese society, though some have got round this by intermarriage with neighbouring villagers. They have been left in limbo, a stateless people, their only hope being that some settlement is reached which will allow them to become citizens of either Bhutan or Nepal.

I listened to dozens of camp-dwellers, hunkered down beneath a banyan tree or on the steps to their cottages, as they recounted how they had been forced to leave Bhutan. I heard of how they had been imprisoned, of intimidation, of how their lands had been confiscated by corrupt Bhutanese officials. No doubt the individuals I talked to had been hand-picked, but they all produced their tattered citizenship cards, land records, photos of the farmhouses they said they had once owned in Bhutan. It was impossible not to be moved by the hopelessness of their situation.

But I also knew that the Bhutanese claim that most of these documents have been forged, or have been stolen, or were invalid in the first place. Most of the people in these camps had been admitted before there was any effective screening in place. Just as there are completely contradictory accounts of who committed the worst atrocities in the south – the Bhutanese army and police, or the 'anti-national terrorists' – so it is impossible to tell what documents are valid unless there is a mutually agreed process of verification. But the people in the camps are against this. Their leaders argue that they have all suffered together, so they should all go back together. Otherwise the exile movement will lose its solidarity. There would be no pot of gold at the end of the rainbow, no reason to sit out another decade as listless camp-dwellers.

The Bhutanese have always insisted on joint verification being carried out inside the camps on the status of all persons claiming to be refugees. They accept that some may have the right to return. And yet, bilateral discussions between Bhutan and Nepal on how this process be carried out have dragged on for years. Another Nepalese delegation arrived while I was in Thimphu.

The king remained adamant that there must first be agreement between the two governments on verification and on what action then be taken. 'Otherwise our decisions would not be taken on logic or what is fair, but solely on political grounds.' But he did promise that once verification was carried out, there would be 'immediate action'.

I had the impression, however, that this was no longer a pressing concern – even though the king has taken on personal responsibility for finding a solution to the 'refugee problem'. Basically, the Bhutanese think they have won. Far more serious is the presence of other armed militants in the jungles of south-eastern Bhutan. These are either members of ULFA (United Liberation Front of Assam) or a fiercely independent tribe known as the Bodos. Both groups demand either independence or greater autonomy from India, and for decades they have been waging a guerilla war against Indian security forces. More recently they had established camps inside Bhutan, and Indian patrols had occasionally followed them across the border 'in hot pursuit'.

Jigme admitted that, 'If this situation persists, then our good relations with India will be severely strained. I have taken full responsibility to resolve the problem.' For while he is no longer head of government and has taken a step back from Bhutan's internal affairs, the king remains in charge of all matters pertaining to national sovereignty and security. And he knows only too well that if India changed its supportive stance towards Bhutan, everything would be undone. All imports must come through India, and practically all exports (including hydro-electricity) go to the Indian market. It was largely because of India's support that Bhutan was able to ride out the 'refugee crisis'. Hence his concern over secessionist groups operating out of Bhutanese territory.

'The Government of India has been very understanding,' he said. 'They know that our security forces cannot push ULFA and Bodo insurgents out of Bhutan. The only way would be by launching attacks on their camps, and they are heavily armed. If India's security forces haven't been able to curb these militants over decades, how can they expect us to do so? Also, you must remember that there are 25 million people in Assam and, whatever political changes occur, they will be our southern neighbours for all time to come.'

On other matters, the king declared himself to be supportive of India's policy. The recent round of nuclear tests conducted by both India and Pakistan, he said, only proved that, 'a nuclear arms capability in South Asia is a fait accompli. There's nothing much any country can do about it.'

As for the concept of a 'Zone of Peace' embracing the Himalayan region – different versions of which have been advanced by both King Birendra and the Dalai Lama – Jigme dismissed it as being 'outdated because nowadays no country can live isolated in peace and security if there are still conflicts within the region as a whole'. He noted that,

'Nepal pursued this concept for many years, but now it is in cold storage.' Bhutan had never been that keen on the idea, anyway, suspecting it might be a ploy for imposing Nepalese hegemony over the region.

At this point, an official bowed himself into the room and whispered something in the king's ear.

'I'm sorry,' he said, turning to me, 'but we must stop now. There are many people waiting to see me.'

Jigme rose and held both my hands in his, wishing me farewell before giving me a final bear hug. Thankfully, this time I managed to avoid getting caught up in the folds of his ceremonial scarf.

I walked through the antechamber and out into a long passage. It was lined with very humble-looking villagers, all of them awaiting a brief audience in which they might present a petition to their king — for a land grant or an amnesty for one of their relatives. Anxiety showed on their faces, and I suddenly felt guilty about keeping these people waiting for so long. But the ADC fell in beside me and ensured we continued at a brisk pace, down another steep wooden staircase and across Tashichodzong's spacious court-yard. It was deserted, the monk body having already left for their winter quarters in Punakha. The sentries saluted at the front gate, where Pema had been waiting patiently.

'Did it go well?' she asked, curious to find out what I had been discussing with her monarch.

'Very well,' I replied. But as we drove back into town, my thoughts turned inwards. He was a hard man to fathom, this King of Bhutan. On one level, he was extremely forthright, always ready to expound his views with a genuine passion rarely found among political leaders, no matter whether they be presidents, prime ministers, or kings. With Jigme, it was difficult to keep the conversation away from the 'big issues'.

On the other hand, he was wary of any intrusions into his family life. He spoke fondly of his children. But his marriage with the four queens, or the influence that this 'new royal family' exerts within Bhutan, were clearly not to be discussed. Perhaps this reluctance to allow any linkage between the very personal world of dynastic politics and his public role goes back to his childhood, when I had first known him. His parents were estranged then, and the struggle between his mother's family, the Dorjis, and other court factions had very nearly plunged the whole of Bhutan into crisis. I could understand why he seeks to avoid any repetition of this, and therefore why in the public arena he sticks to his role as 'The Boss' – or nowadays, Head of State.

Jigme repeatedly stressed that he was an unwilling monarch. But since he had no choice in the matter, he took the responsibilities of kingship very seriously. For him, it was 'the job', and he has applied to it an originality of thought I would never have suspected in the taciturn crown prince I had known. Obviously he had read very broadly, and was keen to introduce rather grand abstractions – the nature of democracy, for instance – into our discussions; for which reason he reminded me vaguely of the 'philosopher-kings' of eighteenth-century Europe.

He is proud not to have copied blueprints for development from the West or other countries, preferring to forge a system 'indigenous to Bhutan'. Because the country lagged so far behind, both he and his father were able to learn from the mistakes of others and set out on a different course. Two common goals of developing countries – democracy and rapid industrialization – have deliberately been avoided. Instead, these two progressive monarchs have in less than fifty years transformed an isolated and feudal society, in most respects unchanged since the seventeenth century, into something that is recognizably modern and yet completely different from any developing country I have seen.

For modern Bhutan remains a society of peasant farmers, onto which has been grafted a reasonably efficient welfare state. Thus far, the country's development has been funded mainly by electricity exports and huge infusions of foreign aid. It remains one of the world's poorest countries; and yet I saw few signs of real poverty or hardship during my travels. The only beggars are religious mendicants or pilgrims outside temples. It is a far cry from what you will find elsewhere in South Asia.

Rather than going for maximum economic growth, King Jigme has declared his goal to be increasing the country's 'Gross National Happiness' – a still imprecise formula which takes in other factors like the environment, social cohesion, and spiritual well-being. These, the king believes, contribute as much to the happiness of his people as material riches. It is a highly original standpoint for any government to take, though its roots may be found in the country's Buddhist traditions.

But now that he has withdrawn from the driving seat in government, what future do these ideas have? The Council of Ministers led by Jigme Thinley endorses much the same policies.

For the time being, there is continuity. The king still retains enormous influence, though his position needs to be defined. He is not, strictly speaking, a constitutional monarch since Bhutan has no written constitution. And while he has worked towards the 'democratization' of politics, the ban on political parties still stands and the country can in no way be described as a fully fledged democracy.

Jigme repeatedly told me that it was up to the Bhutanese people to decide their own future. Eventually, that will probably mean some form of democracy. The constitutional changes he has recently pushed through may be seen as a kind of safety valve which might allow a transition to a more democratic system of government without violent change or revolution. And by distancing the monarchy from this process of change, Jigme has probably gone a long way to ensuring its survival long into the twenty-first century.

I remembered a certain weariness about him when he admitted 'there is only so much that a king can do'. I also suspect that Jigme acted when he did in order to spare his son, the crown prince, from having to take on the same powers and responsibilities that he had shouldered for twenty-six years – and this in a climate that is increasingly dubious about hereditary monarchs exercising real power. Whatever his motives, the fact remains that it is highly unusual for an absolute ruler to bow out voluntarily rather than – as in the case of Nepal – being pushed.

So unusual, indeed, that many ordinary Bhutanese now think their king may be a 'hidden boddhisattva'. They point to the predictions of venerated lamas, to the astrological significance of his birth date, and declare that here was a child predestined to be a great Buddhist ruler. This has now been confirmed by his 'enormous self-sacrifice' in giving up so much of his power.

Religion and power have always been closely entwined in Bhutan, ever since the time of the Great Shabdrung. If King Jigme's experiment holds out, and he goes down in history as the last absolute monarch in the Himalayas, it may well be that he and his successors are venerated in much the same spirt as the Shabdrungs of former years. Through their mothers' lineage, his children are descendants of the last Shabdrung; so perhaps the wheel will turn full circle, and in future the Bhutanese monarchy will become more of a spiritual than a purely temporal force. It is a very Buddhist concept. And in Bhutan, which seems capable of defying conventional wisdom in so many respects, nothing would surprise me.

Epilogue

The Dalai Lama was still living in the Potala when I first set eyes upon the Himalayas. The Kingdom of Bhutan remained closed to outsiders, Nepal was only just beginning to emerge from its self-imposed isolation, and the Chogyal of Sikkim still ruled in his own land, confident of the support of India's prime minister Jawaharlal Nehru. Of the four Himalayan kingdoms my father pointed out, only two still exist – Nepal and Bhutan. A lot can change within a single lifetime.

What has not changed is the overpowering beauty of the Himalayas themselves. I must have fallen under their spell the first time I saw Kanchenjunga; and it was no less potent when I last saw that mountain from the gardens of the Himalayan Hotel in Kalimpong. But it is not just the high mountains that draw me back every year. The wildly plunging foothills with their terraced paddy fields cascading down to a river gorge; the pine-scented air in the cool depths of a forest; the unearthly clarity of light once you pass beyond the cloud belt and onto the high plateau. And then there are the people – valorous, hardy, ever-smiling despite the harshness of their lives – so different from the people of the plains.

I soon began to recognize how the topography of the Himalayan region – the steep foothills and malarial jungles to the south; the vast and inhospitable plateaux beyond – had for centuries kept the inhabitants of these highlands isolated from the outside world. And by journeying through the tangle of mountain spurs and valleys that divide the Himalayas' southern slopes, I could understand why the inhabitants of adjacent valleys had so little contact with each other and hung on to their own distinctive language and customs. I encountered Lobas and Lepchas, Tamangs and Thakalis, Bhotias, Brogpas, Sarchops and Sherpas. The diversity of Himalayan peoples is such that it could keep whole teams of ethnographers busy for decades.

Unfortunately there may not be much time left, for advances in education at the village level invariably corrode such localized languages and cultures. In Bhutan, the teaching of Dzongkha as the national language is a two-edged sword. In Nepal, the process whereby the ethnic minorities are drawn into 'the mainstream' is known as 'sanskritization'; in Sikkim, only Nepali is taught in state schools; in Tibet, instruction at higher levels is in the Chinese language and adheres to the state's ideology. And beyond this, the unstoppable inroads of modernity, the arrival of tourism and video movies and the Internet, all contribute to the erosion of minority cultures. For it will be those who come closest to the mainstream, who learn English or Hindi or Chinese as well as their national and local languages, who will prosper in this new world.

How these traditional societies fare in future depends largely on decisions taken by the central government concerned. In some cases, as in Tibet, the central government appears to be intent on destroying the distinct identity of

469

the Tibetan peoples. In Bhutan, the preservation of traditional Buddhist culture is seen as essential to the country's survival – and therefore to be defended at any cost. Now that Sikkim is part of the world's largest democracy, the indigenous Lepchas and Bhotias are reduced to a permanent minority in their own state and classed as 'tribals'. Nepal's multitude of ethnic minorities have survived through most of the twentieth century thanks to a policy of more or less benign neglect, though since the advent of democracy that too is changing.

Those who rule these minority peoples (even the six million Tibetans are a tiny minority within China) are, in a sense, their custodians. Ultimately, it is up to them whether these traditional cultures survive or not. And in the high country of the Himalayas and the Tibetan plateau, certain branches of human experience – the use of wild herbs and roots in traditional medicine, for instance, or the development of advanced meditation techniques – have survived as nowhere else. In future, these may be found to have benefits for humanity in general – if, that is, their survival is permitted.

For most of the twentieth century, the custodians of these traditions had been kings of one kind or another. Whether it was the theocratic variant of monarchy which prevailed in Tibet (and in Bhutan up to 1907), the Hindu concept of kingship which survives in Nepal but was current throughout the western Himalayas as far as Kashmir before the British left India, or the hereditary Buddhist kings of Sikkim and later Bhutan, some form of monarchy was considered to be the natural form of government. Even today, when these rulers no longer exercise absolute powers, they continue to embody a sense of national identity or, in the Dalai Lama's case, of national aspirations. The very nature of kingship means that it is a natural focus of traditional loyalties and values. Even the King of Mustang, whose territories have been a 'dependent state' of Nepal for centuries, continues to fulfil this role. For all these reasons, I chose to look at the way in which they have emerged from their isolation and sought to adapt to the modern world through the eyes of their kingly rulers.

The ruling monarchs that I spoke to may still be revered in ways that have been forgotten in the West, but they are also politicians. They have no choice. Even King Jigme of Bhutan, who confessed that he never really wanted to be a king and does not believe monarchy to be the best form of government, had no alternative apart from abdication. He simply had to get on with 'the job'. And, while I agree with him about monarchy in principle, I also believe that in some environments or at certain stages in a country's develop-ment, the rule of a benign king is preferable to the overhasty adoption of an already corrupted version of democracy.

King Jigme could talk freely on any issue because, although he has voluntarily stepped back from running Bhutan, he is not subject to the constraints of being a constitutional monarch. It is a very different situation with King Birendra of Nepal. He can no longer afford to be so outspoken, as I discovered when I was finally granted an audience in Narayanhitti Palace. For the past decade he has been a constitutional monarch and every one of his public words and actions is subject to careful scrutiny by elected politicians who would jump at the opportunity to declare that the king had acted unconstitutionally. So Birendra has

471

to be a skilled politician of a different sort, aware of all the nuances and sensitivities of the different political parties and interest groups in Nepal.

The popular image of the Dalai Lama belies the fact that, as head of the Tibetan refugee movement and the supreme embodiment of Tibet's separate identity, he must be a politician and ambassador as well as being a spiritual leader. He was remarkably frank – light-hearted even – about his own death and the crisis of succession that will inevitably follow. And for all his success in building support for the Tibetan cause around the world he has long realized that, at the end of the day, everything depends on China.

While talking with these Himalayan monarchs, I was very much aware that they had all exercised near absolute powers – if not now, then for a part of their lives. Decisions that they took have profoundly affected the way in which their peoples have tried to adapt to the modern world. But in another sense, their influence over events was extremely limited: for once these landlocked kingdoms came out of isolation they became subject to forces over which nobody, not even their rulers, could fully control.

Every one of these countries had changed beyond recognition during the second half of the twentieth century – some by their own volition, others through coercion by an alien power. They had previously survived as more or less independent states mainly because of the weakness or forbearance of their larger neighbours, China and India. All that changed when the Chinese invaded Tibet in 1950. The vast and empty Tibetan plateau, which since time immemorial had acted as a buffer zone between China and the Indian subcontinent, was no longer an effective cordon sanitaire. From then on, the ice-bound heights of the Himalayas became the front line between Asia's aspiring superpowers.

Given the absence of internationally recognized borders, it is hardly surprising they soon came to blows. In 1962, the Chinese army swept over the Himalayan passes and gave India's overconfident military establishment a brutal lesson, before retiring voluntarily behind the McMahon Line. This defeat only spurred India into strengthening its northern defences, both by pushing more military roads into the High Himalaya and by tightening its hold over the smaller independent kingdoms that remained. Sikkim was annexed in 1975; Nepal's monarchy humbled in 1990 following India's economic blockade. Only the Kingdom of Bhutan seems to have enjoyed the consistent support of its larger neighbour to the south.

As justification for their invasions, annexations and meddling in the internal affairs of independent states on either side of the Himalayan divide, both India and China have pointed to the necessity of abolishing feudalism and the old, monarchical system that it supported. Under the guise of improving the well-being of the people, of educating the masses to be 'politically aware' and, in the case of India, of extending to them a variant of Western democracy, they have destabilized traditional highland societies and opened the way for more rapid economic exploitation – usually with little regard for either the environmental consequences or whether such 'development' will actually benefit the local population. And while China's policy of swamping ethnic Tibetans through the 'population transfer' of millions of Han Chinese settlers has been widely criticized, India's 'dumping' of surplus population in Sikkim and other hill states is not so very different. Both stand accused of neo-colonialism.

But can one really defend a system of hereditary monarchy as it was practised in Nepal up to 1990 or in Bhutan to this day – a kind of personal rule in which political liberties and human rights taken for granted in the West have no intrinsic place? Not forever, certainly. But the alternative of full-fledged democracy implies the rapid politicization of highland peoples. This would undermine their traditional sense of community and separate identity, and make it easier for them to be integrated into 'the mainstream' of their larger neighbour. Anthropologists and ethnographers often argue that tribal peoples need to be protected. Might not the same criteria be applied to the more developed Himalayan societies whose customs and value-systems have survived thus far largely because they were protected by kingly rulers?

Neither hereditary monarchy nor the Tibetan practice of rule by reincarnations can find many champions among political theorists these days. They are 'relics from a feudal past' – or so we are told. And yet the people who accept such rule and even protest when changes are introduced, might not they have a better idea of what suits them at their particular stage of development than external commentators?

This raises the whole question of at what stage in a country's modernization external agencies should voice concerns over the absence of Western-style democracy and human rights. Here, the international community appears to be confused. It condemns the 'cultural genocide' and human rights abuses perpetrated by Communist China in Tibet and supports the Dalai Lama's campaign for some form of 'Free Tibet'. At the same time, the European Parliament, UNHCR, Amnesty International and others have condemned the royal Bhutanese government of human rights abuses and 'ethnic cleansing'. And yet, if the Dalai Lama and his supporters ever return to Tibet they would probably go about setting up a constitutional theocracy with a free market and socialist-style welfare programmes. Which is not so very different from what the Buddhist monarchy has achieved in Bhutan over the past fifty years.

Similarly, the reasoning behind Bhutan's expulsion of 'illegal' Nepali-speaking immigrants is much the same as Tibetans' objections to more Chinese settlers – the fear of being swamped by an alien majority and losing for ever the right to be a distinct and independent nation. Exiled Tibetans I talked to made it plain that if Tibet regains meaningful self-rule there will have to be a mass exodus of Han Chinese, and that this would be 'actively encouraged'. Does that lay them open to charges of planning 'ethnic cleansing'?

But all of that lies in a very uncertain future. For the present, the reality is that China and India share a long and highly militarized border along the Himalayan divide, large sections of which are still subject to dispute. Should tensions between the two Asian superpowers escalate into a re-run of the 1962 war, the temptation for the losing side to use limited or 'battlefield' nuclear weapons could become overwhelming. As one senior Indian officer on his way up to a 'think-tank' in Simla explained, 'There is scarcely any civilian population up there.' But if any such war broke out in the Himalayas it would cause an environmental and human catastrophe on such a scale that it is unlikely that either of the remaining 'buffer-states', Bhutan and Nepal, could maintain either their neutrality or their independence.

In an uncertain world, the future of the Himalayan kingdoms and those people who still look to their monarchs to protect their independence and cultural identity, is more uncertain than most. And yet there is an alternative which has been debated in international forums: the Dalai Lama's vision of a demilitarized 'zone of peace' made up of independent or autonomous nation states, Tibet amongst them.

Such a vision may be condemned as being either purely utopian or driven by pure self-interest. It has been derided as encouraging the 'balkanization' of the Himalayan region, creating a series of economically unviable landlocked states (curiously, very similar conditions have not prevented the former Soviet republics of Central Asia from remaining independent). What such a withdrawal from the Himalayan front line would do is restore the buffer zone which has well served the security interests of both regional superpowers for more than two millennia. The fact that India and China are both nuclear powers makes it all the more advisable not to have their armies facing each other on the Roof of the World. Both NATO and Russia have far larger nuclear arsenals, but since their ground forces have ceased conducting potentially threatening military exercises along the old 'Iron Curtain' the whole of Europe has breathed easier.

Regional security is one reason to think seriously about demilitarizing the Himalayas. Another is the well-being of the people who live there and the survival of so many fascinating cultures. The kings and god-kings whom I have interviewed all expressed concern over how the cultural identity of their people might be eroded in future. Each in his own way has done what he can. But in the final analysis, the future of the Himalayan peoples depends on whether India and China draw back from their experiments in neo-colonialism and try to find another way in which their security concerns and economic interests can be satisfied.

Otherwise, much of what is so remarkable about the Himalayan region will disappear over the next half-century. Its rare plants and forests and wildlife are under threat right now; its great diversity of languages and cultures already in decline. To throw away such riches for short-term gain would, I believe, be a disaster for all of humanity.

For these as well as strategic reasons, the power-brokers in Beijing and New Delhi should re-think their plans to exploit the region's natural resources. For them it might seem a distant concern, far down the political agenda. But as with so many 'last frontiers', it will soon be too late for the Himalayas.

GLOSSARY

arra – an alcoholic beverage distilled from barley, wheat or other grain

ahimsa – the principle of non-violence common to most Hindus, Buddhists and Jains, which can be extended to not harming any living creature. Mahatma Gandhi adapted this to non-violent political struggle against British rule.

ambans – powerful ambassadors or pro-consuls sent by the emperors of China to Tibet and other countries over which they claimed suzerainty

Apso – a long-haired Tibetan lapdog

Avalokiteshvara – the Bodhisattva of Compassion, commonly known in Tibet as Chenrezig, who is also the country's protector. The Dalai Lama is believed to be his reincarnation.

chang – a local beverage made from fermented barley, millet, rice or other grain, of roughly the same strength as beer

chashumi – court servants of the kings of Bhutan, chosen for their exceptional size and strength to act as bodyguards and hold their lord in his saddle when riding on steep tracks

chiru – Tibetan antelope

choekye – classical Tibetan, the name given outside Tibet to the language taught in monasteries

chorten – the Tibetan word for a stupa or solid stone or brick-built

479

shrine, usually with a rectangular base and rounded dome, within which are often placed holy relics and other religious treasures. Wayside chortens at the top of mountain passes may be simply a conical pile of stones, to which each traveller adds his own in the hope of a safe journey.

chuba – a heavy woollen outer robe, sometimes fur-lined or made of sheepskin, worn in areas of Tibetan culture

dzo – a domestic animal, the cross between a yak and a cow. Females are known as dri.

hemadatse – a fiery dish of cottage cheese laced with chillies which the Bhutanese eat with most meals, including breakfast

jagir – a temporary land grant awarded by Indian and Nepalese rulers, usually for military service

jaling – a Tibetan musical instrument similar to the trumpet or clarinet

jambi – Bhutanese legal advisers who may assist private individuals in court

jawan – an ordinary soldier, equivalent to private, in the Indian army

Je Khenpo – the Chief Abbot of Bhutan

kadda – a ceremonial white silk scarf normally offered by Tibetan Buddhists to a lama or other dignitary who may then return it with a blessing

kora – the clockwise route around a monastery or sacred place which Buddhists tread in order to gain merit

Karmapa – head of the Kagyu order of Buddhism, normally considered the third highest reincarnation in the Tibetan hierarchy

kukri – the double-curved knife made famous by the Gurkhas, but used throughout Nepal

momos – plump Tibetan ravioli, they are stuffed with meat or vegetables and can either be steamed or fried

Panchen Lama – the second highest reincarnation in Tibet after the Dalai Lama

puri – a small puffed-up Indian bread often eaten at breakfast

raja – an Indian king or ruler

rakshi – an alcoholic liquor made principally in Nepal by distilling rice, wheat or other grains

saddhus – Hindu ascetics or holy men

shastras – ancient Hindu scriptures

shikhar – hunting wild animals

sirdar – the guide or head of an expedition who is in charge of the porters and pack animals

stupa – the Sanskrit word for a solid monument used by Buddhists to house relics or religious treasures (*see* chorten)

suruwal – tight cotton trousers worn by men, part of Nepal's national dress

terton – discoverer of religious treasures

tika – a Hindu blessing which involves smearing the forehead with a coloured paste

topi – the traditional cap worn by Nepali men

tsampa – a roasted barley porridge that is the staple food of most Tibetans

tsechu – a Buddhist festival usually involving masked dances (known as tizi in Mustang)

zhi stones – semi-precious stones with geometric black and white bands that are highly esteemed by people of the Tibetan culture

BIBLIOGRAPHY

Other works consulted but not listed below include government records and publications, articles published separately in newspapers, magazines, scholarly journals or collections, or on an Internet website, as well as any material in languages other than English.

Himalayan region, India and China

Addy, Premen, *Tibet on the Imperial Chessboard* (New Delhi, 1960)

Ahmad, Zahiruddin, *China and Tibet 1708–1959* (London, 1960)

Baid, Rajendra, *Gorkhaland Agitation* (Siliguri, 1988)

Baral, Lok Raj, *Regional Migrations, Ethnicity and Security: The South Asian Case* (New Delhi, 1990)

Barnett, D.A., *China's Far West. Four Decades of Change* (Boulder, Colorado, 1994)

Beckwith, Christopher, *The Tibetan Empire in Central Asia. A History of the Struggle for Great Power among Tibetans, Turks, Arabs and Chinese during the Early Middle Ages* (Princeton, 1987)

Bishop, Peter, *The Myth of Shangri La: Tibet, Travel Writing and the Western Creation of the Sacred Landscape* (Berkeley, 1989)

Bradnock, Robert, *India's Foreign Policy since 1971* (London, 1990)

Byron, Robert, *First Russia then Tibet* (London, 1933)

Cammann, Schuyler, *Trade through the Himalayas: the early British attempts to open Tibet* (Princeton, 1951)

Cassinelli, C.W., & Ekvall, R.B., *A Tibetan Principality: the Political System of Sa-skya* (Ithaca, 1969)

Chaudhury, D.P., *The North-East Frontier of India, 1864–1914* (1978)

Chauhan, R.S., *Struggle and Change in South Asian Monarchies* (New Delhi, 1977)

Coelho, V.H., *Sikkim and Bhutan* (New Delhi, 1967)

Crosette, Barbara, *So Close to Heaven. The Vanishing Buddhist Kingdoms of the Himalayas* (New York, 1994)

Dalvi, J.P., *Himalayan Blunder* (Bombay, 1969)

Dreyer, June Teufel, *China's Forty Million. Minority Nationalities and National Integration in the People's Republic of China* (Harvard, 1976)

—, *China's Political System: Modernization and Tradition* (London, 1993)

Dutt, Subimal, *With Nehru in the Foreign Office* (Calcutta, 1977)

Fleming, Peter, *Bayonets to Lhasa* (London, 1961)

French, Patrick, *Younghusband* (London, 1994)

Fürer-Haimendorf, Christoph von, *Himalayan Traders* (London, 1975)

Ginsberg, George, & Mathos, Michael, *Communist China and Tibet: The First Dozen Years* (The Hague, 1964)

Gould, Sir Basil, *The Jewel in the Lotus: Recollections of an Indian Political* (London, 1957)

Goraon, Eugene, *Nepal, Sikkim and Bhutan* (New York, 1979)

Gupta, K., *The Hidden History of the Sino–Indian Frontier* (Calcutta, 1974)

Hopkirk, Peter, *Trespassers on the Roof of the World* (London, 1982)

Huc, Evariste–Régis, & Gabet, Joseph, *Travels in Tartary, Thibet and China, 1844–46* (London, 1851, 1987)

Jung Chang, *Wild Swans* (London, 1993)

Karan, Pradyuman P., & Jenkins Jr., William M., *The Himalayan Kingdoms: Bhutan, Sikkim and Nepal* (Princeton, 1963)

Kaulback, Ronald, *Tibetan Trek* (London, 1934)

Lall, J.S., & Moddie, A.D. (eds.), *The Himalaya: Aspects of Change* (Oxford, 1981)

Lamb, Alastair, *Britain and Chinese Central Asia: The Road to Lhasa 1767–1905* (London, 1960)

—, *The China–India Border: The Origins of the Disputed Boundaries* (Oxford, 1964)

—, *The McMahon Line: A Study in the Relations between India, China and Tibet* (London, 1966)

Ma Yin, *Questions and Answers about China's Minority Nationalities* (Beijing, 1985)

Malhortra, Inder, *Indira Gandhi: A Personal and Political Biography* (London, 1989)

Markham, Clements R., (ed.), *The Mission of George Bogle to Tibet and the Journey of Thomas Manning to Lhasa* (London, 1879, New Delhi, 1971)

Maxwell, Neville, *India's China War* (London, 1962)

Mehra, Parshotam, *The McMahon Line and After: A Study of the Triangular Contest on India's North-East Frontier between Britain, China and Tibet, 1904–47* (New Delhi, 1974)

—, *The North-Eastern Frontier. A Documentary Study of the Internecine Rivalry between India, Tibet and China, Vol. 1 1906–14, Vol. 2 1914–51* (Bombay, 1980)

Morris, John, *Living with Lepchas* (London, 1938)

Mullik, B.N., *My Years with Nehru: the Chinese Betrayal* (Bombay, 1971)

Palit, D.K., *War in the High Himalaya: The Indian Army in Crisis, 1962* (New Delhi, 1991)

Patel, H.M., *The Defence of India* (Bombay, 1963)

Petech, Luciano, *China and Tibet in the Early Eighteenth Century* (Leiden, 1950, 1971)

Pinn, Fred, *The Road of Destiny. Darjeeling Letters 1839* (Oxford, 1986)

Rahul, Ram, *The Himalayan Borderland* (New Delhi, 1969)

Ray, N.R. (ed.), *Himalaya Frontier in Historical Perspective* (Calcutta, 1986)

Ronaldshay (the Earl of), L.J.L.D., *Lands of the Thunderbolt: Sikkim, Chumbi and Bhutan* (London, 1923)

Rustomji, Nari K., *Enchanted Frontiers: Sikkim, Bhutan and India's North-Eastern Borderlands* (Bombay, 1971)

Seth, Vikram, *From Heaven Lake* (London, 1983)

Shakabpa, W.D., *Tibet: A Political History* (New Haven, 1967)

Short, Philip, *Mao: A Life* (London, 1999)

Singh, Amar Kaur Jasbir, *Himalayan Triangle: A Historical Survey of British India's Relations with Tibet, Sikkim and Bhutan, 1765–1950* (London, 1988)

Snellgrove, David L., *Himalayan Pilgrimage* (Oxford, 1961)

Subba, Tanka B., *Ethnicity, State and Development: A Case Study of the Gorkhaland Movement in Darjeeling* (New Delhi, 1992)

Tamsang, K.P., *The Unknown and Untold Reality about the Lepchas* (Kalimpong, 1983)

Temple, Sir Richard, *Journals Kept in Hyderabad, Kashmir, Sikkim and Nepal* (London, 1887)

Tibet and Peace in South Asia: Proceedings of an International Conference held in New Delhi, India, 12–14 August 1989 (New Delhi, 1991)

Turner, Capt. Samuel, *An Account of an Embassy to the Court of the Teshoo Lama in Tibet: Containing a Narrative of a Journey through Bootan and Part of Tibet* (London, 1800, New Delhi, 1971)

Wessels, Cornelius, *Early Jesuit Travellers in Central Asia 1603–1721* (The Hague, 1924)

White, John Claude, *Sikkim and Bhutan: Twenty-One Years on the North-East Frontier* (London, 1909)

Williamson, Margaret D., *Memoirs of a Political Officer's Wife in Tibet, Sikkim and Bhutan* (London, 1987)

Woodman, Dorothy, *Himalayan Frontiers* (London, 1969)

Younghusband, Sir Francis, *India and Tibet* (London, 1910)

— et al., *The British Invasion of Tibet* (London, 2000)

Bhutan

Aris, Michael, *Bhutan: The Early History of a Himalayan Kingdom* (Warminster & New Delhi, 1979)

—, *Views of Medieval Bhutan: The Diary and Drawings of Samuel Davis, 1783* (London & Washington D.C., 1982)

—, *The Raven Crown: The Origins of Buddhist Monarchy in Bhutan* (London, 1994)

—, & Michael Hutt (eds.), *Bhutan: Aspects of Culture and Development* (1994)

Collister, Peter, *Bhutan and the British* (London, 1987)

Das, Nirmala, *The Dragon Country: The General History of Bhutan* (Bombay, 1974)

Deb, Arabinda, *Bhutan and India: A Study in Frontier Political Relations* (Calcutta, 1976)

Dhakal, D.N.S., & Strawn, Christopher, *Bhutan: A Movement in Exile* (Jaipur, 1994)

Gupta, Shantiswarup, *British Relations with Bhutan* (Jaipur, 1974)

Hickman, Katie, *Dreams of the Peaceful Dragon: A Journey into Bhutan* (London, 1987)

Hutt, Michael (ed.), *Bhutan: Perspectives on Conflict and Dissent* (Gartmore, 1994)

Karan, Pradyuman P., *Bhutan: A Physical and Cultural Geography* (Lexington, 1967)

—, *Bhutan: Environment, Culture and Development Strategy* (1990)

Kohli, Manorama, *India and Bhutan: A Study in Interrelations, 1772–1910* (New Delhi, 1982)

—, *From Dependency to Independence: A Study of Indo–Bhutan Relations* (New Delhi, 1993)

Labh, Kapileshwar, *India and Bhutan* (New Delhi, 1974)

Majumdar, A.B., *Britain and the Himalayan Kingdom of Bhotan* (Patna, 1984)

Mehra, G.N., *Bhutan: Land of the Peaceful Dragon* (New Delhi, 1974)

Office of Tibet, New York, *Report on the Tibetan Refugee Problem in Bhutan* (MS., 1979)

Olschak, Blanche C., *Bhutan: Land of Hidden Treasures* (London, 1971)

—, *Ancient Bhutan: A Study of Early Buddhism in the Himalayas* (Zurich, 1979)

Parmanand, *The Politics of Bhutan. Retrospect and Prospect* (New Delhi, 1992)

Peissel, Michel, *Lords and Lamas: A Solitary Expedition across the Secret Himalayan Kingdom of Bhutan* (London, 1970)

Political Missions to Bootan, comprising the reports of the Hon'ble Ashley Eden, 1864; Capt. R.H. Pemberton, 1837, 1838, with Dr W. Griffith's journal [1837–8]; and the account of Baboo Kishen Kant Bose [1815] (Calcutta, 1865, New Delhi, 1972)

Pommaret, Françoise, *Bhutan* (Hong Kong, 1990)

Rahul, Ram, *Modern Bhutan* (New Delhi, 1971)

—, *Royal Bhutan* (New Delhi, 1983, 1997)

Ramakant & Misra, R.C. (eds.), *Bhutan: Society and Polity* (New Delhi, 1996)

Rennie, David Field, *Bhotan and the Story of the Dooar War* (London, 1866, New Delhi, 1970)

Rose, Leo, *The Politics of Bhutan* (Ithaca, 1977)

Rustomji, Nari, *Bhutan: The Dragon Kingdom in Crisis* (New Delhi, 1978)

Shicklgruber, Christian, & Pommaret, Françoise (eds.), *Bhutan – Mountain Fortress of the Gods* (London, 1997)

Singh, Nagendra, *Bhutan, A Kingdom in the Himalayas* (New Delhi, 1972)

Sinha, Awadesh Coomar, *Bhutan: Ethnic Identity and National Dilemma* (New Delhi, 1991)

Tshewang, Padma, et al., *The Treasure Revealer of Bhutan. Pemalingpa, the Terma Tradition and its Critics* (Kathmandu, 1995)

Ura, Karma, *The Hero with a Thousand Eyes – A Historical Novel* (Thimphu, 1995)

Wangchuck, Her Majesty the Queen Ashi Dorji Wangmo, *Of Rainbows and Clouds* (London, 1999)

Zeppa, Jamie, *Beyond the Sky and the Earth: A Journey into Bhutan* (London, 1999)

Mustang

Adhikary, Surya Mani, *The Khasa Kingdom: A Trans-Himalayan Empire of the Middle Age* (New Delhi, 1988)

Jackson, David P., *The Mollas of Mustang: Historical, Religious and Oratorical Traditions of the Nepalese–Tibetan Borderland* (Dharamsala, 1984)

Peissel, Michel, *Mustang – A Lost Tibetan Kingdom* (London, 1968)

Thapa, Manjushree, *Mustang Bhot in Fragments* (Kathamndu, 1992)

Tucci, Giuseppe, *Journey to Mustang, 1952* (Rome, 1953, Kathmandu, 1982)

Vinding, Michael, *The Thakali: A Himalayan Ethnology* (London, 1998)

Nepal

Adhikari, K.K., *Nepal under Jang Bahadur* (Kathmandu, 1984)

Bajracharya, B.R., Sharma, S.R., & Bakhshi, S.R. (eds.), *Foreign Policy of Nepal* (New Delhi, 1993)

Bajarcharya, Manik Lal, *Birendra – The King with a Difference* (Kathmandu, 1974)

Bhattarai, Madan Kumar, *Diplomatic History of Nepal, 1901–1929* (Kathmandu, 1990)

Bista, Dor Bahadur, *People of Nepal* (Calcutta, 1967, Kathmandu, 1980)

—, *Fatalism and Development: Nepal's Struggle for Modernization* (Calcutta, 1991)

Blake, P.J., Cameron & Seldon, D., *Nepal in Crisis* (New Delhi, 1980)

Brown, T. Louise, *The Challenge to Democracy in Nepal. A Political History* (London, 1996)

Cavenagh, Sir Orfeur, *Rough Notes on the State of Nepal, its Government, Army and Resources* (Calcutta, 1851, 1974)

Chauhan, R.S., *The Political Development in Nepal 1950–70* (New Delhi, 1971)

Gaige, Frederick H., *Regionalism and National Unity in Nepal* (Berkeley, 1975)

Gould, Tony, *Imperial Warriors: Britain and the Gurkhas* (London, 1999)

Hamilton, Francis Buchanan, *An Account of the Kingdom of Nepal and of the territories annexed to this Dominion by the House of Gorkha* (Edinburgh, 1819, New Delhi, 1971)

Hasrat, B.J., *History of Nepal, as Told by its Own and Contemporary Chroniclers* (Hoshiarpur, 1970)

Husain, Asad, *British India's Relations with the Kingdom of Nepal 1857–1947. A Diplomatic History of Nepal* (London, 1970)

Hutt, Michael, *Nepali: a National Language and its Literature* (New Delhi, 1988)

—, (ed.), *Nepal in the Nineties. Versions of the past, visions of the future* (New Delhi, 1994)

Jha, Shree Krishna, *Uneasy Partners: India and Nepal in the Post-Colonial Era* (New Delhi, 1975)

Khanal, Y., *Nepal: Transition from Isolation* (Kathmandu, 1977)

Kirkpatrick, Col. W., *An Account of the Kingdom of Nepaul, being the Substance of Observations Made during a Mission to the Country in the Year 1793* (London, 1811, New Delhi, 1975)

Kreijger, Hugo, *Kathmandu Valley Painting* (London, 1999)

Krishnamurti, Y.G., *His Majesty King Mahendra Bir Bikram Shaha Deva: An Analytical Biography* (n.d.)

Landon, Percival, *Nepal* (London, 1928)

Manandhar, Tri Ratna, *Some Aspects of Rana Rule in Nepal* (Kathmandu, 1983)

Matthiessen, Peter, *The Snow Leopard* (London, 1979)

Oldfield, Henry Ambrose, *Sketches of Nipal, historical & descriptive, with anecdotes of Court Life in the time of Maharaja Jang Bahadur* (London, 1880)

Oliphant, Sir Laurence, *A Journey to Kathmandu with the Camp of Jang Bahadur* (New York, 1852)

Pemble, John, *The Invasion of Nepal: Johan Company at War* (Oxford, 1971)

Petech, Luciano, *Mediaeval History of Nepal* (Rome, 1958, 1984)

Pradhan, Bishwar, *Nepal: A Peace Zone* (Kathmandu, 1982)

Pradhan, Kumar, *The Gorkha Conquests* (Calcutta, 1991)

Raeper, William, & Hoftun, Martin, *Spring Awakening: An account of the 1990 Revolution in Nepal* (New Delhi, 1992)

Raj, Prakash A., *Queens of the Shah Dynasty in Nepal* (Kathmandu, 1997)

Regmi, Dilli Raman, *A Century of Family Autocracy in Nepal* (Banaras, 1958)

—, *Ancient Nepal* (Calcutta, 1960)

—, *Medieval Nepal, 4 vols.* (Calcutta, 1965–66)

—, *Inscriptions of Ancient Nepal, 3 vols.* (New Delhi, 1983)

Regmi, J.C., & Shivakoti, S., *Historical and Biographical Dictionary of the Royal Shah Family* (Kathmandu, 1981)

Regmi, Mahesh Chandra, *Thatched Huts and Stucco Palaces: Peasants and Landlords in 19th Century Nepal* (New Delhi, 1978)

Rose, Leo E., *Nepal: Strategy for Survival* (Berkeley & New Delhi, 1973)

—, & Scholz, John T., *Nepal: Profile of a Himalayan Kingdom* (Boulder, Colorado & New Delhi, 1980)

Sever, Adrian, *Nepal Under the Ranas* (New Delhi, 1993)

BIBLIOGRAPHY

Shaha, Rishikesh, *Modern Nepal: A Political History 1769–1955* (New Delhi, 1990)
—, *Nepali Politics: Retrospect and Prospect* (New Delhi, 1975)
—, *Three Decades and Two Kings. Eclipse of Nepal's Partyless Monarchic Rule* (New Delhi, 1990)
—, *Ancient and Medieval Nepal* (Kathmandu, 1997)
Shrestha, Kusum, *Monarchy in Nepal. The Tribuvhan Era* (Bombay, 1984)
Stiller, Ludwig F., *The Rise of the House of Gorkha* (New Delhi, 1975)
—, *The Silent Cry: The People of Nepal from 1816 to 1839* (Kathmandu, 1976)
—, *Letters from Kathmandu: The Kot Massacre* (Kathmandu, 1981)
Tucci, Giuseppe, *The Discovery of the Mallas* (London, 1962)
Tuker, Sir Francis, *Gorkha: The Story of the Gurkhas of Nepal* (London, 1957)
Vansittart, Capt. Eden, *Notes on the Goorkhas, being a short Account of the Country, History, Characteristics, Clans, etc.* (Calcutta, 1890, New Delhi, 1980)
Whelpton, John, *Jang Bahadur in Europe: the First Nepalese Mission to the West* (Kathmandu, 1983)
—, *Kings, Soldiers and Priests: Nepalese Politics and the Rise of Jang Bahadur Rana, 1830–1857* (New Delhi, 1991)
Wiesner, Ulrich, *Nepalese Temple Architecture* (Leiden, 1978)
Wright, Daniel, *Sketch of the Portion of the Country of Nepal Open to Europeans* (Calcutta, 1877, Kathmandu, 1983)

Sikkim

Basnet, L.B., *Sikkim, a Short Political History* (New Delhi, 1974)
Bhattacharya, B., *Sikkim: The Land and the People* (New Delhi, 1998)
Chopra, P.N., *Sikkim* (New Delhi, 1979)
Das, B.S., *The Sikkim Saga* (New Delhi, 1983)
Datta-Ray, Sunanda K., *Smash and Grab: Annexation of Sikkim* (New Delhi, 1984)
Foring, A.R., *Lepcha – My Vanishing Tribe* (n.d.)

490

Grover, B.S.K., *Sikkim and India: Storm and Consolidation* (New Delhi, 1974)

Jha, Pranab Kumar, *History of Sikkim (1817–1904): Analysis of British Policy and Activities* (Calcutta, 1985)

Kazi, Jigme N., *Inside Sikkim: Against the Tide* (Gangtok, 1993)

Kotturan, George, *The Himalayan Gateway: History and Culture of Sikkim* (1983)

Macdonald, David, *Touring in Sikkim and Tibet* (Kalimpong, 1930, 1943)

Namgyal, Chogyal Thutob & Dolma, T., *History of Sikkim Om Swashti* (MS, 1908)

Parkhurst, C.A., *Sikkim* (London, 1946)

Rao, P. Raghunadha, *Sikkim, The Story of its Integration with India* (New Delhi, 1978)

Risley, H. H., *Gazeteer of Sikkim* (Calcutta, 1894)

Rustomji, Nari, *Sikkim: A Himalayan Tragedy* (New Delhi, 1987)

Sengupta, Nirmalanda, *State Government and Politics of Sikkim* (New Delhi, 1985)

Sinha, A.C., *Politics of Sikkim: A Sociological Study* (Faridabad, 1975)

Tibet

Andrug, Gonpo Tashi, *Four Rivers, Six Ranges – Reminiscences of the Resistance Movement in Tibet* (Dharamsala, 1973)

Aris, Michael, & Kyi, Aung San Suu (eds.), *Tibetan Studies in Honour of Hugh Richardson. Proceedings of the International Seminar of Tibetan Studies, 1979* (London, 1980)

Avedon, John F., *In Exile from the Land of Snows* (New York, 1984)

Barber, Noel, *From the Land of Lost Content. The Dalai Lama's Fight for Tibet* (London, 1969)

Barnett, Robert (ed.), *Resistance and Reform in Tibet* (London, 1994)

Bass, Catriona, *Inside the Treasure House* (London, 1990)

Bell, Sir Charles, *Tibet Past and Present* (Oxford, 1924)

—, *The People of Tibet* (Oxford, 1928)

—, *The Religion of Tibet* (Oxford, 1931)

—, *Portrait of the Dalai Lama* (London, 1946)

Bower, Hamilton, *Diary of a Journey across Tibet* (London 1894, Kathmandu, 1976)

Craig, Mary, *Kundun. A Biography of the Family of the Dalai Lama* (London, 1997)

Dalai Lama, *My Land and My People* (New York, 1962)

—, *The Collected Statements, Interviews and Articles* (Dharamsala, 1982)

—, *Freedom in Exile: The Autobiography of the Dalai Lama* (London, 1990)

—, *Speeches, Statements, Articles and Interviews, 1987–95* (Dharamsala, 1995)

—, *Ancient Wisdom, Modern World. Ethics for a New Millennium* (London, 1999)

—, *Dharamsala and Beijing: Initiatives and Correspondence 1981–1993* (Dharamsala, 1996)

Epstein, Israel, *Tibet Transformed* (Beijing, 1983)

Feigon, Lee, *Demystifying Tibet* (London, 1999)

Ford, Robert, *Captured in Tibet* (London, 1957)

Fürer-Haimendorf, Christoph von, *The Renaissance of Tibetan Civilization* (Oxford, 1989)

Goldstein, Melvyn C., *A History of Modern Tibet, 1913–1951 – The Demise of the Lamaist State* (Berkeley, 1989, New Delhi, 1993)

Goodman, Michael Harris, *The Last Dalai Lama – A Biography* (London, 1986)

Grunfeld, Tom, *The Making of Modern Tibet* (London & New York, 1987)

Gyatso, Palden, & Shakya, Tsering, *Fire Under the Snow* (London, 1997)

Harrer, Heinrich, *Seven Years in Tibet* (London, 1953)

Hi Chang-hao & Kao Yuan-mei, *Tibet Leaps Forward* (Beijing, 1977)

Hilton, Isobel, *The Search for the Panchen Lama* (London, 1999)

Karan, Pradyuman P., *The Changing Face of Tibet. The Impact of Chinese Communist Ideology on the Landscape* (University of Kentucky, 1976)

Lazar, Edward (ed.), *Tibet: The Issue is Independence* (New Delhi, 1994)

Li Tieh-Tseng, *The Historical Status of Tibet* (New York, 1956)

—, *Tibet: Today and Yesterday* (New York, 1960)

McKay, Alexander, *Tibet and the British Raj: The Frontier Cadre, 1904–47* (London, 1997)

Maraini, Fosco, *Secret Tibet* (London, 1952)

Michael, Franz, *Rule by Incarnation: Tibetan Buddhism and its Role in Society and State* (Boulder, Colorado, 1982)

Norbu, Dawa, *Red Star Over Tibet* (London, 1974)

—, *Culture and the Politics of Third World Nationalism* (London, 1992)

—, *Tibet: The Road Ahead* (London, 1997)

Norbu, Jamyang, *Horsemen in the Snow. The Story of Aten and the Khampas' Fight for the Freedom of their Country* (Dharamsala, 1979, London, 1987)

—, *Illusion and Reality: Essays on the Tibetan and Chinese Political Scene from 1978 to 1989* (New Delhi, 1989)

Office of H.H. the Dalai Lama, *Tibetans in Exile 1959–1969. A Report on Ten Years of Rehabilitation* (Dharamsala, 1969)

Pachen, Ani, & Donnelley, Adelaide, *Sorrow Mountain – The Journey of a Tibetan Warrior Nun* (London, 2000)

Palakshappa, T.C., *Tibetans in India. A Case Study of Mundgod Tibetans* (New Delhi, 1976)

Peissel, Michel, *Cavaliers of Kham. The Secret War in Tibet* (London, 1972)

Pema, Jetsun, *Tibet, My Story* (Shaftesbury, 1997)

Petech, Luciano, *Aristocracy and Government in Tibet, 1728–1959* (Rome, 1973)

Qi Yan, *Tibet – Four Decades of Tremendous Change* (Beijing, 1991)

Richardson, Hugh, *Tibet and its History* (Boulder, Colorado, 1984)

— (ed.), *Adventures of a Tibetan Fighting Monk* (Bangkok, 1986)

Samten, Kunga, & Dewatshang, Dorjee Wangdi, *Flight at the Cuckoo's Bequest – The Life and Times of a Tibetan Freedom Fighter* (New Delhi, 1997)

Shakabpa, W.D., *Tibet: A Political History* (New Delhi, 1967, 1986)

Shakya, Tsering, *The Dragon in the Land of Snows* (London, 1999)

Smith Jr., Warren W., *Tibetan Nation. A History of Tibetan Nationalism and Sino-Tibetan Relations* (Boulder, Colorado, 1996)

Snellgrove, David & Richardson, Hugh, *A Cultural History of Tibet* (London, 1968)

Stein, R.A., *Tibetan Civilization* (London, 1972)

Taring, Rinchen Dolma, *Daughter of Tibet* (London, 1970)

Trungpa, Chögyam & Roberts, Esmé Cramer, *Born in Tibet* (London, 1966, 1987)

Tsering, Diki, *Dalai Lama, My Son. A Mother's Story* (London, 2000)

Walt van Praag, Michael C. van, *The Status of Tibet: History, Rights, and Prospects in International Law* (Boulder, Colorado, 1987)

Wang Furen & Suo Wenqing, *Highlights of Tibetan History* (Beijing, 1984)

INDEX

ACAP (Annapurna Conservation Area Project), 244, 249, 265

Aishwarya Rajya Laxmi, Queen of Nepal, 254, 288, 312, 315, 316

Alien's Travel Permits (ATPs), 58–9

ambans (imperial Chinese ambassadors), 66

Amchok Rinpoche, 92–4

Ame Pal, King of Mustang, 207, 229

American Himalayan Foundation, 249, 270

Amnesty International, 411, 450, 456, 457, 475

Anglo-Bhutan War (1864–66), 395–6, 412

Anglo-Nepalese War (1814–16), 331

animism: and Lepcha people, 331; Mongoloid peoples, 42; in Mustang, 213, 228

Annapurna Massif, 170, 205, 206

'April Incident,' in Dharamsala, 85

archery, 19–21, 444–5

Arunachal Pradesh, 43, 87, 427

Astrologer Royal, Nepal, 197–200

Bagmati River, Nepal, 158, 197

Bahadur, Brigadier Chapda, 11

Bahadur, Jang, 184–6, 185, 189

Bahadur Shah, King of Nepal, 183

Baisi principalities, Nepal, 164

Barkhor (old Tibetan quarter in Lhasa), 64–5

Basniats (Gorkha family), 183

Beijing, China, 105, 129, 136, 477

Bengal Duars, 414

Bhadgaon (modern name: Bhaktapur), Nepal, 164, 165, 166, 291

Bhaktapur, *see* Bhadgaon

Bhandari, Gagan Singh, 184–5

Bhattarai, K.P. (Prime Minister of Nepal), 301

Bhote Khosi River, Nepal, 170

Bhotia people, 323, 324, 330, 331, 332, 334, 348, 349, 350, 470

Bhrikuti, Princess of Nepal, 109, 173

Bhutan, 5, 14–46: and Britain, 412–13; civil war in, 394–5; controlled tourism in, 16, 457; and conversion to Buddhism, 41–5; and Dalai Lama, 32–3; death of Sixth Shabdrung, 35–8; disturbances in South, 440–1; 447–50; early Tibetan settlers in, 42–5; education in, 441–3;

Bhutan (*cont.*)
end of absolutism in, 409–10, 453–5; exiled 'Shabdrung', 39–40; farming in, 385–8; fertility blessings in, 425; Great Shabdrung, 24–5, 26, 29–30, 33, 35, 404, 466–7; hydroelectricity project in, 373–4; 'illegal immigrants' in, 364, 371–3, 430–1; and India, 400, 407, 462; king's birthday celebrations in, 419–21, 423; languages in, 420–3, 430, 442; law courts in, 384–5; 'massacre' in Chengmari, 448; modernization of, 362–3, 367, 400–1, 464–5; national sport of archery, 19–21, 444–5; and Nepal, 431; and Nepalis, 449–50; political reform in, 370–1, 424, 465–6; preservation of cultural identity in, 374–5, 470; Punakha Dzong, 27–9, 30; and refugee problem, 372–3, 411, 432, 449–51, 458–61; regency, 34–5; resettlement in, 432–3; royal family of, 7–14, 35, 36–8, 42, 45, 376, 378, 382, 392–7, 399–400, 402, 409–10; and Sikkim, 331; Simtokha Dzong, 24–6; state religion in, 25, 28, 30–1, 33, 423; and Tibet, 30–2; traditional capitals of, 27; treasure discoverers in, 376–8, 388–9; vegetation in, 367–8, 378, 427, 428
Biharis, 347
Birendra Bikram Shah Dev, king of Nepal, 178, 179, 243, 254, 280: audience with, 295–313; 'demonization of', 314–17; incarnation of Vishnu, 159–60; media coverage of, 306; and

multi-party democracy, 288–92, 471–2
Bista, Kirthinidi (Prime Minister), 286–7, 289
'Black Cat' division, 355, 357
Black Mountains, Bhutan, 376, 378, 406, 422
Blair, Tony (Prime Minister), 126
Bodh Gaya (Bihar, India), 207
Bogle, George, 7
'Bollywood' films, 374, 388
Bon religion, 102
Boudhanath, stupa (burial mound) at, 172, 208
Brahmins, 175, 192, 193, 194, 211–12, 243
Britain: and Bhutan, 395–6, 412–13; and Nepal, 166, 177, 181–2, 189; and Sikkim, 331–2
Brogpa nomads, 246, 435–7, 438
Buddhism, 2: in Bhutan, 41–5; Chagzampa, 436; Drukpa sect, 25, 28, 30–1, 33, 423; Gelugpa sect, 30, 33, 44, 58, 89, 143, 330; globalization of, 143; Kagyupa sect, 44, 70, 74, 141–3; in Mustang, 213, 228, 262–3; and Nepal, 173, 311; Nyingmapa sect, 44, 45, 91, 330, 334, 435; and Padmasambhava, 22, 40–1, 74, 226, 238, 242, 335, 377, 382, 389, 443; and Pemalingpa, 376, 377–8, 388–90, 391, 394; and positive action, 152; Sakya sect, 44, 121, 173, 225, 264; in Tibet, 68–75, 91–2; and treasure discoverers (tertons), 376–8, 388–9
Bumthang region, Bhutan, 380–90, 419: dialect in, 422
Bunakha, in Bhutan, 418

Calcutta, 7–8
Camp Hale, Colorado, 97
caste system: and Malla dynasty, 228; Sudra, 158, 195; warriors, 163, 167
Catholic Church, 136–7
Ceauçescu, Nicolae, 290
Central Reserve Police (CRP), 337–8
Changchub Gyaltsen, King of Tibet, 228
Chang Tang desert, Tibet, 75–7
chang (Tibetan-style beer), 216, 218, 327, 426
Changu Lake, Sikkim, 356, 357, 358
Charles, Prince of Wales, 452, 456
chashumi (tall personal attendants), 399
Chaubisi rajas, 168
Chechnya, 149
Chele village, Mustang, 277
Chendebji Chorten, Bhutan, 406–7
Chengmari, Bhutan, 448–9
Chenrezig (Tibetan deity), 125
Chhetris, 165
China, 32: border crossing with Nepal, 53–4; Communism, 145, 308–9; and Dalai Lama, 116, 131, 133–7; human rights in, 103–4, 116, 144, 153, 154; and India, 99, 360, 473, 475–7; and Khampa guerillas, 98–9, 129–30, 148, 256; negotiations with Gyalo Thondup, 100–1, 113; and the Panchen Lama, 38–9, 59–60, 121, 131, 134; and Sakya Lamas, 57–8; and Sikkim, 337; and Tibet, 31, 47, 67–8, 103–6, 113–16, 128–31, 153–4, 400, 472–3
China Youth Travel Service (CTYS), 55–8

chiru (Tibetan antelope), 76
Choekhar valley, Bhutan, 419
Chogyals of Sikkim, 330, 353: Palden Thondup Namgyal (twelfth), 208, 320–5, 322, 336–42, 342–3, 353–4; Phuntsog Namgyal (first), 329–30; Tashi Namgyal, Sir, (eleventh), 353; Thobden, 332; Wangchuck (thirteenth), 328, 344
Chomolhari, 40
Chophel, Thubten, 274–5
Chumbi Valley, 330
Chumey Valley, Bhutan, 425
Chuzom, Bhutan, 418
CIA (Central Intelligence Agency), 97–8, 99, 129, 148, 204, 256, 325
Clinton, Bill (US President), 105, 150
Coburn, Broughton, 270
Communism: in China, 145, 308–9; in Nepal, 303, 309
Cooke, Hope, see Hope, Queen of Sikkim
coronation ceremonies, Nepalese, 194–6, 200
corruption, 118, 370: in Nepal, 303–4, 312; in Sikkim, 346, 355
cronyism, 301, 348
cultural identity, preservation of, 469–70, 477: in Bhutan, 16, 311, 374–5, 420–3, 449; of Brogpa nomads, 438; in Mustang, 263–5; in Nepal, 311–12; in Sikkim, 335; in Tibet, 89–90, 92–4, 110, 111, 112
Cultural Revolution, 68, 70, 92, 110, 113, 114: destruction of Tibetan monasteries, 204

INDEX

Dalai Lama, fifth, Ngawang Lozang
Gyamtsho, 26, 29, 30, 65–6
Dalai Lama, first, 208
Dalai Lama, fourteenth, Tenzin
Gyamtsho, 4, 31–2, 47–8, 67,
68, 468, 472: after his death,
121, 133–8; author's audience
with, 109–23; and China,
112–16; on democracy, 117–18;
and democratization process,
101–2; dual role of, 116–17;
family of, 94–8, 100–3, 122–3;
foundation of monasteries by,
91–2; and Gandhi, 130–2;
Hollywood version of early life,
139–40; internationalizing
strategy of, 103–4, 115; and
Losar Festival, 89–90; and
Nobel Peace Prize, 103; pacifism
of, 113, 122, 124, 128–30, 145,
150; 'presence' and character of,
124–6; and preservation of
Tibetan culture, 89–90, 92–4,
110, 111, 112; and recognition
of other lamas, 141–3; reliance
on 'volunteers', 127–8, 151;
Sikkim cine film of, 328–9; on
socialism, 118–19, 126–7;
Tibetan Youth Congress on,
146–8, 150–1; on Zone of
Peace, 119–20, 476
Dalai Lama, thirteenth, 66–7
Dalai Lamas, 330
Dametsi Monastery, East Bhutan,
435–6
Darjeeling, India, 1, 2, 3, 181–2,
330
Das, B. S., 399
Dasain, Festival of, 187
Dechenchoeling Palace, Bhutan,
451
deforestation, 477: in Bhutan, 417;
in Nepal, 317

Dehra Dun, India, 58, 264
'Delhi Karmapa', 142
democracy, 101–2, 369–70, 473,
474
Dendup, Gaylong Pema, 405
Deneka, Heiko, 386
Deng Xiaoping, 68, 100
Denmark, 104: Crown Prince of,
243
Denzong, the Valley of Rice, see
Sikkim
Dhakal, Ganga Sakar (Liaison
Officer), 211–12, 222–3, 243,
268, 277
Dharamsala, India, 78–82: crimes
in, 85–6; evenings in, 139;
influence of different cultures
on, 83–4; Library and Archives
of Tibetan Works, 92, 93–4
Dhauladhar Range, India, 104–5
Dhaulagiri, Nepal, 205, 206, 237
Dhumri Monastery, Sikkim, 333
Dibya Upadesh, 165, 168
Dilli Bazaar, Kathmandu, 192
Dipendra, Crown Prince, 313
Dochu-La pass, 24, 27, 419
Dolpo region, Nepal, 227, 228
Domkhar Tashichoeling palace,
Bhutan, 397–403
Dorje, Thaye, 142
Dorji Wangmo Wangchuck, Ashi,
Queen of Bhutan, 36, 37
Dorji, Dasho Pem, dzongda of
Bumthang (later of
Wangdiphodrang), 380–90,
424, 447
Dorji, Jigme Palden (Bhutan's
Prime Minister), 11
Dorji, Tashi (Queen's sister), 12, 13
Dorji, Ugyen (Bhutan Agent), 413
Dorji, Yab Ugyen (Queens' father),
37

498

Dorji , Lhendup (Acting Prime Minister), 11, 12
Dr Graham's Homes, Kalimpong, 389
Drapchi Prison, Tibet, 145
Drepung Monastery, India, 87
Drepung Monastery, Tibet, 66
Drigung Festival, 68–75
Druk Desi, 34
Druk National Congress, 39
Druk-Yul Democratic Party, 39
Drukpa church, in Bhutan, 25, 28, 30–1, 33, 44, 423
Duksom, Bhutan, 444
Dukta, Likche ('Leonardo'), 212, 214, 218, 223–4, 237
Dullu Pillar, 227–8
Dungkar Choejey family, 376
Dunhuang (Buddha caves), China, 76
Durbar Squares: Kathmandu, 166, 186–7, 281, 316; Nepal, 165; Patan, 197
Durga Puja, festival of, 178
Dzongkha (Bhutanese national language), 420–3, 449

East India Company (English), 7, 166, 181, 182
East Timor, 149
economic migrants, 346–9: and Bhutan, 373
Eden, Ashley, 412
education, in Bhutan, 441–3
Eisenhower, President Dwight, 286
electricity, 373–4, 387–8, 418, 424, 462
Elgin, James Bruce, 8th Earl of, 82
Enchey Monastery, Sikkim, 336
ethnic cleansing, 364, 447, 458, 475
European Parliament, 373, 475
Everest, Mount, 4, 57, 170, 190

Fabriano, Gentile de, 250
fertility blessings, 425
feudalism: in Mustang, 258–60; necessity of abolition of, 473, 474; in Sikkim, 331, 340
Five-Point Peace Plan, 101, 114
fossil collection, in Mustang, 215, 236
Frederick the Great, King of Prussia, 168
'Friendship Bridge', 53, 170
frisbee, game of, 406
Full Moon Festival, 68–75

gambling, in Mustang, 244
Gamri River, Bhutan, 435, 443
Ganden Monastery, India, 87, 93
Ganden Monastery, Tibet, 66, 69
Gandhi, Indira, 340, 381
Gandhi, Mahatma, 36, 108, 112, 130–1
Gandhi, Rajiv, 381
Gandhi, Sonia, 193
Ganges, River, 170
Gangtok, Sikkim, 7, 320–1, 327, 356
Gankar Pusam, Bhutan, 427
Garwhal region, 228: annexation of, 181
Gelugpa sect, 30, 33, 44, 58, 89, 143, 330
Ghemi, Upper Mustang, 225–6, 233–4
Ghoom, 3
Gilling, Mustang, 276
Golmud, Tibet, 75
Gom Kora, Bhutan, 443–4
Gong An Ju (Public Security Bureau), 58–9, 64
Gongkhang (temple of a protective deity), 26
Gorbachev, Mikhail, 119
Gorkha, hill town of, 317–19

Gorkha Durbar (upper palace), Gorkha, 318–19
Gorkha (Nepal), principality of, 163, 164, 165–9, 317–19: expansion of, 180–1; and invasion of Sikkim, 331; and invasion of Tibet, 171; and Mustang, 230–1, *see also* Shah dynasty
Gorkhaland Movement, 431
Great Schism, 137
Grosny, Chechnya, 149
Guge region, Tibet, 228
Gulf War, prediction of, 199
Gurkhas, 166, 174, 182, 335, 341
Guru Rinpoche, *see* Padmasambhava
Gurung tribe, 228
Gushri Khan, Mongol overlord, 30
Gustavus Adolphus, King of Sweden, 168
Gyanendra, Prince of Nepal, 283–4
Gyantse, Tibet, 60–1
Gyelpo, lama Thangtom (Chagzampa), 436
Gyeltsen, Lam Karma, 384, 425

Han Chinese, 49–50, 65, 145–6, 149, 153, 432, 473, 475
Hanuman (monkey god), 187
hereditary monarchy, 474
Hidayatullah, Chief Justice, 340, 341
Hillary, Sir Edmund, 2
Himachal Pradesh, 83
Himachali people, 85
Himalayas, 468–9: from Bhutan, 27, 427; Nathu-La pass, 359; from Nepal, 169–71; from Tibet, 57; from Tiger Hill, Darjeeling, 3–5; trade across, 206–7, 233, 257
Hindu pilgrims, 206

Hinduism, 163, 164, 193: in Bhutan, 423; Indra Jatra festival, 166; in Mustang, 213, 228; sati rite, 168; tika, 178, 310; Vedic rites, 194, 196
Hollywood films, 139–40, 374, 388
Hope, Queen of Sikkim, 321, 322–3, 325, 343, 354
Hope Leezum, Princess, 325
houses: in Bhutan, 18, 386–7, 417, 435; in Dharamsala, India, 88; in Kathmandu Valley, 172; in Lo Manthang, 241; Mustang, 235; in 'the high country', 221; in Tibet, 64, 77
human rights: agencies, 364, 372, 457–9, 475; in Bhutan, 411, 431, 433, 456–7, 475; in China, 103–4, 116, 144, 153, 154; Dalai Lama and, 128
hunger strikes, 131–2
hydro-electricity, 373–4, 418, 462

illegal immigrants, 364, 371–3, 430–1, 449–50
India, 36, 129: and Bhutan, 400, 407, 462; and China, 99, 360, 473, 475–7; and Himalayan border, 120, 154; Nepali people in, 414; and nuclear testing, 106, 462; and Sikkim, 320, 324–5, 332–3, 336–42, 344, 347–8, 355–7, 474; and Tibetan army recruits, 150; Tibetan refugees in, 86–8, 94–6, 144
Indra Rajya Laxmi, Queen of Nepal, 287
Indra Jatra Festival, 166, 188
Institute of Tibetan Performing Arts, 89
international aid agencies, 304, 457

International Gothic style, 250
International Red Cross, 457

Jaigaon, India, 415
Jakar, Bhutan, 419–20
Jakar Dzong, Bhutan, 382–4
Jampa Lhakhang temple, Bhutan,
41
Jana Andolan, 290–1, 298, 303,
314–16
Jaya Prakash, (last Malla King of
Nepal), 166
Je Khenpo (Chief Abbot of
Bhutan), 27, 28–9
Jhapa, Nepal, 459–60
Jhocchen, Kathmandu, 281
Jigme Dorje Palbar Bista, twenty-
fifth King of Mustang, 207,
253–9, 276: and Buddhism,
262–3; on improved living
standards, 266; and preservation
of culture, 263–5; and road
construction, 270–2
Jigme Dorje Wangchuck, third
King of Bhutan, 11–12, 27,
362–3, 413
Jigme Singe Palbar, Gyalchung
(Crown Prince of Mustang),
208–9, 211, 262, 274, 452–3
Jigme Singye Wangchuck, fourth
King of Bhutan, 32, 45–6,
463–6, 471: at boarding school,
9–10, 363, 365–6; death of
father, 13–14, 366; and end of
absolutism, 409–10, 453–5;
interviews with, 365–75,
452–63
Jigme Wangchuck, second King of
Bhutan, 35, 397–402, 408
John Paul II, Pope, 137, 143
Johnson, President Lyndon B., 286
Jokhang Temple, Tibet, 41, 64,
134

Jomsom, Nepal, 99, 212–13, 232,
257, 278–9
Joshi, Mangal Raj (see also
Astrologer Royal), 197–200
Jumla, Nepal, 228, 229–30,
230–1

Kagbeni, Nepal, 215–18, 230
Kagyu sect, 44, 70, 74, 141–3
Kali, Age of, 196
Kali Gandaki river, Nepal, 206,
214–15, 218, 219, 244, 268,
271, 276, 277
Kalimpong, India, 2, 142, 320,
330, 331, 352, 389, 411–12
Kanchenjunga, Mount, 4, 170,
329, 334, 468
Kangra, India, 181
Karmapa of Kagyu sect, 141–3
Karnataka state, India, 87–8
Kashmir, 120, 172
Kaski, maharajas of (see Lamjung),
189
Kathmandu, Nepal, 157–9:
Gyalchung of Mustang in,
208–9; influence of Thakalis in,
232–3
Kathmandu Valley: and Gorkhas,
164, 165, 166; invasion by
Khasa armies, 228; and Malla
dynasty, 164, 166, 173, 188;
Spring Uprising in, 179, 290–1,
298, 303, 314–16
Kazi, Jigme N. (editor of Sikkim
Observer), 345–8
Kazi, Lhendup Dorji, 324, 338–9,
351–5
Kesang Choden, Ashi, Queen of
Bhutan, 8, 11–12, 19, 363,
382
Keshar Mahal palace, Kathmandu,
191
Kham, eastern Tibet, 330

Khampas, 69–70, 203: guerillas, 97–100, 129–30, 148, 256; revolt in eastern Tibet, 67–8

Khan family, 163–4

Khando, Rinchen, 102

Khasa Mallas (Kings of western Nepal and Tibet), 227–9

kho (Bhutanese national dress), 19–20

Khyeng province, Bhutan, 20, 438

King Tribhuvan Museum, 285, 291

kingship, 470–1

Kirata dynasty, 173

Kirtipur, Nepal, 166

Koirala, B. P., 285

Kora Chorten, 443, 445

Kosygin, Aleksei Nikolayevich (President of USSR), 286

Kot Massacre (1846), Nepal, 185–7

Krishna, 172

Kshatrya (warrior) caste, 163, 167

Kubilai Khan, 57

kukris, 341–2, 448

Kumaon region, India, 181, 228

Kundun (film), 139–40

Kunga Rabden palace, Bhutan, 398–9

Kunley, Drukpa, 377–8

Kurjey temples, Bhutan, 381–2

Kurtoe region, Bhutan, 376: dialect of, 422

Kyengkha dialect, 422

Kyichu Lakhang temples, Bhutan, 13, 41, 42

Kyrung, Nepal, 171

Ladakh monastic estate, Bhutan, 31

Ladakh region, Tibet, 228

Lake Mansovar, Tibet, 206

Lal, B. B., 341

Lamjung, maharajas of, 189

Land of the Thunder Dragon, *see* Bhutan

Langdarma, Prince of Tibet, 45

Langford-Rae, Elisa-Maria (the Kazini), 354

languages, 477: Bhutanese, 420–3, 430, 442; monastic, 423

Laxmi Devi, Queen of Nepal, 184–6

'Leonardo,' *see* Dukta, Likche

Lepcha people: in Bhutan, 43; in Sikkim, 323, 331, 332, 334, 348, 349, 350, 470

Lhamo Dhondup, *see* Dalai Lama, fourteenth

Lhapa sub-sect, 44

Lhasa, Tibet, 47, 48, 63–5, 74: anti-Chinese demonstrations in, 49; King Jigme's education in, 264; protests in, 145, 146; uprising in 1959, 2, 49, 67, 86, 129

Lhasa-Golmud Highway, 75–7

Lhotsampas, 415, 417

Liaison Officer, *see* Dhakal, Ganga Sakar

Library and Archives of Tibetan Works, Dharamsala, 92, 93–4

Licchavi dynasty, 173

Lo, The Land of, 205–6, *see also* Mustang

Lo Ghekar monastery, Mustang, 237–8

Lo Gyalpo, King of Mustang, 207

Lo Manthang, capital of Mustang, 205, 239–73

Loba people, Mustang, 205, 232–3, 257–8: and Khampas, 256; preservation of language, 264; seasonal migration, 266

Lok Sabha (India's lower house), 340

Losar Festival, 79, 86, 88–90, 138–9, 154, 155

Lothshampas, 420, 421, 422

Lujan, Rodolpho, 248–50
Lumbini, Nepal, 163

Machen Lhakang (temple), 29
Mackey, Father, 430, 443
McLeod Ganj (Upper Dharamsala), 82
McMahon, Sir Henry, 170
McMahon Line, 170, 171, 473
Magars (Nepal), 165, 228
Mahabharat Lekh, Nepal, 157
Mahakala (raven-headed deity), 393
Mahakala sanctuary, 439
Mahayana Buddhism, see Buddhism
Mahendra, King of Nepal, 194, 232, 285–8, 309–10
Malla dynasty (of Kathmandu Valley), 164, 166, 173, 188
Malla dynasty (of Western Nepal), 227–9
Manali, India, 39
Mangdelung region, Bhutan, 398–9
Mani Walls, 225, 226, 235, 268
Manjushri, 172
Mao, Chairman, 100, 129, 151
Marang, Mustang, 237
Marshyangdi River, Nepal, 317
Marwaris, 347
Mechi River, Sikkim, 181, 331
media, and Nepalese royal family, 306
Mebatsho (burning lake), Bhutan, 388–90
mental incarnation, 33–4, 35
Middle Way policy, 113–16, 128–9, 146, 152
Milarepa (Buddhist saint), 56
Minyuk dynasty, East Tibet, 330
Misamari camp, India, 87, 92–3
Mollas (monastic texts), 227
'Mon' peoples, 42
monasteries: in Bhutan, 379–80, 390–1, 403–6, 439; destroyed during Cultural Revolution, 204; founded by Dalai Lama in exile, 91–2; in Karnataka state, India, 87, 89; language of, 423; in Lo Manthang, 247–51; in Mustang, 207, 229, 237–8, 272–3, 274–6; in Sikkim, 333–4
Mongar, Bhutan, 429–35
Mongol Khans, 57–8
Mount Kailash, Tibet, 31, 206
Muktinath, holy places at, 215
Murdoch, Rupert, 125
Mustang, 129–30: almost deserted villages in, 235; cave dwellings in, 268–9; under control of Jumla, 229–31; descent to Jomsom in, 273–8; feudalism in, 258–60; flights from, 213, 278–9; geography of, 204–7, 215; and Gorkha, 230–10; journey into, 219–25; Khampa guerillas in, 97–100, 129–30, 148, 256; Lo Ghekar monastery in, 237–8; Malla dynasty in, 227–9; Peissel's account of, 204, 226–7; and preservation of cultural identity, 263–5; and restoration of Thubchhen Gompa, 247–51; road construction in, 270–2; royal house of, 207–8, 226–7, 267; similarity to Tibet, 226; Thakalis in, 231–3; treaty with Gorkha (1789), 230–1

Nagarkot, Nepal, 169–70, 171
Namgyal, Pema (of Netuk House), 327–9, 356
Namgyal Monastery, Dharamsala, 89–90
Namgyal Monastery, Mustang, 239, 272–3

Namgyel, Jigme (Regent of
  Bhutan), 392–4
Naraharinath, Yogi, 227
Narayan Laxmi, Queen of Nepal,
  168
Narayan (manifestation of Vishnu),
  196
Narayanhitti Palace, Kathmandu,
  173–9, 198, 282, 292–4, 295,
  296
Nasal Chowk (royal courtyard,
  Kathmandu), 188
Nathu-La pass, 359
National Assembly (Bhutan), 29,
  370, 372, 409–10, 433, 451,
  455
National Assembly (Tibet in exile),
  102, 128
National Geographic, 204
NATO, 476
Nehru, Jawaharlal, 7, 82, 132, 336,
  400, 468
Nepal, 473: army of, 167, 182;
  Astrologer Royal of, 199–200;
  and Bhutan, 431; and Britain,
  181–2, 189; and China, 99;
  court ceremonials in, 194–6,
  200, 300–1; immigrants in
  Bhutan, 373; Kot Massacre
  (1846), 185–6; media in, 306;
  monarchy/people relationship in,
  308–9; multi-party democracy
  in, 176, 179, 232, 291,
  299–300, 304; palaces in, 161,
  173–9, 187–9, 190–1, 198,
  282, 292–4, 295, 296, 318–19;
  Panchayat system in, 288–91,
  303, 305, 309–10, 314–15;
  preservation of cultural identity
  in, 311–12, 470; Rana
  Oligarchy, 180, 184, 186,
  189–91, 232, 282–4, 308;
  refugee camps in, 458–61; Shah

dynasty in, 160, 164–9, 173,
  180–1, 183–6, 188–9; and
  Sikkim, 331–3, 347; Spring
  Uprising in, 179, 290–1, 298,
  303, 314–16, *see also* Mustang
Nepali National Congress party,
  282–3, 284–5, 287, 300, 303
Neten, Lama Dorje, 403
Netuk House, Sikkim, 327–9, 349
New Age supporters (of Dalai
  Lama), 151
New Delhi, 87, 477
New Labour (Britain), 126–7
Newari craftsmen, 188, 319
Newari people, Kathmandu Valley,
  165, 173
Ngari region, Tibet, 227
Ngedup, Dasho Jambay, 425–6
Ngutuk, Pema (king's bodyguard),
  261–2
Nobel Peace Prize (1989), 103
non-violent struggle (or ahimsa),
  113, 122, 124, 128–30, 145,
  150, 152
Norbu, Thubten Jigme (eldest
  brother of Dalai Lama), 122
Norbulingka (summer palace),
  Tibet, 49
North American Indians, 253
Nubri region, 230
nuclear weapons, 106, 462, 475–6
Nursery for Tibetan Refugee
  Children, 94
Nuwakot, Nepal, 168
Nya-La, Nepal, 222–3
Nyingmapa sect: in Bhutan, 44, 45,
  435; in India, 91; in Sikkim,
  330, 334

Old Palace, Kathmandu, 187–9
orchid cultivation, in Sikkim, 326

Padmasambhava (Buddhist saint), 22, 40–1, 74, 226, 238, 242, 335, 377, 382, 389, 443

pagodas, 173, 188, 197

Pakistan, 76, 120, 337, 462

palaces: in Bhutan, 19, 391–2, 396–7, 397–403, 451; Narayanhitti Palace, 173–9, 198, 282, 292–4, 295, 296; in Nepal, 161, 187–9, 191, 318–19; in Tibet, 49, 65–6, 68, 108, 468

Palden, Prince, 325

Palden Thondup Namgyal, twelfth Chogyal of Sikkim, 208, 320–1, 322, 342–3: overthrow of, 321–5, 336–42, 353–4

Panchayat system, 288–91, 303, 305, 309–10, 314–15

Panchen Lama, 7, 38–9, 59–60, 121, 131, 133

Panday, M. B. (Secretary), 161

Panday, N. R. (Press Secretary), 161–2, 173–8, 191–2, 200–1

Pandes (Gorkha family), 183

Pandey, Mohan Bahadur (Principal Press Secretary), 280, 295, 313

Pandey, Nayan Raj (Royal Preceptor), 192–6

Paro, Bhutan, 18–21: airport, 15–16, 361

Paro Valley, Bhutan, 40

Pashupatinath temple, Nepal, 172, 193, 312

Patan, Nepal, 164, 165, 166, 197, 291

Pathankot, India, 79, 80

Peissel, Michel, 204, 226–7

Pema, Jetsun (sister of the Dalai Lama), 95, 96, 102, 123

Pema Karpo (Drukpa scholar), 25

Pemalingpa (Buddhist saint), 376, 377–8, 388–90, 391, 394

Pemayangtse Monastery, Sikkim, 334–5

Pengyeling Monastery, Tibet, 56

People's Liberation Army of China, 47, 171

Phari Dzong, Tibet, 4, 43, 46, 48, 52

Phuntsholing, Bhutan, 411–12, 415–16

Phuntso Choegron, Ashi, Queen of Bhutan, 382

Phuntsog Namgyal, First Chogyal of Sikkim, 329–30

pilgrims: donation scandal, 312; and Drigung Festival, 68–75; route through Mustang, 206–7

Pliny, 227

Pokhara, Nepal, 103, 212

political prisoners, 77

political reform: in Bhutan, 370–1, 424, 465–6

politics: communism, 145, 303, 308–9; cronyism, 301, 348; Nepalese multi-party system, 176, 179, 232, 291, 299–300, 304; Panchayat system, 288–91, 303, 305, 309–10, 314–15; and religion, 117–18; in Sikkim, 353–5; socialism, 118–19, 126–7; and western democracy, 369–70, 473, 474

Potala (palace), Lhasa, 49, 65–6, 68, 108, 468

Pradhan, K. C., 324, 341, 349–52

Pratrap Singh, King of Nepal, 180

prisoners, political, 77

Prithvi Bir Bikram Shah Dev, King of Nepal, 282

Prithvi Narayan Shah, King of Nepal, 160, 165–9, 180, 188, 293, 318–19

Ptolemy, 227

Public Security Bureau, in Tibet, 58–9, 64
Punakha, Bhutan, 24, 394
Punakha Dzong, 27–9, 30, 38
Purang region, Tibet, 228

Qiang, Xiao, 153

Radi, eastern Bhutan, 429–30
Raj Bhavan (official residence, Calcutta), 7–9
Rajendra, King of Nepal, 184–6
Rajput princes, 163
Ralung Monastery, Tibet, 25, 44
Rana, Keshar Shumsher, 191
Rana, Mohan Shumsher (Prime Minister of Nepal), 284
Rana Bahadur Shah, King of Nepal, 180, 184, 230–1
Rana Oligarchy, Nepal, 180, 184, 186, 189–91, 232, 282–4, 308
Rana palaces, Kathmandu, 161
Rangpo checkpoint, Sikkim, 326, 341
Ratna Rajya Laxmi, Queen of Nepal, 287
Raven Crown of Bhutan, 393, 410
Red House, The (Kagbeni), 216–18
refugees: Bhutanese in Nepal, 372–3, 411, 432, 449–51, 458–61; Tibetan, 31–2, 86–7, 94–6, 144; Tibetan children, 94–6; UNHCR, 372, 457, 458–9, 475
reincarnations, 474: Dalai Lama, 66, 121, 133, 141–3; Pemalingpa, 394; Shabdrung, 33–4, 35, 38–9; Vishnu, 159–60, 164, 196, 294, 310
Research and Analysis Wing (RAW), 324
resettlement policy: Bhutan, 432–3;

Tibet, 49–50, 65, 145–6, 149, 153, 432, 473–4
Reting Lama, 134
Ridol, Queen of Mustang, 255, 270
road construction: in Bhutan, 383; on Lhasa-Golmud Highway, 77; Mustang, 270–2; Tibetan refugees and, 87, 94, 95
Royal Advisory Council, Bhutan, 29
Royal Preceptor, Nepal, 192–6
Russia, 149

St John-in-the-Wilderness, Church of, 82
Saka Monastery, Tibet, 57–8
Sakya tradition, 44, 121, 173, 225, 264
salt monopoly, Mustang, 207, 229–30
Samar, Nepal, 220
Samchi, South Bhutan, 430–2
Sangbochen, Mustang, 222
Sanskrit, 199
Santana, Carlos, 322
Sarchop people, Bhutan, 43, 422, 432, 435, 438
Sarnath, India, 207
satellite television, 426
sati, 168
'Scheduled Tribes', 349–51, 470
science, western, 94
Scorsese, Martin, 139
Sera monastery, India, 87
Sera monastery, Tibet, 66
serfdom, in Bhutan, 362, 400
Shabdrung, Jigme Dorje, sixth, 35–8
Shabdrung, Ngawang Namgyel, Great, 25, 26, 29–30, 33, 35, 208
Shabdrung, Ngawang Namgyel, ninth, 39

Shah, Regent Bahadur, 180
Shah dynasty, Nepal, 160, 173,
    188–9, 208, 232: King Prithvi
    of, 164–9; and Mustang, 230,
    267
shahtoosh wool, 76–7
Sherpas, 264
Sherubtse College, 442–3
Shigatse, Tibet, 56–7, 59, 63, 264
Shumsher, Chandra, 232
Shumsher (branch of Rana family),
    189, 282
Sihanouk of Cambodia, Prince,
    286, 309
Sikhs, 181, 357
Sikkim, 4, 43, 168, 180, 181, 473:
    and British, 331–2; Chogyals of
    (rulers), *see* Chogyals of Sikkim;
    corruption in, 346; economic
    migrants in, 346–9; and India,
    323–5, 332–3, 336–42, 344,
    347–8, 355–7, 474; restricted
    areas in, 355–60; 'Scheduled
    Tribes' in, 349–51, 470;
    vegetation in, 326, 329, 333,
    357–8
Sikkim Democratic Front, 351
Sikkim National Congress, 324
Sikkim Observer, 344–5
Silk Road, 75
silk weaving, 444
Simeon the Stylite (Saint), 197
Simtokha Dzong (Bhutan), 24–6,
    394
Sinchula, Treaty of (1865), 412
Singha Durbar palace, Nepal, 191
Sinja, capital of Malla Empire, 228
Sino-Indian war (1962), 287, 445,
    475
socialism, 118–19, 126–7
Songtsen Gampo, King of Tibet,
    41, 42, 109, 171, 173, 226
Spanish royal family, 278

'Spring Uprising' (1990), 179,
    290–1, 298, 303, 314–16
Strasbourg Proposal (1988), 102,
    115, 128, 151
'Strike Hard' campaign, 115–16
Sudra caste, 158, 195
Sugauli, Treaty of (1816), 181, 182
Surendra, King of Nepal, 184–6,
    189

Taiwan, 105–6: tourists from, 63
Takla, Tsering Dolma (sister of the
    Dalai Lama), 94, 95
Taktsang, Paro Valley, 40, 377
Taktser, Tibet, 48
Tallo Durbar (lower palace),
    Gorkha, 318
Talo Monastery, Bhutan, 35–6
Tamshing Monastery, Bhutan,
    390–1
tangka painting, 93–4
tantrism, 74, 404, 440
Tashi Namgyal, eleventh Chogyal
    of Sikkim, 353
Tashi Yangste, Bhutan, 444–5
Tashichodzong, Bhutan, 23, 362,
    364–5
Tashigang fortress-monastery,
    Bhutan, 436–43, 463
Tashilhunpo Monastery, India, 87
Tashilhunpo Monastery, Tibet,
    59–60
Tatsang Khenpo (Chief Lama), 35
Tawang Monastery, India, 443, 446
Teesta River, Sikkim and West
    Bengal, 181, 331, 412
Teesta Valley, 4, 326
television, 426, 457
temples: in Bhutan, 23, 26, 29, 33,
    40–1, 381–2, 439; in
    Dharamsala, 89; in Nepal, 186,
    193; in Tibet, 56, 64, 106, 134
Tenzin, Dr Sonam, 438–9

Tenzin Jampal Dhadul, Ahan, King of Mustang, 255
Tenzing, Crown Prince of Sikkim, 343
Tenzing Norgay, Sherpa, 2
Terai, Nepal, 157, 158, 168, 171, 182, 228, 284
tertons (treasure discoverers), 376–8, 388–9
Tethong, Tsewang C., 104–7
Thakali, Chandra Bahadur (Private Secretary), 213–14, 246, 247, 251, 252–3, 258
Thakalis, 231–3, 257, 271, 272
Thamel, Kathmandu, 158–9
Thapa, Prime Minister Bhim Sen, 183–4, 185
Thapa, Prime Minister Mathbar Singh, 184
Thapas (Gorkha family), 183
Thekchen Choeling, 107
Thimphu, Bhutan, 14, 21–4, 27, 361–2, 363–4, 407, 418–19, 451–2
Thimphu, dzong commander of, 394
Thingkar, Mustang, 239, 261, 272–3
Thinley, Lyonpon Jigme Y., 450–1, 465
Thinley, Urgyen, 141–2
Thinley, Whangzam, 442
'Third Way' philosophy, 126
Thobden, Chogyal of Sikkim, 332
Thondup, Gyalo (brother of Dalai Lama), 32, 97–8, 100–1, 102, 113, 122
Thousand Buddha Caves, Dunhuang, China, 75–6
Thubchhen Gompa, Lo Manthang, 247–51
Thumsing-La pass, 426, 427, 446
Thurman, Robert, 68

Tiananmen Square, Beijing, 131
Tibet, 4: and Bhutan, 30–2; and China, 31, 47, 67–8, 115–16, 153–4, 400, 472; Dalai Lama theocracy, 65–7; Dalai Lama's inspiration for, 144; Drigung Festival, 68–75; and Khampa guerillas, 69–70, 97–100, 129–30, 148; literature destroyed during Cultural Revolution, 92; and local sanitary habits, 52, 87; and Malla Empire, 228; and negotiations with China, 100–1, 103–6, 113–16, 128–31; police checkpoints in, 61, 62–3; protests inside, 145, 146; and resettlement of Han Chinese, 49–50, 65, 145–6, 149, 153, 432, 473, 475; reunification of, 228–9; and scenario of puppet Dalai Lama, 133–6; and Sikkim, 330; and unofficial trade with Mustang, 233, 257; Upper Mustang's similarity to, 226; Yarlung dynasty, 45, 76
Tibetan Autonomous Region (TAR), 49, 136
Tibetan Children's Village (TCV), 95–6
Tibetan refugees: in Bhutan, 31–2; in India, 86–7, 94–6, 144
Tibetan Welfare Committee, 98
Tibetan Youth Congress, 146–52
Tiger Hill, 3–5
tika (Hindu blessing), 178, 310
Timbuctu, 207
Tito, Marshal, 286
Tizi Festival, 263
Tobgye Tsherling, Dasho, dzongda of Tongsa, 380, 403–4, 447–50
Tongsa Dzong, Bhutan, 379–80, 403–6

Tongsa Penlop (honorific title), 394, 397, 405

tourism: 'baby', 425; in Bhutan, 16, 457; and China Youth Travel Service, 55–8, 60, 64; and effects on Dharamsala, 83–4; in Kathmandu, 281; in Mustang, 210; in Sikkim, 326, 347, 358–9; in Tibet, 55–8, 60, 63, 64

trade: and Mustang, 229, 233, 257, 270–1; between Nepal and India, 290; trans-Himalayan, 206–7

traditional dress: Bhutanese, 19–20; of Brogpa nomads, 437; Nepalese, 175, 414, 415–16

Trailoyka, Crown Prince of Nepal, 189

transhumance, 266, 398

Tribhuvan, King of Nepal, 194, 282, 283–5, 308

Trimshung (Bhutan legal code), 362

Trisuli River, Nepal, 317

Tsangla language, 422

Tsangma, Crown Prince of Tibet, 45

Tsarang, Mustang, 238, 273–6

Tsarang Lama, 274–6

Tsechen Shedrubling Mon Gon Lobdra (monastic school), 264

Tsering, Dawa (Foreign Minister, Bhutan), 364

Tsering, Lhasang (TYC President), 146–52, 153

Tsering, Netyuk, 353

Tshultrim, Dasho Jigme, dzongda of Mongar, 429–33

Tsomgo lake, Sikkim, 356, 357, 358

Tsong people, Sikkim, 349

Tsuglakhang temple, Dharamsala, 89, 107

Tsurphu Monastery, Tibet, 141

Tucci, Giuseppe, 227

Tundikhel Maidan, Kathmandu, 195, 291

Ugyen Pelri Palace, Bhutan, 19

Ugyen Wangchuck, Sir, (first King of Bhutan), 35, 394–7

ULFA (United Liberation Front of Assam), 461, 462

Umayyad arabs, 76

UNHCR (United Nations High Commissioner for Refugees), 372, 457, 458–9, 475

United Nations, 152, 285–6, 310, 363, 450, 458

United States, 97–8, 99, 105, 129, 148, 150, 151

Upper Mustang Conservation and Development Project, 265

Ura, Bhutan, 427, 446

Vedic rites, 194, 196

vegetation: in Bhutan, 367–8, 378, 427, 428; deforestation, 317, 417, 477; in Sikkim, 326, 329, 333, 357–8

videos, 374, 387–8

Vishnu, Lord, 159–60, 164, 196, 294, 310

Walt van Praag, Michael van, 151

Wang Chu river, Bhutan, 417

Wangchuck, Ngagi, 382

Wangchuck, Sir Ugyen, 382–3

Wangchuck, Bhutan's royal house of, 11, 37–8, 45, 392–7

Wangchuck, thirteenth Chogyal of Sikkim, 328, 344

Wangdu, General Gyatso, 99–100

Wangdu, Prince, 255

Wangduchoeling Palace, Bhutan, 391–2, 396–7

Wangyul Dorje, King of Mustang, 267

Wengcheng, Princess, 109

White, John Claude, 7, 396

World Bank, 171

WTO (World Trade Organization), 154

Wutaishan, China, 106

Xian, Imperial capital of, 76

yak butter tea, 72–3, 170, 320

yaks, 358–9, 378, 437

Yale University, United States, 106

Yanki (royal mistress), 11, 12

Yarlung dynasty (Tibet), 45, 76, 227

Yongda, Captain (or Yapo), 334–9, 349–51

Younghusband, Colonel Sir Francis Edward, 60, 171, 396, 407

Yuksom, Sikkim, 329, 333

Zangbo, Dasho Jigme, dzongda of Bumthang, 380–90, 424

Zhangmu, Tibet, 52

Zhou, Mr (of CTYS), 55–8, 60, 64

'Zone of Peace': Dalai Lama and, 119–20, 476; King Birendra and, 288, 298; King Jigme on, 462